ADVANCES IN DIGITAL FORENSICS IV

IFIP – The International Federation for Information Processing

IFIP was founded in 1960 under the auspices of UNESCO, following the First World Computer Congress held in Paris the previous year. An umbrella organization for societies working in information processing, IFIP's aim is two-fold: to support information processing within its member countries and to encourage technology transfer to developing nations. As its mission statement clearly states,

> *IFIP's mission is to be the leading, truly international, apolitical organization which encourages and assists in the development, exploitation and application of information technology for the benefit of all people.*

IFIP is a non-profitmaking organization, run almost solely by 2500 volunteers. It operates through a number of technical committees, which organize events and publications. IFIP's events range from an international congress to local seminars, but the most important are:

• The IFIP World Computer Congress, held every second year;
• Open conferences;
• Working conferences.

The flagship event is the IFIP World Computer Congress, at which both invited and contributed papers are presented. Contributed papers are rigorously refereed and the rejection rate is high.

As with the Congress, participation in the open conferences is open to all and papers may be invited or submitted. Again, submitted papers are stringently refereed.

The working conferences are structured differently. They are usually run by a working group and attendance is small and by invitation only. Their purpose is to create an atmosphere conducive to innovation and development. Refereeing is less rigorous and papers are subjected to extensive group discussion.

Publications arising from IFIP events vary. The papers presented at the IFIP World Computer Congress and at open conferences are published as conference proceedings, while the results of the working conferences are often published as collections of selected and edited papers.

Any national society whose primary activity is in information may apply to become a full member of IFIP, although full membership is restricted to one society per country. Full members are entitled to vote at the annual General Assembly, National societies preferring a less committed involvement may apply for associate or corresponding membership. Associate members enjoy the same benefits as full members, but without voting rights. Corresponding members are not represented in IFIP bodies. Affiliated membership is open to non-national societies, and individual and honorary membership schemes are also offered.

ADVANCES IN DIGITAL FORENSICS IV

Edited by

INDRAJIT RAY

Colorado State University
Fort Collins, Colorado, USA

SUJEET SHENOI

University of Tulsa
Tulsa, Oklahoma, USA

 Springer

Advances in Digital Forensics IV

Edited by Indrajit Ray and Sujeet Shenoi

p. cm. (IFIP International Federation for Information Processing, a Springer Series in Computer Science)

ISSN: 1571-5736 / 1861-2288 (Internet)

ISBN: 978-1-4419-4664-5   e-ISBN: 978-0-387-84927-0

Printed on acid-free paper

9 8 7 6 5 4 3 2 1

springer.com

Contents

PART X   FORENSIC TOOLS

Contributing Authors

Charles Adams is a Professor of Law at the University of Tulsa, Tulsa, Oklahoma. His research interests include intellectual property law and digital forensics.

Yuki Ashino is a Ph.D. student in Computer Engineering at Tokyo Denki University, Tokyo, Japan. His research interests are in the area of digital forensics.

Etienne Barnard is a Senior Researcher in the Human Language Technologies Research Group at Meraka Institute, Pretoria, South Africa. His research interests are in the areas of pattern recognition and artificial intelligence with primary application to the computational modeling of South African languages.

Kenneth Bauer is a Professor of Operations Research at the Air Force Institute of Technology, Wright-Patterson Air Force Base, Ohio. His research interests lie in the areas of automatic target recognition and multivariate statistics.

Paul Burke is a Senior Digital Evidence Research Assistant at the National Center for Forensic Science, University of Central Florida, Orlando, Florida. His research interests include network security, digital forensics and open source operating systems.

Madhusudhanan Chandrasekaran is a Ph.D. candidate in Computer Science and Engineering at the University at Buffalo, Buffalo, New York. His research interests include malware defense, anti-phishing strategies, intrusion detection and digital forensics.

Kam-Pui Chow is an Associate Professor of Computer Science at the University of Hong Kong, Hong Kong, China. His research interests include information security, digital forensics, live system forensics and digital surveillance.

Frederick Cohen is the Chief Executive Officer of Fred Cohen and Associates, Livermore, California. His research interests include information assurance, critical infrastructure protection and digital forensics.

Philip Craiger is an Assistant Professor of Engineering Technology and Assistant Director for Digital Evidence at the National Center for Forensic Science, University of Central Florida, Orlando, Florida. His research interests include information assurance and digital forensics.

Jeremy Daily is an Assistant Professor of Mechanical Engineering at the University of Tulsa, Tulsa, Oklahoma. His research interests include traffic crash reconstruction, solid mechanics, and uncertainty and probabilistic analysis.

David Dampier is an Associate Professor of Computer Science and Engineering and Director of the Southeast Region Forensics Training Center at Mississippi State University, Mississippi State, Mississippi. His research interests include digital forensics, information assurance and software engineering.

Shira Dankner is an M.S. student in Cyber Forensics at Purdue University, West Lafayette, Indiana. Her research interests are in the area of digital forensics.

Alta de Waal is a Senior Researcher in the Human Language Technologies Research Group at Meraka Institute, Pretoria, South Africa. Her research interests include text modeling and Bayesian inference.

Marnita Eaddie is a Major in the U.S. Air Force and a graduate student at the Air Force Institute of Technology, Wright-Patterson Air Force Base, Ohio. Her research interests include cryptography and wireless networks.

Barbara Endicott-Popovsky is the Director of the Center for Information Assurance and Cybersecurity at the University of Washington, Seattle, Washington. Her research interests include network forensics, critical infrastructure protection and secure coding practices.

Paul Fogg received his M.S. degree in Computer Science from the Air Force Institute of Technology, Wright-Patterson Air Force Base, Ohio. His research interests include image matching, digital forensics and databases.

Deborah Frincke is the Chief Scientist for Cyber Security Research in the Computational Sciences Directorate at Pacific Northwest National Laboratory, Richland, Washington. Her research interests include very large system defense, forensics, infrastructure protection, security visualization, SCADA security and information assurance education.

Keisuke Fujita is an M.S. student in Computer Engineering at Tokyo Denki University, Tokyo, Japan. His research interests are in the area of digital forensics.

Rajni Goel is an Assistant Professor of Information Systems and Decision Sciences at Howard University, Washington, DC. Her research interests include information security and privacy, digital forensics and data mining.

Paolo Gubian is an Associate Professor of Electrical Engineering at the University of Brescia, Brescia, Italy. His research areas include integrated circuit design, digital forensics and embedded systems security.

Murat Gunestas is a Ph.D. candidate in Information Technology at George Mason University, Fairfax, Virginia. His research interests include web services security, digital forensics and component-based software engineering.

Mark Hartong is a Senior Electronics Engineer with the Federal Railroad Administration, Washington, DC, and a Ph.D. student in Information Technology at George Mason University, Fairfax, Virginia. His research interests include software engineering, software systems safety, information assurance, control systems security and digital forensics.

Lucas Hui is an Associate Professor of Computer Science at the University of Hong Kong, Hong Kong, China. His research interests include computer security, cryptography and digital forensics.

Zoe Jiang is a Ph.D. student in Computer Science at the University of Hong Kong, Hong Kong, China. Her research interests include information assurance, network security and digital forensics.

Latifur Khan is an Associate Professor of Computer Science at the University of Texas at Dallas, Richardson, Texas. His research interests include data mining, multimedia information management and semantic web and database systems.

Matthew Kiley received his M.S. degree in Information Security from Purdue University, West Lafayette, Indiana. His research interests are in the area of digital forensics.

Renico Koen is an M.S. student in Computer Science at the University of Pretoria, Pretoria, South Africa. His research interests include digital forensics and software design and architecture.

Peter Komisarczuk is a Senior Lecturer of Computer Science at Victoria University, Wellington, New Zealand. His research interests are in the areas of network architectures and protocols, and communications systems.

Xiangwei Kong is a Professor of Electronic and Information Engineering at Dalian University of Technology, Dalian, China. Her research interests include multimedia security, image forensics, image processing and wireless sensor networks.

Michael Kwan is a Ph.D. student in Computer Science at the University of Hong Kong, Hong Kong, China. His research interests include digital forensics, digital evidence evaluation and the application of probabilistic models in digital forensics.

Pierre Lai is a Ph.D. student in Computer Science at the University of Hong Kong, Hong Kong, China. His research interests include cryptography and digital forensics.

Frank Law is a Ph.D. student in Computer Science at the University of Hong Kong, Hong Kong, China. His research interests include digital forensics and time analysis.

Peng Liu is an Associate Professor of Information Sciences and Technology at Pennsylvania State University, University Park, Pennsylvania. His research interests include systems security and survivability, network security, database security and privacy.

Gavin Manes is the President of Oklahoma Digital Forensics Professionals, Inc., Tulsa, Oklahoma. His research interests include digital forensics and critical infrastructure protection.

Christopher Marberry is a Senior Digital Evidence Research Assistant at the National Center for Forensic Science, University of Central Florida, Orlando, Florida. His research interests include digital forensics, computer security and virtualization technologies.

Lodovico Marziale is pursuing an M.S. degree in Mathematics and a Ph.D. in Computer Science at the University of New Orleans, New Orleans, Louisiana. His research interests include digital forensics, machine learning and parallel and concurrent programming.

Mohammad Masud is a Ph.D. candidate in Computer Science at the University of Texas at Dallas, Richardson, Texas. His research interests include data mining and network intrusion detection.

Rodney McKemmish is a Ph.D. candidate in Electrical and Information Engineering at the University of South Australia, Mawson Lakes, Australia. His research interests include digital forensics, electronic discovery and information security.

Fanjie Meng is an M.S. student in Signal and Information Processing at Dalian University of Technology, Dalian, China. Her research interests include digital image processing and image forensics.

Pontjho Mokhonoana is a Researcher at the Council for Scientific and Industrial Research, Pretoria, South Africa. His research interests include digital forensics and mobile technology.

Daniel Molina is a Captain in the U.S. Air Force and a graduate student at the Air Force Institute of Technology, Wright-Patterson Air Force Base, Ohio. His research interests include rootkits, intrusion detection and digital forensics.

Radu Muschevici is an M.Sc. student in Computer Science at Victoria University, Wellington, New Zealand. His research interests include digital forensics and object-oriented programming languages.

Martin Olivier is a Professor of Computer Science at the University of Pretoria, Pretoria, South Africa. His research interests include privacy, database security and digital forensics.

Timothy Pavlic received his graduate degree in Computer and Information Science from the University of South Australia, Adelaide, Australia. His research interests include embedded systems and software architectures.

Gilbert Peterson is an Assistant Professor of Electrical and Computer Engineering at the Air Force Institute of Technology, Wright-Patterson Air Force Base, Ohio. His research interests include digital forensics, steganography, image processing, robotics and machine learning.

Mark Pollitt, Chair, IFIP Working Group 11.9 on Digital Forensics, is a faculty member in Engineering Technology and a principal with the National Center for Forensic Science, University of Central Florida, Orlando, Florida. His research interests include forensic processes, knowledge management and forensic quality management.

Charles Preston is the Chief Operating Officer of SysWisdom LLC, Anchorage, Alaska. His research interests include information assurance, network security and wireless network design.

Golden Richard III is a Professor of Computer Science at the University of New Orleans, New Orleans, Louisiana, and the co-founder of Digital Forensics Solutions, LLC, New Orleans, Louisiana. His research interests include digital forensics, mobile computing and operating systems internals.

Jack Riley is an M.S. student in Computer Science at Mississippi State University, Mississippi State, Mississippi. His research interests include information assurance and digital forensics.

Gregory Roberts is a Captain in the U.S. Air Force and a graduate student at the Air Force Institute of Technology, Wright-Patterson Air Force Base, Ohio. His research interests include cyberspace operations and critical infrastructure communication networks.

Benjamin Rodriguez is a Ph.D. student in Electrical and Computer Engineering at the Air Force Institute of Technology, Wright-Patterson Air Force Base, Ohio. His research interests include digital forensics, signal processing, digital image and video processing, and steganography.

Marcus Rogers is a Professor of Computer and Information Technology at Purdue University, West Lafayette, Indiana. His research interests include psychological digital crime scene analysis, applied behavioral profiling and digital evidence process models.

Vassil Roussev is an Assistant Professor of Computer Science at the University of New Orleans, New Orleans, Louisiana. His research interests include digital forensics, high-performance computing, distributed collaboration and software engineering.

Vidyaraman Sankaranarayanan is a Program Manager at Microsoft Corporation, Redmond, Washington. His research interests include malware defense in the context of user-centered security.

Ryoichi Sasaki is a Professor of Information Security at Tokyo Denki University, Tokyo, Japan. His research interests include risk assessment, cryptography and digital forensics.

Antonio Savoldi is a Ph.D. candidate in Computer Forensics at the University of Brescia, Brescia, Italy. His research interests include digital forensics, steganalysis and embedded systems security.

Christian Seifert is a Ph.D. candidate in Computer Science at Victoria University, Wellington, New Zealand. His research interests include client-side security, client honeypots and digital forensics.

Sujeet Shenoi is the F.P. Walter Professor of Computer Science at the University of Tulsa, Tulsa, Oklahoma. His research interests include information assurance, digital forensics, critical infrastructure protection and intelligent control.

Anoop Singhal is a Senior Computer Scientist in the Computer Security Division at the National Institute of Standards and Technology, Gaithersburg, Maryland. His research interests include network security, web services security, databases and data mining systems.

Nathan Singleton is a B.S. student in Computer Science at the University of Tulsa, Tulsa, Oklahoma. His research interests are in the area of digital forensics.

Jill Slay is the Director of the Defence and Systems Institute Safeguarding Australia Research Laboratory at the University of South Australia, Adelaide, Australia. Her research interests include information assurance, digital forensics, critical infrastructure protection and complex system modeling.

Bhavani Thuraisingham is a Professor of Computer Science at the University of Texas at Dallas, Richardson, Texas. Her research interests include information security and data management.

Benjamin Turnbull is a Postdoctoral Research Fellow at the Defence and Systems Institute Safeguarding Australia Research Laboratory at the University of South Australia, Adelaide, Australia. His research interests include forensic computing, wireless technologies and drug-crime-related electronic analysis.

Tetsutaro Uehara is an Associate Professor of Computing and Media Studies at Kyoto University, Kyoto, Japan. His research interests include high-performance computing, secure multimedia streaming technology, network security and digital forensics.

Shambhu Upadhyaya is a Professor of Computer Science and Engineering at the University at Buffalo, Buffalo, New York. His research interests are in the areas of information assurance, fault diagnosis, fault tolerant computing and VLSI testing.

Rayford Vaughn is the Billy J. Ball Professor of Computer Science and Engineering and a William L. Giles Distinguished Professor at Mississippi State University, Mississippi State, Mississippi. His research interests include information assurance, software engineering and digital forensics.

Harry Velupillai is a Researcher at the Council for Scientific and Industrial Research, Pretoria, South Africa. His research interests include computer security, digital forensics and intrusion detection.

Jacobus Venter is a Senior Researcher at the Council for Scientific and Industrial Research, Pretoria, South Africa. His research interests include digital forensics training, evidence mining and probabilistic methods.

Michael Veth is an Assistant Professor of Electrical and Computer Engineering at the Air Force Institute of Technology, Wright-Patterson Air Force Base, Ohio. His current research focuses on the fusion of optical and inertial systems for navigation and control.

Xinran Wang is a Ph.D. candidate in Computer Science and Engineering at Pennsylvania State University, University Park, Pennsylvania. His research interests include buffer overflow and worm detection, and ad-hoc and sensor network security.

Ian Welch is a Senior Lecturer of Computer Science at Victoria University, Wellington, New Zealand. His research interests include large scale Internet measurements, software emulation and secure auction protocols.

Anthony Whitledge is an attorney who is retired from the U.S. Department of Justice and the Internal Revenue Service. His research interests include digital forensics, data mining and the application of technology to civil and criminal litigation.

Duminda Wijesekera is an Associate Professor of Information and Software Engineering at George Mason University, Fairfax, Virginia. His research interests include information, network, telecommunications and control systems security.

Svein Willassen received his Ph.D. degree in Telematics from the Norwegian University of Science and Technology, Trondheim, Norway. He is currently a Manager at InsideOut AS, a digital forensics company in Oslo, Norway. His research interests include digital forensics and mobile communications.

Siu-Ming Yiu is a faculty member in Computer Science at the University of Hong Kong, Hong Kong, China. His research interests include bioinformatics, computer security, cryptography and digital forensics.

Xingang You is a Professor of Electrical Engineering at Beijing Electrical Technology Applications Institute, Beijing, China. His research interests include multimedia security, signal processing and communications.

Sencun Zhu is an Assistant Professor of Computer Science and Engineering at Pennsylvania State University, University Park, Pennsylvania. His research interests include network and system security, ad-hoc and sensor networks, performance evaluation and peer-to-peer computing.

Matthew Zimmerman is a graduate student at the Air Force Institute of Technology, Wright-Patterson Air Force Base, Ohio. His research interests include virtualization, graphics programming and databases.

Preface

Digital forensics deals with the acquisition, preservation, examination, analysis and presentation of electronic evidence. Networked computing, wireless communications and portable electronic devices have expanded the role of digital forensics beyond traditional computer crime investigations. Practically every type of crime now involves some aspect of digital evidence; digital forensics provides the techniques and tools to articulate this evidence in legal proceedings. Digital forensics also has myriad intelligence applications. Furthermore, it has a vital role in information assurance – investigations of security breaches yield valuable information that can be used to design more secure and resilient systems.

This book, *Advances in Digital Forensics IV*, is the fourth volume in the annual series produced by the IFIP Working Group 11.9 on Digital Forensics, an international community of scientists, engineers and practitioners dedicated to advancing the state of the art of research and practice in the emerging discipline of digital forensics. The book presents original research results and innovative applications in digital forensics. Also, it highlights some of the major technical and legal issues related to digital evidence and electronic crime investigations.

This volume contains twenty-eight edited papers from the Fourth Annual IFIP WG 11.9 Conference on Digital Forensics, held at Kyoto University, Kyoto, Japan, January 28–30, 2008. The papers were selected from forty-two submissions, which were refereed by members of IFIP Working Group 11.9 and other internationally-recognized experts in digital forensics.

The chapters are organized into ten sections: themes and issues, evidence recovery, evidence integrity, evidence management, forensic techniques, network forensics, portable electronic device forensics, event data recorder forensics, novel investigative techniques and forensic tools. The coverage of topics highlights the richness and vitality of the discipline, and offers promising avenues for future research in digital forensics.

This book is the result of the combined efforts of several individuals. In particular, we thank Rodrigo Chandia and Anita Presley for their tire-

less work on behalf of IFIP Working Group 11.9. We also acknowledge
the support provided by Kyoto University, Kyoto, Japan, the Japan Society for the Promotion of Science, the Federal Bureau of Investigation,
National Security Agency and U.S. Secret Service.

INDRAJIT RAY AND SUJEET SHENOI

I

THEMES AND ISSUES

Chapter 1

WHEN IS DIGITAL EVIDENCE FORENSICALLY SOUND?

Rodney McKemmish

Abstract "Forensically sound" is a term used extensively in the digital forensics community to qualify and, in some cases, to justify the use of a particular forensic technology or methodology. Indeed, many practitioners use the term when describing the capabilities of a particular piece of software or when describing a particular forensic analysis approach. Such a wide application of the term can only lead to confusion. This paper examines the various definitions of forensic computing (also called digital forensics) and identifies the common role that admissibility and evidentiary weight play. Using this common theme, the paper explores how the term "forensically sound" has been used and examines the drivers for using such a term. Finally, a definition of "forensically sound" is proposed and four criteria are provided for determining whether or not a digital forensic process may be considered to be "forensically sound."

Keywords: Digital evidence, forensically sound evidence

1.   Introduction

Emerging from the needs of law enforcement in the 1980s, forensic computing (also referred to as digital forensics) has evolved to become an integral part of most criminal investigations. The digital forensic specialist plays a fundamental role in the investigative process – whether it is the forensic analysis of personal computers, cell phones and PDAs belonging to suspects and witnesses, or the acquisition and analysis of network traffic in response to computer security incidents. Forensic computing also plays an increasingly important role in civil litigation, especially in electronic discovery, intellectual property disputes, employment law disputes and IT security incidents.

Please use the following format when citing this chapter:

McKemmish, R., 2008, in IFIP International Federation for Information Processing, Volume 285; *Advances in Digital Forensics IV*; Indrajit Ray, Sujeet Shenoi; (Boston: Springer), pp. 3–15.

In the context of law enforcement, it has been argued that the emergence of forensic computing as a discipline was due to the need to provide technical solutions to legal problems [6]. The technical solution involves the extraction of electronic data by processes that ensure that the resulting product is legally acceptable as evidence. Some scholars argue that legal drivers are the principal force behind shaping the growth and evolution of forensic computing [19]. As in the case of criminal investigations, the need to meet evidentiary requirements also provides a strong stimulus for forensic computing in civil litigation. Not surprisingly, a common element that emerges from forensic computing in criminal and civil matters is the need to produce electronic evidence in a manner that does not detract from its admissibility.

The growing emphasis on admissibility in recent years has caused the focus of the forensic computing discipline to shift to the domain of forensic science. With this shift comes the need to formalize many of the forensic processes and procedures that have been developed in an unstructured or *ad hoc* manner. Evidence of the shift is apparent in NIST's Computer Forensic Tools Testing Program [15] as well as in the work of the Scientific Working Group on Digital Evidence (SWGDE) [20] and the Electronic Evidence Technical Advisory Group of the Australian National Institute of Forensic Science, which is helping integrate the forensic computing function into the forensic science domain [14].

The need to ensure that electronic evidence produced by a forensic process is admissible has given rise to the term "forensically sound" when seeking to describe the reliability of the forensic process. Before exploring what "forensically sound" means, we briefly examine current thinking about the discipline of forensic computing.

2.   What is Forensic Computing?

Numerous digital forensics experts have attempted to define the term "forensic computing." As expected, their definitions are influenced by their perspectives and experience.

In 1999, based on an examination of digital forensic activities by law enforcement agencies from eight countries, McKemmish [12] defined forensic computing as a process encompassing the identification, preservation, analysis and presentation of digital evidence in a legally acceptable manner. Anderson, *et al.* [1] emphasize the scientific nature of forensic computing by defining it as the science of using and analyzing information in order to "reason *post hoc* about the validity of hypotheses which attempt to explain the circumstances or cause of an activity under investigation." On the other hand, Hannan, *et al.* [9] adopt an investigative focus and define forensic computing as a set of processes or procedures focusing on the investigation of computer misuse.

Some definitions of forensic computing focus solely on the underlying legal scope. For example, Casey [5], a computer security and computer crime consultant, postulates a criminal basis for forensic computing by emphasizing that it focuses on establishing how an offense has occurred. On the other hand, Carrier [3], a research scientist and author of several forensic tools, provides a more detailed definition of forensic computing that encompasses the investigative and scientific elements:

> "The use of scientifically derived and proven methods toward the preservation, collection, validation, identification, analysis, interpretation, documentation and presentation of digital evidence derived from digital sources for the purpose of facilitating or furthering the reconstruction of events found to be criminal, or helping to anticipate unauthorized actions shown to be disruptive to planned operations."

Despite the comprehensive nature of his definition of forensic computing, Carrier still restricts its scope to criminal-related activity.

Defining forensic computing is a difficult proposition. After examining various definitions of forensic computing, Hannan [8] concludes that "no single definition can adequately define the current meaning of forensic computing." McCombie and Warren [11] emphasize that digital forensics is fundamentally different from other types of investigations and that major differences exist in the basic definition of forensic computing.

Despite their differences, all the definitions share one common element – the need to maintain the evidentiary weight of the forensic computing product. McKemmish [12] uses the term "legally acceptable," Anderson, *et al.* [1] stipulate the need to meet "evidentiary requirements," and Casey [5] and Carrier [3] refer to digital evidence in the context of legal weight. All these authors highlight the need for a forensic process to maximize the evidentiary weight of the resulting electronic evidence. Indeed, when the evidentiary weight is maximized, the digital forensics community would generally concur that the evidence is forensically sound.

3. Forensically Sound Evidence

To better understand what the term "forensically sound" might actually mean, we first examine the usage of the term. An Internet search quickly shows that the term is used to characterize everything from disk imaging software to a particular approach for extracting computer data. In the context of disk imaging, digital forensics professionals qualify the term by stating that, to be forensically sound, the disk image must be a bit-for-bit copy of the original (i.e., an exact copy). Some go further by adding that the disk imaging process must not only produce an exact copy, but must also include a means for verifying the authenticity of the copy and the reliability of the copying process. Authenticity is typically ensured by using some form of mathematical fingerprinting or hashing that provides a signature for a given block of data. To ensure reliability, it is often advocated that the disk imaging process include an audit trail that clearly records the success or failure of all or part of the copying process. Therefore, one might argue that, in order to be forensically sound, a disk imaging process must satisfy the following requirements:

- The disk imaging process must produce an exact representation (copy) of the original.

- The duplicated data must be independently authenticated as being a true copy.

- The disk imaging process must produce an audit trail.

A more authoritative overview of the disk imaging process is found in NIST's Disk Imaging Tool Specification (Version 3.1.6) [16]. The document specifies a number of mandatory and optional requirements for disk imaging tools. The principal requirements are:

- The tool shall make a bit-stream duplicate or an image of an original disk or partition.

- The tool shall not alter the original disk.

- The tool shall be able to verify the integrity of a disk image file.

- The tool shall log I/O errors.

- The documentation of the tool shall be correct.

When the term "forensically sound" is used to describe the forensic process as a whole, it is done so with two clear objectives:

1. The acquisition and subsequent analysis of electronic data has been undertaken with all due regard to preserving the data in the state in which it was first discovered.

2. The forensic process does not in any way diminish the evidentiary value of the electronic data through technical, procedural or interpretive errors.

It is often the case that to meet these objectives, the concept of "forensically sound" is expressed in terms of a series of steps or procedures to be followed. While this approach is logical and is certainly the most measurable, in reality, it is the lack of uniformity that diminishes its value. Specifically, the steps or procedures often vary from one author to the next and may contain more or less detail. Additionally, the forensic perspective and experience of an author can have a significant bearing on the construction of the forensic process.

For example, consider the difference in the acquisition of data in computer forensics and intrusion forensics cases. In computer forensics, the focus is on obtaining a snapshot of the system at a given point in time (typically using a disk imaging process). In the case of intrusion forensics, the focus is more likely to be on monitoring and collecting data from a network over time. It is, therefore, difficult to advocate taking a disk image of a live system whose state changes over time and where the evidence (network traffic and log files) is in a dynamic state.

Compounding the uncertainty surrounding the meaning and use of the term "forensically sound" is the lack of a clear definition or concise discussion in the digital forensics literature. For example, "Guidelines for the Management of IT Evidence" [7] published by Standards Australia uses the term "forensically sound" in the context of evidence collection, but does not clarify its meaning.

An alternate approach used to qualify forensic processes centers on the adoption of several principles rather than the application of clearly defined steps or processes. The "Good Practice Guide for Computer Based Electronic Evidence" published by the Association of Chief Police Officers (United Kingdom) [13] lists four important principles related to the recovery of digital evidence:

1. No action taken by law enforcement agencies or their agents should change data held on a computer or storage media which may subsequently be relied upon in court.

2. In exceptional circumstances, where a person finds it necessary to access original data held on a computer or on storage media, that person must be competent to do so and be able to give evidence explaining the relevance and the implications of their actions.

3. An audit trail or other record of all processes applied to computer based electronic evidence should be created and preserved. An independent third party should be able to examine those processes and achieve the same result.

4. The person in charge of the investigation (the case officer) has overall responsibility for ensuring that the law and these principles are adhered to.

Similarly, the International Organization on Computer Evidence [10] has specified the following six principles:

1. When dealing with digital evidence, all of the general forensic and procedural principles must be applied.

2. Upon seizing digital evidence, actions taken should not change that evidence.

3. When it is necessary for a person to access original digital evidence, that person should be trained for the purpose.

4. All activity relating to the seizure, access, storage or transfer of digital evidence must be fully documented, preserved and available for review.

5. An individual is responsible for all actions taken with respect to digital evidence while the digital evidence is in his/her possession.

6. Any agency, which is responsible for seizing, accessing, storing or transferring digital evidence, is responsible for compliance with these principles.

The well-known U.S. Department of Justice publication, "Searching and Seizing Computers and Obtaining Electronic Evidence in Criminal Investigations" [22], does not list any principles *per se*. However, the publication does address many of the points discussed above and provides a comprehensive explanation of the forensic process and the related U.S. legal issues.

In a 1999 paper titled "What is Forensic Computing?" McKemmish [12] specified four rules aimed at maximizing the admissibility of digital forensic processes. These rules, which are similar to the principles described above, are:

1. Minimal handling of the original: The application of digital forensic processes during the examination of original data shall be kept to an absolute minimum.

2. Account for any change: Where changes occur during a forensic examination, the nature, extent and reason for such changes should be properly documented.

3. Comply with the rules of evidence: The application or development of forensic tools and techniques should be undertaken with regard to the relevant rules of evidence.

4. Do not exceed your knowledge: A digital forensics specialist should not undertake an examination that is beyond his/her current level of knowledge and skill.

4. Why Define "Forensically Sound?"

Despite the variations in the use of "forensically sound," there remains one universally consistent objective for a digital forensic process – the need to ensure that the end product does not lose its evidentiary weight and, therefore, its admissibility as evidence. Given this overriding consideration, it is not surprising to see an ever increasing number of digital forensics professionals referring to their work product as being derived from a "forensically sound" methodology and/or technology. Indeed, this term is commonly used in affidavits and expert reports, especially when justifying the use of a specific methodology or technology.

The greatest driver to defining the term "forensically sound" may, in fact, come from the legal community. In 2005, the Australian Law Reform Commission (ALRC) released a review of the various Australian uniform evidence acts [2]. The section titled "Reliability and Accuracy of Computer-Produced Evidence" examines the Australian legislative framework that facilitates the proof of electronic evidence. The ALRC analysis identifies several viewpoints. One viewpoint, which relies heavily on the work of Spenceley [21], emphasizes that "a higher threshold for the admission of computer-produced output into evidence [should be] established." Citing Spenceley's research, the ALRC review notes that a question could be raised about the reliability of computer-generated output because "it is impossible to test for either the inaccuracy or accuracy of computer operations, and impossible to give a statistical rate of failure, and that there is therefore no rational basis for assuming a high rate of reliability."

To negate the impact of questions about reliability, the ALRC review notes that "Spenceley builds a case for adopting an approach that relies on implementing a 'redundant mechanism' in the environment in which the computer is used to address the problem of reliability of computer output." The purpose of the redundant mechanism is to prevent or mitigate unreliability by helping "provide some level of verification that a failure in the computer has not occurred." To achieve this goal, the ALRC review cites Spenceley's test of admissibility:

> "It should be demonstrated that: (a) Some mechanism(s) of redundancy (however formulated and implemented) was or were utilized in connection with the production of particular material in the setting in which it was produced; and that (b) It is reasonably likely that any error(s) in the operation of that computer that affected the accuracy of infor-

mation contained in that material would have been detected by such mechanism(s)."

Not surprisingly, when government entities such as ALRC begin to probe the evidentiary value of computer-generated output and, in particular, raise questions about the current reliance on computer-generated output, greater attention is automatically placed on the digital forensic process. Given the variation in the usage of the term "forensically sound" and the focus on the reliability of computer-generated output from an evidentiary perspective, two key questions arise:

- What does "forensically sound" mean?

- How does one know if something is "forensically sound?"

The answer to these questions is important when one considers that the term "forensically sound" is used to not only substantiate a particular forensic technology or methodology, but also to substantiate it in the context of proving the admissibility of the digital forensic output in legal proceedings. This last point makes it all the more critical that there be a clear understanding of what makes something forensically sound.

5. What Does "Forensically Sound" Mean?

The *Compact Oxford English Dictionary* [17] defines the word "forensic" as meaning:

> "(1) relating to or denoting the application of scientific methods to the investigation of crime. (2) of or relating to courts of law."

The same dictionary defines the word "sound" – in the context of "something is said to be sound" – as meaning:

> (1) in good condition. (2) based on reason or judgement. (3) financially secure. (4) competent or reliable. (5) (of sleep) deep and unbroken. (6) severe or thorough."

Utilizing these individual definitions it may be argued that the term "forensically sound" means "the production of reliable electronic evidence before a court of law." In the context of digital evidence, however, the question of reliability is perhaps the key element. Consequently (and given the variations in the use of the term as detailed above), a more concise definition of "forensically sound" is:

> "The application of a transparent digital forensic process that preserves the original meaning of the data for production in a court of law."

The word "transparent" in this definition implies that the reliability and accuracy of the forensic process is capable of being tested and/or verified. The phrase "preserves the original meaning" intimates that the data derived from the forensic process must be capable of being correctly interpreted. In addition to these points, it is worth noting that the term "digital forensic process" covers not only the methodology employed, but also the underlying technology.

5.1   Evaluation Criteria

Reliability and completeness are the two most critical properties of evidence with respect to digital forensic processes. If the reliability and/or completeness of any potential evidence are questionable, its evidentiary value is greatly diminished. Obviously, the question of evidentiary weight and, in particular, admissibility is a legal question that is ultimately determined by the court. Therefore, it is imperative that a digital forensic process be undertaken in manner that does not diminish the authenticity and/or veracity of the evidence.

So what makes a process forensically sound? More specifically, how can a court or lawyer determine if a claim of forensic soundness is legitimate? Given that digital forensic processes comprise many variables, it is difficult to adopt a prescriptive approach that would apply in every circumstance. The solution is to subject the forensic process to several criteria that determine if forensic soundness is an inherent property or merely an unfounded claim. Once a claim of forensic soundness is shown to be appropriate, it becomes a matter of ascertaining the reliability of the electronic evidence.

We propose four criteria for ascertaining the forensic soundness of a digital forensic process. If all four criteria are satisfied, the forensic process possesses the key properties associated with the concept of being forensically sound.

Criterion 1: Meaning

Has the meaning and, therefore, the interpretation of the electronic evidence been unaffected by the digital forensic process?

When potential electronic evidence is acquired and analyzed, it is important that it be preserved in the state in which it was found and that it not be changed by a digital forensic process unless absolutely unavoidable. While the preservation of the data and its associated properties are critical aspects of this concept, they tend to be used in the context of the acquisition of data as opposed to its analysis. Indeed, some digital forensic technologies may result in subtle changes in the way data is presented (e.g., dates and times may be shown in different formats). However, in this case, the raw binary data has not been directly altered; rather, it differs from the original only in the way it is presented. The meaning of the data is unchanged, although its representation may be modified. Thus, the value of the data is not of itself diminished.

Criterion 2: Errors

Have all errors been reasonably identified and satisfactorily explained so as to remove any doubt over the reliability of the evidence?

It is imperative that all software and hardware errors encountered during a digital forensic process be identified and that their impact be clearly identified and explained. Merely saying that there was an error in copying a file is insufficient. The nature of the error, its impact on the accuracy and reliability of the evidence, and any potential interference on the forensic process are all issues that must be discussed. Therefore, a digital forensic process should be designed to avoid undetectable errors wherever possible. Undetectable errors usually arise when a new piece of software is being used during the evidence acquisition or analysis phases. In such circumstances, it is imperative that all the software tools used in the forensic process be properly tested and assessed prior to their use. When an error is identified, it is in the interest of the digital forensic process to ensure that the nature of the error and its impact if any are clearly identified. Failure to do so can affect the reliability of the evidence. Indeed, Casey [4] notes that "forensic examiners who do not account for error, uncertainty and loss during their analysis may reach incorrect conclusions in the investigative stage and may find it harder to justify their assertions when cross-examined."

Criterion 3: Transparency

Is the digital forensic process capable of being independently examined and verified in its entirety?

Given that the results of a digital forensic process are used to substantiate a particular event or activity, it is critical in the interests of natural justice that the entire forensic process be accurate and reliable. To enable such an assessment, it is of paramount importance that the forensic process be transparent and capable of being independently verified. A key element of verification is the ability to reproduce the forensic process under the same conditions with a consistent level of quality being observed each time the process is run [18].

Transparency can be achieved by documenting all the steps, identifying the forensic software and hardware used, detailing the analysis environment and noting any problems, errors and inconsistencies. A key exception occurs when a part of the forensic process is not disclosed for legitimate legal reasons (e.g., public interest immunity); obviously, determining the validity of any exception is at the discretion of the court.

The level of detail required to ensure transparency will, of course, reside in the overall scope and objectives of the forensic process.

Criterion 4: Experience

Has the digital forensic analysis been undertaken by an individual with sufficient and relevant experience?

Fundamental differences exist between how a digital forensics professional undertakes the examination of computer data and how a person unfamiliar with the forensic process performs the same task. For a forensic process to possess the property of forensic soundness, it must have been designed and implemented with due regard to forensic issues. In digital forensics, such a quality is directly derived from the knowledge and skill of the individual performing the forensic analysis. Consequently, if the individual has inadequate experience, it is questionable how he/she could satisfy the court that the meaning of the resulting data has not been affected, or that any errors encountered do not impact the reliability of the resulting evidence.

6.   Conclusions

Electronic data is very susceptible to alteration or deletion. Whether it is an intentional change resulting from the application of some computer process or an unintentional change arising from system failure or human error, the meaning of electronic data can be altered rapidly and easily. Indeed, just as electronic data is created, changed and/or deleted through the normal operations of a computer system, there is the possibility of change arising from the application of an incorrect or inappropriate digital forensic process. Given that the results of such a process may be tendered as evidence, it is critical that every measure be taken to ensure their reliability and accuracy. To this end, a digital forensic process must be designed and applied with due regard to evidentiary issues. Furthermore, it is important that the forensic process be capable of being examined to determine its reasonableness and reliability. It is only when the forensic process is judged to be reliable and appropriate, that a claim of forensic soundness can truly be made.

References

[1] A. Anderson, G. Mohay, L. Smith, A. Tickle and I. Wilson, Computer Forensics: Past, Present and Future, Technical Report, Information Security Research Centre, Queensland University of Technology, Brisbane, Australia, 1999.

[2] Australian Law Reform Commission, Review of the Uniform Evidence Acts, ALRC Discussion Paper 69, Sydney, Australia (www.au stlii.edu.au/au/other/alrc/publications/dp/69/index.html), 2005.

[3] B. Carrier, Defining digital forensic examination and analysis tools using abstraction layers, *International Journal of Digital Evidence*, vol. 1(4), 2003.

[4] E. Casey, Error, uncertainty and loss in digital evidence, *International Journal of Digital Evidence*, vol. 1(2), 2002.

[5] E. Casey, *Digital Evidence and Computer Crime: Forensic Science, Computers and the Internet*, Academic Press, San Diego, California, 2004.

[6] P. Craiger, M. Pollitt and J. Swauger, Law enforcement and digital evidence, in *Handbook of Information Security, Volume 2*, H. Bidgoli (Ed.), John Wiley, New York, pp. 739–777, 2006.

[7] A. Ghosh, *Handbook 171-2003: Guidelines for the Management of IT Evidence*, Standards Australia, Sydney, Australia, 2003.

[8] M. Hannan, To revisit: What is forensic computing? *Proceedings of the Second Australian Computer, Network and Information Forensics Conference*, pp. 103–111, 2004.

[9] M. Hannan, S. Frings, V. Broucek and P. Turner, Forensic computing theory and practice: Towards developing a methodology for a standardized approach to computer misuse, *Proceedings of the First Australian Computer, Network and Information Forensics Conference*, 2003.

[10] International Organization on Computer Evidence, Guidelines for Best Practice in the Forensic Examination of Digital Technology, Digital Evidence Standards Working Group, 2002.

[11] S. McCombie and M. Warren, Computer forensic: An issue of definition, *Proceedings of the First Australian Computer, Network and Information Forensics Conference*, 2003.

[12] R. McKemmish, What is forensic computing? *Trends and Issues in Crime and Criminal Justice*, no. 118 (www.aic.gov.au/publications /tandi/ti118.pdf), 2002.

[13] National High Tech Crime Unit, Good Practice Guide for Computer Based Electronic Evidence, Association of Chief Police Officers, London, United Kingdom (www.acpo.police.uk/asp/policies/Data /gpg_computer_based_evidence_v3.pdf), 2003.

[14] National Institute of Forensic Science, Melbourne, Australia (www .nifs.com.au).

[15] National Institute of Standards and Technology, Gaithersburg, Maryland (www.nist.gov).

[16] National Institute of Standards and Technology, Disk Imaging Tool Specification (Version 3.1.6), Gaithersburg, Maryland (www.cftt .nist.gov/disk_imaging.htm), 2001.

[17] Oxford University Press, *Compact Oxford English Dictionary (Third Edition)*, Oxford, United Kingdom, 2005.

[18] L. Pan and L. Batten, Reproducibility of digital evidence in forensic investigations, *Proceedings of the 2005 Digital Forensic Research Workshop*, 2005.

[19] D. Ryan and G. Shpantzer, Legal aspects of digital forensics (www.danjryan.com/papers.htm), 2002.

[20] Scientific Working Group on Digital Evidence (www.swgde.org).

[21] C. Spenceley, Evidentiary Treatment of Computer-Produced Material: A Reliability Based Evaluation, Ph.D. Thesis, University of Sydney, Sydney, Australia, 2003.

[22] U.S. Department of Justice, Searching and Seizing Computers and Obtaining Electronic Evidence in Criminal Investigations, Computer Crime and Intellectual Property Section, Washington, DC (www.usdoj.gov/criminal/cybercrime/s&smanual2002.htm), 2002.

Chapter 2

APPLYING TRADITIONAL FORENSIC TAXONOMY TO DIGITAL FORENSICS

Mark Pollitt

Abstract   Early digital forensic examinations were conducted *in toto* – every file on the storage media was examined along with the entire file system structure. However, this is no longer practical as operating systems have become extremely complex and storage capacities are growing geometrically. Examiners now perform targeted examinations using forensic tools and databases of known files, selecting specific files and data types for review while ignoring files of irrelevant type and content. Despite the application of sophisticated tools, the forensic process still relies on the examiner's knowledge of the technical aspects of the specimen and understanding of the case and the law. Indeed, the success of a forensic examination is strongly dependent on how it is designed. This paper discusses the application of traditional forensic taxonomy to digital forensics. The forensic processes of identification, classification/individualization, association and reconstruction are used to develop "forensic questions," which are applied to objectively design digital forensic examinations.

Keywords: Digital evidence process, forensic taxonomy, forensic examination

1.   Introduction

Early forensic practitioners from a variety of jurisdictions and backgrounds recognized that evidence stored in electronic form is easily changed with improper handling. In the early 1990s, the International Association of Computer Investigative Specialists (IACIS) promulgated what was, perhaps, the first set of guidelines for digital forensics. The Association of Chief Police Officers (United Kingdom) followed with a good practice guide. Subsequently, the International Organization on Computer Evidence (IOCE) and the G-8 developed a set of principles for computer-based evidence. All these documents stipulate that digital

Please use the following format when citing this chapter:

Pollitt, M., 2008, in IFIP International Federation for Information Processing, Volume 285; *Advances in Digital Forensics IV*; Indrajit Ray, Sujeet Shenoi; (Boston: Springer), pp. 17–26.

evidence be acquired in its totality and that it not be altered during any subsequent examination [8].

These guidelines and principles are reinforced in virtually every digital forensic model. Despite their differences, most forensic models [1–4, 14, 16] follow evidence acquisition with evidence preservation, typically by creating a digital image of the media. Interested readers are referred to [13] for a review of the principal forensic models.

As a result, virtually all forensic examinations start with the totality of the evidence. The examiner is then required to locate, extract and present the material of forensic value. The two fundamental approaches are selection and reduction, and they are often used in combination. Selection involves searching the data (e.g., using string searches) to locate information of probative value. Reduction involves the removal of information that is not of forensic value. This process often uses "negative hashing," where the hash values of known "good" files are used to eliminate unknown files. Negative hashing is facilitated by repositories of file signatures such as those available at the National Software Reference Library [11].

The selection and reduction approaches are both less than optimal. When applying selection, forensic examiners must know, with some degree of specificity, what they are looking for and where it might be located. The irony of this approach is that the more deterministic the approach, the less complete the answer. In the case of reduction, the evidentiary material that remains is often so voluminous as to be unmanageable. To refine their approach to examinations, forensic examiners carefully consider the facts of the case, the elements of the violation and the behavior of computer users. Experiential knowledge is vital to conducting examinations that are efficient and effective, but efforts to objectively identify and articulate this knowledge have not been very successful.

2.   Traditional Forensic Science

Science has provided a foundation for legal proceedings for more than 100 years. During this time, the science practiced in the legal system has differed from traditional scientific endeavors in its form and application, not in its content. Moreover, while traditional science engages the "scientific method" to drive methods of proof, the legal system has demanded additional approaches to ensure the reliability of the evidence, the scientific methods applied and the resulting testimony. These requirements are the result of judicial decisions rather than scientific research and discourse [17].

Edmond Locard, an early 20th century French criminologist, is considered to be the pioneer of modern forensic science. His celebrated "Exchange Principle" postulated that when objects contact one another, there is an exchange of material [5, 9]. A long list of distinguished forensic scientists have added a number of principles to the corpus of forensic scientific knowledge. Nevertheless, there have been surprisingly few attempts to develop ontologies for these principles. This paper draws on two important approaches, Inman and Rudin's Unifying Paradigm of Forensic Science [5] and Lee and Harris' General Concepts in Forensic Science, to further develop a model for digital forensics [7].

3.   Need for Structure

Thomas Kuhn's seminal work, *The Structure of Scientific Revolutions* [6], discussed the importance of paradigms:

> "The study of paradigms is what mainly prepares the student for membership in the particular scientific community with which he will later practice. Because he here joins men who learned the bases of their field from the same concrete models, the subsequent practice will seldom evoke overt disagreement over fundamentals. Men whose research is based on the shared paradigms are committed to the same rules and standards for scientific practice."

The adoption of a paradigm certainly facilitates the instruction of students, but it also allows for the formulation of an accepted practice that adds to the efficiency, effectiveness and reliability of the practitioner's work. The question then becomes: What paradigm?

4.   Application of Traditional Forensic Science

Inscribed on one of four large statues in front of the U.S. National Archives is the quotation: *"What is Past is Prologue."* Many credit Shakespeare for this quotation, but it was, in fact, modified from the original (Act II of *The Tempest*) by John Russell Pope, the architect of the building [10]. It is appropriate that an idea from several hundred years ago that was adapted to modern usage lights the way for the newest forensic science. Traditional forensic science has been developing its paradigm for decades and some of its concepts can be adapted to digital forensics.

Locard's Exchange Principle influenced a number of forensic scientists to develop new ways for looking at evidence. Inman and Rudin [5] have analyzed six of these approaches, categorizing two of them as "principles" and four as "processes."

The two principles are "transfer" and "the divisibility of matter." The first is recognized as Locard's observation; the second was proposed by

Inman and Rudin as a way of explaining the ability to impute characteristics to the whole from a separated piece. It is easy to see how these principles underlie many of the biological, physical and chemical examinations conducted by traditional forensic scientists. The two principles also apply to digital forensics – digital evidence exhibits transference in its interactions and electronic duplicates are representative of the original evidentiary items. But these principles do not have a great deal to offer in terms of developing examination strategies.

On the other hand, the four processes of "identification," "classification/individualization," "association" and "reconstruction" have the potential to be very useful from the perspective of planning digital forensic examinations. The following sections analyze these four processes and discuss how they might be adapted to digital forensics.

4.1   Identification

Inman and Rudin credit Saferstein [15] with defining the concept of identification as the physiochemical nature of the evidence. They note that being able to accurately describe an item or its composition may be sufficient for a given forensic purpose. For example, when the mere presence of illicit drugs is an important element of a crime being investigated, the identification of a white powder as containing cocaine, dextrose and talc may be all that is required.

In the discipline of digital forensics, identification helps describe digital evidence in terms of its context – physically (a particular brand of hard drive), structurally (the number of cylinders, heads and sectors), logically (a FAT32 partition), location (directory and file) or content (a memo, spreadsheet, email or photograph). The presence of metadata or the existence of a particular letter (not necessarily their content) may be probative in an investigation. In other situations, as in child pornography cases, the nature of the content is dispositive. On the other hand, the mere presence of connections between certain computers may demonstrate a key fact in an intrusion case.

Examiners are routinely asked to find evidence on computer storage media, but the tasking is usually done in an investigative context as opposed to a digital context. This places the burden on the examiner to translate the task into an examination plan or strategy. By focusing on the characteristics of the potential evidence, it is possible to search for it in the same way that one looks for cocaine in a drug investigation – by conducting specific examinations.

This process is done best by working backwards. First, we ask, What information is desired? The next logical question is: In what form might this kind of information be stored? Finally, Where might this information be located? Selecting a tool and query that searches in specific locations for limited types of data that have particular characteristics significantly reduces the forensic burden. Simultaneously, it produces "rich" information that may be sufficient for the investigation.

4.2   Classification/Individualization

Inman and Rudin draw on the work of several forensic scientists to explain the concepts of classification and individualization. Classification is an attempt to determine a common origin; individualization uses a set of characteristics to uniquely identify a specimen. The notions are clarified using an example.

A video surveillance camera captures the shooting death of a victim. The perpetrator cannot be identified from the video, but the image is clear enough to identify the type of firearm. A bullet is recovered from the victim and submitted for examination. Based on the bullet's weight and composition, and the size and twist of the rifling marks, the examiner may be able to identify an ammunition manufacturer, the caliber of the weapon and, potentially, its manufacturer. These are all class characteristics, which, on their own, do not link the suspect to the weapon or the weapon to the bullet.

After a suspect is identified, a search reveals a box of unused ammunition and a weapon consistent with the one in the surveillance video. The characteristics of the seized ammunition are identical to the bullet obtained from the victim. As a result, it can be determined that the bullets have a common origin and are therefore "class evidence." The recovered weapon is test-fired and the resulting bullet and the bullet recovered from the victim are microscopically examined. Matching the micro-striations on the bullets allows the examiner to identify the two bullets as coming from the recovered weapon, to the exclusion of all others. This is the process of identification, which yields what is referred to as "individual evidence."

The application of these concepts to digital evidence is relatively straightforward. File systems, partitions and individual files have characteristics that allow for their classification. The location and structure of data on storage media can determine the partition type and the file system. Objects such as file allocation tables, master file tables and inodes define certain file systems. Individual files may have naming conventions as well as internal data structures (headers, footers, metadata, etc.) that determine their origin (common source). An example is a Microsoft Word file, which has a well-documented internal structure. It would be accurate to describe the origin of such a file as being produced by Microsoft Word. All of these are class characteristics. Conversely, a file may be positively identified based on its mathematical signature (i.e., hash value), which corresponds to the process of identification.

4.3   Association

Inman and Rudin bemoan the lack of an accepted definition of the term "association" in the forensic context. They proceed to define it as "an inference of contact between the source of the evidence and a target."

Inman and Rudin use an example where reference fibers are compared with the fibers actually found on a body. When considered in the context of all the facts in the case and all other sources of the same fibers, the examiner may be able to justify a conclusion that the victim had been in contact with a particular source of the fibers.

The physical transfer of evidence is uncommon in digital evidence cases, but it does occur. An item of digital media may be linked to a computer by Windows Registry entries [12]. In malware and intrusion cases, it is often necessary to link the presence of specific files or code to the perpetrator and victim computers. The association of files is also important in intellectual property investigations.

In digital forensics, it is necessary to identify the items (files, data structures and code) that need to be associated and to determine where they might be located and the tools that could be used to locate the items. The required information is then extracted and the associations are presented.

Lee and Harris [7] observe that forensic evidence may demonstrate the commission of a crime (*corpus delicti*) or document the methodology of the crime (*modus operandi*). They identify other modalities, but most of them overlap with the Inman and Rudin taxonomy and are not addressed here. However, Lee and Harris describe one additional area that must be discussed in the context of digital forensics – that of providing investigative leads.

Computers and digital media are potentially valuable sources of lead material. The problem, from the time management and efficacy perspectives, is that it is difficult to define specific goals and objectives for many categories of lead material. Some will be discovered in the normal course of identifying material on known targets. Much will not and will only be linked based on a thorough knowledge of the case, the crime or both. This situation has often been used to justify the assignment of sworn officers to forensic duties. However, the discussion of this issue is beyond the scope of this paper.

4.4   Reconstruction

Inman and Rudin define reconstruction as the "ordering of associations in space and time." Reconstructing a series of events is more common in the engineering fields than in the physical and biological sciences. It is, perhaps, more common in digital forensics than other fields because of the dates and times stamped on metadata pertaining to data, files, file systems and network communications. It is important to recognize, as Inman and Rudin do, that time is often a relative value or ordering rather than a definitive value.

In cases involving the creation and/or alteration of documents or images, the files and file systems may provide information about sequences of events if not the exact dates and times of the events. Comparing file or e-mail metadata may permit the "normalization" of dates and times from multiple computers within a margin of error. Using monitor software, it is possible to observe and document changes to files and file systems that result from the execution of computer code. Generally, the more data points considered and the more consistent the metadata, the more probable that the specific event sequence is correct.

5.   From Principle to Question

Inman and Rudin state:

> "Before the criminalist ever picks up a magnifying glass, pipette or chemical reagent, he must have an idea of where he is headed; he must define a question that science can answer."

This seemingly simple statement in many ways defines the forensic case management problem. It is important to understand how to define an examination as one or a series of investigative or legal questions, which are translated into scientific questions (to use Inman and Rudin's terminology). This suggests a two-part process: defining the legal/investigative questions and then – and only then – defining the digital forensic (scientific) questions.

While this seems obvious, it is not how many examinations are developed. Often, the investigator provides a case synopsis to the examiner and asks the examiner to study the evidence and provide any and all information that might be useful. Sometimes, the examiner will think, even before the investigator has finished speaking, about what could be done. This results in an examination being designed based on what could be done instead of on the specific information that should be located.

The alternative proposed here is to begin by defining the legal or investigative questions that the investigator thinks could be answered from the information contained in the evidence. The examiner may well need to discuss the questions with the investigator, continuously refining the requirements and providing feedback on what is possible, likely and remote. Time spent developing the investigative questions pays off in the ability of the examiner to translate them accurately into an efficient examination plan that is responsive to the legal/investigative questions and that is supported by science. An important part of this discussion is for the examiner and investigator to mutually understand the tasking and the limitations on the potential results. The latter is important for several reasons. Over-reliance on low probability results is misleading, and it may become the weak link in a courtroom presentation. Expending a great deal of examiner effort to produce information of limited value is a poor use of resources. Experience has demonstrated that the process also helps manage investigative expectations.

Once the legal/investigative questions are finalized, the examiner can begin to develop the scientific questions. It is here that the forensic processes discussed above become relevant. Most investigative/legal questions can be translated directly into one or more of the four processes.

For example, several forensic questions can be created to answer whether or not information concerning a particular person is present in a specimen. What name(s) should be searched? Where will information about the person(s) be located? Are there any temporal constraints on when this information might appear? Having answered these questions, the next step is to select a technique or tool that can locate the information.

The above is an example of the identification process. A classification question would involve locating all the images relevant to a certain investigation. Matching an image located online or on another computer to an image found on the specimen computer is an example of individualization.

Investigators could benefit by connecting cameras to images, users to accounts and activities, computers to network connections, and devices to computers. Each of these involves the specification of an association question. Malware, intellectual property and intrusion investigations often rely on the presentation of a sequence of events and the demonstration of cause and effect; these would require the framing of reconstruction questions. When investigative questions are translated into questions based on forensic processes, examiners can develop efficient and objective tests that yield definitive conclusions.

Perhaps the most valuable aspect of this process is that it provides a definitive end to an examination. Many forensic examinations languish because the examiner does not know when the case is finished. If an examination is designed based on what is possible, the examination will never be completed because it is always possible to do more. However, if the questions are defined at the outset, the examination is done when all the questions have been answered. Note that it does not matter what answers are obtained, just that they are accurate.

6. Conclusions

Traditional forensic science has developed an effective and relatively efficient process that has stood the tests of time and the courts. Digital forensics practitioners can learn much from this process. Incorporating the development of forensic questions into the examination process ensures scientific objectivity while simultaneously assisting in case management. Managers can use this approach to leverage their limited resources. Educators can also utilize the approach to ensure compete and consistent results from training programs.

References

[1] V. Baryamureeba and F. Tushabe, The enhanced digital investigation process model, *Proceedings of the Fourth Digital Forensic Research Workshop*, 2004.

[2] N. Beebe and J. Clark, A hierarchical, objectives-based framework for the digital investigation process, *Proceedings of the Fourth Digital Forensic Research Workshop*, 2004.

[3] B. Carrier, Defining digital forensic examination and analysis tools using abstraction layers, *International Journal of Digital Evidence*, vol. 1(4), 2003.

[4] B. Carrier and E. Spafford, Getting physical with the digital investigation process, *International Journal of Digital Evidence*, vol. 2(2), 2003.

[5] K. Inman and N. Rudin, *Principles and Practices of Criminalistics: The Profession of Forensic Science*, CRC Press, Boca Raton, Florida, 2001.

[6] T. Kuhn, *The Structure of Scientific Revolutions*, University of Chicago Press, Chicago, Illinois, 1970.

[7] H. Lee and H. Harris, *Physical Evidence in Forensic Science*, Lawyers and Judges Publishing Company, Tucson, Arizona, 2000.

[8] G. Mohay, A, Anderson, B. Collie, O. de Vel and R. McKemmish, *Computer and Intrusion Forensics*, Artech House, Boston, Massachusetts, 2003.

[9] A. Mozayani and C. Noziglia, *The Forensic Laboratory Handbook: Procedures and Practice*, Humana Press, Totowa, New Jersey, 2006.

[10] National Archives and Records Administration, The Future, College Park, Maryland (www.archives.gov/about/history/building-an -archives/statues/statue-future.html).

[11] National Institute of Standards and Technology, National Software Reference Library, Gaithersburg, Maryland (www.nsrl.nist.gov).

[12] B. Nelson, *Guide to Computer Forensics and Investigations*, Thompson Course Technology, Boston, Massachusetts, 2006.

[13] M. Pollitt, An ad hoc review of digital forensic models, presented at the *Second International Workshop on Systematic Approaches to Digital Forensic Engineering*, 2007.

[14] M. Reith, C. Carr and G. Gunsch, An examination of digital forensic models, *International Journal of Digital Evidence*, vol. 1(3), 2002.

[15] R. Saferstein, *Forensic Science Handbook, Volume II*, Prentice-Hall, Englewood Cliffs, New Jersey, 1988.

[16] P. Stephenson, Modeling of post-incident root cause analysis, *International Journal of Digital Evidence*, vol. 2(2), 2003.

[17] C. Welch, Flexible standards, deferential review: Daubert's legacy of confusion, *Harvard Journal of Law and Public Policy*, vol. 29(3), 2006.

II

EVIDENCE RECOVERY

Chapter 3

RECOVERING DATA FROM FAILING FLOPPY DISKS

Frederick Cohen and Charles Preston

Abstract   As floppy disks and other similar media age, they may lose data due to a reduction in the retention of electromagnetic fields over time, mainly due to environmental factors. However, the coding techniques used to write data can be exploited along with the fault mechanisms themselves to successfully read data from failing floppy disks. This paper discusses the problem of recovering data from failing floppy disks and describes a practical example involving a case of substantial legal value.

Keywords: Floppy disks, field density loss, weak bits, data recovery

1.   Introduction

This paper discusses a method for recovering data from floppy disks that are failing due to "weak bits." It describes a repetitive read technique that has successfully recovered data in forensic cases and discusses the analysis of the results of repetitive reads in terms of yielding forensically-sound data. This technique is not new; however, neither the technique nor the analysis necessary to support its use in legal matters have been published.

The case discussed in this paper involved a fifteen-year-old floppy disk, which contained the only copy of the binary version of a software program that was subject to intellectual property claims of sufficient value to warrant recovery beyond the means normally used by commercial recovery firms. After attempts to read the disk by these firms had failed, the disk was given to the authors to use more rigorous and possibly destructive data recovery methods, subject to court approval.

Several techniques for recovering data from hard-to-read floppy disks are in common use, including reading only relevant sectors from a disk where other sectors fail to read properly, and altering the drive alignment

Please use the following format when citing this chapter:

Cohen, F. and Preston, C., 2008, in IFIP International Federation for Information Processing, Volume 285; *Advances in Digital Forensics IV*; Indrajit Ray, Sujeet Shenoi; (Boston: Springer), pp. 29–41.

to better align the heads with the tracks as originally written. In the case of interest, important data was contained in hard-to-read sectors of the disk, and custom head alignment only marginally altered the recovery characteristics of the disk.

A floppy disk can also be modified to read analog signals and allow the detection thresholds to be altered. Additionally, signals from the read heads can be amplified, rates of rotation can be increased to boost induced currents, and other similar methods can be attempted. But they introduce various problems, including increased time requirements and cost. Furthermore, it is difficult to prove that the methods recover valid data instead of merely turning noise into data.

Other exotic techniques involve analog reads using digital storage scopes, the use of epoxies with suspended fine ferrous material that attach to the media and are visible under a microscope, and the use of magnetic force scanning tunneling microscopy. Some of these techniques are destructive; all are expensive and may result in data loss.

2.   Data Recovery Methodology

The obvious data recovery method is to attempt repeated sector-by-sector reads of a disk; failed sectors are repeated until valid reads are completed. Data from the sectors is then assembled to create a complete image of the disk. This technique has several advantages: (i) it only uses the designed features of the floppy disk drive and, thus, requires very little in the way of explanation or analysis to be considered credible; (ii) it is relatively low cost and takes relatively little time to perform; and (iii) it uses the built-in coding analysis methods and phased lock loops of the floppy drive to decode changes resulting from orientations of charges in areas on the disk. This eliminates the problems involved in explaining coding errors, side band signals, additional introduced errors and other issues associated with building special-purpose hardware.

The specific program used in the case was executed from a bootable White Glove Linux CD, which was kept with the evidence after processing to ensure that the process could be repeated if necessary. The following shell script code was executed:

```
for i in 'count 0 1439'; do
    dd conv$=$noerror bs$=$512 count=1 skip=\$i if=/dev/fd0$>$
    noerr/\$i.out
done
```

The count command counts from the first value (0) to the second value (1,439) in increments of one. For each count value, the noerr command is executed with the conversion option that, in the event of errors, retries are to be attempted an unlimited number of times. The block size is set to 512 (normal block size for such a floppy disk) and a count of one block per execution is used. This is done after skipping count number of blocks from the beginning of the media (in this case the floppy disk /dev/fd0). The output is stored in a file whose name includes the block number (noerr/[count].out, where [count] is the block number and noerr is the directory used to store all the blocks). On each read attempt, a file is created, but unless the file read succeeds with a valid checksum, the file is overwritten on the next attempt.

Reading one sector at a time is beneficial because a single error in a read produces a failure for the entire read. If a single sector takes twenty attempts on average to succeed, reading two sectors would require an average of 400 attempts. Since reading less than one sector does not involve any special execution, this approach minimizes the number of reads and reduces unnecessary wear and tear on the disk while reading it repeatedly until the CRC code and the data match.

When applied to the evidence disk, this process produced different numbers of retry cycles on different sectors. There were no retry cycles on sectors that could be consistently read without errors. For the previously unreadable sectors, the number of retry cycles required ranged from one to more than 70, most of them in the 20 to 30 range. Each sector was stored individually in a file of 512 bytes on a hard disk as it was read, and stored with a filename associated with the sector number as described above. The total number of blocks was 1,440 with 512 bytes each (737,260 bytes of data), corresponding to the entire readable contents of the 720K floppy disk.

The individual files representing the blocks on the evidence disk are independently examinable. Alternatively, they may be assembled in a single file and mounted using a loopback mounting interface or written to a fresh floppy, which can then be read as if it were the original evidence disk. For the case being discussed, the assembly was done using the following program:

```
for i in 'count 0 1439'; do
    dd seek=\$i if=noerr/\$i.out of=noerrdd.out
done
```

The blocks were written to the file at the appropriate locations in the same way as they were read from the evidence disk. Multiple copies were made of the recovered disk for use by all parties. Having read the disk and created forensic duplicates, it is necessary to show that the method is forensically sound.

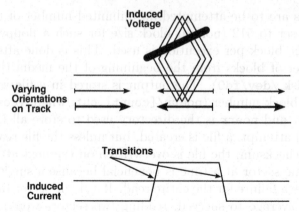

Figure 1. Digital signal encoding on floppy disks.

3. Weak Bits and Floppy Disk Failure Modes

Floppy disks tend to degrade over time and under various environmental conditions such as temperature and humidity. This sometimes results in the presence of so-called "weak bits." Weak bits are caused by degraded electromagnetic orientation alignments or charge densities that reduce voltage and current swings to levels that are too low to reliably trigger transitions in the hardware detectors. Weak bits may also be caused by the physical shifting of magnetic materials under temperature changes, by the growth of organisms on the media, or by friction that abrades portions of the coatings used to retain charges.

Floppy disks typically use the modified frequency modulation (MFM) hardware-level coding [5], in which timed flux density transitions are used to encode bits. Figure 1 illustrates how floppy disks store data. The write head causes magnetic particles to align in one of two orientations along cylinders (concentric circles) at different distances from the center of the platter. Because the circles have different radii, the timings of transitions from one orientation to the other vary with radius. Consequently, lead-in transitions are required to set up an oscillator to synchronize this change detection.

Figure 2 (adapted from [3]) illustrates the mechanisms used to read data from floppy disks. These include a read head, amplifier, pulse generator, phased lock loop, demodulator and additional hardware needed to produce a controller that is usable by a computer at the bus level.

Figure 3 (adapted from [3]) shows the signals that appear at different locations in Figure 2 [3]; it helps clarify the effects of reduced signal levels in the media. As the analog signal (A) degrades, peak pulses

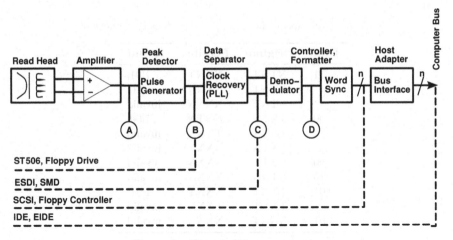

Figure 2. Floppy disk components.

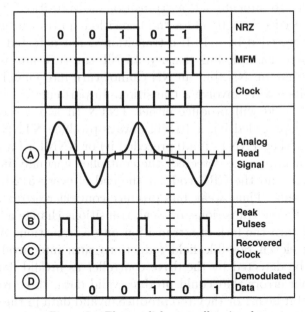

Figure 3. Floppy disk controller signals.

(B) disappear, causing the loss of MFM transitions, which result in demodulated data (D) and phased lock loop desynchronization.

When a floppy disk is being read, changes in field density produce induced currents in the head, which, regardless of the field direction, is seen as a transition (T); the lack of a change at a timing signal produces "no transition" (N). The MFM coding uses a "no transition–transition"

Table 1.   Code space changes from flux density reductions.

Data	Original	Possible	Result
[11]	NTNT	NNNT	1[01]
	NTNT	NTNN	[10]
	NTNT	NNNN	invalid
0[00]	TNTN	NNTN	1[00]
	TNTN	TNNN	invalid
	TNTN	NNNN	invalid
1[00]	NNTN	NNNN	invalid
[10]	NTNN	NNNN	invalid
0[01]	TNNT	NNNT	1[01]
	TNNT	TNNN	invalid
1[01]	NNNT	NNNN	invalid

(NT) sequence to indicate a 1, a "transition–no-transition" (TN) to indicate a 0 preceded by a 0, and a "no transition–no-transition" (NN) to indicate a 0 preceded by a 1. If a transition is not detected because of a loss in electromagnetic flux density, an NT can turn into an NN or a TN can turn into an NN, but an NN cannot turn into an NT or a TN.

Pairs of bits always involve a transition. In particular, a 11 will produce NTNT, a 00 will produce either TNTN (if a 0 preceded it) or NNTN (if a 1 preceded it), a 10 will always produce NTNN, and a 01 will produce either TNNT (if a 0 preceded it) or NNNT (if a 1 preceded it). If no transitions are detected, the controller normally indicates an error condition and the CRC code at the end of every 512-bit block of data is irrelevant. Thus, weak bits produce controller errors due to the inability to observe transitions, or weak transitions change a T to an N. They cannot turn the lack of a transition into a transition. As a result, seven out of eleven possible field reductions turn into invalid codings that should be detected by the drive controller as invalid data. Of the remaining four errors that could produce valid data, three require that the previous bit be a 1 or they too produce invalid data in the controller.

Table 1 shows all the possible changes. In the table, data values represented by T and NT sequences are enclosed in brackets (e.g., [11]) and the required preceding bits are indicated prior to the bracketed pairs (e.g., 1[00]).

None of these errors can produce a transition of the coded data from a 0 to a 1. Thus, a weak bit error can never turn a 0 into a 1; it can only turn a 1 into a 0 or produce an invalid code space output. Additional consistency checks could potentially detect errors such as the transition of 0[00] to 1[00], but the previous 1 bit could not be the result of a

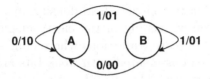

Figure 4. Finite state machine for floppy disk reads.

weak bit (or its coding would be a 0 to 1 transition that a weak bit cannot produce in that position). Therefore, this eliminates the other possible errors that turn 0[01] into 1[01] and 0[00] into 1[00], leaving only the transitions of 1[11] to 1[01] and [11] to [10] due to reduced electromagnetic flux density. If the previous bit was not a 1[NT] or the reduction in flux density reduced the T to an N, then the 1[01] error is also impossible.

Unfortunately, depending on their design, floppy controllers do not always produce error outputs for non-existent transitions. Figure 4 shows the finite state machine for producing output bits based on the current state [5]. Note the lack of state transitions for the 0/11 and 0/01 cases and the 1/10 and 1/11 cases. They are typically designated as "Don't Care" (DC) values, which leaves the designer free to optimize the electronics by ignoring outputs that in theory cannot happen. In practice, a weak transition could produce a change from 0/10 to 0/11; however, the controller would be in State A and this is only identified as a transition for State B. The incomplete specification of error states produces arbitrary behavior depending on the design choice. Fortunately, the CRC code used in floppy disks can compensate for most errors.

Our analysis is based on the assumption that a weakened field density in the locality of a bit cannot trigger a transition; this is worth discussing further. Normally, for a transition to be detected by a floppy disk controller, the electromagnetic field density in one region has to be oriented in one direction while that in the adjacent region has to be oriented in the opposite direction. Which direction is 01 and which direction is 10 coupled with the direction of movement of the disk in the drive dictate whether the drive head gets a positive or negative impulse; but these are not differentiated by the controller – both are considered to be transitions. If a transition from the maximum field density to a zero field density were to trigger a transition, floppy disks would be very unreliable because regions near the tracks are commonly not used and any minor movement in the head could cause such a transition. In addition, the devices are designed so that positive and negative field densities can ensure sound triggering. A half-level density change should not trigger a transition on most floppy disk drives. For this reason, even a maximum field density area adjacent to a zero field density area should not trigger a transition; thus, the weakening of the electromagnetic field strength on the disk should not create transitions where none existed. Of course, the physical phenomena associated with weak bits are analog in nature at this level of granularity. The size of a region of storage on a 720K floppy disk is on the order of 1/8000" in circumference. Because of this relatively high density, most common physical phenomena are unlikely to reduce the field density of one region to near zero while preserving the density of the area next to it at full strength. A scratch could cause this to happen, but then the damage would be permanent and would likely produce the same level of transition on each use.

An electromagnetic field such as that produced by a magnet passing near the disk, a temperature condition or a biological phenomenon is highly unlikely to produce such a dramatic edge condition. There is a strong tendency for these phenomena to produce regions with decreasing effects as a function of distance. This produces a slow transition in field density resulting in a change in field strength with distance that will not normally produce a transition in the floppy disk controller. As a result, it reasonable to assume that no transitions will be created by reductions in electromagnetic field density associated with weak bits, and only the loss of transitions is likely to occur from these physical phenomena.

4.   Code Analysis and Error Rates

In addition to the MFM coding, floppy disks also use a CRC code at the end of each sector after it is written. This is highly likely to be inconsistent when certain classes of errors occur in portions of the sector. It is easy to detect single bit flips, multiple bit flips in close proximity and several other combinations of bit flips. According to Freeman [1]:

> "Any bit error term E(x) which is an exact multiple of P(x) will not be detected. This is the case for the two-bit error 10000001, where the two bad bits are 7 bits apart. Note that 10000001 = (1011) (1101)(11). The allowable separation between two bad bits is related to the choice of P(x). In general, bit errors and bursts up to N bits long will be detected for a prime P(x) of order N. For arbitrary bit errors longer than N bits, the odds are 1 in 2N than a totally false bit pattern will nonetheless lead to a zero remainder. In essence, 100% detection is assured for all errors E(x) not an exact multiple of P(x). For a 16-bit CRC, this means:
>
>> 100% detection of single-bit errors
>>
>> 100% detection of all adjacent double-bit errors
>>
>> 100% detection of any errors spanning up to 16 bits
>>
>> 100% detection of all two-bit errors not separated by exactly $2^{16}-1$ bits (this means all two-bit errors in practice!)

For arbitrary multiple errors spanning more than 16 bits, at worst 1 in 216 failures, which is nonetheless over the 99.995% detection rate."

If we assume that the CRC is intact, the available error modes from weak bits are such that the degradation mechanism would have to produce reduced flux densities exactly 32 transition distances from each other for the CRC code to fail to detect pairs of errors. Reductions in flux density producing lost transitions in adjacent bits or other sequences of less than 32 transition areas (representing 16 bits of data) are detected by CRC codes with 100% accuracy unless they range over large areas, in which case they would produce invalid codes in the MFM decoding mechanism. Thus, the physical phenomena that produce weak bits are very unlikely to create conditions under which data from a sector correctly matches the CRC code and no MFM coding error is produced, but an alteration from the loss of a transition occurs.

This implies that if weak bits cause errors and a successful read of the data with matching CRC code is completed, it is highly likely that the data recovered accurately reflects the data written to that sector. While it is difficult to calculate the probability, it is certainly less than the probability of errors associated with MFM or CRC alone. In other words, there is no known synergistic effect that can cause one of them to correct an error produced by the other.

The method used tends to support the contention that disk failures are caused by weak bits. Specifically, if another mechanism was in play (e.g., alignment errors or mechanical defects in the original writer), then the realignment process would have yielded better or worse data instead of nearly identical error behavior. If bits were not written at all or if a typical contemporaneous weak bit writing mechanism were used, the levels would be unlikely to vary across such a wide range of re-reads. The fact that different numbers of re-reads are needed at different locations on the disk indicates that the failure mechanism produces errors distributed over a range of electromagnetic field losses, e.g., as a result of overheating due to improper storage, contamination by fungi or the loss of data with age, all of which take place over time rather than instantaneously. These are precisely the sorts of errors that the CRC codes were designed to detect.

One issue that must be addressed is the potential that repeated reads could eventually lead to a valid CRC code and no MFM errors, which would result in false sector data being accepted as legitimate. This particular scenario, because it involves weak bits, is less complicated to analyze than a scenario in which random changes are made. Specifically, the changes associated with weak bits tend to be all in one direction, which eliminates transitions and, thus, changes of 1's to 0's. The probability of lost transitions causing detections is at least 17/22 for each transition based on Table 1 (number of invalid transitions versus number of rows). Because of the nature of the CRC coding, errors that go undetected must be in quantities larger than 16 bits and distributed across the sector data area, or as combinations of the sector data area and the CRC area with a probability no higher than 1 in 216. Since the CRC and MFM methods are not correlated in any way as far as we are aware, a reasonable assumption is that the probability of both methods failing to detect a change due to reduced electromagnetic density is no greater than 1 in $2^{16} \times (5/22)^{16}$, which is less than 1 in 1,015. The probability of encountering an erroneous data recovery is low enough that even for hundreds of retries, there is almost no chance that false recovery would occur.

The above analysis ignores retries during actual recovery. Many read errors were corrected after a relatively small number of re-reads, ranging from 1 to 15 retries, with a few samples having more retries. Several sectors could be read only after about 80 retries; none took significantly more than 80 retries. Since the floppy drive does three retries per reported retry, the actual number of attempts was about 240. Exact figures are unavailable because of court orders and the examination cannot be repeated because there is no way to create another equivalent disk. It is somewhat disturbing that many sectors had on the order of 80 retries and the individuals who received the disk indicated that certain portions of the recovered blocks were corrupted. Future research should attempt to understand this problem.

The well-known birthday paradox [2] appears to be relevant to the case at hand. According to the paradox, if a group of 23 people has randomly distributed birthdays, the probability is about $\frac{1}{2}$ that two of them have the same birthday. Furthermore, the 50% probability of matching birthdays occurs when the number of samples is approximately 1.1 times the square root of the sample size (for large sample sizes). For a 16-bit CRC (65,536 possible values), the value $1.1 \times \sqrt{65536}$ is 281.6. Therefore, as the number of reads approaches 282, the probability of a collision is about 50%. However, the CRC situation is slightly different from the birthday paradox because the CRC values are not selected without replacement in the sample. Furthermore, plots of the birthday paradox, which has no known closed-form solution, show that the probability changes more or less linearly around the square root; thus, it would be unexpected to have a peak near the square root.

Some other mechanism is possibly at work, but we do not know what it is. The birthday paradox does not explain the uneven distribution of recoveries. Moreover, the CRC results are not necessarily generalizable to weak bit failures that produce less than random results. If a floppy drive is unable to detect coding errors at the level of transitions and the "Don't Care" (DC) states of the finite state machine that decodes the content do not produce errors, other sources of error likely exist, which is a potential weakness of the technique.

5.   Correcting Errors

As discussed above, some blocks that are read successfully after about 80 retries are suspect. However, the errors produced by weak bits are still limited, which is very helpful.

Two approaches for error correction may be considered. One is to perform the re-read process repeatedly and match the results from multiple runs to determine if there is consistency in some portion of the bits decoded across multiple runs. The other is to determine which bits could have been altered. Unfortunately, repeated reads cause a floppy disk to degrade further because of mechanical wear. This is especially problematic when only one evidence sample exists.

At this time, we have not analyzed the errors produced by weak bits with consistent CRC codes. However, we have investigated the reconstitution of the original content, albeit to a limited extent.

Note that only 1-0 transitions can occur and only in particular locations within bit sequences. In particular, a 1-0 transition can only occur when a 11 turns into a 10 or 01, which is denoted as 11-[10/01]. Moreover, patterns appearing on decoded disk content cannot all result from lost transitions. Therefore, the candidates for lost transition changes are very limited and specific bits can be definitively determined not to have resulted from a flux density loss.

One approach for revealing the bits that could and could not have been altered by such faults is to examine all possible 11-[10/01] transitions in each re-read block and identify those that form valid parts of the code space both before and after transitions are lost. An observed 11 or 00 cannot come from such a change, so all pairs of 1's and 0's can be eliminated from the analysis, reducing the number of possible faults on a random content block by 50%.

Substantial improvements are possible when the language is known and the language has redundancy. The typical content of English, for example, is on the order of 2.3 bits per byte [4]. This means that if four bits per byte are potentially corrupted and each of the two remaining pairs could only have been produced by one of two codings, all of the original text should be recoverable. For example if the original text is

$This_8$ = 124 150 151 163 (Initial 0 bit stops intra-word effects)

124_8 = 01 010 100_2 (No valid weak bit errors)

150_8 = 01 101 $000_2 \rightarrow$ 00 101 000_2 = 50_8 = '(' = T(is

151_8 = 01 101 001_2 (No valid weak bit errors)

163_8 = 01 110 $011_2 \rightarrow$ 00 110 011_2 = 63_8 = '3' = Thi3

163_8 = 01 110 $011_2 \rightarrow$ 01 010 011_2 = 123_8 = 'S' = ThiS

163_8 = 01 110 $011_2 \rightarrow$ 01 100 011_2 = 143_8 = 'c' = Thic

163_8 = 01 110 $011_2 \rightarrow$ 01 110 010_2 = 162_8 = 'r' = Thir

163_8 = 01 110 $011_2 \rightarrow$ 01 110 001_2 = 161_8 = 'q' = Thiq

Figure 5. Procedure for inverting faults.

"This" in ASCII, only a few outputs can arise from missing transitions. Note that all intra-byte pairings include a 0 because ASCII is a seven-bit code and, thus, the initial 0 bit stops any 1-0 transitions from crossing the byte boundaries.

Double bit errors can be produced by weak bits in this situation, and they produce new valid codes, resulting in additional codes for "s" in "This" only. There are also other valid codes that can produce these same values from different lost transactions. For example, 161_8 (01 110 001_2) can be produced by 11 110 001 and a wide range of other values that involve turning 0's into 1's. The procedure for inverting these faults involves generating the set of all possible source bytes and eliminating those that do not make sense in the language.

The procedure for inverting faults is illustrated in Figure 5. For example, several different characters can replace the "q" in "Thiq," but the only valid ones in English would be "n" and "s," corresponding to "Thin" and "This," respectively. The code for "n" is 110_8 or 01 001 000_2, which cannot produce 161_8 through any combination of missed transitions. Similarly, "Thir," "Thic," "ThiS," and "Thi3" cannot be generated from "Thin," but can be generated from "This" with only 1-0 transitions. Extending this to the word as a whole, "T" and "i" cannot be altered by 1-0 failures from missed transitions, and other sources of "(" (50_8) that fit in the English word "T?i?," where the second "?" must be transformable into any one of the identified values are again limited.

6. Conclusions

The multiple read technique is effective at recovering data from failing floppy disks. It produces accurate results with a high probability in a reasonable amount of time with relatively low damage to the original evidence. Because the technique relies on normal floppy disk reads using standard unmodified equipment, it is easier to implement than exotic methods and less likely to be challenged in court.

The principal disadvantage of the technique is that repeated reads cause wear and tear. Another disadvantage is that the technique does not reveal the specific mechanism of failure even if it produces reasonable results. Also, large numbers of reads may not produce valid results for a sector, requiring the technique to be terminated manually and restarted at the next sector. Furthermore, the possibility exists that repeated reads could produce invalid data that matches the CRC codes without creating invalid MFM codes in the controller. Fortunately, in cases where the numbers of re-reads are on the order of hundreds or where reads can be completed with questioned data, the limits on 11-[10/01] transitions and language redundancy can be used to correct errors.

Avenues for future work involve automating the decoding and analysis processes and conducting a detailed investigation of multiple errors in CRC codes. While the data recovery technique is applicable to all MFM-coded media, it does not apply directly to other storage media (e.g., hard drives and CD-ROMs). Our future research will attempt to develop reliable data recovery techniques for modern storage media.

References

[1] R. Freeman, *Practical Data Communications*, John Wiley and Sons, New York, 1995.

[2] D. Knuth, *The Art of Computer Programming – Sorting and Searching*, Addison-Wesley, Reading, Massachusetts, 1973.

[3] H. Leimkuller, Computer evidence analysis and recovery of magnetic storage media data, *Proceedings of the Twenty-Ninth IEEE International Carnahan Conference on Security Technology*, pp. 147–153, 1995.

[4] C. Shannon, A mathematical theory of communications, *Bell Systems Technical Journal*, vol. 27, pp. 379–423; vol. 27, 623–656, 1948.

[5] P. Siegel, Recording codes for digital magnetic storage, *IEEE Transactions on Magnetics*, vol. 21(5), pp. 1344–1349, 1985.

Chapter 4

EXTRACTING EVIDENCE USING GOOGLE DESKTOP SEARCH

Timothy Pavlic, Jill Slay and Benjamin Turnbull

Abstract   Desktop search applications have improved dramatically over the last
three years, evolving from time-consuming search applications to instantaneous search tools that rely extensively on pre-cached data. This
paper investigates the extraction of pre-cached data for forensic purposes, drawing on earlier work to automate the process. The result is
a proof-of-concept application called Google Desktop Search Evidence
Collector (GDSEC), which interfaces with Google Desktop Search to
convert data from Google's proprietary format to one that is amenable
to offline analysis.

Keywords: Google Desktop Search, evidence extraction

1.   Introduction

Current desktop search utilities such as Windows Desktop Search,
Google Desktop Search and Yahoo! Desktop Search differ from earlier
tools in that user data is replicated and stored independently [1, 10].
Unlike the older systems that searched mounted volumes on-the-fly, the
newer systems search pre-built databases, accelerating the search for
user data with only a nominal increase in hard disk storage [5]. The
replication of data in a search application has potential forensic applications – data stored independently within a desktop search application
database often remains after the original file is deleted.

In previous work [9], we examined the forensic possibilities of data
stored within Google Desktop Search; in particular, we discussed the
extraction of text from deleted word processing documents, thumbnails
from deleted image files and the cache for HTTPS sessions. However, the
format of the extracted data files does not allow for simple interpretation
and analysis; therefore, the only sure method of extracting data was via

Please use the following format when citing this chapter:

Pavlic, T., Slay, J. and Turnbull, B., 2008, in IFIP International Federation for Information Processing, Volume 285;
Advances in Digital Forensics IV; Indrajit Ray, Sujeet Shenoi; (Boston: Springer), pp. 43–50.

the search application interface. We also showed that it was possible to maintain the forensic integrity of the extracted data by disabling certain components of the Google Desktop Search application. But this data could only be accessed using manual keyword searches submitted via the application interface.

This paper presents a more efficient technique for extracting data from desktop search utilities. The discussion focuses on Google Desktop Search, but the concepts are applicable to other desktop search applications. The resulting proof-of-concept application, Google Desktop Search Evidence Collector (GDSEC), automates the data extraction process and enables investigators to copy data from Google Desktop Search files in a forensically-sound manner without having to conduct manually searches using the interface.

2.   Google Desktop Search

Google Desktop Search was released in 2004. The original version was designed only for Windows XP. Currently, versions are available for Windows Vista, Linux and Mac OS X.

The Windows version of Google Desktop Search was designed for single users. However, when Google Desktop Search was installed and run by an administrator in a multi-user environment, the program would index and search all files regardless of their ownership. This potential security flaw received widespread media coverage [6, 8].

Security concerns have been raised about the integration of Google Desktop Search with Google's Internet search engine, but these vulnerabilities have not been exploited [3]. Attention has also focused on the privacy issues related to Google Desktop Search's approach of copying local data to external machines for faster search [2].

This work focuses exclusively on the Windows-based implementation of Google Desktop Search, the most widely used application. The Macintosh and Linux versions of Google Desktop Search operate very differently. Note that Google Desktop Search is executed under Windows NT/2000 and later versions because it uses libraries that are available only in more recent platforms.

Google Desktop Search has three executables, `GoogleDesktopIndex` `.exe`, `GoogleDesktopSearch.exe` and `GoogleDesktopCrawl.exe`. The `GoogleDesktopSearch.exe` executable is the main program of the search suite; it operates by setting up an HTTP server on local port 4664 and controls all user interactions. The `GoogleDesktopCrawl.exe` program traverses the file structure on the hard disk and reports changes to `GoogleDesktopIndex.exe`. `GoogleDesktopIndex.exe` interfaces with persistent storage files, `GoogleDesktopCrawl.exe` and the Microsoft Indexing Service. The Indexing Service sends notifications when files are changed; this information is used by `GoogleDesktopCrawl.exe` to determine the files that may require updating. Note that Google Desktop Search creates a registry key at `HKEY_USERS\SID\Software\Google \Google Desktop` where `SID` is the unique user SID. Several options are provided, including locations for file storage.

The Google desktop searching utility allows third-party additions to its software, which facilitates the customization of search parameters. However, third-party additions must use the Google API to customize all settings via the Google program, meaning that direct communication with the database that stores files is not permitted. Google provides a software development kit (SDK) for Google Desktop Search that contains five APIs. The SDK is based on the COM model, allowing any programming language supporting COM to be used to develop plug-ins that utilize the APIs.

Google Desktop Search supports the ability to encrypt the data store that contains cached items. However, further examination has revealed that the application merely invokes Windows NTFS encryption for the folder containing user data. Since the computer is being examined for forensic purposes, we assume that some measure of access is guaranteed.

3.   Google Desktop Search Evidence Collector

This section describes the Google Desktop Search Evidence Collector (GDSEC) tool. It highlights the methods developed for accessing and extracting data, and for storing results. Also, it discusses how evidence collection can be conducted in a forensically-sound manner.

3.1   Accessing Data

Several methods are available for accessing data from desktop search applications. The ordering of access methods from a forensic integrity perspective (best to worst) are:

- Accessing files directly.

- Accessing files using an interpreter.

- Extracting data using API mechanisms provided by the original application.

- Extracting data using the API.

- Searching for data using the API.

Directly accessing and interpreting any files created by a desktop search utility is the preferred method from a forensic perspective because it ensures that all the stored information is available without using an intermediate system. In addition, the data is much more easily extracted using existing digital forensic tools.

The issue with accessing files directly or using an interpreter is that it is difficult to determine the format of the files, which is required to ensure that all the data can be extracted in its original form. Of course, the format can be reverse engineered, but unless the software developer is involved, reverse engineering may have to be performed repeatedly because the format often changes between releases.

Extracting data via an API is less preferable than accessing the data directly. Using an API requires the original Desktop Search program to execute in a forensically-sound manner. The primary advantage is that it permits more thorough extraction of data from the given file format than screen scraping or manual searching.

Our previous research [9] was unsuccessful at determining the file structure to an adequate level of detail. We were, therefore, unable to access the data directly from within Google Desktop Search. However, the following method can be used to access file data in a forensically-sound manner:

Data Access Method

1 Copy the Google Desktop Search storage folder (default is `c:\Documents and Settings\username\Local Settings\Application Data\Google\Google Desktop Search`) from the source machine to the Google Desktop Search folder on the analysis machine.

2 Rename the file `GoogleDesktopCrawl.exe` to `GoogleDesktopCrawl.exe2` on the analysis machine; this prevents the file from loading.

3 Open the Google Desktop Search program and ensure that no email programs are loaded on the analysis machine.

4 After the Google Desktop Search program has loaded on the analysis machine, navigate to the storage folder and change the file attributes of the files to read-only; this allows the Google Desktop Search program to close without editing any files.

This data access method is time consuming; the only options are to manually search for keywords using the user interface or to screen scrape the information to another search tool. In either case, there is no means to ensure that all the data has been extracted. The problem is acerbated by the fact that Google Desktop Search performs a strict search, i.e., the entire word being searched must be present for a hit to occur (searching for "bana" does not return results with "banana").

As mentioned earlier, Google Desktop Search provides several APIs to enable third-party applications to be used for data search and collection. Also of interest is Google Desktop's interface mechanism, which uses a web interface on a local host web server; this web server receives all user queries and functions as the main user interface to the application. Since a web server is a common service with a standardized access method, it provides another method for accessing data maintained within Google Desktop's storage mechanism. Thus, an HTTP-based extraction application can be used to submit queries to Google Desktop Search and retrieve results.

Extracting information from Google Desktop Search via an HTTP server was deemed to be the most effective method. Several APIs are available that enable data to be retrieved in raw HTML or XML formats. Our GDSEC prototype uses GDAPI, a Java-based API for querying the Google Desktop Search web server.

3.2   Analyzing Output Data

Google Desktop Search was used on a test database containing a variety of file types. Our analysis revealed that Google Desktop Search records file-type-specific metadata (e.g., movie lengths and bit rates, and image resolutions) in a common set of fields, which means that the value of the fields are ambiguous.

The SDK documentation supplied by Google [4] describes an option for viewing search results in an XML format. Specifically, by appending the string &format=xml to the end of a search result page, the results can be viewed as a formatted XML page; this helped us to understand the data that is retrieved for each filetype. Every search result has a standard set of XML elements. File-specific metadata is stored in the *snippet* element as a single string, which could be parsed if required.

Google Desktop Search (version 2) enables items to be viewed in a timeline format, which lists the files indexed on each day. Implementing this feature requires metadata (e.g., timestamps) to be stored. A *time* element (with date and time information) was discovered in the XML search results. Examination of the SDK revealed it to be the date/time that the item was indexed and cached by Google Desktop Search, rather than a timestamp extracted from the computer's file system metadata (e.g., file creation time or time of last modification).

3.3   Extracting Data

Google Desktop Search does not offer a wildcard search feature. A linear search requires an identifier for the indexed entries. However, although Google Desktop Search has identifiers, we were unable to format search requests based on item identifiers. In any case, item identifiers would have to be discovered by issuing queries before they could be used in queries; this doubles the computational requirements.

Consequently, our experiments used brute force search with a dictionary containing a small set of words designed to test the ability of the application to handle query results that contained references to files discovered by previous queries. The keywords in the dictionary were chosen to correspond to the test files used to evaluate the application and validate the extraction process.

3.4   Storing and Querying Extracted Data

GDSEC was developed as a proof-of-concept application for extracting data. Consequently, the results are simply stored in text files. The search application initially stores the retrieved results in memory as result objects before writing them to files. Each result object is simply an encapsulated collection of strings and integers used to represent every XML element available from a Google Desktop Search query result. A red-black binary tree is used to manage all the result objects with the *url* XML element (which points to a file on the file system or the Internet) of the search result used as the unique identifier. After a query is issued, result objects are created for each result and an attempt is made to add them to the tree based on their URLs. A file that has already been discovered in a previous query is not added to the tree.

The text files generated as output contain a list of all the elements extracted from the XML results along with the information related to the elements. Cached content is also appended to the end of the text output. The file names of output files are based on the last component of the URL (usually the file name and extension). For cached files with the same name that reside in different directories, an extra numerical character is appended to the file extensions of the output files to make them unique. Illegal file name characters such as "?" that appear in a URL (due to web pages with parameters) are replaced with the "_" character. The text files are generated in a separate folder on the file system. Each folder is given a unique name by using its creation time; this ensures that all subsequent output requests are written to different folders.

Table 1.   Google Desktop Search data.

Filename	Match	Filename	Match
dbc2e.ht1	Yes	Dbdam	Yes
Dbdao	Yes	Dbeam	Yes
Dbeao	Yes	Dbm	Yes
dbu2d.ht1	Yes	dbvm.cf1	Yes
dbvmh.ht1	Yes	fii.cf1	Yes
Fiid	Yes	fiih.ht1	Yes
Hp	Yes	hpt2i.ht1	Yes
rpm.cf1	Yes	rpm1m.cf1	Yes
rpm1mh.ht1	Yes	rpmh.ht1	Yes
uinfo_data	No		

3.5   Verifying Forensic Soundness

It is important to verify that the GDSEC application is forensically sound and that the extracted data can be used as evidence. The verification process used a controlled indexing test and a hash value comparison.

The first test used a controlled indexing environment to verify that GDSEC retrieved data without modifying it. A partition was created on a test system with multiple files named EVIDENCE.txt containing the text string "criminal activity." Google Desktop Search was configured to only index this partition. After the indexing was completed, GDSEC was launched with instructions to perform the dictionary search and to write all the retrieved items to a text file. This text file contained all the XML search results and the cached content retrieved from the cache URL. The cached content that was recovered contained the strings "criminal activity," which proved that no data was modified during extraction.

Next, it was necessary to verify that no other data was modified during the extraction process. As part of the controlled indexing test, when the file was indexed, Google Desktop Search was terminated and MD5 hash values [7] were generated for all the data files used by the search application. The application was then re-executed and the remainder of the controlled indexing test was performed. When this was completed, Google Desktop Search was once again terminated and a second set of MD5 hash values was generated for the data files.

Table 1 shows the results of the hash value matching test. Only file uinfo_data was altered; all the other files had the same hash values before and after extraction and were, therefore, unaffected. The file uinfo_data stores user information about the search application and no actual cached content. Therefore, although this file was altered by

Google Desktop Search, the loss of integrity is known and explained, and does not impact the extraction of cached content.

4.   Conclusions

Google Desktop Search Evidence Collector (GDSEC) is a prototype tool designed to collect data from the files used by Google Desktop Search in a forensically-sound manner. The current version of GDSEC interacts with Google Desktop Search to extract information. However, the preferred extraction technique from a forensic point of view is for the application to directly access files; future research will investigate this issue with the goal of implementing the capability in GDSEC. Other avenues for improvement include interfacing GDSEC with an SQL database to provide the ability to conduct additional searches of the retrieved information and implementing routines to retrieve cached content for items that have multiple cached versions (e.g., websites that are visited frequently).

References

[1] B. Cole, Search engines tackle the desktop, *IEEE Computer*, vol. 38(3), pp. 14–17, 2005.

[2] Electronic Frontier Foundation, Google copies your hard drive – Government smiles in anticipation (www.eff.org/press/archives /2006/02/09), February 9, 2006.

[3] T. Espiner, Google admits Desktop security risk, ZDNet UK (news .zdnet.co.uk/internet/security/0,1000000189,39253447,00.htm), February 20, 2006.

[4] Google, Google Desktop (desktop.google.com).

[5] S. Olsen, Google unveils Desktop Search, CNET News.com (www.news.com/2100-1024_3-5408765.html), October 14, 2004.

[6] B. Posey, Working with NTFS encryption (www.brienposey.com /kb/working_with_ntfs_encryption.asp), 2002.

[7] R. Rivest, MD5 message-digest algorithm, RFC 1321 (www.ietf.org /rfc/rfc1321.txt), 1992.

[8] T. Spring, Google Desktop Search: Security threat? PC World (blogs.pcworld.com/staffblog/archives/000264.html), 2004.

[9] B. Turnbull, B. Blundell and J. Slay, Google Desktop as a source of digital evidence, *International Journal of Digital Evidence*, vol. 5(1), 2006.

[10] X1 Technologies, X1 Desktop Search (pro.x1.com/?source=Yahoo).

Chapter 5

EVALUATION OF REGISTRY DATA REMOVAL BY SHREDDER PROGRAMS

Harry Velupillai and Pontjho Mokhonoana

Abstract   Shredder programs attempt to overcome Window's inherent inability to erase data completely. A shredder is useful when one needs to transfer ownership or dispose of a computer, but it can be exploited by a suspect for the purpose of wiping incriminating evidence. Most shredder programs claim to remove all traces of data. This paper examines these claims by conducting forensic examinations of computers on which shredder programs were used.

Keywords: Shredder tools, Windows Registry, data removal

1.   Introduction

It is difficult to completely remove all traces of data from a computer system [9]. In the case of Microsoft Windows, for example, much of the "erased" data is recoverable, even when it is not visible from the Windows Explorer interface. For example, traces of a program remain after deleting it using Window's Add/Remove Programs function. Generally, the residual data takes little space and users are not concerned about this data unless it affects system performance.

The situation has changed with the release of digital forensic tools [10], which enable users to locate, recover and interpret deleted data. Initially, forensic tools were only available to law enforcement personnel; now, high performance tools are available to all at relatively low cost. The implications are obvious – data must not simply be removed, it must be removed securely. Also, data should be removed from locations that may not be quite so obvious.

Shredder programs were developed to address Window's inherent inability to erase data completely. These programs claim to wipe all traces of sensitive data, including data residing in locations that normal users

Please use the following format when citing this chapter:

Velupillai, H. and Mokhonoana, P., 2008, in IFIP International Federation for Information Processing, Volume 285; *Advances in Digital Forensics IV*; Indrajit Ray, Sujeet Shenoi; (Boston: Springer), pp. 51–58.

would not access (e.g., the Windows Registry). This paper examines the effectiveness of shredder programs available on the market. In particular, it evaluates their ability to completely remove Windows Registry entries. Several digital forensic tools, including a hex editor, are used to determine if deleted entries are still visible after shredder programs are executed.

2.   Windows Registry

The Windows Registry is a directory that stores settings and options for all the hardware, software and users of a Windows system. Changes to control panel settings, file associations and installed software and applications are maintained in the registry. The registry files are in continuous use when the machine is running; changes to the registry are made in real time and timestamps are changed only at shutdown. Registry data is stored in multiple files whose names and locations differ according to the specific Windows edition [2, 6].

- **Windows 3.11:** The registry is stored in only one file Reg.dat, which is located in the directory C:\Windows.

- **Windows 95/98:** The registry consists of two files, User.dat and System.dat, which are stored in the directory C:\Windows.

- **Windows ME:** The registry consists of three files, User.dat, System.dat and Classes.dat, which are stored in the directory C:\Windows.

- **Other Windows Versions:** The registry of Windows versions released after Windows ME (excluding Vista) have six files, Default, Sam, Security, Software, System and Userdiff, which are stored in the directory %SystemRoot%\System32\Config. Note that these files do not have extensions. In addition, each user has two files, Ntuser.dat and Usrclass.dat, stored in the corresponding user profile directory.

The problem with registry data is that the user knows where the files are located, but he cannot wipe them because they are vital to Windows – he might as well re-install the operating system. This is why shredder programs are required.

3.   Shredder Programs and Forensic Tools

This section describes the shredder programs and digital forensic tools used in our experiments.

3.1 Shredder Programs

Numerous shredder programs are available from commercial sources or are downloadable from the Internet. We selected two representative programs, CCleaner [13], which is available as freeware; and Registry Washer [14], a commercial product.

3.2 Forensic Analysis Tools

Several digital forensic tools [8] were used to evaluate the ability of the shredder programs to delete registry data.

- **Ultimate Toolkit:** This popular toolkit from Accessdata [4] consists of the FTK Imager, Registry Viewer, Password Recovery Toolkit (PRTK), Distributed Network Attack (DNA) and Forensic Toolkit (FTK). Only the FTK Imager and Registry Viewer were used in our tests.

- **FTK Imager:** FTK Imager is a forensic tool for recovering evidence from a target machine [1]. The tool can create physical and logical images of drives in a number of formats. In addition, it can extract registry files from a running machine. Because FTK Imager accesses the drive directly instead of via the operating system interface, it is able to acquire the locked system files used by the registry.

- **Registry Viewer:** The Registry Viewer is a forensic tool for viewing all Windows Registry files [3]. It provides access to user data, hardware and software information, URL/MRU lists and the Protected System Storage Provider.

- **Regedit:** This Windows Registry editor is a built-in utility for viewing and editing registry entries [12]. Regedit permits the addition, modification and deletion of registry entries.

4. Experimental Setup and Results

The experiments involved installing and then uninstalling eMule [7], a popular peer-to-peer program. While peer-to-peer programs can be used for illegal activities, our focus was on determining whether or not the shredder programs could remove all traces of eMule from the Windows Registry.

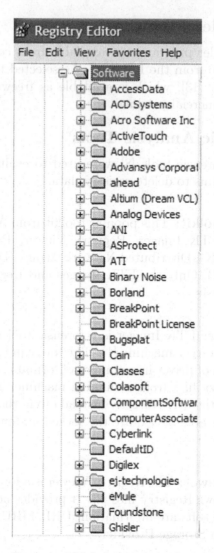

Figure 1. eMule key in the registry.

4.1   Installation

When installed, eMule creates eight entries in file `Ntuser.dat` in the Windows Registry. Note that Windows Registry folders are called "keys."

- **Entry 1 (Key):** The eMule key is located at `Software\Emule` (Figure 1). Entries 2, 3 and 4 are located inside this key.

Name	Type	Data
(Default)	REG_SZ	(value not set)
Install Path	REG_SZ	C:\Program Files\eMule
Installer Language	REG_SZ	1033
UsePublicUserDirectories	REG_DWORD	0x00000002 (2)

Figure 2.   Entries 2, 3 and 4 in the Registry

- **Entry 2 (String Value):** This entry is found in `Software\Emule` `\Install Path` (Figure 2). The first entry `Default` is ignored because it is created by the Windows Registry, not by eMule; also, it does not contain any data. Of the three entries created under the eMule key, only Entry 2 holds sensitive data.

- **Entry 3 (StringValue):** This entry is found in `Software\Emule` `\Installer Language`.

- **Entry 4 (Dword Value):** This entry is found in `Software\Emule` `\UsePublicUserDirectories`.

- **Entry 5 (Key):** This entry is at `Software\Microsoft\Windows` `\CurrentVersion\Explorer\MenuOrder\StartMenu\Programs\E mule`.

Name	Type	Data
(Default)	REG_SZ	(value not set)
Order	REG_BINARY	08 00 00 00 02 00 00 00 8a 02 00 00 01 00 00 00 05 00 00 00 70 00 00 00 00 0...

Figure 3.   Entry 6 in the registry.

- **Entry 6 (Binary Value)** This entry, created under Entry 5, is at `Software\Microsoft\Windows\CurrentVersion\Explorer` `\MenuOrder\StartMenu\Programs\Emule\Order`. Figure 3 shows the entry; note that the default entry is ignored.

- **Entry 7 (String Value):** This entry is at `Software\Microsoft\` `Windows\ShellNoRoam\MuiCache\C:\Program Files\eMule\emu le.exe`. This entry points to the location of the eMule executable and it is added only if eMule is executed.

- **Entry 8 (String Value):** This entry is at `Software\Microsoft\` `Windows\ShellNoRoam\MuiCache\O:\LocalDriveC\downloads\e Mule0.48a-Installer.exe`. It points to the location of the eMule installation file.

Table 1.   Comparison of shredder programs.

Entry	Windows	CCleaner	Registry Washer
1	Removed		
2	Removed		
3	Removed		
4	Removed		
5		Not Removed	Not Removed
6		Not Removed	Not Removed
7		Removed	Removed
8		Conditional Removal	Conditional Removal

4.2   Uninstallation

Several entries are removed after Windows is used to uninstall eMule. However, Entries 5,6,7 and 8 remain.

4.3   Evaluation of Shredder Programs

Both the shredder programs removed Entry 7. Entry 8 was removed only when the eMule installer had been deleted or moved to a different directory. However, both programs did not remove Entries 5 and 6. The results are summarized in Table 1.

Analysis of the results sheds light on how shredder programs work and why they fail to remove all traces of a program. Shredders attempt to find data that should be removed mainly by searching for broken links. This is why Entry 8 was removed only when the installation file had been deleted or moved. Entries 5 and 6 were not removed because they did not contain links to programs, just data used by programs.

4.4   Forensic Acquisition

The final step in the experiments was to use forensic tools to see if the deleted portions of the registry could be reconstructed. Our tests showed that it was not possible to recover any data deleted by the two shredders or manually using Regedit. The fact that the data deleted using Regedit was also not recoverable indicates some other mechanism is at work – perhaps the way Windows stores and changes registry files. We intend to investigate this issue in future work.

5.   Advantages and Limitations

Using shredder programs has several advantages. CCleaner was very effective at wiping the detailed history maintained by Windows. Also,

CCleaner's secure deletion facility enables users to delete data as well as to overwrite the sectors that held the data to prevent any recovery [5, 9]. Moreover, it allows users to choose the number of overwrites based on the sensitivity of the data being erased [11].

Windows stores the search terms used by most applications. Therefore, when Regedit is used to delete registry entries, search data pertaining to these entries is saved – and is easily recovered. Unlike Regedit, the shredder programs do not leave any such traces.

The shredder programs examined in this work have certain limitations. The most serious limitation is the lack of user input. In particular, users cannot submit program names or terms that should be located and removed. For example, Entries 5 and 6 could easily have been deleted if the shredder programs allowed users to enter the specific entries they want erased from the registry

Regedit addresses this issue by permitting manual deletion. But this is problematic because, as described above, Windows stores the search terms used to locate the registry entries. Ironically, attempting to delete entries creates additional entries that must be deleted.

Finally, the shredder programs do not wipe all the data. As verified by our experiments, traces of eMule remained even after it was uninstalled and the shredder programs were executed.

6. Conclusions

Shredder programs are useful tools, but they are unable to erase all traces of potentially sensitive Windows Registry data. The manual deletion of data is an option, but the process of searching for the data to delete leaves traces. The burden, therefore, falls on the user to understand the nature and locations of the data that remain on a computer system. Short of wiping the entire hard drive, there is no way to remove all the sensitive data and references to its existence.

Acknowledgements

This research was supported by the Council for Scientific and Industrial Research of the Republic of South Africa.

References

[1] AccessData, FTK Imager, Lindon, Utah (www.accessdata.com).

[2] AccessData, Registry quick find chart, Lindon, Utah (www.access data.com).

[3] AccessData, Registry Viewer, Lindon, Utah (www.accessdata .com).

[4] AccessData, Ultimate Toolkit, Lindon, Utah (www.accessdata .com).

[5] H. Berghel, and D. Hoelzer, Digital village: Disk wiping by any other name, *Communications of the ACM*, vol. 49(8), pp. 17–21, 2006.

[6] H. Carvey, *Windows Forensics and Incident Recovery*, Addison-Wesley, Boston, Massachusetts, 2004.

[7] eMule.org, eMule (www.emule-project.net).

[8] G. Francia and K. Clinton, Computer forensics laboratory and tools, *Journal of Computing Sciences in Colleges*, vol. 20(6), pp. 143–150, 2005.

[9] S. Garfinkel and A. Shelat, Remembrance of data passed: A study of disk sanitization practices, *IEEE Security and Privacy*, vol. 1(1), pp. 17–27, 2003.

[10] W. Harrison, D. Aucsmith, G. Heuston, S. Mocas, M. Morrissey and S. Russelle, A lessons learned repository for computer forensics, *International Journal of Digital Evidence*, vol. 1(3), 2002.

[11] N. Joukov, H. Papaxenopoulos and E. Zadok, Secure deletion myths, issues and solutions, *Proceedings of the Second ACM Workshop on Storage Security and Survivability*, pp. 61–66, 2006.

[12] Microsoft Help and Support, Windows Registry information for advanced users, Microsoft Corporation, Redmond, Washington (support.microsoft.com/kb/256986).

[13] Piriform, CCleaner (www.ccleaner.com).

[14] Right Utilities, Registry Washer (www.rightutilities.com).

III

EVIDENCE INTEGRITY

III

EVIDENCE INTEGRITY

Chapter 6

USING BOOT CONTROL TO PRESERVE THE INTEGRITY OF EVIDENCE

Keisuke Fujita, Yuki Ashino, Tetsutaro Uehara and Ryoichi Sasaki

Abstract   This paper describes Dig-Force2, a system that securely logs and stores evidentiary data about the operation of a personal computer. The integrity of the logged data is guaranteed by using chained hysteresis signatures and a trusted platform module (TPM) that prevents unauthorized programs or tampered programs from executing. Experiments indicate that the Dig-Force2 system is both efficient and reliable.

Keywords: Evidence integrity, hysteresis signatures, boot control

1.   Introduction

Personal computers are often used as instruments of electronic crime. This makes it important to securely log and store evidentiary data pertaining to computer operations for use in legal proceedings [8].

To address this issue, we have previously developed Dig-Force [3], a system that reliably records data about personal computer use on the computer itself. Dig-Force uses chained signatures to maintain the integrity of evidentiary data. Dig-Force is effective even when it is installed on a standalone computer located outside a protected network.

One problem with Dig-Force is that it is difficult to ensure that the personal computer user cannot alter programs and data on the computer. In particular, it is necessary to detect program or data tampering and to guarantee that only authorized programs are executed. This paper describes an enhanced version of the Dig-Force system (Dig-Force2) that securely logs and stores evidentiary data pertaining to computer use. The integrity of the logged data is preserved using chained hysteresis signatures and a trusted platform module (TPM) that prevents unau-

Please use the following format when citing this chapter:

Fujita, K., Ashino, Y., Uehara, T. and Sasaki, R., 2008, in IFIP International Federation for Information Processing, Volume 285; *Advances in Digital Forensics IV*; Indrajit Ray, Sujeet Shenoi; (Boston: Springer), pp. 61–74.

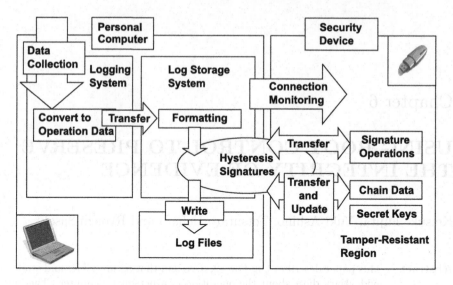

Figure 1. Dig-Force architecture.

thorized programs or tampered programs from executing. Experiments indicate that the new system is both efficient and reliable.

2. Dig-Force

This section describes the operating assumptions, architecture and processing flow of the Dig-Force system.

2.1 Operating Assumptions

The primary functions of Dig-Force are to log data about personal computer operations without any failure, and to detect tampering of the logged data even when it is done by the personal computer operator.

Dig-Force was designed to operate under three principal assumptions: (i) no programs or data on the personal computer should be modified by its operator, (ii) although the computer operator may perform unauthorized operations, neither the administrator nor the verifier ever perform unauthorized operations, and (iii) the computer operator never passes the security device (described below) to a third party.

2.2 Architecture

The Dig-Force architecture is presented in Figure 1. It consists of three principal subsystems:

- **Security Device:** The security device contains a tamper-resistant area to prevent the chained hysteresis signatures from being modified. The device also performs hysteresis signature operations.

- **Logging System:** The logging system collects operational information, which is preserved in a log storage system. The logging system also records that the security device is always installed on the personal computer. Note that the computer cannot be operated without the security device.

- **Log Storage System:** The log storage system communicates with the security device and stores the hysteresis signatures with the logged data. The logged data is intended to serve as evidence in legal proceedings. However, since the data is easily coped, erased or modified, chained hysteresis signatures are used instead of independent digital signatures to ensure the security and integrity of the logged data.

A hysteresis signature is a digital signature with a chained structure [6], i.e., each signature is dependent on the preceding signatures. A successful attack involving the alteration of data would require all the hysteresis signatures preceding and following the data to be adjusted. Thus, a hysteresis signature is more secure and reliable than a traditional digital signature.

The security device enables Dig-Force to defend against "restoration attacks," which are effective against hysteresis signatures [3]. Such an attack occurs when an intruder deletes the suffixes of log file data and performs a series of operations to update the log file.

2.3   Processing Flow

Dig-Force's processing flow has three phases: configuration, operation and verification. Three entities are involved: the system administrator who makes the initial settings, the personal computer operator, and the verifier who checks the logs stored on the computer.

- **Configuration Phase:** During this phase, the system administrator uses the security device to create public/private key pairs and stores the private keys in the tamper-resistant area of the security device. The administrator also determines the initial values of the chain data and stores them in the tamper-resistant area. Next, the administrator sends the public keys and the initial values of the chain data to the verifier. Finally, the administrator delivers the personal computer installed with the logging system, log storage system and security device to the operator.

- **Operation Phase:** The operator uses the personal computer received from the system administrator. The logging system confirms that the security device is installed, after which it collects operational data and passes it to the log storage system.

  The log storage system accumulates the logged data, communicates with the security device, applies the hysteresis signatures to the logged data, writes the chain values, signatures and logged data to the log file, and stores the chained hash values in the security device.

  Upon completing a session, the personal computer operator saves his documents and the log file on storage media, and submits the storage media and security device to the verifier.

- **Verification Phase:** The verifier applies the hash function to the final chain data contained in the submitted log file and computes the hash values. The verifier then compares these hash values with those contained in the security device. Next, the verifier checks the signatures using the initial values from the configuration phase and the chain values, signatures and logged data stored in the log file.

3.   Implementation Issues

It is difficult to guarantee that users cannot modify programs or data on a personal computer. A malicious user with sufficient expertise could alter the Dig-Force program itself so that it does not detect tampering. To address this threat, Dig-Force should be tamperproof and computer operations should be monitored to ensure that only the "correct" versions of authorized programs execute. This can be implemented using a white list containing the digital signatures of approved programs, which are provided by a trusted third party.

Another important requirement is to implement boot control functionality that prevents unauthorized programs from executing. To accomplish this, we use features provided by Microsoft Windows XP, which is used as the development and operational environment. In particular, we leverage the multiple hierarchies that Windows XP provides from the hardware layer all the way up to the application layer (Figure 2).

In general, there are three ways to implement the reliable monitoring of programs on a personal computer. These involve using: (i) the operating system, (ii) a device driver located within the operating system kernel (Figure 2), and (iii) APIHook, a service program that hooks the Windows API, changes the processing and monitors application program start-up.

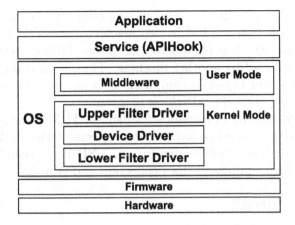

Figure 2. Windows XP hierarchy.

Although the operating system is the most desirable option for monitoring unauthorized programs, Windows XP does not offer the required functionality. Therefore, we considered the device driver and APIHook solutions. Ultimately, we selected APIHook because it was easier to implement.

APIHook is a service program that executes in the application layer; therefore, there is always the risk that it can be tampered with. It is difficult to tamper with or delete the APIHook program on a computer because APIHook is automatically set to execute first. However, if the hard drive is transferred to another computer, the APIHook program on the drive can be modified or deleted. To address this issue, we have developed an enhanced version of Dig-Force, called Dig-Force2, which engages a trusted platform module (TPM) as an additional safeguard.

TPMs are integrated circuit chips with security hardware that protect certain areas of the chips from being tampered with. A TPM mounted on the motherboard of a personal computer can function as a coprocessor accessible from the CPU via the low pin count bus. The Trusted Computing Group (TCG) [10] defines several functions for a TPM. These include: (i) creating, storing and conducting encryption/decryption and signature operations with RSA keys, (ii) performing hashing operations, (iii) generating random numbers, (iv) maintaining information on platform state, and (v) providing adequate non-volatile and volatile memory for storing data.

A TPM that is mounted in a personal computer is machine specific. Therefore, if a TPM in a computer is removed and replaced with another TPM, an authentication error results and the computer will not start up.

Thus, the TPM can be used to uniquely identify a particular computer. The encryption key in a TPM is also machine specific. Therefore, the hard drive data, which is enciphered using the TPM's encryption key, cannot be deciphered by another machine. Thus, even if the hard drive is moved to another personal computer, it is not possible to delete or otherwise tamper with the APIHook program.

There are two additional reasons for using a TPM. First, apart from the TPM, there is no need to incorporate a special device in the personal computer. Second, an auxiliary device (e.g., USB device) can be removed by mistake, which terminates data collection and storage.

4.   Dig-Force2

We have designed the Dig-Force2 system to address the limitations of Dig-Force. Dig-Force2 employs a TPM as its security device rather than eToken [2], which is used by Dig-Force. This section describes the operating assumptions, architecture and processing flow of Dig-Force2.

4.1   Operating Assumptions

Dig-Force2 is designed to operate under two primary assumptions: (i) since the monitoring program is a service that operates under the administrator's authority, it cannot be halted by a computer user whose authority is lower than that of the administrator, and (ii) the BIOS, operating system and monitoring program software are reliable; since the monitoring program starts up right after the operating system, it is difficult for an unauthorized individual to alter the monitoring program, which features APIHook functions.

4.2   Architecture

Dig-Force2 has five main components (Figure 3):

- **Logging System:** The logging system collects operational information, which is maintained in a log storage system. The logging system also records that the auxiliary device is always installed on the personal computer.

- **Log Storage System:** The log storage system adds timestamps and formats the operational data received from the logging system. Then, it interacts with the TPM to apply hysteresis signatures to the formatted data and writes the data to a log file.

- **Auxiliary Device:** The auxiliary device must be inserted into the personal computer in order for the computer to operate. The

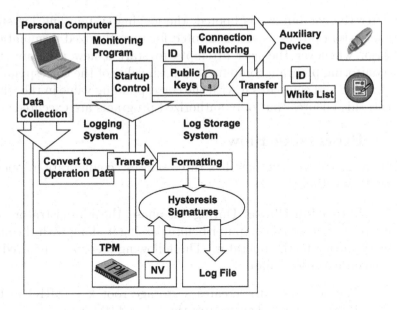

Figure 3.   Dig-Force2 architecture.

auxiliary device stores the hash values ("white list") of authorized programs and IDs that identify users along with the digital signatures of the hash values and IDs (signed by the administrator).

- **Trusted Platform Module:** The TPM performs the hysteresis signature operations. It has a tamper-resistant area that protects the chain data that forms the signature keys and signature history.

- **Monitoring Program:** The monitoring program is started as a service at the uppermost authority of the operating system, which prevents the computer operator from terminating the program. The monitoring program checks that the auxiliary device is mounted on the computer; the computer cannot be operated without this device. The program then computes the hash values of the .exe files of the logging and log storage systems and compares them with the values in the white list; the computer is permitted to start only if the values match. Note that before the white list is used, the digital signature provided by the administrator or a trusted third party is verified. The monitoring program also reads the ID from the auxiliary device that identifies the computer operator and compares it with its pre-set value; the computer can be operated only if the IDs match.

After the computer has booted, the logging system and log storage system processes are monitored for unauthorized termination. Also, whenever the user attempts to start a new program, the monitoring program computes the hash value of the corresponding .exe file and compares it with the corresponding value in the white list; this ensures that only authorized programs are executed.

4.3   Processing Flow

Dig-Force2's processing flow has three phases: configuration, operation and verification.

- **Configuration Phase:** During this phase, the administrator configures the personal computer before passing it along with the auxiliary device to the operator. The following steps are involved in the configuration phase:

  - The administrator creates a storage root key (SRK) in the TPM; this root key secures the other TPM keys.

  - The administrator creates a secret key (S) in the TPM that is used for the hysteresis signatures and a public key (P) used for signature verification. These keys are encrypted using SRK and stored on the computer's hard drive.

  - The administrator specifies an arbitrary initial value (R1) for the chain data and stores it in the TPM's non-volatile memory.

  - The administrator sends the initial values that become the chain data to the verifier.

  - The administrator stores in the auxiliary device the white list and the IDs used by the monitoring program to identify individuals.

  - The administrator sets up the public key used for verifying the white list and the IDs that identify individuals in the monitoring program.

  - Finally, the administrator installs the monitoring system and the logging and log storage systems on the personal computer.

- **Operation Phase:** During this phase, the auxiliary device is mounted on the personal computer, and the monitoring program and the logging and log storage systems are started. Figure 4 illustrates the processing flow of the monitoring program. The following steps are involved:

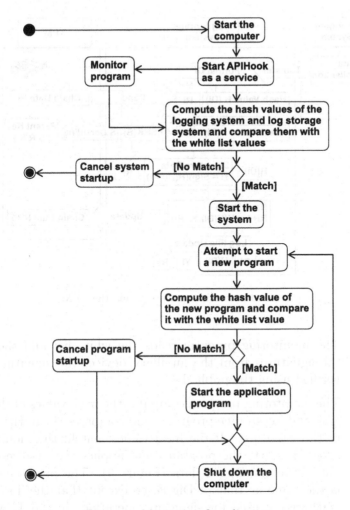

Figure 4. Monitoring flow diagram.

- The operator mounts the auxiliary device on the computer.

- The monitoring program is started as a service program after the operating system has started.

- The monitoring program checks that the auxiliary device is mounted; if the device is not mounted, the monitoring program locks the computer.

- The monitoring program reads the IDs that identify individuals and their digital signatures from the auxiliary device. The monitoring program verifies the digital signatures; the computer works only if this verification is successful.

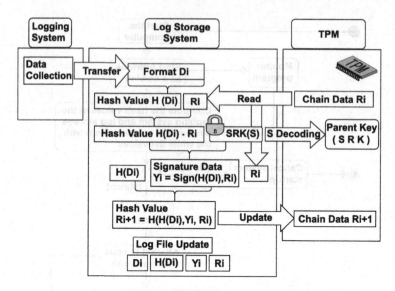

Figure 5. Hysteresis signatures using the TPM.

- The monitoring program reads the white list and the digital signatures from the auxiliary device; the signatures are verified using the public key.

- The monitoring program computes the hash values of the logging and log storage programs and compares them with those in the white list. If the hash values match, the monitoring program starts the programs and applies the hysteresis signatures to the logged data (Figure 5). The processing flow is the same as that of Dig-Force except that the TPM key (SRK(S)) is used for signature operations in the TPM and the chain data is stored in the TPM's non-volatile memory.

- The monitoring program checks the other programs (.exe files) to ensure that unauthorized programs do not start. Also, whenever the operator attempts to start a program, the monitoring program hooks the API and computes the hash value of the program; the program is permitted to execute only if this hash value matches its white list value.

- **Verification Phase:** The verifier receives the personal computer with the TPM and the auxiliary device from the operator. The verification of digital signatures in the TPM is similar to that for Dig-Force, except that the chain data stored in the TPM's non-volatile memory is used along with the TPM keys. This confirms

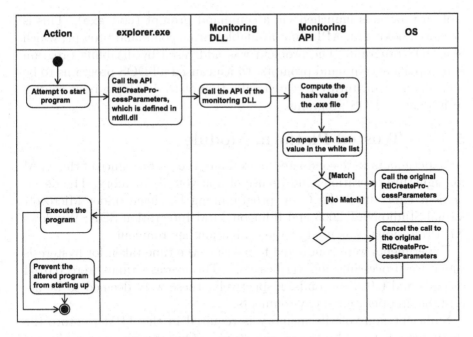

Figure 6.   Boot control flow diagram.

that the monitoring program is operating in a reliable manner, ensuring that only authorized programs are executed.

5.   Functional Experiments

Functional tests of the monitoring program and TPM were conducted to verify the effectiveness and practicality of Dig-Force2.

5.1   Monitoring Program

An experiment was conducted to test the program start-up control function provided by APIHook. APIMonitor [4] was used to identify the APIs invoked during program start up (we discovered that more than ten APIs are called when a program is started). We hooked some of these APIs and changed their processing flow. One of these APIs is RtlCreateProcessParameters, which is defined in ntdll.dll. Figure 6 illustrates how this particular API is hooked to control booting.

We wrote a prototype program that implemented the processing flow in Figure 6 based on information provided in [1]. The program was used to experiment with boot control. It was able to prevent unauthorized programs from starting up. However, it was unable to exert boot control on programs launched via a command prompt (`cmd.exe`). This is because hooking an API is not available with a command prompt, which is a DOS program. The problem was addressed by disabling program start-up using command prompts, which caused all DOS programs to be unavailable. Our future research will attempt to develop a boot control technique for DOS programs.

5.2   Trusted Platform Module

Experiments were conducted to evaluate the performance of the TPM for signature operations and its use of non-volatile memory. The development effort used the C++ programming language under Microsoft Visual Studio.NET 2003 and Infineon TPM Integration SDK; Windows XP Professional was used as the evaluation environment.

Experiments were conducted to measure the time taken for hysteresis signature processing and verification. The average times were 0.0764 seconds and 0.0295 seconds, respectively; these were deemed to be acceptable in operational environments.

Sufficient non-volatile memory is required in the TPM to store the chain data for the hysteresis signatures. Our experiments confirmed that 20 bytes of non-volatile memory were available in the TPM.

5.3   Possible Attacks

This section describes five attacks that can impact Dig-Force2 along with the corresponding countermeasures.

- **Attack 1:** This attack launches a malicious program that modifies the logged data and/or signatures. The attack is defeated by ensuring that the monitoring program checks every program and only permits authorized programs to execute.

- **Attack 2:** This attack tampers with or deletes the monitoring program after transferring the hard drive on which it resides to another computer. The hard drive is then returned to the original computer. Thus, the monitoring program is unable to prevent unauthorized programs from executing. The attack is defeated by enciphering the monitoring program using the TPM's encryption function and public key so that it cannot be decrypted on another computer.

- **Attack 3:** This attack halts the logging program and/or log storage program, preventing Dig-Force2 from collecting evidentiary data. The attack is defeated by having the monitoring program check the programs' execution status and automatically restart the programs if they are terminated.

- **Attack 4:** This attack modifies the white list so that the monitoring program permits an unauthorized program to execute. The attack is defeated by using digital signatures that employ the administrator's private key; the monitoring program uses the corresponding public key to verify the signatures and detect alterations.

- **Attack 5:** This attack alters the chain data stored in the non-volatile memory of the TPM. It is defeated by ensuring that the monitoring program prevents unauthorized programs (that access the non-volatile memory) from executing.

6. Conclusions

Dig-Force2 is an efficient and reliable system for collecting data about computer operations for use in legal proceedings. The integrity of the evidentiary data is ensured by using chained hysteresis signatures and a TPM that prevents unauthorized programs from executing.

Our future research will focus on enhancing the Dig-Force2 system. One issue is that the white list contains only the names of authorized programs and their hash values. However, it is also necessary to consider DLLs and plug-ins because tampering with these components can cause unauthorized programs to execute. We will attempt to augment the white list by incorporating the hash values of approved DLLs and plug-ins [9]. Another important issue is to harden the monitoring program against attacks. A promising approach is to use BitLocker in Windows Vista [5] to encrypt the hard drive that contains the monitoring program.

Acknowledgements

The authors wish to thank IBM Japan and Infineon Technologies, Japan for their assistance with TCG technology.

References

[1] K. Aiko, Kenji's Homepage (ruffnex.oc.to/kenji).

[2] Aladdin Knowledge Systems, Petach Tikva, Israel (www.aladdin .com).

[3] Y. Ashino and R. Sasaki, Proposal of digital forensic system using security device and hysteresis signature, *Proceedings of the Third International Conference on Intelligent Information Hiding and Multimedia Signal Processing*, pp. 3–7, 2007.

[4] R. Batra, API Monitor (www.rohitab.com/apimonitor).

[5] Microsoft Corporation, BitLocker Drive Encryption, Redmond, Washington (www.microsoft.com/windows/products/windowsvista /features/details/bitlocker.mspx).

[6] K. Miyazaki, S. Susaki, M. Iwamura, T. Matsumoto, R. Sasaki, H. Yoshiura, Digital document sanitizing problem, *Institute of Electronics, Information and Communication Engineers Technical Reports*, vol. 103(195), pp. 61–67, 2003.

[7] J. Richter, *Advanced Windows*, Microsoft Press, Redmond, Washington, 1997.

[8] R. Sasaki, Y. Ashino and T. Masubuchi, A trial for systematization of digital forensics and proposal on the required technologies, *Japanese Society of Security Management Magazine*, April 2006.

[9] SignaCert, Independent IT Controls, Portland, Oregon (japan.signa cert.com).

[10] Trusted Computing Group, Beaverton, Oregon (www.trustedcom putinggroup.org).

Chapter 7

HYPOTHESIS-BASED INVESTIGATION OF DIGITAL TIMESTAMPS

Svein Willassen

Abstract   Timestamps stored on digital media play an important role in digital investigations. However, the evidentiary value of timestamps is questionable because timestamps can be manipulated or they could refer to a clock that is erroneous or improperly adjusted. This paper presents a formalism for defining clock hypotheses based on historical adjustments to clocks, and for testing the consistency of the hypotheses with respect to stored timestamps. Two consistency tests are proposed for justifying clock hypotheses without having to rely on timestamps from external sources.

Keywords: Digital investigations, timestamps, causality, clock hypothesis testing

1.   Introduction

A timestamp is a recorded representation of a specific moment in time. In digital computing, a timestamp is a recorded representation of a specific moment in time in a digital format. This representation is either stored on digital media or is transmitted on a network designed to convey digital data.

Timestamps play an important role in digital investigations. They are traditionally used to place the timestamped event at a specific moment in time, thereby facilitating event reconstruction. The identification that a certain event on a computer took place at a specific time makes it possible to correlate the event with other events occurring outside the computer system. These external events may have occurred in another digital system or in the physical world. A Windows system hard drive in a typical digital investigation can contain tens or hundreds of thousands of timestamps.

Please use the following format when citing this chapter:

Willassen, S., 2008, in IFIP International Federation for Information Processing, Volume 285; *Advances in Digital Forensics IV*; Indrajit Ray, Sujeet Shenoi; (Boston: Springer), pp. 75–86.

Stored timestamps may not accurately reflect the times that the events occurred. A timestamp is always relative to the setting of the clock that generates it. Unfortunately, clocks are not completely reliable. They may drift, generating timestamps that are increasingly different from those generated by other clocks. Clocks may also fail or may produce incorrect timestamps. Furthermore, clocks on most systems can be adjusted by users intentionally or accidentally. Consequently, timestamps generated by the same clock cannot be reliably compared unless it can be shown that the clock was not adjusted during the time period between the creation of the timestamps. Timestamps generated by different clocks are reliably compared by computing the difference between the clocks and verifying that the clocks were not adjusted.

Timestamps are vital to reconstructing events in digital forensic investigations. But they cannot be relied upon as evidence without considering all the factors that may lead to errors. This paper describes a formalism for defining and testing the consistency of clock hypotheses. Carrier's hypothesis-based investigation model [2] is used to test the evidentiary value of timestamps. In this model, the history of the medium under investigation is the complete set of configurations, states and events that have occurred during the lifetime of the medium. The data directly observable by the investigator is the final state of the medium, and it includes observations of all timestamps stored on the medium and the clock. The ability to test clock hypotheses increases the evidentiary value of timestamps even when clocks are erroneous, improperly adjusted or are known to have failed.

2.   Related Work

The problem of timestamp interpretation has been studied by several researchers. Schatz and colleagues [6] have analyzed clock synchronization in enterprise computer networks. They suggest that clock drift can be mitigated by correlating timestamps stored in the web cache with records obtained from web servers. Other researchers [1, 7] also advocate the use of correlation methods for timestamps stored on target computers that were created by other clocks (e.g., timestamps in dynamically generated web pages). These methods provide correlations for the periods during which the cached data exists on the target computers. They are able to confirm or refute hypotheses about a clock in the period for which correlation data exists, but they may be unable to provide reasonable evidence to refute certain hypotheses (e.g., that the timestamps have been changed or that the clock has been adjusted during the period for which no correlation data exists). Correlation with server records is only possible when such data exists and the forensic investigator has legal access to this data.

Gladyshev [4] studied the use of causality properties to establish a time period during which an event may have occurred. In his approach, time boundaries can be established when an event that occurred at an unknown or uncertain time is causally preceded and succeeded by events whose times of occurrence are known. When investigating a target computer, the events whose occurrence times are known must come from external sources. Our approach also uses the notion of causality, but it does not require time references from external sources.

3. Hypothesis-Based Timestamp Investigation

This section discusses the main concepts underlying hypothesis-based timestamp investigation.

3.1 Causality

Causality – the relationship between cause and effect – can be formally expressed as a mathematical relation between events. Lamport [5] was the first to use the *happened-before* relation ($\rightarrow$) for ordering events pertaining to executing processes and message passing. Lamport's definition was generalized by F'.ige [3] to encompass process creation and termination as well as synchronous and asynchronous message passing.

Gladyshev [4] proposed an extended definition of *happened-before* for digital investigations. According to Gladyshev, $e_1 \rightarrow e_2$ if e_2 uses the result of e_1 or e_1 precedes e_2 in the usual course of business of some organization or during the normal operation of a machine. This definition is useful because digital investigations require the reconstruction of events both within and external to computer systems.

Gladyshev's definition of the *happened-before* relation uses the terms, "usual course of business" and "normal operation," which are open to interpretation. In contrast, our definition of the relation directly captures the notion of causality.

Definition. Let e_1 and e_2 denote events and let $\rightarrow$ represent the *happened-before* relation. If $e_1 \rightarrow e_2$, then the occurrence of e_1 is necessary for e_2 to occur because e_2 depends on the effects of e_1.

Examples of causality captured by the *happened-before* relation are:

- "e_1 produces an item that is a necessary input for e_2."
  This is equivalent to Gladyshev's definition "e_2 uses the result of e_1." The definitions of Lamport and Fidge are also covered by this example.

- "e_1 and e_2 are events in a computer program where e_2 uses data produced by e_1."

  Since events that occur when computer programs execute use items produced by other events in the same program (e.g., variables, data stored in memory, registers and stack pointers), many events that occur during program execution can be expressed using the *happened-before* relation. This is a special case of "e_1 produces an item that is a necessary input for e_2." The definition of *happened-before* also captures events related to processes modeled by Lamport and Fidge with the exception of events that do not use results from each other. This exception makes the definition suitable for modern computer systems in which the execution order of program statements can be modified by compilers and processors when the instructions do not depend on the results of each other.

3.2   Time

Time is considered to be a fundamental quantity because it is not defined in terms of other quantities. However, it is measurable via comparisons with periodic events such as those occurring in clocks. Examples of periodic events are the swings of a pendulum (pendulum clock), movement of the earth (sundial) and microwave emission (atomic clock). We assume that every event has a moment in time associated with it and these moments in time can be ordered using the $<$ and $=$ relations.

Definition. Let e be an instantaneous event in the domain of events E, and let T be the domain of time. The function $t(e) : E \mapsto T$ provides the moment in time at which event e occurred.

We assume that causality is preserved in time, i.e., no event can causally depend on an event occurring at the same time or at a later time than itself. This notion is expressed explicitly using the *happened-before* relation ($\rightarrow$):

$$t(e_i) \leq t(e_j) \Rightarrow e_j \nrightarrow e_i. \tag{1}$$

This assumption captures the intuitive relationship that exists between causality and time. If such causal relationships were allowed, then events in the future would affect events in the past, which has not been shown to occur in the real world.

For two events that satisfy the *happened-before* relation ($\rightarrow$), Equation 1 implies that:

$$e_i \rightarrow e_j \Rightarrow t(e_i) < t(e_j). \tag{2}$$

This equation imposes an ordering in time on events related via the $\rightarrow$ relation. However, it does not imply any ordering in time for events not related by $\rightarrow$. Also, $t(e_i) < t(e_j)$ does not imply that $e_i \rightarrow e_j$. Events may occur at different moments in time without being related by $\rightarrow$. On the other hand, if two moments in time, $t(e_1)$ and $t(e_2)$, are ordered such that $t(e_1) < t(e_2)$, events occurring at those moments in time cannot be causally connected in reverse such that $e_2 \rightarrow e_1$.

3.3 Clocks

A clock is a device designed to provide its owner with an approximation of time that is sufficiently coherent to allow the owner to measure and compare time periods. Also, a clock is sufficiently consistent with other clocks to allow its owner to perform actions concurrent with other clock owners without continuous coordination. The definition of a clock should reflect the possibility of clock drift and adjustment discussed in Section 1.

Definition. Let V be the domain of time values produced by a clock. A clock function is defined as $c(t) : T \mapsto V$.

The definition of a clock function does not impose any restrictions on clock values as a function of time. For example, even if $t_1 < t_2$, it may well be the case that $c(t_1) > c(t_2)$. Also, even if $t_1 < t_2 < t_3$, the relationship $c(t_1) = c(t_2) = c(t_3)$ may hold. The latter situation could occur if the events at t_1, t_2, t_3 are so close together in time that the clock is unable to differentiate between them.

3.4 Timestamped Events

A timestamped event is an event for which there exists a timestamp value in domain V of time values. The timestamp value can be represented as a function of the event. A timestamp is created when an event makes a copy of the value provided by a clock. The timestamps in a set of timestamped events are not necessarily related to the same clock.

Definition. Let E be a set of timestamped events and let V be the domain of time values. The function $\tau_c(e) : E \mapsto V$ is defined such that $\tau_c(e_i) = c(t(e_i))$, where $\tau_c(e_i)$ is the timestamp associated with the event e_i relative to clock c.

A timestamp in the above definition is the value of the producing clock at the time of the event. The timestamp thus reflects the clock's representation of time at that particular moment. The definition of timestamps as a function of events and clocks makes it possible to reason about timestamps and clocks.

3.5 Ideal and Non-Ideal Clocks

An ideal clock is one that can only go forward. A non-ideal clock is a clock that is not ideal.

Definition. Let I be the set of ideal clocks. An ideal clock $c(t) \in I$ satisfies the properties:

$$\forall i \forall j (t(e_i) < t(e_j) \;\; \Rightarrow \;\; c(t(e_i)) \leq c(t(e_j)))$$
$$\forall i \forall j (t(e_i) = t(e_j) \;\; \Rightarrow \;\; c(t(e_i)) = c(t(e_j))).$$

An ideal clock has a monotonically increasing clock function. However, note that the values, $c(t(e_i))$ and $c(t(e_j))$, produced for two different moments in time, $t(e_i)$ and $t(e_j)$ (where $t(e_i) < t(e_j)$), may be equal. Many clocks express moments in time as discrete values. A discrete clock with limited resolution may represent two moments that are close in time using the same clock value.

Theorem 1. *Timestamps produced by all ideal clocks $c \in I$ satisfy the property:*

$$e_i \rightarrow e_j \Rightarrow \tau_c(e_i) \leq \tau_c(e_j).$$

Proof: An ideal clock satisfies the property:

$$\forall i \forall j (t(e_i) < t(e_j) \Rightarrow c(t(e_i)) \leq c(t(e_j))).$$

That is, for events e_i and e_j occurring at times $t(e_i)$ and $t(e_j)$:

$$t(e_i) < t(e_j) \Leftrightarrow c(t(e_i)) \leq c(t(e_j)).$$

Upon replacment, we obtain:

$$e_i \rightarrow e_j \Rightarrow c(t(e_i)) \leq c(t(e_j)).$$

Since $\tau_c(e_i) = c(t(e_i))$, we obtain the result:

$$e_i \rightarrow e_j \Rightarrow \tau_c(e_i) \leq \tau_c(e_j).$$

$\square$

The monotonicity property of ideal clocks ensures that two causally connected events timestamped by the same ideal clock have timestamps such that the timestamp of the latter event is never less than the timestamp of the former event.

3.6   Clock Hypothesis Formulation

In order to test if a certain theory holds for a clock, it is necessary to formulate a hypothesis about the clock function. The clock hypothesis, denoted by $c_h(t)$, is then tested against the set of observed timestamps.

Definition. A clock function $c(t)$ has two components, an ideal clock function $b(t)$ and a function $d(t)$ that represents the deviation from the ideal clock:

$$c(t) = b(t) + d(t).$$

The ideal clock $b(t)$ is called the base clock; $d(t)$ is the difference between the base clock and the clock of interest. Two clocks with a common base clock can be compared by examining their deviations. It is sometimes useful to express the time of an event in terms of the base clock. This is done by subtracting $d(t)$ as follows:

$$b(t) = c(t) - d(t). \tag{3}$$

3.7   Observed Event Sets and Correctness

During a digital investigation of a computer system, the investigator may observe a number of timestamped events that are based on the same clock. Some of these events will be causally connected. The set of observed timestamped events is called the "observation set."

Definition. An observation set O is a set of timestamped events that are related to one clock $c_o(t)$.

An observation set typically has a large number of timestamped events with a large number of causal connections. The data in an observation set is used to determine whether or not a clock hypothesis holds.

Definition. A clock hypothesis $c_h(t)$ for an observation set O is correct if $c_o(t) = c_h(t)$ for all t, i.e.,

$$c_o(t) = c_h(t) \Rightarrow \forall e_i(\tau_{c_o}(e_i) = c_h(t(e_i))).$$

If a clock hypothesis is correct, then all occurrences of timestamps must match the values predicted by the hypothesis. The correctness property can, therefore, be used to devise techniques for testing whether or not a clock hypothesis is correct.

Theorem 2. In a correct clock hypothesis $c_h(t)$ the timestamps of all causally connected events $e_i \rightarrow e_j$ in an observation set O must be such that the timestamp of the first event minus the deviation from a common base is not greater than the timestamp of the latter event minus the deviation from a common base, i.e.,

$$e_i \rightarrow e_j \Rightarrow \tau_{c_o}(e_i) - d_h(t(e_i)) \leq \tau_{c_o}(e_j) - d_h(t(e_j)).$$

Proof: Let $c_h(t)$ be a correct clock hypothesis. Let $b(t)$ be a common base for $c_h(t)$ and $c_o(t)$. Then,

$$b(t) = c_h(t) - d_h(t)$$

$$b(t) = c_o(t) - d_o(t).$$

Thus,

$$c_h(t) - d_h(t) = c_o(t) - d_o(t).$$

Also, since $c_h(t)$ is correct, we have $c_h(t) = c_o(t)$. Therefore,

$$d_h(t) = d_o(t)$$
$$b(t) = c_o(t) - d_h(t).$$

Upon inserting the definition, we obtain:

$$b(t(e)) = \tau_{c_o}(e) - d_h(t(e)).$$

Note that $b(t)$ is an ideal clock. According to Theorem 1, ideal clocks satisfy the property:

$$e_i \rightarrow e_j \Rightarrow c(t(e_i)) \leq c(t(e_j)).$$

Inserting the expression for $b(t)$ yields the result:

$$e_i \rightarrow e_j \Rightarrow b(t(e_i)) \leq b(t(e_j))$$
$$e_i \rightarrow e_j \Rightarrow \tau_{c_o}(e_i) - d_h(t(e_i)) \leq \tau_{c_o}(e_j) - d_h(t(e_j)).$$

$\square$

Conversely, if the property examined in Theorem 2 does not hold, the hypothesis is incorrect.

Theorem 3 (Test-A). *If a pair of causally connected events $e_i \rightarrow e_j$ exist in an observation set O for which the timestamp of e_i minus the hypothesis deviation from a common base is larger than the timestamp of e_j minus the hypothesis deviation from a common base, then the clock* *hypothesis is incorrect, i.e.,*

$$\exists e_i \exists e_j ((e_i \to e_j) \wedge (\tau_{c_o}(e_i) - d_h(t(e_i)) > \tau_{c_o}(e_j) - d_h(t(e_j))))$$

$$\Rightarrow c_o(t) \neq c_h(t).$$

Proof: Let $c_h(t)$ be a clock hypothesis and O be an observation set with clock $c_o(t)$. Let (e_a, e_b) be a pair of events in O such that $e_a \to e_b$ and $\tau_{c_o}(e_a) - d_h(t(e_a)) > \tau_{c_o}(e_b) - d_h(t(e_b))$. Assume that $c_h(t)$ is correct, then $c_h(t) = c_o(t)$. Since $c_h(t)$ is correct, according to Theorem 3 we have:

$$e_i \to e_j \Rightarrow \tau_{c_o}(e_i) - d_h(t(e_i)) \leq \tau_{c_o}(e_j) - d_h(t(e_j)).$$

But for $i = a$ and $j = b$, we have assumed that:

$$(e_a \to e_b) \wedge (\tau_{c_o}(e_a) - d_h(t(e_a)) > \tau_{c_o}(e_b) - d_h(t(e_b))). \tag{4}$$

This contradicts the result from Theorem 2. Therefore, if Equation 4 holds, $c_h(t)$ cannot be correct. No assumptions or restrictions are imposed on events a and b; a and b could, therefore, be any event in the observation set O. For any event e_i and e_j, if Equation 4 holds, $c_h(t)$ cannot be correct. Consequently,

$$\exists e_i \exists e_j ((e_i \to e_j) \wedge (\tau_{c_o}(e_i) - d_h(t(e_i)) > \tau_{c_o}(e_j) - d_h(t(e_j))))$$

$$\Rightarrow c_o(t) \neq c_h(t).$$

$\square$

Example 1. Consider the default clock hypothesis, which assumes that the clock of the target computer has always been equal to civil time, say UTC. Then $c_h(t) = b_h(t)$ and $d_h(t) = 0$. Let the observed set consist of timestamps for four events e_1 through e_4 where $e_1 \to e_2$ and $e_3 \to e_4$:

$$
\begin{aligned}
\tau_{c_o}(e_1) &= \text{Jan 12, 2003, 12:46:34} \\
\tau_{c_o}(e_2) &= \text{Apr 21, 2004, 10:22:38} \\
\tau_{c_o}(e_3) &= \text{Feb 9, 2003, 22:16:04} \\
\tau_{c_o}(e_4) &= \text{Dec 12, 2002, 02:46:32}
\end{aligned}
$$

If Test-A is applied for $i = 3$ and $j = 4$, we obtain:

$$(e_3 \to e_4) \wedge (\tau_{c_o}(e_3) > \tau_{c_o}(e_4)).$$

Since $d_h(t) = 0$, the test fails. Thus, the default hypothesis is incorrect for this observation set.

The result can be explained informally as follows: Since e_4 must have happened after e_3 and the timestamp of e_4 represents an earlier time than the timestamp of e_3, it cannot be the case that the clock was not adjusted between these two events.

Theorem 4 (Test-B). *In a clock hypothesis $c_h(t)$, for values c' of $c_h(t)$ for which $c_h(t) = c'$ has no solution, the existence of any timestamps in the observation set O with value $\tau_{c_o}(e_i) = c'$ implies that $c_h(t)$ is incorrect.*

Proof: Let $c_h(t)$ be a clock hypothesis and O an observation set with clock $c_o(t)$. Let e_a be an event in O and let $\tau_{c_o}(e_a) = c'$ be the timestamp of e_a. Furthermore, let c' have a value such that $c_h(t) = c'$ has no solution. If $c_h(t)$ is correct, $c_h(t) = c_o(t)$. Also,

$$\forall e_i(\tau_{c_o}(e_i) = c_h(t(e_i))).$$

This means that for $i = a$:

$$\tau_{c_o}(e_a) = c_h(t(e_a)).$$

This is a contradiction because $\tau_{c_o}(e_a) = c'$ and $c_h(t) = c'$ has no solution. Therefore, if $\tau_{c_o}(e_a) = c'$ and $c_h(t) = c'$ has no solution, then $c_h(t)$ cannot be correct.

$\square$

3.8   Clock Hypothesis Consistency

Theorems 3 and 4 can be used to refute a clock hypothesis for an observation set O based on the timestamps of events in O. In the case of Test-A (Theorem 3), a clock hypothesis is incorrect when observations of timestamps for two causally connected events are not ordered correctly by the clock hypothesis being tested. On the other hand, Test-B (Theorem 4) stipulates that a clock hypothesis is incorrect when timestamps are observed that cannot be produced by the clock hypothesis because it is a discontinuous function. By iterating over all events and event pairs, every timestamp can be checked for consistency using Test-A and Test-B.

The tests can refute a clock hypothesis, but they cannot prove that it is correct. This leads to the following definition of a consistent clock hypothesis.

Definition. Given a set of tests Z, a clock hypothesis is consistent under Z with an observation set O if no test $z \in Z$ shows that the hypothesis is incorrect for O. A clock hypothesis is inconsistent under Z with an observation set O if it is not consistent under Z with O.

The distinction between the definitions of a correct hypothesis and a consistent hypothesis is useful in the context of digital investigations. In a correct clock hypothesis, all possible time values are always based on the clock of interest. Such a hypothesis can only be verified if the clock has been observed at every moment in its history. This is inconceivable for the clock on a target machine in a digital investigation. Therefore, at best, the investigator can attempt to establish a consistent clock hypothesis. In such a hypothesis, none of the timestamps of the events in O used in the tests in Z are able to show that the hypothesis is incorrect. Nevertheless, the presence of large numbers of timestamps and causally connected events in O impose strict constraints on a consistent hypothesis, which can be used to justify the hypothesis. The more data available in O that is supplied to the tests in Z, the greater the justification provided to the consistent clock hypothesis.

3.9 Clock Hypothesis as a Scientific Hypothesis

In Carrier's hypothesis based investigation model [2], a digital investigation is a process that formulates and tests hypotheses to answer questions about digital events and/or the state of digital data. According to Carrier, an investigative process is scientific if the hypothesis is scientific and is tested by conducting experiments. Carrier cites Popper in that the "criterion of the scientific status of a theory is its falsifiability or refutability or testability."

The question here is whether or not the methods for clock hypothesis formulation and testing adhere to these criteria. From the previous discussion, a clock hypothesis is a theory that is falsifiable and therefore testable. The clock hypothesis theory thus meets the requirements of a scientific theory. The hypothesis forbids certain things from happening, i.e., the occurrence of timestamp configurations described in Test-A and Test-B. The two tests examine the evidence to refute hypotheses. They do not look for confirmation; instead, they seek to detect inconsistencies. Even when a test does not refute a hypothesis, the testing has value as a serious but unsuccessful attempt to falsify the hypothesis, which can be viewed as offering a certain amount of confirming evidence.

4. Conclusions

Timestamps of computer and network events are routinely used for incident reconstruction in digital forensic investigations. However, their evidentiary value can be questioned because they are easily manipulated and the clocks used to create them could have been erroneous or improperly adjusted. The proposed formalism enables digital forensic investigators to define clock hypotheses based on historical adjustments to clocks and to test the consistency of the hypotheses with respect to stored timestamps. When the number of timestamps is large and many of the timestamped events are causally related, the consistency tests place clock hypotheses under close scrutiny. Even when a test does not refute a hypothesis, its mere application provides important confirming evidence. Clock hypothesis specification and testing is readily implemented in a software tool. Such a tool would enable investigators to verify the evidentiary value of timestamped data. Also, it could be used to investigate alternative hypotheses related to incident reconstruction, such as those postulated by prosecutors and defense attorneys.

References

[1] C. Boyd and P. Forster, Time and date issues in forensic computing – A case study, *Digital Investigation*, vol. 1(1), pp. 18–23, 2004.

[2] B. Carrier, A hypothesis-based approach to digital forensic investigations, Technical Report 2006-06, Center for Education and Research in Information Assurance and Security, Purdue University, West Lafayette, Indiana, 2006.

[3] C. Fidge, Logical time in distributed computing systems, *IEEE Computer*, vol. 24(8), pp. 28–33, 1991.

[4] P. Gladyshev and A. Patel, Formalizing event time bounding in digital investigations, *International Journal of Digital Evidence*, vol. 4(2), 2005.

[5] L. Lamport, Time, clocks and the ordering of events in a distributed system, *Communications of the ACM*, vol. 21(7), pp. 558–565, 1978.

[6] B. Schatz, G. Mohay and A. Clark, A correlation method for establishing the provenance of timestamps in digital evidence, *Digital Investigation*, vol. 3(S1), 98–107, 2006.

[7] M. Weil, Dynamic time and date stamp analysis, *International Journal of Digital Evidence*, vol. 1(2), 2002.

Chapter 8

IMPROVING DISK SECTOR INTEGRITY USING K-DIMENSION HASHING

Zoe Jiang, Lucas Hui and Siu-Ming Yiu

Abstract   The integrity of data stored on a hard disk is typically verified by computing the chained hash value of disk sector data in a specific order.
However, this technique fails when one or more sectors turn bad during
storage, making it impossible to compute their hash values. This paper presents a k-dimension hashing scheme, which computes and stores
multiple hash values for each hard disk sector. The hash values for each
sector are computed in different ways; thus, when a hard disk develops
bad sectors, it is still possible to verify the integrity of the data in the
unaffected sectors. The paper also discusses how hashing parameters
may be tuned to achieve desirable properties, including minimizing the
probability that the integrity of a sector cannot be verified because other
sectors have gone bad.

Keywords: Evidence integrity, hard disks, hash values, k-dimension hashing

1.   Introduction

This paper focuses on a common, but important, problem in digital
forensic investigations: Suppose certain data was written to a hard disk
when it was created for evidentiary purposes; after a period of time –
say one month – how could one prove that the hard disk contents are
the same as before?

The straightforward scheme is to calculate a chained hash value of
all the data in all the sectors in a specific sequence. This hash value
is digitally signed and stored in a secure location. At some point in
the future, when the integrity of the hard disk must be evaluated, the
chained hash value is recomputed and compared with the previous value.
If the two hash values match, the hard disk content is assumed not to

Please use the following format when citing this chapter:

Jiang, Z., Hui, L. and Yiu, S.-M., 2008, in IFIP International Federation for Information Processing, Volume 285;
Advances in Digital Forensics IV; Indrajit Ray, Sujeet Shenoi; (Boston: Springer), pp. 87–98.

have been modified; if the values do not match, data in one or more disk sectors is somehow different from the original data.

The chained hashing scheme fails when the stored hard disk develops one or more bad sectors. A hash value cannot be computed for a bad sector and, consequently, the chained hash value for the entire hard disk cannot be calculated. Moreover, as disk capacity increases, the number of sectors increases, which makes the chained hashing scheme less attractive.

This paper describes an improved hashing scheme, which computes and stores multiple hash values for hard disk sectors. Specifically, hash values computed in different ways are available for verifying the integrity of a sector. Thus, when a hard disk develops one or more bad sectors, it is still possible to verify the integrity of the data in the unaffected sectors.

2.   Background

This section describes the physical structure of hard disks and discusses hashing techniques for verifying the integrity of stored data.

2.1   Hard Disk Structure

A hard disk has one or more platters for storing data. Each platter has two read/write heads, one for the top face of the platter and the other for the bottom face. A platter is divided into tens of thousands of tightly-packed concentric circles called tracks. A cylinder is the set of tracks at which the heads are currently located.

Since tracks hold far too much information to be suitable as the smallest individually-addressable units of storage on a disk, each track is further divided into sectors that typically hold 512 bytes of data. Modern hard disks may have several thousand sectors in a single track.

An individual sector is traditionally addressed using an ordered CHS triple containing the cylinder, head and sector numbers (Figure 1). Due to the 8.4 GB limit of the Int 13h interface, modern drives are no longer specified using the CHS mode. Instead, they are addressed at the logical level using logical block addressing (LBA). At the physical level, however, most modern hard disks still use the CHS mode. Therefore, by accessing the integrated disk controller, which automatically translates LBA to the physical geometry, it is possible to match CHS triples to the physical hard disk characteristics [7].

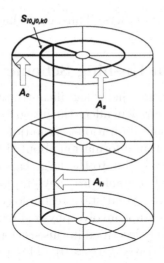

Figure 1. Hard disk structure.

2.2 Verifying Hard Disk Integrity

Most digital forensic tools (e.g, EnCase [3] and DESK [1]) use the chained hashing scheme to verify the integrity of data on hard disks. A change to just one bit in a sector, file or hard disk causes the hash value to be different [2].

Kornblum [5] recently proposed the context triggered piecewise hashing (CTPH) scheme to identify modified versions of known files (where data may have been inserted, modified or deleted). Although the CTPH scheme was designed for files, it can be applied to hard disks – a bad sector is considered to correspond to the portion of a file that has been modified. However, the CTPH scheme has high computational time requirements of $O(n \log n)$ where n is the size of the data being hashed. It is, therefore, not feasible to apply CTPH to large capacity hard disks (e.g., those exceeding 120 GB).

Jiang, *et al.* [4] have proposed a 3-dimension hashing scheme with better performance than the CTPH technique. This scheme computes multiple hash values to reduce the impact of bad sectors on disk integrity verification while requiring only a linear $(O(n))$ increase in computational time. The 3-dimension hashing scheme calculates hash values for: (i) all sectors with the same cylinder and head numbers (A_s in Figure 1) for all cylinder and head numbers; (ii) all sectors with the same cylinder and sector numbers (A_h in Figure 1) for all cylinder and sector numbers; and (iii) all sectors with the same head and sector numbers (A_c in Figure

1) for all head and sector numbers. Thus, every hash value that is stored has a physical meaning.

3.   *k*-Dimension Hashing Scheme

The 3-dimension hashing scheme significantly reduces the probability that one or more bad sectors will affect the integrity verification of a hard disk. However, it has some limitations. A major drawback is that it is not always possible to obtain information about the physical structure of the hard disk; this is mainly due to the large capacities of modern hard disks and the diversity of technologies they employ [7]. For example, a USB thumb drive that uses solid state technology requires an integrity checking scheme that does not involve physical drive characteristics.

The *k*-dimension scheme described in this section extends 3-dimension hashing by using an arbitratry k $(k > 0)$. This provides more freedom to design hashing schemes, including schemes that do not rely on the physical characteristics of hard disks. The only requirement is that the sectors in a hard disk being verified form a sequence.

Let N be the total number of disk sectors in a hard disk, and let p be the probability that any one disk sector becomes a bad sector after some period of time. We investigate the fail probability (P_f) of an integrity proof of a disk sector. This occurs when all the hash values involving the disk sector cannot be computed because other sectors involved in the hash computations have gone bad.

A 1-dimension hashing scheme is the trivial case that computes one hash value for all N sectors. The integrity proof of a disk sector is viable only when all the sectors are good sectors, which occurs with probability $(1 - p)^{(N-1)}$. Consequently, the fail probability P_f is $1 - (1 - p)^{(N-1)}$.

For a 2-dimension scheme, the N sectors give rise to an $N_1 \times N_2$ (2-dimensional) array where N_1 and N_2 are integers such that $N_1 \times N_2 = N$. The minimum value of P_f occurs when $N_1 = N_2 = N^{1/2}$. In this case, the probability P_f is equal to $1 - \{(1 - p)^{[N^{(\frac{1}{2})} - 1]}\}^2$.

Similarly, for a *k*-dimension hashing scheme, where the sectors form a *k*-dimensional array, the minimum value of P_f occurs when the size of each dimension N_k is equal to $N^{1/k}$. Therefore, for a *k*-dimension scheme with $k \geq 1$, $P_f = \{1 - (1 - p)^{[N^{(\frac{1}{k})} - 1]}\}^k$.

Note that extra hash values must be stored when implementing the *k*-dimension hashing scheme. In general, the total number of hash values *(Num)* stored is equal to $k \cdot N^{(\frac{k-1}{k})}$.

Increasing the number of dimensions k decreases the fail probability P_f, but the number of hash values Num also increases. It is, therefore, necessary to examine how P_f may be reduced while Num is also reduced.

One strategy is to divide the N disk sectors into j blocks ($j \geq 1$) and apply the k-dimension hashing scheme to each individual block. This strategy is simple and effective. Even in the 1-dimension case, by setting j to N, the probability P_f can be reduced to 0 with Num set equal to $N!$ This is the absolute minimum value of P_f; therefore, it is necessary to consider the combined effect of the dimension size k and the number of blocks j.

Upon substituting the number of blocks j in place of the number of disk sectors N, the fail probability for the k-dimension hashing scheme is given by:

$$P_f = \{1 - (1 - p)^{[(\frac{N}{j})^{(\frac{1}{k})} - 1]}\}^k. \tag{1}$$

The corresponding number of hash values to be stored is given by:

$$Num = j \cdot k \cdot (\frac{N}{j})^{(\frac{k-1}{k})}. \tag{2}$$

4. Analysis of k-Dimension Hashing

Tables 1–4 present the fail probabilities and the numbers of hash values required to be stored for various values of N (number of sectors) and p (probability that a sector becomes bad).

To simplify the presentation and related discussion, the data in Tables 1–4 is plotted to create the graphs in Figures 2 through 7. Figures 2 and 3 present the data in Table 1. Figures 2 and 4 present the data in Table 2. Figures 5 and 6 present the data in Table 3. Figures 5 and 7 present the data in Table 4. Note that Figures 2, 3 and 4 correspond to $N = 1.152e8$ while Figures 5, 6 and 7 correspond to $N = 3.6e8$.

As expected, increasing the number of dimensions k while keeping the number of blocks j fixed yields a lower fail probability P_f. However, the data also reveals that, when k is increased by 1, P_f drops by a value of approximately p. This anomaly can be partially explained by simplifying Equation 1 above. Given that $(1 - e)^m$ can be approximated by $1 - em$ when e is very small and integer $m > 1$, the equation for P_f simplifies to:

$$\{p \cdot [(N/j)^{(1/k)} - 1]\}^k.$$

Upon further simplification and ignoring the -1 term, P_f is given by:

$$p^k \cdot (N/j).$$

Table 1. P_f and Num for $N = 1.152e8$, $p = 1e - 5$.

j/k		1-D	2-D	3-D	4-D
1e0	P_f	1	$1.04e-2$	$1.10e-7$	$1.11e-12$
	Num	1	2.15e4	7.10e5	4.45e6
1e1	P_f	1	$1.10e-3$	$1.10e-8$	$1.07e-13$
	Num	1.00e1	6.79e4	1.53e6	7.91e6
1e2	P_f	1	$1.00e-4$	$1.10e-9$	$1.02e-14$
	Num	1.00e2	2.15e5	3.30e6	1.41e7
1e3	P_f	$6.84e-1$	$1.00e-5$	$1.10e-10$	$9.21e-16$
	Num	1.00e3	6.79e5	7.10e6	2.50e7
1e4	P_f	$1.09e-1$	$1.00e-6$	$1.00e-11$	$7.67e-17$
	Num	1.00e4	2.15e6	1.53e7	4.45e7
1e5	P_f	$1.14e-2$	$1.08e-7$	$8.50e-13$	$5.42e-18$
	Num	1.00e5	6.79e6	3.30e7	7.91e7
1e6	P_f	$1.14e-3$	$9.47e-9$	$5.80e-14$	$2.68e-19$
	Num	1.00e6	2.15e7	7.10e7	1.41e8
1e7	P_f	$1.05e-4$	$5.73e-10$	$2.00e-15$	$5.03e-21$
	Num	1.00e7	6.73e7	1.50e8	2.50e8
1e8	P_f	$1.52e-6$	$5.37e-13$	$1.10e-19$	$1.68e-26$
	Num	1.00e8	2.15e8	3.30e8	4.45e8
N	P_f	0	0	0	0
	Num	1.15e8	2.30e8	3.50e8	4.61e8

Table 2. P_f and Num for $N = 1.152e8$, $p = 1e - 10$.

j/k		1-D	2-D	3-D	4-D
1e0	P_f	$1.15e-2$	$1.15e-12$	$1.14e-22$	$1.11e-32$
	Num	1	2.14e4	7.10e5	4.45e6
1e1	P_f	$1.15e-3$	$1.15e-13$	$1.14e-23$	$1.10e-33$
	Num	1.00e1	6.79e4	1.53e6	7.91e6
1e2	P_f	$1.15e-4$	$1.15e-14$	$1.12e-24$	$1.02e-34$
	Num	1.00e2	2.15e5	3.30e6	1.41e7
1e3	P_f	$1.15e-5$	$1.15e-15$	$1.08e-25$	$9.22e-36$
	Num	1.00e3	6.79e5	7.10e6	2.50e7
1e4	P_f	$1.15e-6$	$1.13e-16$	$1.01e-26$	$7.68e-37$
	Num	1.00e4	2.15e6	1.53e7	4.45e7
1e5	P_f	$1.15e-7$	$1.09e-17$	$8.53e-28$	$5.42e-38$
	Num	1.00e5	6.79e5	3.30e7	7.91e7
1e6	P_f	$1.14e-8$	$9.47e-19$	$5.78e-29$	$2.68e-39$
	Num	1.00e6	2.15e7	7.10e7	1.41e8
1e7	P_f	$1.05e9$	$5.73e-20$	$1.99e-30$	$5.03e-41$
	Num	1.00e7	6.79e7	1.53e8	2.50e8
1e8	P_f	$1.52e-11$	$5.37e-23$	$1.13e-34$	$1.68e-46$
	Num	1.00e8	2.45e8	3.30e8	4.45e8
N	P_f	0	0	0	0
	Num	1.15e8	2.30e8	3.50e8	4.61e8

Table 3. P_f and *Num* for $N = 3.6e8$, $p = 1e - 10$.

j/k		1-D	2-D	3-D	4-D
1e0	P_f	1	$3.00e-2$	$3.50e-7$	$3.50e-12$
	Num	1	$3.79e4$	$1.52e6$	$1.05e7$
1e1	P_f	1	$3.40e-3$	$3.50e-8$	$3.41e-13$
	Num	$1.00e1$	$1.20e5$	$3.27e6$	$1.86e7$
1e2	P_f	1	$3.53e-4$	$3.50e-9$	$3.28e-14$
	Num	$1.00e2$	$3.79e5$	$7.04e6$	$3.30e7$
1e3	P_f	$9.73e-1$	$3.56e-5$	$3.40e-10$	$3.05e-15$
	Num	$1.00e3$	$1.20e6$	$1.50e7$	$5.88e8$
1e4	P_f	$3.02e-1$	$3.56e-6$	$3.30e-11$	$2.66e-16$
	Num	$1.00e4$	$3.79e6$	$3.30e7$	$1.05e8$
1e5	P_f	$3.50e-2$	$3.48e-7$	$2.90e-12$	$2.07e-17$
	Num	$1.00e5$	$1.20e7$	$7.00e7$	$1.86e8$
1e6	P_f	$3.60e-3$	$3.23e-8$	$2.30e-13$	$1.27e-18$
	Num	$1.00e6$	$8.79e7$	$1.50e8$	$3.32e8$
1e7	P_f	$3.00e-4$	$2.50e-9$	$1.20e-14$	$4.41e-20$
	Num	$1.00e7$	$1.20e8$	$3.30e8$	$5.88e8$
1e8	P_f	$3.00e-5$	$8.05e-11$	$1.50e-16$	$2.03e-22$
	Num	$1.00e8$	$3.79e8$	$7.99e8$	$1.05e9$
N	P_f	0	0	0	0
	Num	$4.00e8$	$7.20e8$	$1.10e9$	$1.44e9$

Table 4. P_f and *Num* for $N = 3.6e8$, $p = 1e - 10$.

j/k		1-D	2-D	3-D	4-D
1e0	P_f	$3.54e-2$	$3.60e-12$	$3.60e-22$	$3.50e-32$
	Num	1	$3.79e4$	$1.52e6$	$1.05e7$
1e1	P_f	$3.60e-3$	$3.60e-1$	$3.60e-23$	$3.42e-33$
	Num	$1.00e1$	$1.20e5$	$3.27e6$	$1.86e7$
1e2	P_f	$4.00e04$	$3.60e-14$	$3.50e-24$	$3.28e-34$
	Num	$1.00e2$	$3.79e5$	$7.04e6$	$3.30e7$
1e3	P_f	$4.00e-5$	$3.59e-15$	$3.50e-25$	$3.05e-35$
	Num	$1.00e3$	$1.20e6$	$1.50e7$	$5.88e8$
1e4	P_f	$4.00e-6$	$3.56e-16$	$3.30e-26$	$2.66e-36$
	Num	$1.00e4$	$3.79e6$	$3.30e7$	$1.05e8$
1e5	P_f	$4.00e-7$	$3.48e-17$	$2.90e-27$	$2.07e-37$
	Num	$1.00e5$	$1.20e7$	$7.00e7$	$1.86e8$
1e6	P_f	$4.00e-8$	$3.23e-18$	$2.30e-28$	$1.27e-38$
	Num	$1.00e6$	$8.79e7$	$1.50e8$	$3.32e8$
1e7	P_f	$4.00e-9$	$2.50e-19$	$1.20e-29$	$4.41e-40$
	Num	$1.00e7$	$1.20e8$	$3.30e8$	$5.88e8$
1e8	P_f	$3.00e-10$	$8.05e-21$	$1.50e-31$	$2.03e-42$
	Num	$1.00e8$	$3.79e8$	$7.99e8$	$1.05e9$
N	P_f	0	0	0	0
	Num	$4.00e8$	$7.20e8$	$1.10e9$	$1.44e9$

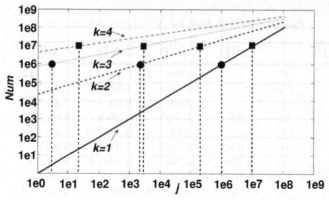

Figure 2.   Num versus j for N = 1.152e8.

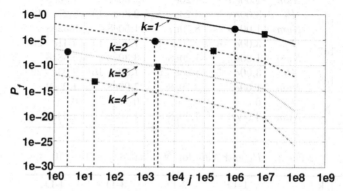

Figure 3. P_f versus j for $N = 1.152e8$, $p = 1e - 5$.

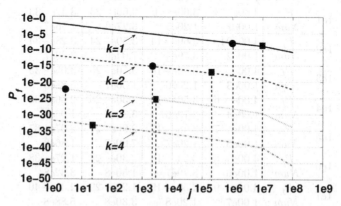

Figure 4. P_f versus j for $N = 1.152e8$, $p = 1e - 10$.

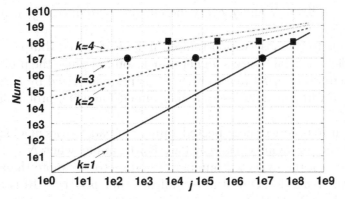

Figure 5.   *Num* versus j for $N = 3.6e8$.

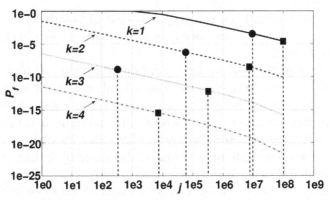

Figure 6. P_f versus j for $N = 3.6e8$, $p = 1e - 5$.

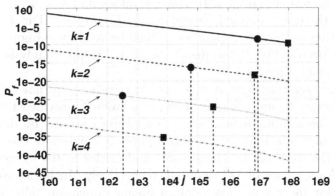

Figure 7. P_f versus j for $N = 3.6e8$, $p = 1e - 10$.

Therefore, for fixed N and j, every increment in k reduces P_f by a factor of p.

This leads to the observation that even if j is changed (but not by too much), it is beneficial to use a higher dimension to reduce the probability P_f. The reduction in P_f due to higher k is parameterized by p. Specifically, it is advantageous to use a higher dimension when probability p is low.

Note that in practice the expected number of bad sectors in a hard disk is low and the probability p is very low. For example, when $N = 1.152e8$ and $p = 1e - 5$, the expected number of bad sectors is more than 1,000, which is not realistic. Our studies indicate that $p = 1e - 10$ is a more realistic value. Nevertheless, the data corresponding to $p = 10e - 5$ is presented to show the behavior of the hashing scheme for a p value that is not very small.

Another observation from the graphs is that although P_f is expected to drop to zero for $j = N$, this does not occur even when j is close to N (see Figures 4 and 7).

Figures 2–4 can be used to determine the appropriate number of dimensions to be used given a fixed *Num* (number of hash values to be stored). First, Figure 2 is used to determine the number of blocks (j) for each dimension value (k) that will require *Num* hash values. Next, Figure 3 or 4 is used to determine the probabilities P_f corresponding to the j values for each value of k. Finally, the value of k that yields the lowest fail probability P_f is selected.

To illustrate the methodology, consider a fixed *Num* value of $1e7$. The four squares in Figure 2 identify the points with this *Num* value and $k = 4, 3, 2$ and 1. The j values of these four points are recorded. Next, the four points in Figure 3 with these j values and $k = 4, 3, 2, 1$ are identified (these are marked as squares in Figure 3). The P_f values corresponding to these four points can then be read from Figure 3. The lowest fail probability P_f occurs for $k = 4$. Similar analysis can be performed using Figures 5–7.

Upon investigating several different *Num* values, we have observed that it is better to use a higher dimension value k provided that *Num* is at least the minimum number of hash values needed by dimension k. Two examples in Figures 2–4 and Figures 5–7 illustrate the effect of increasing the dimension. The squares and circles in the figures correspond to *Num* values of $1e7$ and $1e6$, respectively. In both cases, it is clear that for the given *Num* value, a higher dimension value k yields a lower fail probability P_f. Upon comparing the two groups of points (squares and circles), it is apparent that a higher j value produces a lower fail probability P_f for the same dimension k.

5.   Observations

Our analysis indicates that k-dimension hashing is very effective at reducing the fail probability P_f. For example, the fail probability for 10 blocks (with $p = 1e - 10$ and $N = 1.152e8$) reduces from $1.15e - 2$ in the straightforward scheme of using one hash value for the entire hard disk to $1.10e - 33$ when 4-dimension hashing is used. This is a drastic decrease in fail probability. Similar reductions occur for other parameter settings.

Our findings can be summarized in the following recommendations. If the minimization of the fail probability P_f is the principal goal and *Num* hash values can be stored, where *Num* < N (number of disk sectors), then it is best to use the highest possible k-dimension hashing scheme. On the other hand, if *Num* is close to or larger than N, then the 1-dimension hashing scheme with $P_f = 0$ is the best choice.

Note that these recommendations ignore the overhead involved in handling large numbers of hash values, especially when the hash values have to be digitally signed (as in many digital forensic tools [1, 3]). The Merkle hash tree [6] is a low overhead approach for signing multiple hash values [8]. Nevertheless, it is important to investigate the effect of the overhead involved in digital signing on the choice of dimension.

6.   Conclusions

The k-dimension hashing scheme is a robust technique for verifying the integrity of data stored on hard disks. The scheme computes the hash values for each sector in multiple ways; thus, when one or more sectors go bad, it is still possible to verify the integrity of the data in the unaffected sectors. Our future research will investigate applications of k-dimension hashing to enhancing evidence preservation and detecting evidence tampering with high probability.

Acknowledgements

This research was partially supported by the Research Grants Council of the Hong Kong Special Administrative Region under Project Nos. HKU 7136/04E and HKU 7132/06E.

References

[1] K. Chow, C. Chong, K. Lai, L. Hui, K. Pun, W. Tsang and H. Chan, Digital evidence search kit, *Proceedings of the First International Workshop on Systematic Approaches to Digital Forensic Engineering*, pp. 187–194, 2005.

[2] J. Foster and V. Liu, Catch me, if you can, presented at *Black Hat Japan 2005* (www.blackhat.com/presentations/bh-usa-05/bh-us-05-foster-liu-update.pdf), 2005.

[3] Guidance Software, EnCase, Pasadena, California (www.guidance software.com).

[4] Z. Jiang, L. Hui, K. Chow, S. Yiu and P. Lai, Improving disk sector integrity using a 3-dimension hashing scheme, *Future Generation Communication and Networking*, vol. 2, pp. 141–145, 2007.

[5] J. Kornblum, Identifying almost identical files using context triggered piecewise hashing, *Proceedings of the Sixth Digital Forensic Research Workshop*, 2006.

[6] R. Merkle, A certified digital signature, *Proceedings of the Ninth International Cryptology Conference*, pp. 218–238, 1989.

[7] The PC Guide, Hard Disk Drives (www.pcguide.com/ref/hdd).

[8] M. Wang, S. Yiu, L. Hui, C. Chong, K. Chow, W. Tsang, H. Chan and K. Pun, A hybrid approach for authenticating MPEG-2 streaming data, *Proceedings of the International Workshop on Multimedia Content Analysis and Mining*, pp. 203–212, 2007.

IV

EVIDENCE MANAGEMENT

Chapter 9

CLASS-AWARE SIMILARITY HASHING FOR DATA CLASSIFICATION

Vassil Roussev, Golden Richard III and Lodovico Marziale

Abstract   This paper introduces "class-aware similarity hashes" or "classprints," which are an outgrowth of recent work on similarity hashing. The approach builds on the notion of context-based hashing to create a framework for identifying data types based on content and for building characteristic similarity hashes for individual data items that can be used for correlation. The principal benefits are that data classification can be fully automated and that *a priori* knowledge of the underlying data is not necessary beyond the availability of a suitable training set.

Keywords: Similarity hashing, class-aware similarity hashing, classprints

1.   Introduction

The problem of identifying the type of data inside a container (e.g., file or disk image) has been studied for several years with few positive results. Indeed, the ability to identify the underlying type of the data without the help of file system metadata is very useful in data recovery operations (file carving), especially as a means for validating the attempted data recovery. For example, if a tool runs into text data while attempting to carve a JPEG file, it is clear that the process is not on the right track. This is important because data carving is routinely applied to target images to recover (fragments of) deleted data and is often a valuable source of information.

Another related problem is automated data correlation. Targets often contain several terabytes of data, making it necessary to quickly separate potentially relevant data from irrelevant data. The best strategy is to use prior accumulated data to make the separation. Traditional forensic investigations use large, sophisticated databases (e.g., for fingerprints and DNA) to quickly zero in on relevant data. In digital forensics,

Please use the following format when citing this chapter:

Roussev, V., Richard III, G. and Marziale, L., 2008, in IFIP International Federation for Information Processing, Volume 285; *Advances in Digital Forensics IV*; Indrajit Ray, Sujeet Shenoi; (Boston: Springer), pp. 101–113.

success has come from using databases of hash values of known system and application files, such as those maintained by NIST [6]. But it is debatable if this approach will work when the databases contain billions of hash values – would it be necessary to compute clusters just to perform hash searches?

Traditional, file-based (cryptographic) hashing is useful but fragile; it needs the exact binary representation of all versions of the objects of interest. Several schemes have been proposed to address this issue. Kornblum [5] has proposed a context-based approach that dynamically splits a file into individually hashable chunks from which a composite hash is produced. While the use of a hash-based context – which can be traced to early research in information retrieval [1, 3] and is derived from Rabin's original work [8] – is a proven technique, the rest of the scheme lacks robustness. Recently, we proposed a more robust approach [9] based on Bloom filters [2], but it lacks an elegant mechanism for splitting up arbitrary targets.

In [10] we refined the approach to create the multi-resolution similarity (MRS) hashing scheme that can be applied to arbitrary targets. The scheme clearly identifies similarities in data files that would be classified by a human as being related (e.g., different drafts of the same document). Also, the MRS hashing scheme can identify the presence of a contained file (e.g., JPEG) inside a larger target (e.g., raw drive image) without metadata or any other assistance from the file system.

An MRS hashing tool has significant performance advantages stemming from the fact that it requires only a single sequential pass over an image. In contrast, other file-based tools require access to file metadata, which results in non-sequential disk access patterns.

Figure 1 illustrates the effects of non-sequential access on the throughput of a modern hard drive, as measured by Intel's IOMeter tool. As little as 2% randomness in the workload can produce a 30% performance penalty; 5% randomness can cut performance in half. With hard drive capacities outpacing bandwidth and latency improvements [7], forensic targets are increasing in size faster than the ability of forensic tools to process them in a timely manner.

This paper discusses the use of class-aware similarity hashing to address these issues. Empirical results using a custom tool show that class-defining features can be automatically extracted for several classes of commonly-used file types. In other words, it is practical to define common file types solely based on syntactic features of their binary representations.

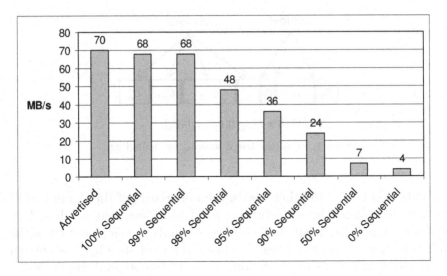

Figure 1. Hard drive throughput for WDC WD5000KS (500 GB).

2.   Similarity Hashing

This section briefly summarizes recent work on similarity hashing. Interested readers are referred to [10] for additional details.

Block-level hashing is the most basic scheme for determining the similarity of binary data. The technique generates and stores cryptographic hashes for blocks of a chosen fixed size (e.g., 512 bytes). Block hashes from two different sources can then be compared and, by counting the number of blocks in common, a measure of similarity may be determined. The principal advantages of this scheme are that it is supported by existing hashing tools and that it is computationally efficient; in fact, the hash computations are faster than disk I/O.

However, block-level hashing has certain limitations when applied to discover file similarity. The success of the technique depends heavily on the physical layout of the files being similar. However, the insertion, deletion or modification of just one character at the beginning of a file could render all the block hashes different. Also, block hashes do not help identify if an object (e.g., JPEG image) is embedded in a file (e.g., Microsoft Word document). In short, block hashing is too fragile and negative results do not reveal any useful information.

Kornblum [5] proposed context-triggered piecewise hashing to address the limitations of block-level hashing. The idea is to identify content markers, called "contexts," within (binary data) objects and to store the sequence of hashes for each of the pieces (or chunks) in between

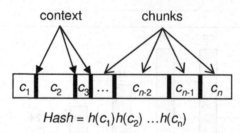

$$Hash = h(c_1)h(c_2) \ldots h(c_n)$$

Figure 2.   Context-based hashing or "shingling."

contexts (Figure 2). In other words, the boundaries of the chunk hashes are not determined by an arbitrary fixed block size but are based on object content. The hash of the object is simply a concatenation of the individual chunk hashes. Thus, if a new version of the object is created by localized insertions and deletions, some of the original chunk hashes will be modified, reordered or deleted, but enough will remain in the new composite hash to identify the similarity.

To identify a context, Kornblum's **ssdeep** implementation uses a rolling hash over a window of c bytes that slides over the target. If the t lowest bits of the hash (the trigger) are all equal to one, a context is detected, the hash computation of the preceding chunk is completed and a new chunk hash is started. The value of t depends on the size of the target because **ssdeep** generates a fixed-size result. Intuitively, a larger t value produces less frequent context matches and reduces the granularity of the hash.

We recently proposed Bloom filter similarity hashing [9], a scheme utilizing Bloom filters to derive object similarity. This scheme uses the (known) structure of an object to break it into components, which are individually hashed and placed in a Bloom filter. Using the mathematical properties of filters, we demonstrated analytically and empirically that the bitwise comparison of filters yields a useful measure of the similarity between the binary representations of two or more objects.

In subsequent work [10], we combined Bloom filter similarity hashing with context-based object decomposition ("shingling" [3]) to handle arbitrary binary data. We also devised a standardized multi-resolution scheme called MRS hashing that allows objects of arbitrary size to be hashed without loss of resolution. Moreover, the scheme allows different-sized objects to be compared; for example, it is possible to search for the remnants of a 1 MB file inside a 100 GB target.

MRS hashing is very memory efficient due to the use of Bloom filters; hash values are no more than 0.5% of target size. Thus, the complete MRS hash of a 500 GB hard drive can fit in the main memory of a modern workstation. From the point of view of performance, MRS hashing is no more expensive than block-level MD5 hashing, even when the unoptimized version of MD5 is used. The comparison step is very efficient and can be sped up by using lower resolution for large targets and/or delegating comparisons to a graphics processor (e.g., NVidia G80); this can speed up the process twenty times.

3. Class-Aware Similarity Hashing

As discussed in the preceding section, MRS hashes provide a sensitive and tunable means for finding similarities among binary data objects. But why are these objects similar? From our previous work, it appears that MRS hashing works reasonably well for user-generated artifacts (e.g., .jpg, .doc and .pdf files) in that the objects identified as being similar stand out from other objects in their class.

However, this is not the case for other classes of objects such as applications and system libraries. When applied in its original form, MRS hashing finds too many applications/libraries to be similar, which limits its usefulness. Note that these matches are not false positives; the binary representations of the objects are indeed similar. The observed syntactic similarities are generally artifacts of the particular file format (common headers, etc.) used by the compiler and statically-linked libraries. For example, we discovered (to our surprise) that most of the libraries sampled had repetitive functions. In other words, the same function code was present multiple times. These functions tend to be small and are likely compiler artifacts. Nonetheless, they increase the binary similarity, but are not necessarily indicative of semantic similarity.

Therefore, the fundamental problem is: Is it possible to effectively separate the class-common features (hashes) of an object from its characteristic individual features? Solving this problem would permit the definition of an object class (e.g., Microsoft Word documents) as a set of context-based hashes that are commonly found in such objects. Furthermore, it would lead to at least three important applications:

- The data recovery process is enhanced by eliminating at least some of the false positive results that plague virtually all file carving tools.

- The similarity hashing scheme is enhanced by separating the class-common hashes from object-specific hashes; this would yield more focused similarity results.

- An unstructured target can be searched to estimate the number of objects of different types without reading the file system. Information can be obtained after a single sequential pass over the target; partial results could be presented while the operation is underway. This would help in a triage process, which is often faced with a large volume of data.

In addition to aiding regular digital forensic investigations, the latter two applications could help in tricky legal situations where search and seizure must be balanced against privacy concerns. The judicial system has not as yet directly addressed the bounds of what is a reasonable search in the digital world. Nevertheless, the capabilities listed above could provide cause for search, e.g., a disk contains a file that is similar to something relevant or the drive contains a large number of pictures. Just as important, the capabilities could help rule out unlikely candidates.

This paper focuses on the validation of the concept of class-aware similarity hashing. In particular, it attempts to verify the existence of class-specific features that can be captured via hashing, to quantify the number and coverage of these features, and to cross-validate the features by comparing their performance for other classes of objects.

4.   Empirical Study

The empirical study used a custom tool that implemented a counting Bloom filter with a single hash function. This is equivalent to using a hash table whose values correspond to the number of data chunks that hash to the particular hash key. The procedure used is a variant of the original MRS hashing scheme.

For each file, given parameters c and t:

1. Hash a sliding window of size c with the djb2 hash function.

2. If the t rightmost bits are all set to 1, declare a new context match and compute an MD5 hash of the data chunk between the previous context and the current one, and place it in the counting Bloom filter; advance the window by the minimum chunk size (2^{t-2}) and go to Step 1.
   Otherwise, slide the window by one position.

3. If the end of file is reached, exit.
   Otherwise, go to Step 1.

In the case of low-entropy data, a single file often contributes the same hash value multiple times. To address this problem, a local filter is created for each file and the number of hash value contributions is limited to one per key (this is added to the total in the master table). Note that this problem is not due to MRS hashing because it does not use a counting filter.

The next step is to build a histogram which, for a given number k, gives the number of filter locations that have a count k (i.e., k files contain that hash). Based on the histogram, a notion of "coverage" is defined for threshold r – the number of files that contain a hash that has a count of at least r in the master table. Intuitively, it is desirable to obtain maximum coverage with the fewest number of features, so the search starts at the highest frequency and goes down in order. This approach does not guarantee minimal coverage in terms of the number of hashes, but it works fairly well in practice. Two other terms, "relative coverage" and "coverage size," are defined. The "relative coverage" is the fraction of objects covered by hashes with count of at least r. The "size" of a coverage is the number of hashes participating in the coverage.

Seven file sets were used in the empirical study. The first three file sets, whose contents were obtained at random from the Internet, were also used in our previous work [10]. The remaining four file sets contain standard system files as described below.

- *doc:* This set contains 355 files varying in size from 64 KB to 10 MB (total 298 MB).

- *xls:* This set contains 415 files varying in size from 64 KB to 7 MB (total 257 MB).

- *jpg:* This set contains 737 files varying in size from 64 KB to 5 MB (total 121 MB).

- *win-dll:* This set contains 1,243 files (total 141 MB) from a fully-patched WindowsXP `system32` directory varying in size from 3 KB to 640 KB.

- *win-exe:* This set contains 343 files (total 46 MB) from the WindowsXP `system32` directory varying in size from 1 KB to 17 MB.

- *cyg-bin:* This set contains 1,272 files (total 192 MB) from the `bin` directory of Cygwin 2.4 (including all executable files) varying in size from 3 KB to 7.6 MB.

- *ubu-bin:* This set contains 445 files (total 63 MB) from the `/usr/bin` directory of a fully-patched Ubuntu 6.06; the files varied in size from 16 KB to 3.85 MB.

4.1   First-Order Analysis

The first task was to verify the hypothesis that data from different file types exhibits common features that can be captured via context-based

Table 1.   First-order analysis of user data.

doc			xls			jpg		
Hashes	Cov %	Cover	Hashes	Cov %	Cover	Hashes	Cov %	Cover
1	52	188	1	59	245	1	28	212
2	54	195	3	83	345	4	52	388
3	59	212	4	92	382	5	54	400
4	91	325	5	94	394	10	59	439
5	91	325	6	97	403	38	72	536
6	93	331	7	97	406	42	75	557
8	93	333	23	100	415	65	78	579
9	93	333				81	79	585
10	94	334				90	81	604
12	97	346				122	85	629
15	97	347				405	88	653
20	99	352				3857	98	729
774	100	355						

hashing. One feature is a hash value that is common to a set of data objects of a specific class. The coverage of this feature includes all the objects that contain the feature at least once. Ideally, a relatively small set of features should cover as much as possible of the reference set.

First, we ran our custom tool against a set of 600 files (256 KB each) of random data. The results showed that only two features were common to five different files; all the other features were common to no more than two files. This result is expected – random data should not exhibit any features. High-entropy data objects (e.g., compressed and/or encrypted objects) should exhibit similar results.

Table 1 summarizes the results for three common types of user-created data: Microsoft Word documents (*doc*), Microsoft Excel spreadsheets (*xls*) and JPEG images (*jpg*). All the hash values were generated using similarity hashing as described in Section 4 with the parameters $c = 8$ and $t = 5$. The first column presents the number of hashes in the cover, the second provides the relative coverage (percentage of the file set covered) and the third gives the absolute number of files covered. Thus, the row {5, 91, 335} means that the top five ("most popular") hashes cover 335 files, which constitute 91% of the files in the reference set. Note that several intermediate rows are not shown for reasons of space; only data that represents important trends is presented. Also, the rows presented in boldface represent the coverage chosen for the cross-analysis study in the next section.

Table 2. First-order analysis of system executables.

win-dll			win-exe			cyg-bin			ubu-bin		
Hashes	Cov %	Cover	Hashes	Cov %	Cover	Hashes	Cov %	Cover	Hashes	Cov %	Cover
1	41	510	1	44	151	1	11	146	1	53	239
2	58	733	3	46	158	2	22	285	2	64	285
4	68	853	4	77	265	36	30	384	3	78	351
9	71	886	5	78	267	49	36	458	4	82	365
17	75	933	6	79	271	90	41	529	6	84	377
43	**80**	**1004**	7	80	273	105	49	624	9	85	379
122	85	1061	8	86	295	144	55	706	**33**	**91**	**407**
541	90	1120	11	87	296	276	61	778	50	91	409
2478	95	1193	**12**	**89**	**305**	**654**	**67**	**853**	1100	92	412
5390	97	1215	56	90	306	1947	72	921	3208	93	416
14208	98	1228	139	91	310	3332	75	958	5820	93	417
36716	99	1237	332	95	324	7013	80	1022	6648	94	419
			453	95	325	16913	86	1096	9192	95	424
			987	96	329	29985	89	1138	42238	97	435
			9873	98	334	65119	93	1190			

The results show that *doc* and *xls* files have compact and easily identifiable feature hash sets or "classprints" that represent the types. In the case of *doc* files, only 20 feature hashes are required to provide 99% coverage. The top four give 91% coverage, so choosing the cut-off point can be somewhat subjective. The results are not as good for *jpg* files, where a substantially larger feature set is required to cover the reference files. Intuitively, the larger the feature set, the more instance-specific the features it includes.

In all cases, the feature set was kept relatively small and the inflection point was chosen so that the rate at which features need to be added was greater than the rate at which coverage was increased. For example, in the *jpg* case, the increase from 10 to 38 hash values yields an increase in coverage from 59% to 72%; the next step, from 38 to 42 is relatively small and yields a correspondingly modest improvement from 72% to 75%. However, the increase from 42 to 65 only yields an improvement of 75% to 78%. Therefore, 42 was chosen as the cut-off point for the experiments in the next section.

The analysis of system executables shows some interesting results (Table 2). The sets were chosen so they had various degrees of commonality. Specifically, all the sets primarily contain executable code for the Intel x86 architecture. Although other resources could be bundled into an

Table 3. Feature set intersection.

	doc	xls	jpg	win-dll	win-exe	cyg-bin	ubu-bin
doc		3 (17%)					
xls	3 (43%)						
jpg							
win-dll					9 (21%)	1 (2%)	
win-exe				9 (75%)			
cyg-bin				1 (0.2%)			1 (0.2%)
ubu-bin						1 (3%)	

executable, these are relatively small system utilities that are unlikely to contain much beyond code. The *win-dll, win-exe* and *cyg-bin* file sets all contain Microsoft Windows code. The *cyg-bin* files correspond to the Windows portion of the utilities under Unix/Linux, which are contained in the *ubu-bin* file set. Both these types of files are compiled using gcc.

The main observation is that it is easy to identify the inflection points for the *win-dll, win-exe* and *ubu-bin* file sets, but not for the *cyg-bin* set. Part of the reason could be that *cyg-bin* contains more files than two of the other sets; however, *win-dll* has about the same number of files and does not have the same problem. The reference cover that was picked has substantially more hash values (654) than for any of the other sets, still the coverage is much lower – only 2/3 of the reference set.

In summary, the observed data shows that it is possible to define a class-common feature set based on similarity hashes. The next task is to establish whether or not these features are "class-defining," i.e., they are generally not present among the features of other classes.

4.2   Second-Order Analysis

Clearly, if the class-common features that are discovered are shared by multiple classes, their analytical value is significantly diminished. A second-order analysis was undertaken because there were reasons to believe that some of the chosen sets may share features.

For completeness, all 21 possible (unordered) pairs of feature sets were compared, and their intersections were computed in relative and absolute terms. The results are presented in Table 3, which only shows the non-zero elements. The table is symmetric in terms of the absolute numbers; the figures in parentheses correspond to the intersections as a fraction of the total number of features for the associated set (row). For example, the *xls* and *doc* sets have three features in common, which represents 43% of all features for the *xls* files and 17% of the features for the *doc* files.

The results indicate that the {*doc, xls*} and {*win-dll, win-exe*} file set pairs cannot be considered independent, which is not entirely unexpected. Nevertheless, just one feature from the intersection can provide a useful hint about the content of a target because it helps eliminate a large number of possibilities.

4.3   Estimating Drive Content

The next test involved the application of the *doc* feature set to estimate the number of .doc files in a 7.2 GB Windows partition residing on a personal laptop. First, the reference set was examined and the average number of features matched by each file was computed. Next, the number of matches against the unknown target was used to estimate the number of .doc files in the Windows partition.

As it turned out, the original reference set was not ideal for this purpose – it contained many files that had a very large number of feature matches (the "top" file had 547 matches). Upon closer review, it was discovered that this file contained a huge amount of repetitive information. Clearly, a more systematic approach for selecting reference sets would help avoid problems in such pathological cases.

Nonetheless, the median of nine feature matches per file was taken and applied to the target Windows partition that had yielded 298 feature matches. Thus, it was estimated that there were $298/9 = 33$ Microsoft Word documents on the partition. The actual count was 68, so the estimate was off by a factor of two.

The approach has some potential, but more research is needed to improve and validate this technique. Still, it is notable that features from a training set were applied to a completely unknown and unrelated target; this is evidence that the identified features are generic class features.

Another interesting point pertains to the throughput of the operation. The single-threaded, unoptimized version of the code was able to perform the search in 2 hours and 44 minutes, corresponding to a rate of 45 MB/s. This is significant because the code is parallelizable so 2-4 threads on a dual- or quad-core processor should keep up with the sustained 80-100 MB/s transfer rate of current large-capacity HDDs. In other words, valuable information could be obtained during the initial cloning of a target without incurring any latency overhead. Furthermore, the operation is constrained by hash value generation, so estimates for multiple types of data could easily be performed in a single run with virtually no impact on performance.

5.   Conclusions

Class-aware similarity hashing is an attractive technique for automatically extracting class-defining feature sets (classprints) and for identifying data types based on content. Our empirical study demonstrates that classprints can be generated for several common file types; in other words, the file types can be defined solely in terms of syntactic features of their binary representation. The overall scheme requires a modest amount of storage during the extraction phase and a negligible amount for the classprints. Experiments indicate that hashing rates above 1 Gbit/s can be sustained; this exceeds the transfer rates of current generation high-capacity (500 GB+) hard drives. The hashing scheme also enables investigators to ask very generic questions about targets without violating privacy concerns. In fact, it is possible to discover whether or not a drive contains documents (or document remnants) of a particular type without examining file names or metadata.

References

[1] S. Brin, J. Davis and H. Garcia-Molina, Copy detection mechanisms for digital documents, *Proceedings of the ACM SIGMOD International Conference on the Management of Data*, pp. 398–409, 1995.

[2] B. Bloom, Space/time tradeoffs in hash coding with allowable errors, *Communications of the ACM*, vol. 13(7), pp. 422–426, 1970.

[3] A. Broder, S. Glassman, M. Manasse and G. Zweig, Syntactic clustering of the web, *Proceedings of the Sixth International World Wide Web Conference*, pp. 391–404, 1997.

[4] A. Broder and M. Mitzenmacher, Network applications of Bloom filters: A survey, *Internet Mathematics*, vol. 1(4), pp. 485–509, 2005.

[5] J. Kornblum, Identifying almost identical files using context triggered piecewise hashing, *Proceedings of the Sixth Digital Forensic Research Workshop*, 2006.

[6] National Institute of Standards and Technology, National Software Reference Library, Gaithersburg, Maryland (www.nsrl.nist.gov).

[7] D. Patterson, Latency lags bandwidth, *Communications of the ACM*, vol. 47(10), pp. 71–75, 2004.

[8] M. Rabin, Fingerprinting by Random Polynomials, Technical Report TR-15-81, Center for Research in Computing Technology, Harvard University, Cambridge, Massachusetts, 1981.

[9] V. Roussev, Y. Chen, T. Bourg and G. Richard III, md5bloom: Forensic file system hashing revisited, *Proceedings of the Sixth Digital Forensic Research Workshop*, 2006.

[10] V. Roussev, G. Richard III and L. Marziale, Multi-resolution similarity hashing, *Proceedings of the Seventh Digital Forensic Research Workshop*, 2007.

Chapter 10

APPLYING TOPIC MODELING TO FORENSIC DATA

Alta de Waal, Jacobus Venter and Etienne Barnard

Abstract   Most actionable evidence is identified during the analysis phase of digital forensic investigations. Currently, the analysis phase uses expression-based searches, which assume a good understanding of the evidence; but latent evidence cannot be found using such methods. Knowledge discovery and data mining (KDD) techniques can significantly enhance the analysis process. A promising KDD technique is topic modeling, which infers the underlying semantic context of text and summarizes the text using topics described by words. This paper investigates the application of topic modeling to forensic data and its ability to contribute to the analysis phase. Also, it highlights the challenges that forensic data poses to topic modeling algorithms and reports on the lessons learned from a case study.

Keywords: Digital investigation, analysis phase, evidence mining, topic modeling

1.   Introduction

The four major phases in digital investigation are acquisition, examination, analysis and reporting [14]. The value of the information obtained in digital investigations has been questioned by several researchers [1, 11]. In particular, they argue that the analysis phase, where most of the actionable evidence is gathered, lacks sufficient definition and support in terms of principles, methods and tools [14, 17]. Knowledge discovery and data mining (KDD) has the potential to enhance the analysis phase [14, 17]. The use of KDD principles and tools in digital investigations is referred to as "evidence mining" [17].

Textual artifacts are important in many digital investigations [1, 11]. These "documents" include e-mails, reports, letters, notes, text messages, etc. In a typical case, the evidence set may contain thousands

Please use the following format when citing this chapter:

de Waal, A., Venter, J. and Barnard, E., 2008, in IFIP International Federation for Information Processing, Volume 285; *Advances in Digital Forensics IV*; Indrajit Ray, Sujeet Shenoi; (Boston: Springer), pp. 115–126.

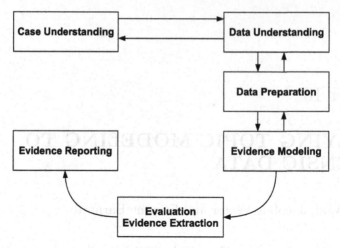

Figure 1. CRISP-EM process.

of documents. Often, a very small proportion of these documents are relevant and an even smaller proportion of the relevant documents may contain actionable evidence. Manually processing thousands of text documents to discover evidence is a difficult and time-consuming task.

Expression-based searches are often used to analyze digital data. Such searches require a good understanding of the evidence being sought. Furthermore, the retrieved information is not ranked (e.g., based on relevance to the case). Thus, latent evidence – evidence that exists but is not directly accessible to the investigator – will not be found. Evidence mining, on the other hand, uses KDD principles and techniques to uncover electronic artifacts that assist in developing crime scenarios [17]. These artifacts include known evidence as well as latent evidence.

CRISP-EM, a specialization of the CRISP-DM process [5], is intended to support evidence mining [17]. The work described in this paper falls within the scope of the data preparation phase of CRISP-EM (Figure 1). Data preparation covers all the activities involved in constructing a data set used for event reconstruction and modeling. Data set construction is a challenging task that involves a trade-off between selecting relevant data and losing vital information used for event reconstruction. A summary of the data would be extremely useful to an investigator; it would facilitate better understanding of the data content and assist in focusing the data preparation task on gathering relevant data.

Topic modeling is a powerful latent variable analysis technique that can help associate relevant documents by modeling the underlying (latent) topics in a collection of text documents. Additionally, it suggests prevalent themes within the text, thereby providing a useful summary of the document collection. As a KDD technique, topic modeling has the potential to discover latent evidence that is often missed by expression-based searches. However, digital evidence is non-homogeneous in terms of format and content, which poses unique challenges to KDD techniques. This paper investigates the primary issues involved in applying topic modeling to forensic data. Also, it examines the utility of topic modeling in a real investigation.

2.   Topic Modeling

Large collections of digital data are widely available and are growing at an incredible pace. Attempting to understand the meaning of the data is a difficult task and, in general, the first option is to perform expression (keyword) searches. However, the results of these searches do not adequately describe the meaning of the data collection, especially when the user has limited insight into the collection. A summary of the collection that encapsulates the main topics within the data would be very useful [12]. An example of a data collection is a text corpus of newspaper articles. For this corpus, a list of topics might include politics, sport, finance, culture and local news.

A text corpus is a collection of documents, each with an underlying semantic context. The semantic context refers to the intended meaning of a document and develops as the document is generated. For example, a newspaper article reports on a news event and, as the article is read, the reader becomes aware of the ideas the reporter intended to communicate. The "hidden" semantic context is represented by the words of a document. Topic modeling, which addresses the retrieval of semantic context from a text corpus, can be formalized as a statistical inference problem. Given a set of data (words), the latent semantic context from which it was generated can be inferred [7]. A topic is defined as a probability distribution over words. In statistical terms, a topic model is a latent variable model where the latent variables describe the topics [2].

Figure 2 presents an example involving two topics from a subset of the TREC AP corpus [8]. The ten words with the highest probabilities for each topic are presented along with their probabilities. These top-10 words describe the two topics. Topic A clearly has to do with financial markets whereas Topic B deals with a naval incident in Saudi Arabia.

The fundamental assumption in topic modeling is that the semantic context of a document is a mixture of topics [7]. A "bag-of-words" approach is commonly adopted for topic modeling, which means that a document is treated as a collection of words while ignoring the structure of the document. The output of the bag-of-words approach is a Word

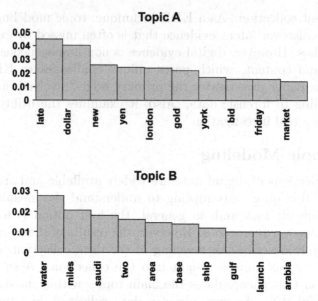

Figure 2. Word probability distributions for two topics (top 10 words).

× Document frequency matrix where cell$_{ij}$ represents the frequency of word$_i$ in document$_j$.

3.   Topic Modeling Applied to Forensic Data

When applied to text data, topic modeling provides a summary of the documents by describing the latent topics in the data as illustrated in Figure 2. This leads to two useful outputs: a verbal summary of the topics and a visual representation of the document space.

3.1   Topic Modeling Process

Figure 3 illustrates the six-level process involved in applying topic modeling to the analysis of real forensic data. Each level represents a different data set. Level 1 represents the original forensic data set. Levels 2 through 4 represent data sets generated during data filtering. Data pre-processing produces a Word × Document matrix (Level 5), which is the input for topic modeling. The Level 6 data set represents the results of topic modeling.

3.2   Data Sets

The data sets produced during the topic modeling process can be described in parallel with the levels in the process graph in Figure 3.

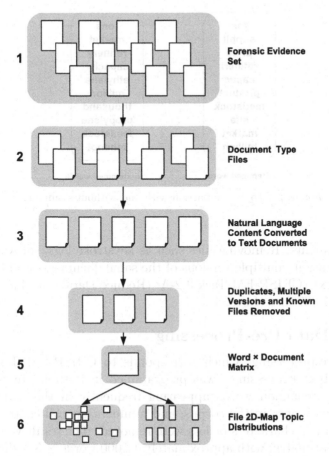

Figure 3. Topic modeling output and interpretation scheme.

- The text corpus (Level 1) was taken from a real investigation. It contained more than 100,000 entities such as documents, operating system files, deleted entities and page files.

- The data set and data type were selected according to CRISP-EM Task 3.1-A (Select Sites/Equipment/Device) and CRISP-EM Task 3.1-B (Select Types of Data to be Included). All the document files (.doc, .txt, .pdf, .html and .rtf) in the evidence set were extracted using FTK. The files were restricted to allocated or logical files. This data set (Level 2) contained 12,483 documents.

- The data set was reduced to documents with natural language content according to CRISP-EM Task 3.2-A (Reduce Data). After converting the documents to text files (CRISP-EM Task 3.5-A (Convert Data Formats)), the data set (Level 3) contained 1,661

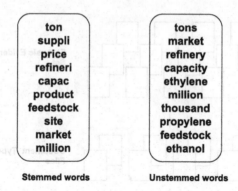

ton	tons
suppli	market
price	refinery
refineri	capacity
capac	ethylene
product	million
feedstock	thousand
site	propylene
market	feedstock
million	ethanol

Stemmed words   **Unstemmed words**

Figure 4. Topic comparison with and without stemming.

documents. Removing files such as keystroke logs, software documentation, multiple versions of the same documents and files with no text (CRISP-EM Task 3.2-A: (Reduce Data)) produced a data set of 837 files (Level 4).

3.3   Data Pre-Processing

Data pre-processing, which corresponds to CRISP-EM Task 3.3-D (Perform Text Processing), was programmed in Python. In this step, stop words (common words appearing frequently in the text), words occurring only once in the corpus, and numbers, special characters and words with two characters or less were removed. The result was a Word × Document matrix with approximately 11,000 words × 837 documents (Level 5). This matrix was the input for the topic modeling step.

3.4   Experimental Setup

Early in experiments it became clear that forensic data poses unique challenges for topic modeling. A major challenge is the use of stemming, i.e., reducing derived words to their stems. For example, the words, "waiting," "waits" and "'waited," are reduced to their stem, "wait." The Porter stemming algorithm [15] in the Natural Language Toolkit of Python was used to perform stemming. Stemming was planned as a standard pre-processing task, but the stemmed words hampered the intelligibility and interpretation of topic distributions.

We ran two experiments. The first applied stemming to words. The second used inflections and derived versions of words without stemming.

Figure 4 presents the results obtained with and without stemming. It is important to understand the influence that stemming has on the interpretation of results. If stemming hampers an investigator from grasping

Topic 4	Topic 7	Topic 17	Topic 5
investigation	product name*	internet	meeting
act	rw	click	company name*
matter	dea	we	action
section	chemicals	use	team
state department*	site	page	va
terms	products	operating system*	report
public	chemical	version	end
following	germany	search	surname*
pty	units	file	name*
government	group	document	discussion

*Information changed due to sensitive nature of original data

Figure 5. Sample topics modeled from forensic data.

the gist of a topic because he/she is unable to see the original unstemmed word, then it is more appropriate to develop topics without stemming. This is despite the fact that not using stemming increases the dimensionality of the problem.

Several topic models are available, each with different assumptions about the distribution of topics [7]. The Latent Dirichlet Allocation (LDA) model assumes that the set of topics has a Dirichlet distribution. It produces a more reasonable mixture of topics compared with earlier approaches that do not use explicit models [2].

Our experiments used LDA as the topic model. For simplicity, the number of topics was fixed at 20. In the future, the LDA model will be extended by defining the number of topics as a random variable; this will permit the model to infer the natural number of topics inherent in the text corpus. The Matlab Topic Modeling Toolbox [6] was used to perform LDA topic modeling.

3.5 Experimental Results

The output of topic modeling is a Word × Topic matrix and a Topic × Document matrix, which correspond to the data set at Level 6 (Figure 3).

- **Word × Topic Matrix:** Each column of this matrix represents a topic as a probability distribution over words. The top-10 words (words with the highest probabilities) provide a good description of a topic. Listing the top-10 words for each topic provides a summary of the document collection. Figure 5 presents sample topics modeled from forensic data. Topic 17 deals with computer use and

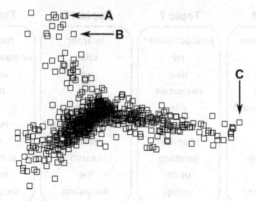

Figure 6.   Visualization of documents in a 2D map.

Internet access/search. Topic 5 relates to company meetings that were attended by a specific individual.

- **Topic × Document Matrix:** Each column of this matrix represents a mixture of topics for a document. The mixture of topics describes the semantic context or gist of the document [7]. Documents with similar topic distributions are closely related in terms of semantic context. This "relatedness" of documents can be visualized in a 2D map, which presents the symmetrized Kullback-Leibler divergence [10] between each pair of topic distributions. (The Kullback-Leibler divergence measures the difference between two probability distributions.) Classical multidimensional scaling is used to visualize all pairwise document distances in the 2D map. Figure 6 shows a 2D visualization of the forensic document collection, where each block represents a document. Documents A and B are closely related based on their mixtures of topics (semantic context). On the other hand, Documents A and C differ significantly in terms of their semantic context. Thus, if Document A is relevant to the case at hand, the investigation should focus on Document B rather than Document C. A similar 2D map can be generated for topics to convey the relatedness between topics. In general, if a topic is identified as being relevant to a case, other topics can be prioritized for investigative purposes based on their proximity to the original topic in the 2D map.

4.   Forensic Benefits

Topic modeling can assist digital forensic analysts and investigators in several ways. In large cases, with multiple data sets from multiple sites, performing topic modeling on natural language data can provide analysts and investigators with valuable information about the semantic context of the data. A summary of the natural language data also enables investigators to prioritize the data to be analyzed. A 2D map helps identify closely related documents that would not typically be identified via keyword searches. The map also assists in expanding the set of relevant documents. Moreover, the topics can be used to augment the existing keyword set. When an existing keyword is a top-10 word for a topic, the other words defining the topic can be included in the keyword set. Note that such an expansion of the keyword set is based on the actual characteristics of the forensic data, not on prior knowledge of the case.

5.   Lessons Learned

Topic modeling is a promising technique because it reduces the quantity of data to be reviewed by human analysts and suggests prevalent themes within a set of documents to be analyzed. Although much research remains to be done on algorithm development and performance evaluation, our work has shown that even off-the-shelf algorithms can function very well. One issue that deserves attention is the design of performance metrics that reflect modeling goals. This is a significant challenge for standard applications of topic models [16], more so for digital forensic applications. The metrics should reflect the requirements of the forensic environment (e.g., intelligibility to human analysts and salience of detected topics).

Our study identified several other practical matters.

- Many documents have multiple versions. Treating these versions as independent documents increases the computational overhead and skews the results (topics). On the other hand, attempting to detect the different versions of each document is a difficult problem. For example, it is not clear how to deal with two documents that have a small overlap or how to merge different versions of documents without losing relevant information.

- Named entities (e.g., person names, locations and organizations) have high evidence potential, but need to be treated with care. We recommend that named entities be recognized [9] and removed from documents temporarily (to exclude them from data pre-processing tasks such as stemming and removal of stop words). Newman, *et al.* [13] have combined topic models and named entity recognizers to jointly analyze named entities and topics. This enables topics to be used to relate entities, which provides a wealth of information on people, organizations and locations mentioned in the text corpus.

- Documents written in different languages may be present in a corpus. Such documents should be treated separately for several reasons, e.g., investigators may not be proficient in all the languages, data pre-processing tasks such as stemming and spell checking are language-dependent, and existing algorithms cannot perform topic modeling across languages. An automated system (see, e.g., [3]) may be used to separate documents written in different languages.

- Stemming reduces the number of parameters in a corpus and consolidates semantically-related words. Also, it increases the number of occurrences of individual words in a corpus, which leads to better modeling. However, as discussed earlier, using stemming on forensic data may hamper the understanding of topic distributions. It may, therefore, be advisable to revert to the original words when presenting topics to an investigator.

- "Known files" (e.g., `readme.txt` and other help files, license agreements, etc.) must be removed from a corpus to reduce the amount of spurious data presented to the analyst. This can be done very efficiently by screening known documents using hash values.

- Spelling mistakes add parameters to the model and give rise to incorrect word statistics (the count for one word is assigned to multiple variants). However, it is difficult to automate spell checking in a reliable manner, especially in an informal context where important neologisms and jargon could be transcribed incorrectly. It may be preferable to have low precision as opposed to correcting spelling mistakes in an incorrect manner. This matter deserves further investigation.

- It is standard practice in topic modeling to remove words that occur only once in a corpus. This usually leads to the removal of approximately 5% of the vocabulary of a corpus. However, when this practice was applied to the forensic data set, approximately 50% of the vocabulary was removed, suggesting that valuable information was discarded in the process. A better way for dealing with unique words is needed for topic modeling to be successfully applied to forensic corpora.

- Text corpora used for topic modeling are typically homogeneous (e.g., news articles, conference proceedings and book chapters). Forensic corpora, on the other hand, are generally mixtures of documents, reports, letters, email bodies and faxes. It is important to modify topic modeling approaches to better handle non-homogeneous data, e.g., by avoiding the bias towards longer documents inherent in the statistical models used by current approaches.

6.   Conclusions

This paper has reported on a case study of topic modeling applied to forensic data very early in an actual investigation. No evidence was discovered in this investigation, but the analysis indicates that, with certain refinements, topic modeling can be very useful for discovering the semantic context of text documents in a forensic corpus and for summarizing document content. Future research will investigate the role of metadata in forensic corpora and the application of topic modeling on corpora from different types of cases. Also, topic modeling algorithms will be augmented to address the temporal characteristics of data and the evolution of topics and changes in their importance [12, 18].

References

[1] N. Beebe and J. Clark, Digital forensic text string searching: Improving information retrieval effectiveness by thematically clustering search results, *Digital Investigation*, vol. 4S, pp. S49–S54, 2007.

[2] D. Blei, A. Ng and M. Jordan, Latent Dirichlet allocation, *Journal of Machine Learning Research*, vol. 3, pp. 993–1022, 2003.

[3] G. Botha, V. Zimu and E. Barnard, Text-based language identification for the South African languages, *Proceedings of the Seventeenth Annual Symposium of the Pattern Recognition Association of South Africa*, 2006.

[4] E. Casey, *Digital Evidence and Computer Crime*, Academic Press, London, United Kingdom, 2000.

[5] P. Chapman, J. Clinton, R. Kerber, T. Khabaza, T. Reinartzrysler, C. Shearer and R. Wirth, CRISP-DM 1.0: Step-by-Step Data Mining Guide, The CRISP-DM Consortium, SPSS, Chicago, Illinois (www.crisp-dm.org/CRISPWP-0800.pdf), 1999.

[6] T. Griffiths and M. Steyvers, Finding scientific topics, *Proceedings of the National Academy of Sciences*, vol. 101(1), pp 5228–5235, 2004.

[7] T. Griffiths, M. Steyvers and J. Tenenbaum, Topics in semantic representation, *Psychological Review*, vol. 114(2), pp. 211–244, 2007.

[8] D. Harman, Overview of the first text retrieval conference, *Proceedings of the First Text Retrieval Conference*, pp. 1–20, 1992.

[9] A. Louis, A. de Waal and J. Venter, Named entity recognition in a South African context, *Proceedings of the Annual Conference of the South African Institute of Computer Scientists and Information Technologists*, pp. 170–179, 2006.

[10] D. Mackay, *Information Theory, Inference and Learning Algorithms*, Cambridge University Press, Cambridge, United Kingdom, 2003.

[11] C. McCue, *Data Mining and Predictive Analysis: Intelligence Gathering and Crime Analysis*, Butterworth-Heinemann, Burlington, Massachusetts, 2007.

[12] Q. Mei and C. Zhai, Discovering evolutionary theme patterns from text: An exploration of temporal text mining, *Proceedings of the Eleventh ACM SIGKDD International Conference on Knowledge Discovery and Data Mining*, pp. 198–207, 2005.

[13] D. Newman, C. Chemudugunta, P. Smyth and M. Steyvers, Analyzing entities and topics in news articles using statistical topic models, *Proceedings of the Intelligence and Security Informatics Conference*, pp. 93–104, 2006.

[14] M. Pollitt and A. Whitledge, Exploring big haystacks: Data mining and knowledge management, in *Advances in Digital Forensics II*, M. Olivier and S. Shenoi (Eds.), Springer, New York, pp. 67–76, 2006.

[15] M. Porter, An algorithm for suffix stripping, *Program*, vol. 13(3), pp. 130–137, 1980.

[16] L. Rigouste, O. Cappe and F. Yvon, Inference and evaluation of the multinomial mixture model for text clustering, *Information Processing and Management*, vol. 43(5), pp 1260–1280, 2007.

[17] J. Venter, A. de Waal and N. Willers, Specializing CRISP-DM for evidence mining, in *Advances in Digital Forensics III*, P. Craiger and S. Shenoi (Eds.), Springer, New York, pp. 303–315, 2007.

[18] X. Wang and A. McCallum, Topics over time: A non-Markov continuous-time model of topical trends, *Proceedings of the Twelfth ACM SIGKDD International Conference on Knowledge Discovery and Data Mining*, pp. 424–433, 2006.

V

FORENSIC TECHNIQUES

Chapter 11

FORENSIC ANALYSIS OF VOLATILE INSTANT MESSAGING

Matthew Kiley, Shira Dankner and Marcus Rogers

Abstract   Older instant messaging programs typically require some form of installation on the client machine, enabling forensic investigators to find a wealth of evidentiary artifacts. However, this paradigm is shifting as web-based instant messaging becomes more popular. Many traditional messaging clients (e.g., AOL Messenger, Yahoo! and MSN), can now be accessed using only a web browser. This presents new challenges for forensic examiners due to the volatile nature of the data and artifacts created by web-based instant messaging programs. These web-based programs do not write to registry keys or leave configuration files on the client machine. Investigators are, therefore, required to look for remnants of whole or partial conversations that may be dumped to page files and unallocated space on the hard disk. This paper examines the artifacts that can be recovered from web-based instant messaging programs and the challenges faced by forensic examiners during evidence recovery. An investigative framework for dealing with volatile instant messaging is also presented.

Keywords: Instant messaging, forensic analysis, volatile information, artifacts

1.   Introduction

The popularity of instant messaging has exploded during the last decade. From a humble beginning as a UNIX command line application, instant messaging has become one of the most popular forms of communication. During the period of growth, traditional client-based messaging programs such as AOL Instant Messenger (AIM) have dominated. In fact, active AIM subscribers currently number more than 50 million [15]. However, newer web-based programs are becoming increasingly popular. E-Buddy, a web-based messaging program, has 35 million desktop subscribers and more than five million mobile users [1].

Please use the following format when citing this chapter:

Kiley, M., Dankner, S. and Rogers, M., 2008, in IFIP International Federation for Information Processing, Volume 285;
Advances in Digital Forensics IV; Indrajit Ray, Sujeet Shenoi; (Boston: Springer), pp. 129–138.

Due to its popularity and purported privacy, instant messaging is being exploited by criminals, especially online predators.

Web-based and mobile messaging services are valuable sources of evidence. However, dealing with volatile instant messaging requires entirely different investigative procedures. Forensic analysis no longer involves merely locating archived or deleted messages, and stored "buddy" lists.

This paper presents a brief overview of volatile instant messaging and discusses approaches for conducting an investigation involving a web-based messaging program. Artifacts and other forensically-significant information that can be obtained from four popular web-based instant messaging programs are examined in detail. Finally, an investigative framework for dealing with volatile instant messaging is outlined.

2.   Volatile Messaging

Techweb [12] defines instant messaging as the process of "exchanging text messages in real-time between two or more people logged into a particular instant messaging service." Volatile instant messaging, on the other hand, is a relatively new concept, which has not been formally defined. We adopt an operational definition for the concept: "real-time messaging between two or more people using a web interface." This means that a user with access to a public terminal or web browser can engage in instant messaging without having to access a traditional client like AOL Instant Messenger or MSN. Implied in the definition is the concept of volatility. After the web browser is closed or the machine is shut down, no records of user activity or chat log archives are (conceivably) retained. This is the primary difference between volatile instant messaging and its traditional counterpart.

Traditional instant messaging relies on the existence of an installed client program (e.g., Yahoo Messenger or MSN). Most programs require the user to enter an online handle and password from a previously created account. However, this information can be falsified as little, if any, verification is performed [7]. The one benefit of user authentication (i.e., "logging in") is that the messaging server can archive the IP address of the user [15]. This makes it possible to pinpoint a user to a specific computer or geographical location.

The messaging server typically marks the user as online upon successful authentication and sign on. The program then displays a list of currently logged on "buddies" from the user's contact list. Although the first message is sent through the main servers, subsequent messages originate directly from the client machine, reducing traffic to the messaging servers [5]. This poses a potential problem in forensic investigations because conversations are not logged by messaging servers.

The upside of client-based messaging is that information can be recovered from a suspect's machine. Recent studies [2, 4, 10] report that the forensic analysis of instant messaging programs provides a variety of evidence, including chat logs, file transfers and registry artifacts.

Web-based only or volatile messaging programs require a different investigative approach from client-based messaging programs. This is because there are no installed programs and very little data may remain after a browser is closed. The next section examines four popular web-based only messaging programs and discusses what, if any, evidence may be retained and recovered.

3.   Methodology

This paper reports on the results of tests conducted on four web-based instant messaging programs: (i) AIM Express, (ii) Google Talk, (iii) Meebo, and (iv) E-Buddy. The four web-based programs were chosen because of the popularity of their service and instant messaging client. The tests used a Dell Latitude 600 laptop with 1 GB RAM, Windows XP Professional Service Pack 2 and a 60 GB hard disk formatted with NTFS. Internet Explorer version 6.0.2900.2180 was used as the web browser for chat communications.

AIM Express and Google Talk are web-based clients that run their own protocol [13]. Meebo and E-Buddy, on the other hand, are browser-based clients that rely on other instant messaging services (e.g., Yahoo, MSN or AOL) [3].

The machine settings were verified prior to conducting the tests. The default virtual memory size was set at 768 MB to 1,536 MB, and the registry was checked to ensure that the page file is not erased during shut down [9]. Test data was created by conducting three different conversations for each messaging program. The conversations were limited to two participants and lasted three to four minutes. The frequency of the conversations closely imitated real-life scenarios; suspects generally engage in multiple, short conversations with their victims. The conversations were initiated by another machine, after which the laptop user replied to the message with unique phrases that would help identify the conversation.

The first step in the forensic examination was to acquire a bit-stream image of the laptop. Access Data's Forensic Toolkit (FTK) Imager version 2.5.1 and a Tableau T5 IDE write blocker with a 2.5 inch adapter were used for image acquisition. After acquiring and verifying the im-

Table 1.   Unique phrases used as keywords.

AOL	Google Talk	Meebo	E-Buddy
bannnnanas	fuzzie logyck	meebomeebo	functionza
weirdtheme	spaces spled wrong	thisfoodisok	documnt this consrvation
this is a space	toomany	generastso	999-222-2222

age of the laptop hard drive under FTK Imager, the file was indexed using FTK version 1.7.1 build 07.06.22. Prior to reviewing the image, a keyword list containing distinct phrases used during the conversations was created (Table 1). Keyword searches based on the list were run on the indexed drive, resulting in a relatively fast sweep of the hard drive image. Unfortunately, this yielded fewer results than expected, making it necessary to perform a live (un-indexed) search with FTK.

Runtime DiskExplorer for NTFS version 3.03 was then used to examine the hard drive image at a lower level. Sector-by-sector searches were conducted to find the distinct phrases used during the conversations. This method was necessary due to the nature of volatile messaging. After the browser is closed and the page file contents are erased, data often resides in unallocated space until the operating system re-allocates the cluster. Performing a cursory search using an indexed image typically yields limited results in the case of volatile messaging.

Table 2.   Artifacts from volatile messaging clients.

Program	Time Estimate	Conversation Details	Screen Names	Buddy List Details
AIM Express	X	X	X	X
Google Talk	X	X	X	X
Meebo	X			
E-Buddy	X		X	

4.   Results

Table 2 lists the artifacts discovered in the four volatile messaging clients. Evidence of forensic value was retrieved from every volatile messaging client; however, complete chat logs were not recoverable.

Artifacts were found in various Internet file caches used by Internet Explorer. Each cache holds a different piece of data. The History.IE5 directory contains an Index.dat file, which maintains a log of the user's Internet history without caching the content. This file is crucial to reconstructing a suspect's browsing history because the file contains the URL of the site visited, the last time the page was visited, and the number of times the page was viewed [6]. Also, several sub-directories within History.IE5 show the date ranges for the logged entries.

The Temporary Internet Files\Content.IE5 sub-directory stores cached web pages and images that the user has viewed, and makes them readily accessible should the site be visited again. This was implemented to reduce the time needed to load web pages; however, it also provides the forensic examiner with valuable information about user activity. In addition, the Cookies sub-directory contains files that web pages place on the user's computer. These "cookies" are used by web sites to track user behavior and maintain personalized settings.

Many of the remaining artifacts were found in the drive free space (i.e., unallocated space on the drive). They consisted of screen names and, in the case of AIM Express, fragments of the buddy list. Snippets of AIM Express and Google Talk conversations were also found in the same location. Windows XP is known to use this space to store data that does not have to remain in memory or be saved on the hard drive. Note that this data is eventually overwritten.

Screen names were found in the pagefile.sys set of files. The operating system uses a page file to store information that should be in physical memory, but is not because it is used infrequently. The size of the page file is variable, but within a specified range; by default, the Windows XP range is 756 MB to 1,512 MB [14]. The forensic implications of modifying this range were not investigated in this study.

4.1   AIM Express

AIM Express left behind several artifacts, including snippets of conversations, details of the buddy list and approximate times when the conversations took place. The buddy list is extremely helpful in forensic investigations; this list can be used as a reference point to establish a social network. The approximate times of conversations can be estimated based on Index.dat entries made by AIM Express; these times can be used to construct timelines and sequences of key events.

Snippets of the other user's conversations and the buddy list were also found in the file slack and pagefile.sys file (Figure 1). This seems to agree with the observations of Dickson [2], except that this data was found on the hard disk rather than in RAM. In traditional instant messaging programs, such as AIM, chat logs are stored in files under locations specified by the user or in default locations such as the Program Files directory. Web-based conversations, unless specifically logged by

```
300 | 20 20 20 20 20 3c 2f 73 63 72 69 70 74 3e 0d 0a | </script>
310 | 3c 73 63 72 69 70 74 3e 74 72 79 20 7b 20 70 61 | <script>try { pa
320 | 72 65 6e 74 2e 61 6f 6c 2e 63 65 2e 5f 43 6f 6d | rent.aol.ae._Com
330 | 65 74 2e 63 6f 6d 65 74 28 7b 69 6d 45 76 65 6e | et.comet({imEven
340 | 74 3a 7b 73 52 65 6d 6f 74 65 55 73 65 72 3a 27 | t:{sRemoteUser:'
350 | 4d 65 6c 65 72 79 54 6f 64 27 2c 73 45 76 65 6e | MeleryTod',sEven
360 | 74 3a 27 6d 73 67 52 65 63 65 69 76 65 64 27 2c | t:'msgReceived',
370 | 73 4d 73 67 3a 27 3c 68 74 6d 6c 3e 3c 66 6f 6e | sMsg:'<html><fon
380 | 74 20 46 41 43 45 3d 5c 78 32 32 61 72 69 61 6c | t FACE=\x22arial
390 | 5c 78 32 32 3e 3c 66 6f 6e 74 20 43 4f 4c 4f 52 | \x22><font COLOR
3a0 | 3d 5c 78 32 32 23 30 30 30 30 30 30 5c 78 32 32 | =\x22#000000\x22
3b0 | 3e 6d 69 6e 69 20 63 6f 6f 6c 65 72 3c 5c 78 32 | >mini cooper<\x2
3c0 | 66 66 6f 6e 74 3e 3c 5c 78 32 66 68 74 6d 6c 3e | ffont><\x2fhtml>
3d0 | 27 2c 73 4e 65 74 3a 27 61 69 6d 27 7d 7d 29 7d | ',sNet:'aim'}})}
3e0 | 20 63 61 74 63 68 28 65 29 20 7b 7d 20 20 20 20 | catch(e) {}
```

Figure 1. Conversation snippet from slack space.

```
27e0 | 7b 22 61 69 6d 49 64 22 3a 22 77 6f 6c 66 6d 67 | {"aimId":"wolfmg
27f0 | 39 37 30 22 2c 20 22 64 69 73 70 6c 61 79 49 64 | 970", "displayId
2800 | 22 3a 22 77 6f 6c 66 6d 67 39 37 30 22 20 22    | ":"wolfmg970" "
2810 | 73 74 61 74 65 22 3a 22 6f 6e 6c 69 6e 65 22 2c | state":"online",
2820 | 20 22 70 72 6f 66 69 6c 65 4d 73 67 22 3a 22 3c | "profileMsg":"<
2830 | 64 69 76 20 73 74 79 6c 65 3d 5c 22 62 61 63 6b | div style=\"back
2840 | 67 72 6f 75 6e 64 2d 63 6f 6c 6f 72 3a 20 23 66 | ground-color: #f
2850 | 66 66 66 66 66 5c 22 3e 3c 73 70 61 6e 20 73 74 | fffff\"><span st
2860 | 79 6c 65 3d 5c 22 66 6f 6e 74 2d 73 69 7a 65 3a | yle=\"font-size:
2870 | 20 30 2e 39 30 65 6d 3b 20 66 6f 6e 74 2d 66 61 | 0.90em; font-fa
2880 | 6d 69 6c 79 3a 20 27 41 72 69 61 6c 27 5c 22 3e | mily: 'Arial'\">
2890 | 26 71 75 6f 74 3b 49 6e 20 79 6f 75 72 20 66 61 | &quot;In your fa
28a0 | 63 65 2c 20 53 70 61 63 65 20 43 6f 79 6f 74 65 | ce, Space Coyote
28b0 | 21 26 71 75 6f 74 3b 20 2d 48 6f 6d 65 72 3c 62 | !&quot; -Homer<b
28c0 | 72 2f 3e 3c 62 72 2f 3e 3c 73 70 61 6e 3e 3c 3c | r/><br/></span><
28d0 | 73 70 61 6e 20 73 74 79 6c 65 3d 5c 22 62 61 63 | span style=\"bac
28e0 | 6b 67 72 6f 75 6e 64 2d 63 6f 6c 6f 72 3a 20 23 | kground-color: #
28f0 | 66 66 66 66 66 66 3b 20 66 6f 6e 74 2d 73 69 7a | ffffff; font-siz
2900 | 65 3a 20 30 2e 39 30 65 6d 3b 20 66 6f 6e 74 2d | e: 0.90em; font-
2910 | 66 61 6d 69 6c 79 3a 20 27 41 72 69 61 6c 27 5c | family: 'Arial'\
2920 | 22 3e 3c 61 20 68 72 65 66 3d 5c 22 68 74 74 70 | "><a href=\"http
2930 | 3a 2f 2f 77 77 77 2e 66 6c 69 63 6b 72 2e 63 6f | ://www.flickr.co
2940 | 6d 2f 70 68 6f 74 6f 73 2f ██ ██ ██ ██ 33 38    | m/photos/████38
2950 | 30 2f 5c 22 3e 68 74 74 70 3a 2f 2f 77 77 77 2e | 0/\">http://www.
2960 | 66 6c 69 63 6b 72 2e 63 6f 6d 2f 70 68 6f 74 6f | flickr.com/photo
2970 | 73 2f ██ ██ ██ ██ 2f 3c 2f 61 3e 3c             | s/██████/</a><
2980 | 2f 73 70 61 6e 3e 3c 2f 64 69 76 3e 22 2c 20 22 | /span></div>", "
2990 | 70 72 65 73 65 6e 63 65 49 63 6f 6e 22 3a 22 68 | presenceIcon":"h
29a0 | 74 74 70 3a 2f 2f 6f 2e 61 6f 6c 63 64 6e 2e 63 | ttp://o.aolcdn.c
29b0 | 6f 6d 2f 61 69 6d 2f 69 6d 67 2f 6f 6e 6c 69 6e | om/aim/img/onlin
29c0 | 65 2e 67 69 66 22 7d 2c 20 7b 22 61 69 6d 49 64 | e.gif"}, {"aimId
```

Figure 2. Screen name and profile message in `fetchBuddyInfo.htm` file.

the user, are stored in temporary Internet directories that may or may not remain after the browser is closed. If these directories have been deleted or overwritten, more powerful forensic tools are required to view conversations in drive free space or file slack.

The `fetchbuddyInfo.htm` file, which is found under the `Temporary Internet Files\Content.IE5` directory within the profile's local settings, contained expanded buddy list information for the screen names obtained from the laptop (Figure 2). This information is valuable in cases where additional profile evidence is necessary. A profile often lists personal interests and hobbies, possibly even a home address. In addition, the expanded profile can provide investigative clues about the suspect's behavior and potential contacts, and help determine geographic areas of activity.

The `Index.dat` entries in `Temporary Internet Files\Content.IE5` show the screen name of the user as well as the time of the conversation. This allows an investigator to make an estimate of when the conversation took place. Finally, the user's screen name can be found in the following files: `$Logfiles`, `$MFT records`, `username@aimexpress.aol[1].txt` and `aimtoday.aim[1].txt`. Although these files may not provide crucial evidence, they can be used to corroborate other events.

4.2 Google Talk

Google Talk left several artifacts in the `Temporary Internet Files\Content.IE5` directory, e.g., the `accountinfo.htm` file, which displays the screen name used to sign on to Google. More importantly, the data gathered from slack space showed portions of all three conversations from both parties. These conversations were found by running keyword searches on the unique phrases used to distinguish the conversations. It is important to note that un-indexed searches were used to obtain these results; a normal indexed search yielded no results. Entries made in the `Index.dat` file within the `History.IE5` directory were also discovered. These entries can be used to correlate the time the user logged into gmail and the interface through which Google Talk was accessed.

4.3 Meebo and E-Buddy

Details about Meebo and E-Buddy conversations could not be found. The two programs function as true volatile messaging clients – virtually all the information about a conversation disappears after it ends. This is partly due to the heavy use of JavaScript on both websites. By maintaining a constant server-side connection via JavaScript, the site is able to maintain the appearance of a desktop application [8]. However, this has the effect of limiting the amount of information that can be gathered from the hard drive. Ultimately, the most useful artifacts found were the `Index.dat` entries, which showed when the E-Buddy and Meebo websites were accessed. In addition, the `ebuddy.htm` file in the `Temporary Internet Files` folder retains the screen name that the user used to sign on to the service.

5.   Investigative Framework

Having discussed the artifacts that can be recovered from web-based instant messaging programs, we present a preliminary framework for investigators. This framework has three phases: recognition, formulation and search.

- **Recognition:** The first step in searching for evidence of volatile messaging is to identify if and when a web-based instant messaging conversation took place using the suspect machine. This is accomplished by searching for the existence of temporary Internet files or `Index.dat` entries that indicate the suspect signed on to a messaging service. For example, AIM conversations are indicated in temporary Internet files (e.g., `fetchBuddyInfo.htm`) while Google Talk conversations are identified by the presence of the `AccountInfo.htm` file. In situations where the Internet history or cache have been erased or are unavailable, manual indexed and non-indexed searches using the files mentioned above or search terms such as `.Ebuddy` may also yield results. Note that E-Buddy uses named servers (e.g.,"Kentucky") for logging in clients.

- **Formulation:** The formulation phase uses data gathered from the recognition phase to populate the list of possible screen names and other keywords used as input in the search phase. Snippets of previous instant messaging conversations may also be used to populate the list. In addition, any unique or misspelled words known by the investigator should be included in the list of search terms as they are likely to be found in chat conversations [11].

- **Search:** The search phase uses indexed and un-indexed searches to locate volatile messaging artifacts. Fast indexed searches that use the list created during the formulation phase should be performed first. If the results are inconclusive or incomplete, "live" or un-indexed searching is necessary. This is especially true for items found in slack or unallocated space because text residing in these locations may not be properly indexed by the forensic tool. The results from this phase can be used in subsequent searches.

The most challenging aspect of an examination is finding proof that a volatile messaging conversation ever took place. However, once evidence of this activity is found, search terms may be compiled and executed. Complete conversations may never be uncovered. Nevertheless, extensive live and un-indexed searches often yield successful results.

6. Conclusions

Web-based instant messaging presents challenges for forensic examiners due to the volatile nature of the data and artifacts created by the messaging programs. Forensic evidence is recoverable after these programs have been used, but investigators must know certain elements of the conversations in order to perform string searches. Even so, time-consuming sector-by-sector searches are required to uncover all the potential evidence.

Our research has revealed that several useful items of information can be recovered; these include the list of user contacts, snippets of conversations and the approximate time of the last conversation. In most cases, multiple instances of these items are found; they can be used to help corroborate other pieces of evidence found on the target system. The investigative framework proposed for the four web-based instant messaging programs considered in our study formalizes the task of evidence recovery. However, additional research is required to test the validity of this framework on other browsers and instant messaging clients.

Acknowledgements

This work was partially supported by the National Science Foundation under ITR Grant No. 0428554.

References

[1] Australian IT, E-Buddy gets growth message (www.ebuddy.com/pr ess/auit_article.pdf), November 7, 2006.

[2] M. Dickson, An examination into AOL Instant Messenger 5.5 contact identification, *Digital Investigation*, vol. 3(4), pp. 227–237, 2006.

[3] A. Ghag, Top 10 web-based instant messengers (www.tech2.com/india/topstuff/websites-internet/top-10-webbased-instant-messeng ers/2892/0), 2006.

[4] W. Gillam, Instant messaging artifacts for cyber investigations, Unpublished manuscript, Department of Computer and Information Technology, Purdue University, West Lafayette, Indiana, 2006.

[5] A. Grossman, No don't IM me: Instant messaging, authentication, and the best evidence rule, *George Mason Law Review*, vol. 13(6), pp. 1309–1340, 2006.

[6] K. Jones and R. Belani, Web browser forensics, Part 1 (securityfoc us.com/infocus/1827), 2005.

[7] D. Juhnke and D. Stenhouse, Instant messaging: What you can't see can hurt you (in court) (www.forensics.com/pdf/Instant _Messaging.pdf), 2005.

[8] Meebo, Meebo Forum (forum.meebo.com/viewtopic.php?t=12476).

[9] Microsoft Corporation, How to clear the Windows paging file at shutdown, Microsoft Help and Support, Redmond, Washington (sup port.microsoft.com/kb/314834), 2007.

[10] New York State Computer Forensic Workgroup, Messaging: A forensic view, presented at the *Ninth Annual New York State Cyber Security Conference* (www.cscic.state.ny.us/security/confer ences/security/2006/Presentations/hurbanek.swf), 2006.

[11] J. Reust, Case study: AOL Instant Messenger trace evidence, *Digital Investigation*, vol. 3(4), pp. 238–243, 2006.

[12] Techweb, Instant messaging (www.techweb.com/encyclopedia/defi neterm.jhtml?term=instantmessaging), 2007.

[13] H. Tschabitscher, Top 10 free email services (email.about.com/cs /freeemailreviews/tp/free_email.htm).

[14] D. Waddington and D. Hutchison, Resource partitioning in general purpose operating systems: Experimental results in Windows NT, *ACM SIGOPS Operating Systems Review*, vol. 33(4), pp. 52–74, 1999.

[15] Yahoo! IP address (info.yahoo.com/privacy/us/yahoo/ipaddress/de tails.html), 2008.

Chapter 12

TIMELY ROOTKIT DETECTION DURING LIVE RESPONSE

Daniel Molina, Matthew Zimmerman, Gregory Roberts, Marnita Eaddie and Gilbert Peterson

Abstract   This paper describes a non-intrusive rootkit detection tool designed to support forensic investigations that involve the live analysis of computer systems. The tool, which does not require pre-installation, correlates outputs from multiple system data gathering utilities. Test results indicate that the tool successfully detects several well-known rootkits, including Hacker Defender, AFX, Vanquish, FU and FUto.

Keywords: Rootkit detection, live response

1.   Introduction

Rootkits enable attackers to have undetected access to computer systems; they hide an attacker's presence by manipulating system data and/or operating system code. These malicious programs hamper digital forensic investigations – evidence that is collected carefully may still be compromised by active rootkits. In particular, rootkits may prevent forensic tools from gathering accurate information. Addressing this issue requires investigators to run more intrusive tools that can alter the system state.

This paper describes a rootkit detection tool designed for live analysis that minimizes system modification. The tool, which does not require pre-installation, correlates outputs from multiple system data gathering utilities. The detection tool has proved to be effective against five rootkits: Hacker Defender [8], AFX [14], Vanquish [17], FU [15] and FUto [16]. In the tests, these rootkits were hiding a backdoor (Back Orifice 2000 [19]) and a folder containing four files.

Please use the following format when citing this chapter:

Molina, D., Zimmerman, M., Roberts, G., Eaddie, M. and Peterson, G., 2008, in IFIP International Federation for Information Processing, Volume 285; *Advances in Digital Forensics IV*; Indrajit Ray, Sujeet Shenoi; (Boston: Springer), pp. 139–148.

2.　　Rootkits

Rootkits are programs that enable attackers to have undetected access to computer systems. The term "root" comes from the UNIX world where "root" is the highest level of privilege afforded to a user. Originally written for UNIX, rootkits now target a variety of operating systems.

A rootkit typically incorporates Trojaned system processes and scripts that automate the actions involved in compromising systems [12]. Rootkits often attempt to be untraceable by hiding files, network connections, memory addresses and registry entries. Some rootkits are embedded in other programs or media as in the case of the rootkit found in Sony CDs in 2005 [4].

Windows rootkits – like those that target UNIX systems – seek the highest possible privilege level. Windows runs on the Intel x86 architecture, which employs a memory protection scheme using four rings (Rings 0–3). Ring 0, which has the highest level of privilege, represents the memory space where the operating system kernel and drivers reside. Ring 3 has the lowest privilege level and represents the memory space where user applications reside.

Stealthy rootkits tend to operate at a lower ring than Ring 3 where rootkit detection and prevention software typically operates. Hoglund [7] and Rutkowska [18] note that placing a rootkit detector in a lower ring increases the detection rate. On the other hand, a rootkit that executes in a lower ring than a detector can control or fabricate the information gathered by the detector, which enables the rootkit to remain hidden.

The rootkit detection technique described in this paper correlates outputs from multiple system data gathering utilities. These utilities are executed from user space (Ring 3) without prior installation.

2.1　　Rootkit Categories

Rootkits are categorized as kernel, library, user-level, hardware-level and virtual machine based rootkits. Some rootkits fall in multiple categories, e.g., those with kernel and user-level components.

- Kernel Rootkits: These rootkits add additional kernel code and/or replace a portion of kernel code to enable them to obtain stealthy control of computer systems.

- Library Rootkits: These rootkits achieve stealth by modifying system libraries used by user and/or kernel applications [2].

- User-Level Rootkits: These rootkits, also called application-level rootkits, are programs that modify system files or binaries on disk [11].

- Hardware-Level Rootkits: These rootkits attempt to subvert computer systems at the lowest level. They are extremely difficult to implement, but Heasman [6] has demonstrated that such rootkits are possible. We do not attempt to detect hardware-level rootkits because of their complexity and lack of availability.

- Virtual Machine Based Rootkits (VMBRs): These rootkits attempt to take control of the virtual machine monitor (VMM), which lies between the hardware and operating system. Thus, VMBRs are able to control requests to the hardware that originate from the upper levels. A VMBR typically modifies the boot sequence and loads itself instead of the chosen VMM or operating system. After it is loaded, the rootkit loads the host operating system as a virtual machine. An example of a VMBR is SubVirt [9].

A VMBR is difficult to detect during live analysis because rootkit detection software is executed within the virtual machine. Software running on the target machine cannot access the state of a VMBR [9]. From the user's perspective, a VMBR is in a hidden VMM where malware can operate without interference. A VMBR thus has the ability to access all keystrokes, network packets, memory allocations, system events, etc. We do not attempt to detect VMBRs because of their complexity and lack of availability.

2.2   Rootkit Hiding Techniques

Kernel and user-level rootkits apply various hiding techniques, either individually or in combination. The principal hiding techniques are:

- Patching: This technique involves static or dynamic modification of binaries. Static patching is also used by software crackers to bypass software protection and registration methods.

- Hooking: This technique redirects or alters the normal flow of execution of a program by modifying one or more function calls in memory. Hacker Defender is an example of a rootkit that uses hooking.

- Direct Kernel Object Manipulation: This technique exploits the way the Windows OS schedules processes. Malicious processes are hidden by removing their entries from the doubly linked list used by the Windows Object Manager [7]. FU and FUto are examples of rootkits that use this hiding technique.

2.3   Rootkit Detection Techniques

Rootkit detectors fall in one or more of the following categories [21]:

- **Signature Based Detectors:** These detectors scan system files for rootkit fingerprints.

- **Heuristic/Behavioral Based Detectors:** These detectors check for deviations from normal system behavior.

- **Cross-View Based Detectors:** These detectors compare system parameters obtained in two or more different ways to detect inconsistencies or anomalies.

- **Integrity Based Detectors:** These detectors compare the current snapshot of a system to a known trusted snapshot.

- **Hardware-Based Detectors:** These detectors employ direct memory access to retrieve data, which is scrutinized for rootkit fingerprints.

At the time of writing this paper, software-based rootkit detectors have components that execute from user space, kernel space or both. A detector is much more effective when it runs at a level below the rootkit. For example, if a rootkit only executes in user space then the detector has a better chance of detecting the rootkit from kernel space.

Kernel-level rootkits can be identified by a detector that coexists with the rootkit in kernel space or by a hardware-based detector. However, such detectors cannot be used during a live response because they affect evidence integrity.

Some anti-virus programs include rootkit detection features. For example, F-Secure Internet Security 2005 offers "manipulation control," a behavior-blocking mechanism that prevents malicious processes from manipulating other processes [5].

Some of the well-known rootkit detectors are:

- **BlackLight:** This Windows rootkit detector identifies rootkit files, folders and processes, but not hidden registry keys [20]. It offers a removal option for detected rootkits; however, this feature must be used with care to avoid problems with the computer system.

- **RootkitRevealer:** This Windows tool detects rootkits by performing a high level scan from user space and a raw disk scan; the results of the two scans are compared for anomalies. The tool reports differences in the Windows registry and file system. However, it does not have any rootkit removal capabilities [20].

- IceSword: This Windows tool suite includes a process viewer, startup analyzer, port enumerator and other utilities. The tool only provides data, leaving rootkit identification to the user [20].

- Chkrootkit: This UNIX shell script checks specific system binaries to determine if a rootkit has been installed [10].

- Rootkit Hunter: This UNIX rootkit detector performs MD5 comparisons of critical system files and searches for known rootkit files, hidden files and suspicious information in loadable kernel modules. Also, it checks file permissions and scans plain text and binary files for strings that indicate the presence of rootkits [1].

3.   Live Response Analysis

Digital forensic investigators typically employ live analysis tools (e.g., FRED or Helix) to collect evidence from running systems. However, even if the evidence is collected carefully and documented diligently, it may be compromised by active rootkits.

Forensic investigators must be cognizant of how user-level and kernel-level rootkits affect the integrity of computer systems. User-level rootkits alter the security subsystem and display inaccurate information; they intercept system calls and filter output APIs to hide processes, files, system drivers, network ports, registry keys and paths, and system services [3]. Kernel-level rootkits usurp system calls, hide processes, registry keys and files, and redirect calls to Trojan functions [13].

Due to the increasing threat of rootkits and their impact on computer systems, digital forensic investigators must strive to detect rootkits in a timely manner. Rootkit detection tools can aid investigators in determining if rootkits are present and which data may have been compromised. Some of these tools have to be installed before a system is exposed to a hostile environment. Installing a rootkit detector during live analysis can dramatically alter the state of the system.

Once a computer system is turned off, a rootkit cannot actively hide itself or other information that could indicate its presence. A forensic investigator may, therefore, conduct an off-line analysis of the computer image and search for signatures that reveal the presence of rootkits. However, even if a rootkit is detected, the investigator may have difficulty determining whether or not the rootkit was active.

4.   Rootkit Detection System

The Windows rootkit detection system described in this section uses open source utilities that perform a system scan from user space. These utilities, which do not have to be pre-installed, are executed via a batch script that runs each utility and sends its output to a separate file. After the batch script completes, data from the output files is correlated by an automated analysis program to identify discrepancies. A Java-based GUI with a file parser is used to generate a report of the discrepancies. Because the utilities are executed from trusted media, it is important that the GUI and parser utility also run from trusted media. This is accomplished by using a Java Runtime Environment (JRE) located on the trusted media source.

The rootkit detector provides investigators with the ability to initiate a batch job that invokes all the command line utilities and scans the output files for potential threats. The outputs of the utilities are analyzed for (i) differences between output files that should display identical information, and (ii) combinations of discrepancies that could indicate possible threats. While it is simple to classify all of the differences between the outputs, it is difficult to categorize and assess all possible combinations of discrepancies. Therefore, the detector focuses on certain key differences and combinations of these differences.

Figure 1 illustrates the identification of discrepancies. The scenario involves identifying the presence of a hidden file called `secret.hide` by examining directory listings produced by two different tools (`dir` and `ls`). This method is effective at discovering files hidden by the Vanquish rootkit.

Having identified the discrepancies in the output files, predefined detection rules are applied to determine if the discrepancies indicate the presence of a rootkit. Figure 2 presents a scenario where three discrepancies have been identified: Discrepancy A comes from comparing the outputs of `dir` and `ls.exe`, Discrepancy B comes from comparing the outputs of `pslist.exe` and `handle.exe`, and Discrepancy C comes from comparing the outputs of `dir` and `handle.exe`. Information about the discrepancies is passed to the detection rules (as in Figure 2), which determine if a rootkit is present or not.

5.   Results

The Windows-based rootkit detection tool was tested on a system running Windows XP with Service Pack 2. To make the testing process consistent, the victim system was run on VMWare, which enables malicious code (e.g., rootkits) to be executed without infecting the host operating system. In addition, it enables the user to start or stop a test image quickly and reliably, and to go back to previous snapshots.

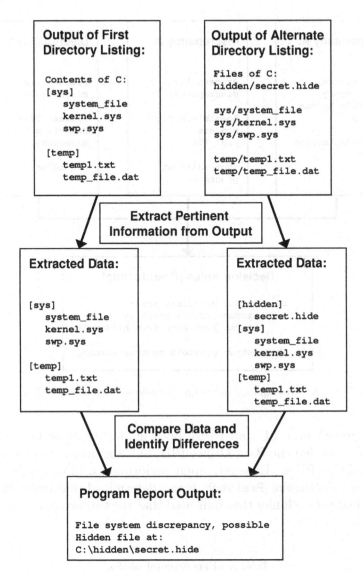

Figure 1. Identification of discrepancies.

Initial tests involved running the batch script and analyzing each output file for evidence of a rootkit. The output file of `handle.exe` clearly indicated the presence of the Hacker Defender rootkit via a non-existent process with a PID and an object named Hacker Defender. The AFX and Vanquish rootkits were also detected during initial testing.

The next step was to perform tests against rootkits that employed more sophisticated hiding techniques (i.e., kernel-level subversion). The

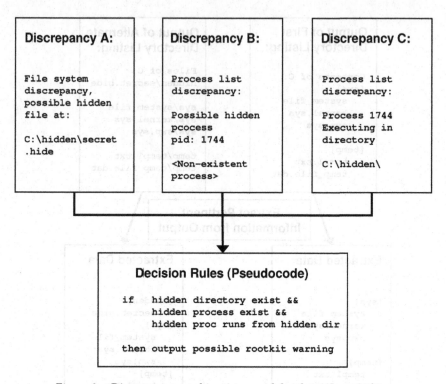

Figure 2. Discrepancy combinations used for detecting rootkits.

rootkits tested were FU and FUto, both hiding the Back Orifice PID. The tool identified the Back Orifice PID, but was unable to identify the FU and FUto PIDs. However, upon performing a directory listing of the folder C:\Windows\Prefetch, it was determined that bo2K.exe and FU.exe had prefetch files that indicated that the two programs had been executed.

Table 1. Experimental results.

Rootkit	Rootkit PID	Bo2k PID	Bo2k Port	Hidden Data
Hacker Defender	Found	Found	Not Found	Found
AFX	Found	Found	Not Found	Found
Vanquish	N/A	N/A	N/A	Found
FU	Not Found	Found	Not Found	N/A
FUto	Not Found	Found	Not Found	N/A

Table 1 summarizes the experimental results. The principal result is that Back Orifice was detected for all the user-level and kernel-level rootkits tested. However, the rootkit detection tool was unable to locate Back Orifice's open ports.

6. Conclusions

Evidence collected during live analysis of systems can be compromised by active rootkits. Digital forensic investigators need automated tools that can detect rootkits during live response investigations of computer systems. The rootkit detection tool described in this paper has proved to be relatively effective in tests. Specifically, the tool was able to identify the PIDs of the Hacker Defender, AFX, and Vanquish rootkits, the PIDs of their backdoors and the folders they were attempting to hide. Tests against the FU and FUto rootkits were not as successful; the only evidence obtained was the name of the executable FU.exe in the prefetch folder. On the other hand, the PID and file name of Back Orifice were easily detected although FU and FUto were attempting to hide this information.

Topics for future research include performing experiments with other rootkits and backdoors, conducting an exhaustive examination of the Windows API to identify all the alternative ways for obtaining system information, and investigating rootkit detection in UNIX environments.

Acknowledgements

This research was supported by the Anti-Tamper Software Protection Initiative Technology Office, Sensors Directorate, U.S. Air Force Research Laboratory. The views expressed in this paper are those of the authors and do not reflect the official policy or position of the U.S. Air Force, U.S. Department of Defense or the U.S. Government.

References

[1] M. Boelen, Rootkit Hunter (www.rootkit.nl/projects/rootkit_hunt er.html).

[2] A. Chuvakin, An Overview of Unix Rootkits, iALERT White Paper, iDefense Labs, Chantilly, Virginia, 2003.

[3] K. Dillard, What are user-mode vs. kernel-mode rootkits? (search windowssecurity.techtarget.com/originalContent/0,289142,sid45_gc i1086469,00.html), 2005.

[4] J. Evers, Microsoft will wipe Sony's rootkit, CNET News.com, November 13, 2005.

[5] F-Secure, The Threat – Rootkits, Helsinki, Finland (www.virus.fi /blacklight/rootkit.shtml).

[6] J. Heasman, Implementing and Detecting a PCI Rootkit, Next Generation Security Software, Sutton, United Kingdom, 2006.

[7] G. Hoglund and J. Butler, *Rootkits: Subverting the Windows Kernel*, Addison-Wesley, Boston, Massachusetts, 2005.

[8] Holy_Father, Hacker Defender (hxdef), 2005.

[9] S. King, P. Chen, Y. Wang, C. Verbowski, H. Wang and J. Lorch, SubVirt: Implementing malware with virtual machines, *Proceedings of the IEEE Symposium on Security and Privacy*, pp. 314–327, 2006.

[10] J. Levine, B. Culver and H. Owen, A methodology for detecting new binary rootkit exploits, presented at the *IEEE SouthEastCon Technical Conference*, 2003.

[11] J. Levine, J. Grizzard and H. Owen, Detecting and categorizing kernel-level rootkits to aid future detection, *IEEE Security & Privacy*, vol. 4(1), pp. 24–32, 2006.

[12] K. Mandia, C. Prosise and M. Pepe, *Incident Response and Computer Forensics*, McGraw-Hill/Osborne, Berkeley, California, 2003.

[13] S. McClure, J. Scambray and G. Kurtz, *Hacking Exposed: Network Security Secrets and Solutions*, Osborne/McGraw-Hill, Berkeley, California, 2001.

[14] Rootkit.com, AFX Rootkit (www.rootkit.com).

[15] Rootkit.com, FU Rootkit (www.rootkit.com).

[16] Rootkit.com, FUto Rootkit (www.rootkit.com).

[17] Rootkit.com, Vanquish Rootkit (www.rootkit.com).

[18] J. Rutkowska, Introducing Stealth Malware Taxonomy, Technical Report, COSEINC Advanced Malware Labs (invisiblethings.org /papers/malware-taxonomy.pdf), 2006.

[19] Sourceforge.net, Back Orifice 2000 (www.bo2k.com).

[20] Tech Support Alert, Rootkit Detection and Removal (www.pcsupp ortadvisor.com/rootkits.htm), 2006.

[21] A. Todd, J. Benson, G. Peterson, T. Franz, M. Stevens and R. Raines, Analysis of tools for detecting rootkits and hidden processes, in *Advances in Digital Forensics III*, P. Craiger and S. Shenoi (Eds.), Springer, Boston, Massachusetts, pp. 89–105, 2007.

VI

NETWORK FORENSICS

Chapter 13

IDENTIFYING AND ANALYZING WEB SERVER ATTACKS

Christian Seifert, Barbara Endicott-Popovsky, Deborah Frincke,
Peter Komisarczuk, Radu Muschevici and Ian Welch

Abstract   Client honeypots can be used to identify malicious web servers that attack web browsers and push malware to client machines. Merely recording network traffic is insufficient to perform comprehensive forensic analyses of such attacks. Custom tools are required to access and analyze
network protocol data. Moreover, specialized methods are required to
perform a behavioral analysis of an attack, which helps determine exactly what transpired on the attacked system. This paper proposes a
record/replay mechanism that enables forensic investigators to extract
application data from recorded network streams and allows applications
to interact with this data in order to conduct behavioral analyses. Implementations for the HTTP and DNS protocols are presented and their
utility in network forensic investigations is demonstrated.

Keywords: Network forensics, malicious web servers, client honeypots

1.   Introduction

Network forensic readiness involves "maximizing the ability of an environment to collect credible digital evidence while minimizing the cost
of incident response" [11]. The goal is to simplify network forensic tasks
without sacrificing the quality of digital evidence. This can be achieved
using specialized techniques and tools as well as by embedding forensic
capabilities in networks, thus "operationalizing" network forensic readiness [1].

This paper examines network forensic readiness in the context of malicious web servers. Malicious web servers push malware to client machines – so called "drive-by-downloads" – by exploiting web browsers.
A previous study [10] used client honeypots to find malicious servers on

Please use the following format when citing this chapter:

Seifert, C., Endicott-Popovsky, B., Frincke, D., Komisarczuk, P., Muschevici, R. and Welch, I., 2008, in IFIP
International Federation for Information Processing, Volume 285; *Advances in Digital Forensics IV*; Indrajit Ray, Sujeet
Shenoi; (Boston: Springer), pp. 151–161.

the Internet. However, once identified, the attack origin and mechanism, and the actions performed by the malware could not be explained.

A major challenge is to extract and interact with application data from recorded network streams. In particular, it is difficult to demonstrate and analyze attacks because the streams have to be piped via network channels through the client application to execute the identical code path that made an attack possible. Since the attack source code is not readily available, analyzing system behavior (referred to as "behavioral analysis") is the primary means to infer the inner workings of an attack.

Network and application protocols do not support the replay of network data to analyze how an attack impacted an application or system. This inability has contributed to inadequate network forensic readiness in the context of client-side attacks.

This paper presents a custom solution using web and DNS proxies and demonstrates its utility in network forensic investigations. The solution, however, is specific to the HTTP and DNS protocols [3, 7] and is not easily generalizable. This is why the paper also calls for the support and implementation of a record/replay mechanism in these protocols to provide a generic network forensic solution.

2.   Background

This section discusses the problems posed by malicious web servers and the overall lack of forensic readiness to cope with attacks.

2.1   Malicious Web Servers

Our previous study [10] concerned itself with identifying "drive-by-downloads," an emerging type of attack executed by malicious servers on client machines. These attacks target vulnerabilities in client applications and usually alter the state of the client machine without user consent. Typically, the malicious server installs malware on the client machine without the user's knowledge.

Our work concentrated on identifying malicious web servers that attack web browsers. The mere retrieval of a malicious web page with a vulnerable browser results in a successful compromise of the client machine. The web environment was chosen because these attacks are currently the most common type of drive-by-downloads.

We identified malicious web servers using high-interaction client honeypots. Such a honeypot uses a dedicated operating system to drive a vulnerable browser to interact with a potentially malicious web server. After each interaction, the operating system is checked for unauthorized state changes, e.g., new executable files in the startup folder. If any

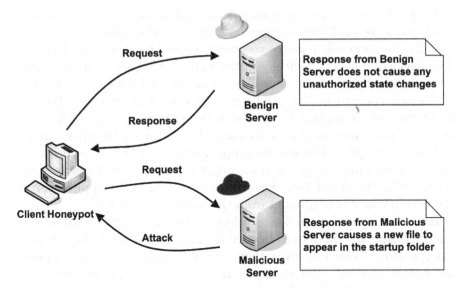

Figure 1. Client honeypot.

unauthorized state changes are detected, the server is classified as malicious (Figure 1).

Twelve instances of a high-interaction client honeypot were used to inspect about 300,000 web pages over a three-week period. A total of 306 malicious URLs were identified that successfully attacked a standard installation of Microsoft Windows XP SP2 with Internet Explorer 6.0 SP2. The malicious servers took control of the machine and primarily installed malware that attempted to defraud the user.

Unauthorized state changes to the client machines were recorded when the client honeypots identified malicious web servers. In addition, network data was collected using the `tcpdump` tool [6] and stored in `libpcap` data files. This data contained all the network traffic sent to and from a client honeypot, including HTTP and DNS requests and responses. Interested readers are referred to [10] for more details about the use of high-interaction client honeypots.

2.2   Forensic Analysis

Analysis of network and application data (DNS records, HTML pages and IP source addresses) helps identify the servers involved in attacks and their role in the attacks. Also, the inspection of HTML pages reveals embedded source code, which could provide information about attack mechanisms.

In general, an attack incorporates an exploit that targets a vulnerability and a payload that is executed after the vulnerability is exploited. Usually, the embedded source code only implements the initial exploit. The payload, which is typically in the form of a binary, requires behavioral analysis to determine how it operates. Behavioral analysis requires the attack code to be executed again on the client machine, but this is difficult to accomplish for several reasons, including server location, server domain name and security context. Opening a web page from a web server is quite different from opening it as a file. A page that is opened from a previously-saved file might not trigger. In fact, to trigger successfully, the attack code has to be sent to the client application via the network as if it originated from the malicious server.

Recorded network data does not lend itself to straightforward forensic analysis. Application data embedded in `libpcap` files has to be extracted using custom tools; but, even then, the data may not directly support behavioral analysis. For example, HTML pages extracted with these tools cannot be fed to a browser to provide information about if and how the attack occurred.

Note that it is difficult to develop an application that interacts with a malicious server in order to analyze an attack. This is because the dynamic nature of the network makes malicious web servers appear different over time. Also, it is often the case that hackers implement fluctuations to hide attack sources and hinder forensic investigations of attacks. As a result, forensic analyses of attacks must be based on the data recorded during the initial identification of malicious web servers.

2.2.1 Replaying Network Data.

In order to replay network traffic at the transport layer, recorded packets must be placed back on the wire. The technique involves splitting the network flow into server traffic and client traffic. After one side of the flow, say client traffic, is selectively placed on the wire, the server would have to recognize a request as if it originated from a client and provide the normal response.

Separating the network flow into client and server packets is an easy task. It is done by filtering the network flow by client source or server IP address. However, having the client or server interactively respond to the replayed network traffic is not a capability that is normally supported by the transport layer of a network protocol such as TCP [5] (regardless of whether IPv4 [4] or IPv6 [2] is employed).

Several mechanisms of the TCP protocol are responsible for this. TCP is a stateful protocol that uses a three-way handshake to establish a connection between a client and server. First, the client sends a TCP packet to the server with the ACK flag set. The server acknowledges

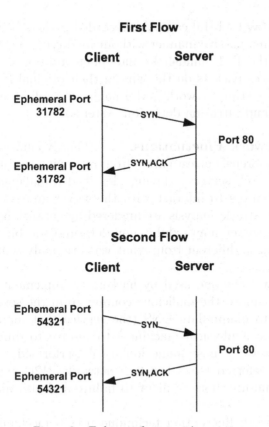

Figure 2. Ephemeral port assignment.

this connection request by sending a TCP packet with the ACK and SYN flags set. The connection is established when the client sends a TCP packet with the ACK flag set. Sequence numbers are exchanged during the handshake to identify the other party in each communication. Thus, connections cannot be established when TCP traffic is replayed by placing only one side of the network flow on the wire.

Another difficulty is posed by ephemeral ports that are created by the client to accept response packets from the server during the process of establishing a connection. In other words, the client application temporarily becomes a server. An ephemeral port is dynamically assigned in the high port range with each connection as shown in Figure 2. This port remains closed when no connection is being established. Replaying network traffic against the client requires matching the temporarily-opened ephemeral port with the destination port specified in TCP packets. Without this matching, the traffic would not reach the client application.

The tcpreplay tool [14] can place recorded packets back on the wire, but it does so in a passive manner without modifying the recorded packets to address the TCP handshake and ephemeral port assignment constraints. It places packets on the wire in their original form mainly for the purpose of testing network performance and inline security devices (e.g., firewalls and intrusion detection systems).

2.2.2   Network Fluctuations.   The dynamic nature of networks prevents forensic investigators from retrieving the original content from malicious web servers. Having identified a malicious web server, subsequent attempts to interact with the server and retrieve information to support attack analysis are hindered by network fluctuations. In particular, the server may exhibit non-deterministic behavior, providing content that is different from what was originally sent to the client application.

The simplest technique used by hackers to implement network fluctuations is to remove the malicious content from the server. A second mechanism is to manipulate DNS (the service that maps host names to IP addresses of physical machines) to resolve to different physical machines whenever a host name lookup is performed. Such network structures are referred to as fast-flux networks [12]. This makes the attack infrastructure more resilient to failure and also hinders forensic investigations.

A third network fluctuation technique uses a mechanism known as "IP tracking." Exploitation kits deployed on web servers, such as Mpack v0.94 [9], can be configured to trigger only during the initial contact with a malicious web server. Subsequent interactions with the web server from the same IP address provide the identical, albeit benign, web pages. Thus, the malicious web server that launched an attack on the client honeypot appears to be benign to the forensic investigator.

3.   Proposed Solution

Our solution engages a record/replay mechanism in which recorded data is played back through the client application (Figure 3). This makes it much easier to extract relevant information from the data. Instead of writing a custom forensic analysis application, the existing functionality of the client application can be used to extract information from network data. Moreover, replaying recorded data through the client application supports behavioral analysis.

As mentioned above, implementing a record/replay mechanism at the network transport layer poses several challenges. Therefore, our solution

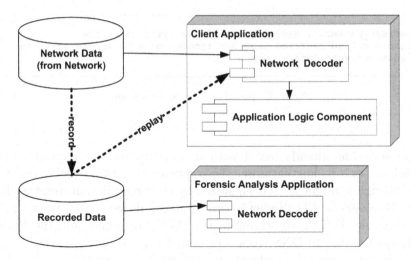

Figure 3. Record/replay mechanism.

uses the application layer to implement record/replay. Specifically, all client application and malicious web server communications are routed through a proxy that records all the application data. The proxy, if instructed to replay the stored data instead of fetching it from the actual server, can repeatedly replay the server responses to the client.

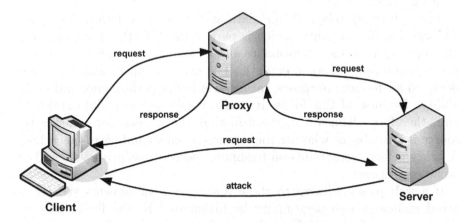

Figure 4. Proxy architecture.

The top portion of Figure 4 presents the proxy architecture. The architecture supports forensic analysis because the proxy server stores all the data during the initial operation of the client honeypot. In particular, it is possible to perform a behavioral analysis of the attack code using a browser. The browser makes the HTTP request, which is routed via the proxy. Since the proxy already knows the response, it returns the server

```
refresh_pattern . 999999 100\% 999999 override-expire
ignore-reload override-lastmode ignore-no-cache ignore-no-store
ignore-private ignore-auth
```

Figure 5. Squid configuration options.

response it has already saved without passing another request to the malicious server. Furthermore, the application data is easily retrieved even though it might have been stored by the proxy in a proprietary format. Browsers and DNS clients can obtain and decode the proxy data. For example, WGET could obtain the HTTP response, and the HOST tool could translate DNS responses stored on the proxy server. Thus, our solution reuses the code of existing tools, eliminating the need to procure custom tools for extracting and analyzing application data.

3.1   Proxy Solution

Web browsing uses two application protocols (HTTP and DNS). Consequently, two proxy solutions are implemented: a web proxy that routes and stores HTTP data and a DNS proxy that performs the same operations on DNS data.

The web proxy relays HTTP data and stores this data in its cache. The caching functionality, which is part of the HTTP/1.1 specification [3], improves response performance and availability, and permits disconnected operation (to some extent). The caching functionality was not designed for forensic purposes, rather to enhance performance and availability. Because of this focus, it is also concerned with data staleness and, therefore, defines a mechanism that checks whether a newer resource is available or whether the resource itself should never be cached. A proxy utilizes constraints on freshness and security/privacy as well as cache correctness.

If a web proxy adheres to these functional requirements strictly, a saved malicious web page might be invalidated by the freshness constraint and fetched again from the server upon a subsequent request. In contrast, our solution attempts to use the web proxy for storage rather than caching without applying the mechanisms defined in the HTTP/1.1 specification. In particular, it uses Squid [15], an open source web proxy implementation. Squid is highly configurable and permits deviations from the HTTP/1.1 specification. In fact, the forensic requirements for the web proxy can be achieved using the Squid configuration settings shown in Figure 5.

DNS proxies, similarly to web proxies, are designed to store DNS responses in their caches for a predefined period of time. Once the validity of a DNS response has expired, the DNS proxy must perform another DNS lookup on the actual DNS server. Again, an implementation is needed that can override this behavior. This can be done using `pdnsd` [8], a simple DNS daemon with permanent caching designed to deal with unreachable or down DNS servers (e.g., in dial-up networking). The purging of older cache entries can be prevented by setting the maximum cache size to a high value (e.g., using the configuration option `perm_cache=204800`).

3.2 Limitations

The proposed solution has some limitations. First and foremost, it is not easily applicable to other network data. The HTTP and DNS protocols are based on a simple request/response model. Since the protocols were designed at a time when dial-up networks dominated, caching proxies were incorporated to conserve resources and increase reliability. Proxy storage capabilities facilitate forensic data collection and analysis; however, they are unlikely to be provided by modern protocols. For example, peer-to-peer protocols and other popular protocols such as SSH do not have a simple request/replay structure, which makes it difficult to offer proxy record/replay capabilities.

Second, the proxy solution does not provide the same interactivity as a real server. State information (e.g., for authentication) is held by the client and is usually conveyed back to the server in the form of a cookie. While a proxy is able to store this information, a client would have to adhere to the same request sequence to solicit the same responses. For example, if a client accesses a web page after authentication, it would have to be re-authenticated before it could access the same web page from the server at a later time; this is because the required authentication information is missing from the request. Furthermore, the proxy solution will not work when encryption is used by the two communicating parties.

Finally, interacting with a server via a proxy might solicit different server responses. This is not a concern in a forensic setting. However, because the data sent to the client is recorded by the proxy, this might pose a problem when searches are performed using a client honeypot. Specifically, a server might check for the existence of a proxy and not behave maliciously if such a proxy is encountered as a precautionary measure. Figure 4 illustrates this situation. The top flow shows a client application interacting with a server via a proxy. The server detects the proxy set-up and, therefore, delivers a benign web page. The bottom flow shows a client interacting directly with the server. The server does not detect a proxy that potentially records data and believes it is free to launch the attack.

4.   Conclusions

Identifying and analyzing web server attacks are difficult tasks due to the lack of forensic readiness of network protocols. Our custom proxy-server-based record/replay solution adds network forensic readiness capabilities to client honeypots. The solution supports the examination of application data by reusing the capabilities of the clients that consume the data. It also permits the data to be sent interactively to client applications to perform behavioral analyses of attacks, which provide a more complete picture of attack mechanisms and impact.

While forensic capabilities have been implemented at the application layer using existing proxy solutions, we believe a generic solution could be implemented at the network transport layer. The difficulty in implementing such a solution is primarily due to the fact that existing protocols were not designed with network forensic readiness in mind. We believe that incorporating forensic requirements during protocol design is instrumental to achieving network forensic readiness.

References

[1] B. Endicott-Popovsky, D. Frincke and C. Taylor, A theoretical framework for organizational network forensic readiness, *Journal of Computers*, vol. 2(3), pp. 1–11, 2007.

[2] S. Deering and R. Hinden, RFC 2460: Internet Protocol Version 6 (IPv6) Specification (www.faqs.org/rfcs/rfc2460.html), 1998.

[3] R. Fielding, J. Gettys, J. Mogul, H. Frystyk, L. Masinter, P. Leach and T. Berners-Lee, RFC 2616: Hypertext Transfer Protocol – HTTP/1.1 (www.ietf.org/rfc/rfc2616.txt), 1999.

[4] Information Sciences Institute, RFC 791: Internet Protocol, University of Southern California, Los Angeles, California (www.faqs.org /rfcs/rfc791.html), 1981.

[5] Information Sciences Institute, RFC 793: Transmission Control Protocol, University of Southern California, Los Angeles, California (www.faqs.org/rfcs/rfc793.html), 1981.

[6] V. Jacobson, C. Leres and S. McCanne, tcpdump (www.tcpdump .org).

[7] P. Mockapetris, RFC 1035: Domain Names – Implementation and Specification (www.ietf.org/rfc/rfc1035.txt), 1987.

[8] T. Moestl and P. Rombouts, **pdnsd** – Proxy DNS server (www.phys .uu.nl/~rombouts/pdnsd/index.html).

[9] C. Seifert, Know your enemy: Behind the scenes of malicious web servers (www.honeynet.org/papers/wek), 2007.

[10] C. Seifert, R. Steenson, T. Holz, Y. Bing and M. Davis, Know your enemy: Malicious web servers (www.honeynet.org/papers/mws), 2007.

[11] J. Tan, Forensic readiness (www.arcert.gov.ar/webs/textos/forensic _readiness.pdf), 2001.

[12] The Honeynet Project and Research Allicance, Know your enemy: Fast-flux service networks (www.honeynet.org/papers/ff/fast-flux .pdf), 2007.

[13] A. Turner, **flowreplay** design notes (synfin.net/papers/flowreplay .pdf), 2003.

[14] A. Turner, **tcpreplay** (tcpreplay.synfin.net/trac).

[15] D. Wessels, H. Nordstroem, A. Rousskov, A. Chadd, R. Collins, G. Serassio, S. Wilton and C. Francesco, Squid web proxy cache (www.squid-cache.org).

Chapter 14

FORENSIC WEB SERVICES

Murat Gunestas, Duminda Wijesekera and Anoop Singhal

Abstract   Choreography, orchestration and dynamic invocation allow new web services to be composed from existing ones. However, these compositions create service interdependencies that can be misused for financial fraud and other illegal purposes. When a misuse is reported, investigators have to navigate through collections of logs to recreate the invocation scenario in order to evaluate the misuse claims. We propose the creation of forensic web services that can securely maintain transaction records between web services. An independent entity could use the stored records to reproduce the complete transaction history when investigating a misuse claim.

Keywords: Web services, service oriented architecture, transaction forensics

1.   Introduction

Web services are being used for many commercial, government and military purposes. New web services can be created by seamlessly integrating existing web services using techniques such as choreography, orchestration, dynamic invocation and brokering. These service-level compositional techniques create complex dependencies between web services of different organizations. When they are exploited, multiple servers and organizations are affected, resulting in considerable financial loss and infrastructure damage.

Investigating web service incidents requires that the dependencies between service invocations be retained in a neutral and secure manner so that the alleged activity can be recreated while preserving evidence that could lead to and support prosecution. Evidence extracted from web servers, such as XML firewall alerts from endpoint services and web server log records, have limited forensic value. Defendants can claim

Please use the following format when citing this chapter:

Gunestas, M., Wijesekera, D. and Singhal, A., 2008, in IFIP International Federation for Information Processing, Volume 285; *Advances in Digital Forensics IV*; Indrajit Ray, Sujeet Shenoi; (Boston: Springer), pp. 163–176.

that they did not send the messages in question or that the plaintiffs altered the logs to make their cases.

To address these issues, we propose Forensic Web Services (FWSs), which preserve the evidence needed to recreate composed web service invocations independent of the parties with vested interests. Note that a simple non-repudiation argument with multiple log records has no forensic value. Also, web service forensics cannot be treated as a bilateral problem between two web services because of dynamic compositions. Consequently, FWSs provide web-service-based forensic capabilities to web services. This requires FWSs to be integrated with web services that require them; these web services are referred to as customer web services. In order to do so, FWSs provide a centralized service access point to customer services. The information retained by FWSs as a trusted third party can be provided to forensic examiners. Previous proposals for monitoring web services [6] and generating evidence [10, 16, 26] are primarily for business purposes. We are not aware of similar applications that support forensic investigations.

Organizations that are tightly integrated through web transactions and processes can benefit from FWSs in many ways. They can hold their partner services accountable when their vulnerabilities affect transaction confidentiality, availability, etc. Also, the details of malicious activity can impact punitive measures and damage claims. We show that non-repudiable logging of critical information exchanges is an effective way to meet these needs. Some logging and processing approaches already exist for web services [5, 6, 28]. Also, Sremack [30] has proposed an approach for conducting online investigations. However, these approaches do not employ a trusted third party to generate and preserve evidence or offer conclusive evidence as provided by the FWS framework.

2.   Web Service Attacks

Numerous web service attacks, such as WSDL/UDDI scanning, parameter tampering, replays, XML rewriting, man-in-the-middle attacks, eavesdropping and routing detours have been identified [7–9, 17, 18, 20, 27] and characterized (see, e.g., [31, 33]). To motivate the need for FWSs, we discuss the cross-site scripting (CSS) attack [9], which is presented in Figure 1. An attacker with stolen credentials injects malicious data, invoking an update operation on a weather service that stores a script (including instructions to steal cookies) in web browsers. Next, a web application, say Portal Web Application in Figure 1, retrieves this malicious data when invoking a get operation and publishes weather information to its subscribers in HTML, thereby making the

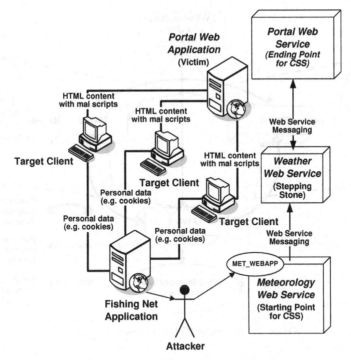

Figure 1. Cross-site scripting attack.

subscribers send their personal information (stored in cookies) to the attacker's Fishing Net Application.

3. Forensic Web Services Framework

The Forensic Web Services (FWSs) framework consists of two services. One generates pairwise evidence when transactions occur between pairs of web services. The other composes evidence generated from pairwise transactions and creates complex transaction scenarios on demand.

The FWSs framework uses trusted third parties that sit in between transactions. To obtain forensic services, all web services must sign up with a FWS (Figure 2), and all FWSs agents must cooperate by providing relevant pairwise transactional evidence that they have stored. Four roles are involved in the process: sender, receiver, operator FWS and non-operator FWS. The operator FWS refers to a FWS selected by either party to manage the steps listed below; the non-operator FWS belongs to the other party. A FWSs registry is available to locate all registered FWSs servers. FWSs systems must satisfy the following requirements:

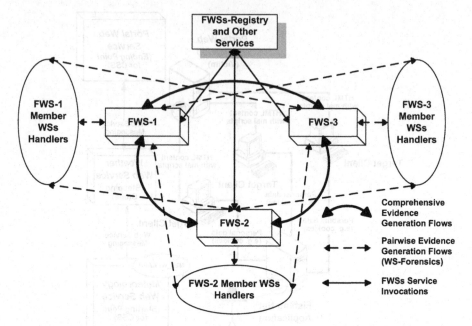

Figure 2.   Forensic Web Services framework.

- The web service call stack must be enriched with a WS-Forensics layer.

- A message format is required to communicate with WS-Forensics layer messages and store them in FWSs servers.

- All web services must use a client agent that re-routes their transactional messages through FWSs servers.

- The underlying system must provide a trust base and cryptographic services.

The web service stack has three layers: the bottom layer consists of SOAP messages, the middle layer WS-SecureConversations and the top layer WSDL specifications (Figure 3). A forensic layer is added between the middle and top layers to re-route transactions through FWSs servers. The sender web service and receiver web service communicate using their WSDLs independently of the underlying WS-Forensics layer.

WS-Forensics uses the following message format:

⟨#session|#message|#signatureK(#session|#message/sequence
|#message/envelope)⟩

where # refers to the points in XML format, | denotes concatenation and / points to the subparts of elements. Also, "session" identifies a

Figure 3. WS-Forensics stack.

WS-Forensics conversation and "message" is the upper layer content and its sequence number in the conversation. Both endpoints (sender and receiver) sign a session.

FWSs store messages in two formats: LogRecordIndex (LRI) and LogRecord (LR) without signatures, where LRI records a single fwsMessage, LR stores entire WS-Forensics sessions, including all fwsMessages delivered to and/or generated by FWSs. LRIs are stored at both endpoints while LRs are stored only at the operator FWS. FWSs also timestamp all messages. LR contains a record index with the final timestamp, status and the last sequence value of the conversation. All transaction information is reliably intercepted and re-routed through FWSs servers using sender and receiver processes positioned in front of each web service endpoint. The sender process uses the FWSs handler exposed by the forensics layer, adds the extra routing information to conform with the WS-Forensics message format and passes it to the WS-SecureConversation or WS-Trust handler exposed by the WS-Trust layer. Similarly, the receiver process verifies the signatures, extracts the SOAP message and passes it to the intended service or port type.

WS-Forensics is designed to run over a secure layer with the following services (that are already satisfied by WS-Trust [21] and WS-SecureConversation [22]):

- **Authentication:** Senders, receivers and FWSs nodes.

- **Delegated Authentication:** As a trusted third party, FWSs nodes authenticate themselves to the receiver on behalf of the sender.

- **Channel Confidentiality and Integrity:** FWSs nodes must ensure the confidentiality and integrity of channels between senders and receivers.

- **Reliability:** Messages in channels between FWSs nodes and customer nodes must be reliable.

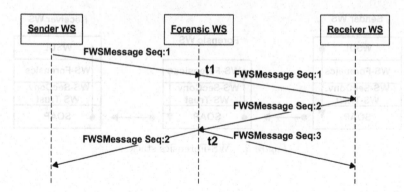

Figure 4. Operator FWS managing SELP.

4.   Collecting Pairwise Evidence

FWSs collect pairwise transactional evidence using the Simple Evidence Layer Protocol (SELP) [10]. Four roles are employed: sender, receiver, operator FWS and non-operator FWS. The following steps are performed by the operator FWS (see Figures 4 and 5):

1. The operator FWS receives MsgSeq.1, which contains ⟨#session| #message|#signatureSender-K(#session|"1"|#env)⟩.

2. It validates and stores the message, creates an LR and LRI for MsgSeq.1 and notifies the non-operator FWS.

3. It forwards MsgSeq.1 to the receiver and starts a timer.

4. If the response MsgSeq.2 does not reach in time, the operator FWS signs MsgSeq.-1(⟨#session|#message|#signatureFWS-K(#session |"-1"|#env)⟩), stores the message and sends it back to the sender; also, it creates an LRI, which is sent to the non-operator FWS. However, if MsgSeq.2 (⟨#session|#message|#signatureReceiver-K (#session|"2"|#env)⟩) arrives on time then, it stores the message and forwards it to the sender; also, it creates an LRI, which is sent to the non-operator FWS.

5. It creates, signs and sends MsgSeq.3 (⟨⟨#session|#message|#signa tureFWS-K(#session|"3"|#env)⟩) to the receiver. It also stores the message in the LR and sends the LRI to the non-operator FWS. Dependencies between stored data are maintained using LRIs.

The SELP protocol and FWSs event logs retain the evidence required to verify the sender's claims of timely transmission, the receiver's claims

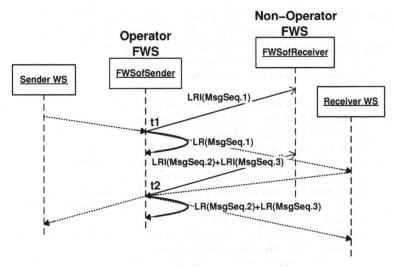

Figure 5. Operator FWS storing pairs.

not to have received messages in a timely manner, either party's claims of non-availability of the other party, and any contractual violations.

5.   Creating Evidence for Scenarios

This section describes the main data types and algorithms used to collect and preserve evidence of pairwise transactions involving web services.

FWSs store information exchanged between pairs of services in LRI tables that are used to generate service dependencies expressed as a dependency graph. Dependency graph nodes have the complex type *WebServiceNode*, where each *WebServiceNode* has a unique ID and field *NodeLevel*, which expresses the degree of adjacency of the node to the root of the graph. The field *NodeThreshold* expresses the maximum degree of adjacency from the root. The edges of the graph are represented using the complex data type *LogRecordEdge* with *SenderID* and *ReceiverID* attributes. An authorized requestor generates evidence bags by providing the required arguments using *generateEvidenceBagPortType*, a port that calls other FWSs to collect dependent evidence residing in its log records. FWSs use *StorageService*, *MembershipQueryService*, *SecurityService*, *EvidenceBagService* and other auxiliary internal services. The FWSs Registry manages the member registration processes. The operation *getFWSPortType* called by the FWSs nodes retrieves the ID

1. **partnerLinks**: SecurityService; VirusScannerService;
        SignatureDetectionSrv; RootFWS; Requestor; FWSRegistry
2. **variables**: EvidenceBagIn; EvidenceBagOut; LogRecordEdges;
        DependentsBagIn; DependentsBag;
        LogRecordEdgesForEvidenceGraph;
3. **begin**
4.   receive EvidenceBagIn from Requestor
5.   invoke getFWSs(RootWS) in FWSRegistry
6.   assign RootFWS partnerLink
7.   assign EvidenceBagIn to DependentsBagIn
8.   invoke collectDependents(DependentsBagIn) in RootFWS
9.   assign DependentsBag to LogRecordEdges
10.   assign distinct ArrayOfFWSTTP from LogRecordEdges
        ←!– Invokes a set of FWSTTPs to get actual LREs by their LRIs →
        ←!– using flowN loop structure →
11.   **flowN** N='countNodes(' ArrayOfFWSTTP '...)' indexVariable='index'
12.   partnerLink: OwnerFWSOfLogRecords
13.   variables: LogRecordEdgesOutput
14.   assign OwnerFWSOfLogRecords partnerLink
15.   invoke getLogRecordsByValue in OwnerFWSOfLogRecords
16.   receive LogRecordEdgesOutput as getLogRecordsByValue callback
            ←!———————— Stores the result ————————→
17.   append LogRecordEdgesForEvidenceGraph
                from LogRecordEdgesOutput
18.   **end** of flowN
19.   assign LogRecordEdgesForEvidenceGraph to EvidenceBagOut
20.   invoke scan(EvidenceBagOut) in VirusScannerService
21.   invoke detect(EvidenceBagOut) in SignatureDetectionSrv
22.   invoke signAndEncrypt(EvidenceBagOut) in SecurityService
23.   reply EvidenceBagOut to Requestor
24. **end**

Figure 6. Building evidence bags.

of the registered FWS of any web service. The operation *registryInfo-PortType* is used for member registration and de-registration.

FWS build digital evidence bags [11] using the pseudo BPEL algorithm presented in Figure 6 [14]. First, a requestor starts building digital evidence bags (Line 4) by invoking the *generateEvidenceBag* process with the suspected root *WebServiceNode*, *StartTime* (defines the start time), *TimeThreshold* (defines the time range) and *NodeThreshold* (defines the node range), which are included in the *EvidenceBagIn* message. In Lines 5–8, the FWS gets the FWS that controls the root node, which is the start point for the collection process. The FWS assigns the address of the rootFWS partner link and continues by invoking the *collectDependents* process, which runs recursively over many FWSs with the *DependentsBagIn* message as parameter (see Figure 7 for details). *Depen-*

←!– Starts extracting values (timeThreshold, nodeThreshold, etc.) →
←!– from DependentsBagIn and initializes creating the →
←!– WebServiceNodes and LogRecordEdges instances of GRAPH →
1. baseTime = startTime - timeThreshold
2. **for each** logRecordIndex LRI in FWS {
3.   timeThreshold=timeTreshold - (startTime - LRI.timeStamp)
4.   startTime=LRI.timestamp
5.   **for each** webServiceNode WS in GRAPH {
6.   **if** (SenderWS | ReceiverWS ∈ LRI & LRI ∉ GRAPH
              & R.timestamp ≥ baseTime & WS.nodeLevel
              ≤ WS.nodeThreshold) {
7.   Add LRI as edge into GRAPH
8.   **if** (LRI's partner web service PWS ∉ GRAPH) {
9.   PWS.nodeLevel=WS.nodeLevel+1
10.   PWS.nodeThreshold=nodeThreshold
11.   Add the PWS into GRAPH }
12.   **if** (LRI's PWS ∉ this.FWS & LRI's PWS ∉ GRAPH) {
13.   NeighbourFWS = getFWS(PWS)
14.   NeighbourFWS.collectRecords(DependentsBagIn)
15.   Merge DependentsBagOut into GRAPH}}}}
16. **return** GRAPH in DependentsBagOut format

Figure 7. Collecting dependent processes.

dentsBagIn is assigned the values in the *EvidenceBagIn* message in Line 7. The FWS is returned a final *DependentsBag* message by the children of the recursive call and the returned message contains *LogRecordEdges* only with index information (LRI). In order to convert *LogRecordEdges* with LRIs into *LogRecordEdges* containing LRs (actual contents of messages), the *generateEvidenceBag* process first extracts distinct *fwsttps* from *LogRecordEdges* into an array in Line 10. In Lines 11–8, the flowN structure in BPEL is used to create dynamic parallel execution scopes for each *fwsttp.location*. For each *fwsttp.location*, dynamic partner links *OwnerFWSOfLogRecords* are also created. Then, *getLogRecordsByValue* operations in these partner links are invoked for each parallel scope and the results are combined in the *LogRecordEdgesForEvidenceGraph*. *LogRecordEdgesForEvidenceGraph* is assigned to *EvidenceBagOut*, which constitutes the actual *EvidenceGraph* document. Other bookkeeping procedures such as scanning and signature verification are applied between Lines 20 and 22. Finally, a response is sent to the requestor in Line 23.

The *generateEvidenceBag* process in Figure 6 is a wrapper of the *collectDependents* process inspired by King and Chen's dependency graph algorithm [15] and Wang and Daniels' evidence graph generation algorithm [32]. The algorithm in Figure 6 first creates instances of *WebSer-*

viceNodes and *LogRecordEdges* and loads the *DependentsBagIn* message into these objects setting the *WebServiceNode* part as a root node for the execution of the algorithm. All the other values in the input message are loaded into the corresponding variables (e.g., *timeThreshold* and *nodeThreshold*). After the initialization phase, the algorithm listed in Figure 7 is used. The created objects *WebServiceNodes* and *LogRecord-Edges* are the nodes and edges of the dependency graph (GRAPH). The GRAPH is constructed based on two facts. First, the algorithm traverses the LRIs in decreasing order of time to search for dependent web service nodes among the sender/receiver fields of the log records; these are inserted into *LogRecordEdges*, which sets the *SenderID*, *ReceiverID* and *DependencyDirection* attributes provided their timestamp is within the time threshold. Second, when a new partner web service is found in the LRIs, it is added to the *WebServiceNodes* object only if the current web service node's *nodeLevel* is less or equal to *nodeThreshold*.

6.   Related Work

To the best of our knowledge, no distributed forensic framework exists for investigating interrelated web services. However, the research efforts discussed in this section share some common features with our objectives and/or methods.

The FWSs design is influenced by WS-NRExchange [26], especially its implementation of fair non-repudiation using the Coeffey-Saidha protocol [4]. However, unlike FWSs, WS-NRExchange does not address choreography and service compositions.

Herzberg and Yoffe [10] proposed the use of an evidence layer for e-commerce transactions located on top of the transport layer. The FWSs framework incorporates their SELP specification, which was designed for the evidence layer.

FWSs use trusted third parties for pairwise evidence generation as do Coffey and Saidha [4]. Certified e-mail protocols [19] have also been used without trusted third parties [16]. Onieva and co-workers [23] proposed the use of inline trusted third parties for e-commerce transactions with multi-recipient cases through these intermediaries, but not for forensic applications. Bilal and colleagues [3] have used BPEL to implement a non-repudiation protocol for web services; however, their solution does not use trusted third parties and, therefore, lacks message content handling capabilities.

FWSs use handlers in an existing web service architecture [1, 2, 12, 24]. Axis2 [25] also implements web service standards such as Rampart for WS-SecureConversation, Rahas for WS-Trust, Sandesha2 for WS-RM, and Kandula for WS-Coordination [13].

WSLogA [5] tracks web service invocations by logging them using SOAP intermediaries. However, unlike FWSs, it does not have a distributed collection mechanism for gathering comprehensive forensic evidence from services sharing multiple servers.

Research in the area of network forensics has also inspired the design of the FWSs framework. These include Wang and Daniels' use of intrusion detection system alerts to generate evidence graphs for network forensic analysis [32] and ForNet's use of router logs in its distributed network forensics framework [29].

7. Conclusions

Composed, choreographed and stand-alone web services span many applications. Consequently, the exploitation of a vulnerability in one service can impact many other services. The Forensic Web Services framework supports the investigation of attacks and the assignment of blame. This capability is provided as a service to other web services by logging service invocations. All the logged data is preserved in a digital evidence bag, which can be used to recreate attacks in a forensically-sound manner.

References

[1] Apache Software Foundation, Axis2 Architecture Guide (ws.apache.org/axis2/0_95/Axis2ArchitectureGuide.html), 2006.

[2] BEA Systems, Specifying SOAP handlers for a web service, BEA WebLogic Workshop Help (Online), San Jose, California (edocs.bea.com/workshop/docs81/doc/en/core/index.html).

[3] M. Bilal, J. Thomas, M. Thomas and S. Abraham, Fair BPEL processes transaction using non-repudiation protocols, *Proceedings of the IEEE International Conference on Services Computing*, pp. 337–340, 2005.

[4] T. Coffey and P. Saidha, Non-repudiation with mandatory proof of receipt, *ACM SIGCOMM Computer Communication Review*, vol. 26(1), pp. 6–17, 1996.

[5] S. da Cruz, L. Campos, M. Campos and P. Pires, A data mart approach for monitoring web services usage and evaluating quality of services, *Proceedings of the Twenty-Eighth Brazilian Symposium on Databases*, 2003.

[6] S. da Cruz, M. Campos, P. Pires and L. Campos, Monitoring e-business web service usage through a log based architecture, *Proceedings of the IEEE International Conference on Web Services*, pp. 61–69, 2004.

[7] Y. Demchenko, L. Gommans, C. de Laat and B. Oudenaarde, Web services and grid security vulnerabilities and threats analysis and model, *Proceedings of the Sixth IEEE/ACM International Workshop on Grid Computing*, 2005.

[8] S. Faust, SOAP web services attacks (www.net-security.org/dl/arti cles/SOAP_Web_Security.pdf), 2003.

[9] D. Green, Attacking and defending web services, presented at the *Nebraska CERT Conference* (www.certconf.org/presentations /2006/files/TA2.pdf), 2006.

[10] A. Herzberg and I. Yoffe, The Delivery and Evidence Layer, Report 2007/139, Cryptology ePrint Archive (eprint.iacr.org/2007/139 .pdf), 2007.

[11] C. Hosmer, Digital evidence bag, *Communications of the ACM*, vol. 49(2), pp. 69–70, 2006.

[12] IBM Corporation, JAX-RPC handlers collection, Armonk, New York (publib.boulder.ibm.com/infocenter/wasinfo/v6r0/index.jsp? topic=/com.ibm.websphere.pmc.express.doc/sibusresources/JAXR PC Handler_CollectionForm.html), 2007.

[13] C. Jayalath and R. Fernando, A modular architecture for secure and reliable distributed communication, *Proceedings of the Second International Conference on Availability, Reliability and Security*, pp. 621–628, 2007.

[14] M. Juric, *Business Process Execution Language for Web Services*, Packt Publishing, Birmingham, United Kingdom, 2006.

[15] S. King and P. Chen, Backtracking intrusions, *ACM SIGOPS Operating Systems Review*, vol. 37(5), pp. 223–236, 2003.

[16] S. Kremer, O. Markowitch and J. Zhou, An intensive survey of fair non-repudiation protocols, *Computer Communications*, vol. 25(17), pp. 1606–1621, 2002.

[17] J. Mallery, J. Zahn, P. Kelly, W. Noonan, E. Seagren, P. Love, R. Kraft and M. O'Neill, *Hardening Network Security*, McGraw-Hill/Osborne, Emeryville, California, 2005.

[18] M. McIntosh and P. Austel, XML signature element wrapping attacks and countermeasures, *Proceedings of the Second ACM Workshop on Secure Web Services*, pp. 20–27, 2005.

[19] S. Micali, Certified e-mail with invisible post offices, presented at the *Sixth Annual RSA Data Security Conference*, 1997.

[20] W. Negm, Anatomy of a web services attack: A guide to threats and preventative countermeasures (www.bitpipe.com/detail/RES /1084293354_294.html), 2004.

[21] OASIS Web Services Secure Exchange Technical Committee, WS-Trust V1.0, OASIS (www.oasis-open.org/committees/download .php/16138/oasis-wssx-ws-trust-1.0.pdf), 2006.

[22] OASIS Web Services Secure Exchange Technical Committee, WS-SecureConversation 1.3, OASIS (docs.oasis-open.org/ws-sx/ws-sec ureconversation/200512/ws-secureconversation-1.3-os.html), 2007.

[23] J. Onieva, J. Zhou, M. Carbonell and J. Lopez, Intermediary non-repudiation protocols, *Proceedings of the IEEE International Conference on E-Commerce Technology*, pp. 207–214, 2003.

[24] Oracle, Using JAX-RPC handlers, *Oracle Application Server Web Services Developer's Guide*, Redwood Shores, California (download.oracle.com/docs/cd/B31017_01/web.1013/b28974/jaxrpchand lers.htm), 2006.

[25] S. Perera, C. Herath, J. Ekanayake, A. Ranabahu. D. Jayasinghe, S. Weerawarana and G. Daniels, Axis2: Middleware for next generation web services, *Proceedings of the IEEE International Conference on Web Services*, pp. 833–840, 2006.

[26] P. Robinson, N. Cook and S. Shrivastava, Implementing fair non-repudiable interactions with web services, *Proceedings of the Ninth IEEE International EDOC Enterprise Computing Conference*, pp. 195–206, 2005.

[27] J. Rosenberg and D. Remy, *Securing Web Services with WS-Security: Demystifying WS-Security, WS-Policy, SAML, XML Signature and XML Encryption*, Sams Publishing, Indianapolis, Indiana, 2004.

[28] M. Rouached and C. Godart, Analysis of composite web services using logging facilities, *Proceedings of the Second International Workshop on Engineering Service-Oriented Applications: Design and Composition*, pp. 74–85, 2006.

[29] K. Shanmugasundaram, N. Memon, A. Savant and H. Bronnimann, ForNet: A distributed forensics network, *Proceedings of the Second International Workshop on Mathematical Methods, Models and Architectures for Computer Networks Security*, pp. 1–16, 2003.

[30] J. Sremack, Investigating real-time system forensics, *Proceedings of the First International Conference on Security and Privacy for Emerging Areas in Communication Networks*, pp. 25–32, 2005.

[31] A. Vorobiev and J. Han, Security attack ontology for web services, *Proceedings of the Second International Conference on Semantics, Knowledge and Grid*, p. 42, 2006.

[32] W. Wang and T. Daniels, Building evidence graphs for network forensics analysis, *Proceedings of the Twenty-First Annual Computer Security Applications Conference*, pp. 254–266, 2005.

[33] W. Yu, P. Supthaweesuk and D. Aravind, Trustworthy web services based on testing, *Proceedings of the IEEE International Workshop on Service-Oriented System Engineering*, pp. 159–169, 2005.

Chapter 15

DETECTING REMOTE EXPLOITS USING DATA MINING

Mohammad Masud, Latifur Khan, Bhavani Thuraisingham, Xinran Wang, Peng Liu and Sencun Zhu

Abstract   This paper describes the design and implementation of DExtor, a data-mining-based exploit code detector that protects network services. DExtor operates under the assumption that normal traffic to network services contains only data whereas exploits contain code. The system is first trained with real data containing exploit code and normal traffic. Once it is trained, DExtor is deployed between a web service and its gateway or firewall, where it operates at the application layer to detect and block exploit code in real time. Tests using large volumes of normal and attack traffic demonstrate that DExtor can detect almost all the exploit code with negligible false alarm rates.

Keywords: Server attacks, exploit code, data mining, attack detection

1.   Introduction

Remote exploits are often used by attackers to gain control of hosts that run vulnerable services or software. Typically, an exploit is sent as an input to a remote vulnerable service to hijack the control flow of machine instruction execution. Attackers sometimes inject executable code in the exploit that is run after a successful hijacking attempt. We refer to such remote code-carrying exploits as "exploit code."

Several approaches have been proposed for analyzing network flows to detect exploit code [1, 4, 8–11]. An attack can be prevented if an exploit is detected and intercepted while it is in transit to a server. This approach is compatible with legacy code and does not require changes to the underlying computing infrastructure. Our solution, DExtor, follows this strategy. In particular, it uses data mining to address the general problem of exploit code detection.

Please use the following format when citing this chapter:

Masud, M., Khan, L., Thuraisingham, B., Wang, X., Liu, P. and Zhu, S., 2008, in IFIP International Federation for Information Processing, Volume 285; *Advances in Digital Forensics IV*; Indrajit Ray, Sujeet Shenoi; (Boston: Springer), pp. 177–189.

Exploit code usually consists of three parts: (i) a NOP sled at the beginning of the exploit, (ii) a payload in the middle, and (iii) return addresses at the end. The NOP sled is a sequence of NOP instructions; the payload contains the attack code; the return addresses point to the code to be executed. Thus, exploit code always carries some valid executables in the NOP sled and payload. It is considered to be an "attack input" to the corresponding vulnerable service; inputs that do not exploit a vulnerability are referred to as "normal inputs." For example, in the case of a vulnerable HTTP server, benign HTTP requests are normal inputs while requests that exploit a vulnerability are attack inputs. If we assume that normal inputs only contain data, then exploit code detection reduces to a code detection problem.

Chinchani and Berg [1] justify this assumption by maintaining that "the nature of communication to and from network services is predominantly or exclusively data and not executable code." However, certain exploits do not contain code (e.g., integer overflow exploits and return-to-libc exploits); we do not consider such exploits in this work. It is also worth mentioning that exploit code detection is fundamentally different from malware detection, which attempts to identify the presence of malicious content in an executable.

Our data mining approach uses three types of features to differentiate between attack inputs and normal inputs. They are: (i) useful instruction count, (ii) instruction usage frequency, and (iii) code vs. data length. The process has several steps. First, training data consisting of attack inputs and normal inputs is collected. Next, the training examples are disassembled. Following this, the three types of features are extracted from the disassembled data. Several classifiers (Support Vector Machine (SVM), Bayes Net, Decision Tree (J48) and Boosted J48) are then trained and the best classifier is selected as the classification model. When DExtor is deployed in a networking environment, it intercepts inputs destined to the network service and tests them against the classification model; attack inputs are blocked in real time.

DExtor has several advantages over existing exploit code detection techniques. DExtor is compatible with legacy code and transparent to the services it protects. The current version operates on Windows platforms with the Intel 32-bit architecture, but can be adapted to any operating system and hardware simply by modifying the disassembler. Also, DExtor does not require any signature generation and matching. Finally, DExtor is robust against most attack-side obfuscation techniques.

DExtor also has forensic applications. For example, it can be used to analyze network traffic sent to a server before a crash or compromise.

This helps determine whether the incident was caused by a code-carrying exploit and also assists in identifying the source of the attack.

2. Related Work

Several techniques have been proposed for detecting exploits in network traffic and protecting network services. The three main categories of techniques are signature matching, anomaly detection and machine-code analysis.

Signature matching is used in intrusion detection systems such as Snort [8] and Bro [4]. These systems maintain a signature database of known exploits; an alert is raised when traffic matches a signature in the database. Signature-based systems are easy to implement, but they are defeated by new exploits as well as by polymorphism and metamorphism. DExtor does not use signature matching to detect exploit code.

Anomaly detection techniques identify deviations in traffic patterns and raise alerts. Wang and co-workers [11] have designed PAYL, a payload-based system that detects exploit code by computing several byte-level statistical measures. Other anomaly-based detection systems are an enhanced version of PAYL [10] and FLIPS [5]. DExtor differs from anomaly-based systems in two respects. First, anomaly-based systems are trained using normal traffic characteristics and detect deviations from these characteristics; DExtor considers both normal and attack traffic in building its classification model. Second, DExtor uses instruction patterns instead of raw byte patterns to construct its classification model.

Machine code analysis techniques apply binary disassembly and static analysis of network traffic to detect the presence of executables. DExtor falls in this category. Toth and Kruegel [9] have used binary disassembly to find long sequences of executable instructions and identify the presence of a NOP sled. DExtor also applies binary disassembly, but it does not need to identify a NOP sled. Like DExtor, Chinchani and Berg [1] detect exploit code based on the assumption that normal traffic should contain no code. They apply disassembly and static analysis, and identify several structural patterns and characteristics of code-carrying traffic. However, unlike DExtor, their detection approach is rule based. SigFree [12] also disassembles inputs to server processes and applies static analysis to detect the presence of code. It applies a code abstraction technique to locate useful instructions in the disassembled byte stream and raises an alert when the useful instruction count exceeds a predetermined threshold. DExtor applies the same disassembly technique as SigFree, but does not use a fixed threshold. Instead,

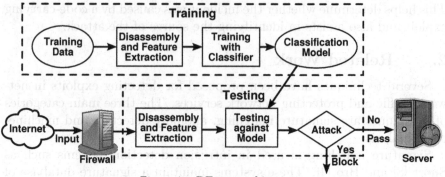

Figure 1. DExtor architecture.

it applies data mining to extract features and uses them to distinguish between normal traffic and exploits.

3.   DExtor

This section describes the DExtor architecture and its main components.

3.1   DExtor Architecture

DExtor is deployed in a network between a network service and its gateway or firewall (Figure 1). It is first trained offline with real instances of attacks (e.g., exploits) and normal inputs (e.g., HTTP requests), and a classification model is constructed. Training consists of three steps: disassembly, feature extraction and classification. When it is deployed in a network, DExtor intercepts and analyzes all inputs to the service in real time; inputs that are identified as attacks are blocked.

3.2   Data Disassembly

The disassembly algorithm is similar to that used by SigFree [12]. Each input to the server is considered to be a byte sequence. There may be more than one valid assembly instruction sequences corresponding to a given byte sequence. The disassembler uses an "instruction sequence distiller" to filter redundant and illegal instruction sequences. The main steps of this process are:

- Step 1: Generate instruction sequences

- Step 2: Prune subsequences

- Step 3: Discard smaller sequences

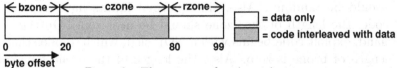

Figure 2. Three zones of an input instance.

- Step 4: Remove illegal sequences

- Step 5: Identify useful instructions

3.3 Feature Extraction

Feature extraction is the heart of DExtor's data mining approach. Three important features are used: (i) useful instruction count, (ii) instruction usage frequency, and (iii) code vs. data length.

- **Useful Instruction Count:** The useful instruction count (UIC) is the number of useful instructions found in Step 5 of the disassembly process. This feature is important because a real executable should have a large number of useful instructions; on the other hand, pure data should have no useful instructions.

- **Instruction Usage Frequency:** The instruction usage frequency (IUF) is the frequency of an instruction in a normal or attack sample. Intuitively, normal data should not have any bias toward any specific instruction or set of instructions. Thus, normal data should have a random IUF distribution. On the other hand, since exploit code performs specific (malicious) activities, it must have a bias toward a set of instructions and its IUF distribution should have some pattern.

- **Code vs. Data Length:** Exploit code has a NOP sled, payload and return addresses. Consequently, each input instance is divided into three zones: beginning zone (bzone), code zone (czone) and remainder zone (rzone) (Figure 2). Typically, the bzone corresponds to the first few bytes of an input that could not be disassembled and contains only data. The czone follows the bzone and contains the bytes that were successfully disassembled; it probably contains some code. The rzone contains the remaining bytes in the input that cannot be disassembled; it generally contains only data.

  The normalized lengths (in bytes) of the three zones should have different distributions for normal inputs and attack inputs. Intuitively, normal inputs should have the czone at any location with equal probability, implying that the bzone and rzone distributions should be random. Also, since normal inputs have little to no code, the length of the czone should be near zero. On the other hand, exploit code begins with a NOP sled, which implies that the length of bzone is zero. Also, the length of the czone for exploit code should be greater than that for normal inputs. Thus, the differences in the distributions of zone lengths for normal and attack inputs can be used to identify the type of input.

3.4   Feature Combination

The features computed for each input sample are: (i) UIC – a single integer, (ii) IUF – k integers denoting the instruction frequencies (k is the number of different instructions in the training data), and (iii) CDL – three real numbers corresponding to the lengths of bzone, czone and rzone. Thus, $k + 4$ features are considered: the first $k + 1$ feature values are integers and the last three are real numbers. These $k + 4$ features constitute the combined feature vector for an input instance.

3.5   Classification

The Support Vector Machine (SVM), Bayes Net, Decision Tree (J48) and Boosted J48 are used for classification. The SVM classifier is robust to noise and high dimensionality; also, it can be fine-tuned to perform efficiently in a problem domain. The Bayes Net classifier is capable of finding the interdependencies existing between different attributes. The Decision Tree (J48) classifier has an excellent feature selection capability, and requires much less training and testing time than other classifiers. The Boosted J48 classifier is useful because of its ensemble methods.

4.   Experimental Setup and Results

This section describes the experimental setup and results.

4.1   Data Set

The data set contained real exploit code as well as normal traffic to web servers. Strong efforts were undertaken to ensure that the data set was as diverse, unbiased and realistic as possible.

The exploit code was obtained by generating twenty unencrypted exploits using the Metasploit framework [7]. Next, nine polymorphic engines (ADMmutate [6], clet [2], Alpha2, CountDown, JumpCallAdditive, Jumpiscodes, Pex, PexFnstenvMov and PexFnstenvSub) were applied to the unencrypted exploits. Each polymorphic engine was used to generate 1,000 exploits, yielding a collection of 9,000 exploits.

The normal inputs were traces of HTTP requests/responses to/from a web server. The traces were collected by installing a client-side proxy that monitored and captured all incoming and outgoing messages. More than 12,000 messages containing HTTP requests and responses were collected. The responses comprised text (.javascript, .html, .xml), applications (x-javascript, .pdf, .xml), images (.gif, .jpeg, .png), audio (.wav), and flash content.

Two types of evaluation were performed on the data. First, five-fold cross validation was conducted to measure the accuracy and the false positive and false negative rates. Second, the performance of the classifiers was tested on new exploits. This was done by training a classifier using the exploits generated by eight of the nine polymorphic engines and testing it using the exploits generated by the ninth engine. The test was performed nine times by rotating the polymorphic engine that was tested. Normal examples were distributed in the training set and test set in equal proportions.

4.2   Experiments

The experiments were run on a 2 GHz Windows XP machine with 1 GB RAM. The algorithms were written in Java and compiled with JDK version 1.5.0_06. The Weka ML Toolbox [13] was used for the classification tasks. SVM classification used the C-Support Vector Classifier (C-SVC) with a polynomial kernel and $\gamma = 0.01$. Bayes Net used a simple estimator with $\alpha = 0.5$ and a hill-climbing search for the network learning. J48 used tree pruning with $C = 0.25$. Ten iterations of the AdaBoost algorithm were performed to generate ten models. Each of the three features was tested alone on a classifier (with the classifier being trained and tested with the same feature).

4.3   Results

Three metrics were used to evaluate the performance of DExtor: accuracy (ACC) and the false positive (FP) and false negative (FN) rates. ACC is the percentage of correctly classified instances, FP is the percentage of negative instances incorrectly classified as positive instances, and FN is the percentage of positive instances incorrectly classified as negative instances.

Table 1 presents the performance of the classifiers for various features. The highest accuracy (99.96%) was obtained for DExtor's combined feature (Comb) with the Boosted J48 classifier. The other features have lower accuracies than the combined feature for all the classification techniques. Also, the combined feature has the lowest false positive

Table 1. Performance of classifiers for different features.

Feature	IUC	IUF	CDL	Comb
Metric	ACC/FP/FN	ACC/FP/FN	ACC/FP/FN	ACC/FP/FN
SVM	75.0/3.3/53.9	99.7/0.2/0.1	92.7/12.4/0.6	99.8/0.1/0.2
Bayes Net	89.8/7.9/13.4	99.6/0.4/0.4	99.6/0.2/0.6	99.6/0.1/0.9
J48	89.8/7.9/13.4	99.5/0.3/0.2	99.7/0.3/0.3	99.9/0.2/0.1
Boosted J48	89.7/7.8/13.7	99.8/0.1/0.1	99.7/0.3/0.5	99.96/0.0/0.1
SigFree		38.5/0.2/88.5		

rate (0.0%) obtained with Boosted J48. The lowest false negative rate was also obtained for the combined feature (0.1%). In summary, the combined feature with Boosted J48 classifier produced near perfect detection.

The last row of Table 1 shows the accuracy and false alarm rates of SigFree with the same data set. SigFree used UIC with a fixed threshold of 15. It has a low false positive rate (0.2%), a high false negative rate (88.5%) and an overall accuracy of only 38.5%.

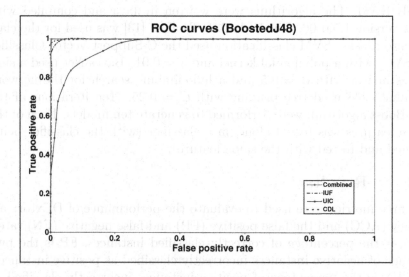

Figure 3. ROC curves for different features with BoostedJ48.

Figure 3 shows the receiver operating characteristic (ROC) curves for different features with the BoostedJ48 classifier. The area under the curve (AUC) is the highest for the combined feature (which is 0.999). The ROC curves for the other classifiers have similar characteristics; they are not presented due to space limitations.

Table 2. Effectiveness at detecting new exploits.

Classifier	SVM	BNet	J48	BJ48
Metric	ACC/FP/FN	ACC/FP/FN	ACC/FP/FN	ACC/FP/FN
Admutate	86.4/0.2/31.7	57.4/0.0/100	98.2/0.0/4.3	99.7/0.0/0.6
Alpha2	99.9/0.07/ 0.0	56.4/0.0/100	56.4/0.0/100	56.4/0.0/100
Clet	100/0.0/0.0	99.6/0.07/0.8	99.9/0.1/0.0	99.9/0.07/0.0
CountDown	99.8/0.4/0.0	100/0.0/0.0	100/0.0/0.0	99.8/0.3/0.0
JmpCallAdditive	100/0.0/0.0	98.1/0.0/4.6	99.9/0.1/0.0	100/0.0/0.0
JumpisCode	99.4/0.08/1.4	96.2/0.08/8.8	99.9/0.07/0.0	99.9/0.07/0.1
Pex	99.7/0.2/0.4	99.4/0.0/1.4	99.8/0.2/0.2	99.8/0.1/0.3
PexFnStenvMov	99.9/0.0/0.0	99.1/0.0/2.1	99.9/0.07/0.1	99.9/0.0/0.2
PexFnStenvSub	99.7/0.2/0.3	99.3/0.0/1.7	99.8/0.08/0.1	99.9/0.08/0.0

Table 2 shows DExtor's ability to detect new kinds of exploits. Each row reports the detection accuracies and false alarm rates for one particular engine-generated exploit. As described earlier, each classifier was trained using the exploits generated by the eight other engines and tested using exploits from the ninth engine. For each engine, the training set contained 8,000 exploits and about 10,500 randomly selected normal samples, and the test set contained 1,000 exploits and about 1,500 randomly chosen normal samples. The results in Table 2 show that all the classifiers successfully detected the new exploits with an accuracy of 99% or higher.

The total training time was less than 30 minutes, including disassembly time, feature extraction time and classifier training time. This amounts to about 37 ms per kilobyte of input. The average testing time for the combined feature set was 23 ms per kilobyte of input, including disassembly time, feature value computation time and classifier prediction time. SigFree, on the other hand, required 18.5 ms for testing each kilobyte of input. Since training is performed offline, DExtor requires only 24% more running time than SigFree. Thus, the price-performance trade-off is in favor of DExtor.

4.4 Analysis of Results

Figure 4 (left-hand side) shows the IUF distributions of the 30 most frequently used instructions in normal inputs and attack inputs. Clear differences are seen in the two distributions. The first five instructions have high frequencies (> 11) for attack inputs, but have zero frequencies for normal inputs. The next sixteen instructions in attack inputs have frequencies close to two while the corresponding frequencies for normal

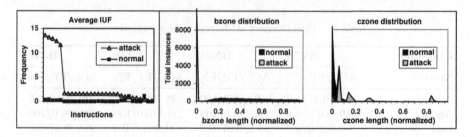

Figure 4. Instruction usage frequencies and zone length distributions.

inputs are again near zero. An attacker who intends to write exploit code that mimics normal inputs should avoid using these 21 instructions, but it is difficult to create exploits without using these instructions.

Figure 4 also presents the distributions of the CDL feature values. The histograms show the numbers of input samples having specific lengths (as a fraction of total input size) for bzone (center) and czone (right-hand side). The histograms are generated by dividing the entire range of normalized bzone and czone lengths ([0, 1]) into 50 equal-sized bins, and counting the number of input instances that fall in each bin. Note that most of the attack samples in the bzone histogram have values in the first bin (i.e., [0, 0.02)); on the other hand, the bzone values for normal samples are spread over all the bins. Therefore, an attacker wishing to mimic normal traffic should craft exploits that do not have any code in the first 10% of the exploit; but this is difficult to accomplish because exploits begin with a NOP sled. Similarly, the czone histogram shows that most of the normal samples have czone values in the range [0, 0.05] whereas attack samples mostly have czone values greater than 0.05. Therefore, in order to mimic normal traffic, an attacker should keep his code length within 5% of the exploit's length. For a 200-byte exploit, this leaves only 10 bytes for the attack code – including the NOP sled, making it extremely difficult to write the exploit.

5.   DExtor Characteristics

This section discusses the robustness of DExtor's exploit code detection methodology along with its limitations.

5.1   Robustness

DExtor is immune to instruction re-ordering because instruction order is not considered in exploit code detection. Also, detection is unaffected by the insertion of junk instructions as this only serves to increase the frequencies of the junk instructions. Likewise, DExtor is immune to instruction replacement as long as all the most frequently used instruc-tions are not replaced. DExtor is also robust against register renaming and memory re-ordering because registers and memory locations are not considered in exploit detection. Obfuscation by inserting junk bytes can affect the disassembler, especially when junk bytes are inserted at lo-cations that are not reachable at run-time. However, this problem is addressed by the recursive traversal strategy employed by the disassem-bly algorithm [3].

5.2 Limitations

DExtor is partially affected by branch function obfuscation, which obscures the control flow of an executable so that disassembly cannot proceed. Currently, there is no general solution to this problem. When branch function obfuscation is present, DExtor is likely to produce frag-mented code blocks, missing some of the original code. This does not impact detection unless the missed blocks contain large numbers of in-structions.

DExtor is certainly limited by its processing speed. Currently, DEx-tor has a throughput of 42 KB/sec in a real environment. Such a low throughput is unacceptable for an intrusion detection system that must handle several gigabits per second. Fortunately, DExtor is intended to protect just one network service, which requires much less throughput.

Nevertheless, the throughput issue can be addressed using faster hard-ware and optimizing all the software components (disassembler, feature extractor and classifier). Also, certain incoming traffic can be excluded from analysis. For example, because exploit code is typically a few kilo-bytes in length, bulk inputs to the server with size greater than a few hundred kilobytes are unlikely to be exploit code. Both these solutions should increase DExtor's throughput sufficiently to enable it to operate effectively in real-time environments.

6. Conclusions

DExtor uses data mining very effectively to detect and block exploit code. Designed to operate at the application layer, DExtor is positioned between the server and its gateway or firewall. It is completely trans-parent to the service it protects, and can be deployed as a stand-alone component or coupled with a proxy server. DExtor is robust against most attack-side obfuscation techniques. Tests using large volumes of normal and attack traffic demonstrate that DExtor can detect exploit code with very high accuracy and negligible false alarm rates. Further-more, DExtor is able to detect new types of exploits with high accuracy.

DExtor is also useful in forensic investigations, especially in determining whether a crash or compromise was caused by a code-carrying exploit. In addition, it can assist in identifying the source of the exploit.

Acknowledgements

This research was supported by the Air Force Office of Scientific Research under Contract No. FA9550-06-1-0045 and by the National Science Foundation under CAREER Grant No. CNS-0643906.

References

[1] R. Chinchani and E. Berg, A fast static analysis approach to detect exploit code inside network flows, *Proceedings of the Eighth International Symposium on Recent Advances in Intrusion Detection*, pp. 284–308, 2005.

[2] T. Detristan, T. Ulenspiegel, Y. Malcom and M. von Underduk, Polymorphic shellcode engine using spectrum analysis, *Phrack*, vol. 11(61), 2003.

[3] C. Kruegel, W. Robertson, F. Valeur and G. Vigna, Static disassembly of obfuscated binaries, *Proceedings of the Thirteenth USENIX Security Symposium*, pp. 255–270, 2004.

[4] Lawrence Berkeley National Laboratory, Bro intrusion detection system, Berkeley, California (bro-ids.org), 2007.

[5] M. Locasto, K. Wang, A. Keromytis and S. Stolfo, FLIPS: Hybrid adaptive intrusion prevention, *Proceedings of the Eighth International Symposium on Recent Advances in Intrusion Detection*, pp. 82–101, 2005.

[6] S. Macaulay, ADMmutate: Polymorphic shellcode engine (www.ktwo.ca/security.html), 2007.

[7] Metasploit, The Metasploit Project (www.metasploit.com).

[8] Snort.org, Snort (www.snort.org).

[9] T. Toth and C. Kruegel, Accurate buffer overflow detection via abstract payload execution, *Proceedings of the Fifth International Symposium on Recent Advances in Intrusion Detection*, pp. 274–291, 2002.

[10] K. Wang, G. Cretu and S. Stolfo, Anomalous payload-based network intrusion detection and signature generation, *Proceedings of the Eighth International Symposium on Recent Advances in Intrusion Detection*, pp. 227–246, 2005.

[11] K. Wang and S. Stolfo, Anomalous payload-based network intrusion detection, *Proceedings of the Seventh International Symposium on Recent Advances in Intrusion Detection*, pp. 203–222, 2004.

[12] X. Wang, C. Pan, P. Liu and S. Zhu. SigFree: A signature-free buffer overflow attack blocker, *Proceedings of the Fifteenth USENIX Security Symposium*, pp. 225-240, 2006.

[13] Weka, Weka 3: Data mining software in Java, University of Waikato, Hamilton, New Zealand (www.cs.waikato.ac.nz/ml/weka).

VII

PORTABLE ELECTRONIC DEVICE FORENSICS

Chapter 16

USING SENSOR DIRT FOR TOOLMARK ANALYSIS OF DIGITAL PHOTOGRAPHS

Martin Olivier

Abstract   Dust particles that collect on the image sensors of digital cameras often leave marks on the pictures taken with these cameras. The question
therefore arises whether these marks may be used for forensic identification of the camera used to take a specific picture. This paper considers
the question by investigating the impact of various camera and lens factors, such as focal length and recording format. A matching technique
involving grid overlay is proposed and the probability of false positive
matches is quantified. Initial results indicate that toolmark analysis
based on sensor dirt has potential as a forensic technique for camera
identification.

Keywords: Digital cameras, sensor dirt, toolmark analysis

1.   Introduction

The occurrence of dirt on the optical sensors of digital single lens
reflex (DSLR) cameras is a problem that is well known to professional
and amateur photographers [6]. These cameras have interchangeable
lenses; when a lens is removed, the potential exists for dust to enter the
film chamber of the camera. In addition, dust may stick to the rear of
a newly-attached lens. Dust particles introduced into a DSLR camera
often make their way to the camera sensor, an electrically-charged device
that attracts particulate matter.

Dirt typically consists of silica, quartz, metallic, fiber and/or organic
particles [4]. The term "dust" is commonly used to refer to these particles, but "dirt" or "contaminants" is arguably a more descriptive term.
In the case of photocopier identification, marks left by such particles are
referred to as "trash" marks [9]. We prefer to use the term "dirt," but
use it interchangeably with the term "dust" in this paper.

Please use the following format when citing this chapter:

Olivier, M., 2008, in IFIP International Federation for Information Processing, Volume 285; *Advances in Digital
Forensics IV*; Indrajit Ray, Sujeet Shenoi; (Boston: Springer), pp. 193–206.

While dirt marks are a nuisance to photographers, they are potentially useful to forensic investigators. Since the marks appear on more or less any picture taken from the time particles stick to the image sensor to the time they are removed, they can help identify the specific camera that was used to take a picture of interest.

It is necessary to consider a number of provisos. Dirt may have been washed from a sensor after a picture was taken – just like fingerprints can be wiped from a murder weapon. Alternatively, the sensor could have been cleaned before a picture was taken, causing the picture to have no distinguishing marks – just like using gloves may prevent fingerprints from being left on a murder weapon. It is possible that the image could have been edited before it was "published," and such editing may have (purposefully or inadvertently) removed the distinguishing marks. Despite these shortcomings, we contend that sensor dirt has the potential to be useful in digital forensic investigations. The fact that it is common knowledge how to avoid leaving fingerprints at crime scenes has not made fingerprint evidence any less useful in criminal investigations.

Some modern cameras have mechanisms that prevent dirt from collecting on image sensors. However, as will be argued below, the problem (or opportunity) persists. In fact, some cameras are delivered with dirt on their sensors. Since removing dirt requires some skill, these cameras may carry the distinguishing marks for the rest of their lives.

This paper is intended as an early analysis of the extent to which sensor dirt may be used to associate a picture with a given camera. Two aspects are considered. The first is the impact of aperture, focal length and related factors on the appearance of sensor dirt in a picture. The second is how artifacts in a picture may be matched with a camera based on the dirt currently present on its image sensor.

2.　　Background

Toolmark analysis is a well-established branch of forensic science [7]. In the physical world, a tool may impress its form on another object or leave scratch marks as it rubs against the other object [9, 12]. In ballistics, for example, the firing pin impresses a mark on the cartridge that may be used to identify the firearm. As the round travels through the barrel, "striations" are scratched on it by imperfections in the barrel.

It is also important to distinguish between class and individual characteristics [9, 12]. The grooves in the barrel of a firearm produce marks on a round that travels through it; these marks may be shared by other firearms in the class (e.g., firearms of the same caliber or firearms made by the same manufacturer). On the other hand, striations on a round are caused by random imperfections in the barrel of the firearm that fired the round and are, therefore, unique to that firearm.

Digital cameras also leave marks on the images they produce. One example is image resolution (more specifically, image dimensions), which is determined by the sensor. Digital cameras also add metadata about images using EXIF tags [2] that typically include the camera make and model. Another example of a class characteristic is the image file format (usually JPEG). Also, some of the compression parameters may be specific to a class of cameras [10]. In the case of DSLR cameras (and some high-end compact cameras), the image may alternatively (or in addition) be recorded in the proprietary format of the vendor [6]. The term "RAW" is often used to refer to these formats. Since most RAW formats are specific to camera manufacturers, they may also be used to identify the class of camera that took a RAW-format picture.

The focus of this paper is on individual characteristics. Sensor dirt – like metal particles in the barrel of a firearm – are positioned by chance and should, therefore, be unique to a particular camera.

The identification of imaging equipment from the marks left by particles is not new. The photocopier used to make a specific copy may be identified by the "trash" marks on the copy [9]. However, a DSLR camera, unlike most other imaging systems, has large variations in the manner in which it may be used – in particular, the ability to be used with different lenses at various settings. The impact of a small aperture setting on the visibility of dirt marks is well known. We are not aware of any other work that has considered the impact of other settings in the forensic context.

Our strategy is to empirically determine the impact of various DSLR camera settings on the manner in which dirt marks are recorded. Once the variations are known, it becomes possible to state accurately whether a mark on an image could have been caused by a particle on a sensor or whether it is possible that two marks on two images could have been caused by the same particle. During this second phase, it becomes necessary to locate marks on images, and the work done to locate and eliminate such marks becomes useful. Zhou and Lin [14], for example, have conducted a detailed investigation of the formation and subsequent removal of artifacts caused by sensor dust.

Dirik, *et al.* [5] have proposed an approach for camera identification based on sensor dust. Their approach is to identify possible marks on pictures and then compare the marks on different pictures.

Our approach is closer to that of Zamfir, *et al.* [13], although their primary intention is to correct blemishes rather than to match a photograph to a camera. They have derived a theoretical model that predicts the position and size of artifacts on an image depending on the aperture and focal length. The calculations depend on calibration images to determine certain camera and lens properties. In contrast, we approach these measurements in an empirical manner, which enables us to consider more dimensions, such as image encoding. Our work also does not assume that the suspect lens is available for calibration. Unfortunately, for reasons of space, it is not possible to present a detailed comparison of the theoretical results of Zamfir, *et al.* with our empirical results. Such a comparison, which is clearly important, is left for future work.

Interested readers are referred to the books by Collins [6] and Hedgecoe [8] for additional information about photography, and to the Pentax K10D DSLR manual [11] for details about the camera used in this work.

3.   Artifacts

A spot caused by sensor dirt is referred to as a mark or "artifact." The appearance of an artifact may be influenced by various factors. Photographers are well aware that artifacts are more noticeable at small apertures. However, the largest aperture at which an artifact may be useful for forensic purposes is not yet known. This section presents an empirical study of the effect of aperture size and other factors on artifacts. Key factors that may impact the usefulness of an artifact include lens focal length, sensor sensitivity (or film speed), lens nature (zoom as opposed to fixed focal length), dirt on the rear lens element and the degree of "busyness" of the image in the area of an expected artifact.

It is probable that all these factors are to some extent dependent on one another. For example, the usability of an artifact at a given aperture may depend on sensor sensitivity. This gives rise to a multidimensional problem where a huge number of combinations have to be tested. However, since this is a preliminary study, the factors are considered independently instead of in combination. Also, the results reported in this paper are based on a single camera. Nevertheless, we believe that our study provides some useful insights while containing the complexity.

3.1   Experimental Setup

Our experiments used a Pentax K10D DSLR camera with an SMC Pentax-D FA Macro 50mm F2.8 set at F32 that was manually focused on a sheet of white paper 50cm away. Image quality was set to "best" and shake reduction was turned off. Filtered daylight in a simple light tent was used and the white balance set to daylight. Sensor sensitivity was set to ISO 100. We refer to the camera used in the experiments as the "experimental camera" and the picture of the white sheet as a "sensor shot." In the experiments described below, the base setup was used with all settings kept constant, except for the factor being considered, which was varied over a range of values.

A 20" LCD screen with 1,400 × 1,050 resolution was used to view the images. The resolution of the image sensor in the experimental camera was 3,872 × 2,592; this means that effectively 1,400 × 937 pixels (about 1.3 megapixels) were used to view the approximately 10 megapixels produced by the image sensor. Since each pixel on the screen represented approximately eight sensor pixels, small marks (in the region of eight or fewer pixels) would not have been observed.

To reduce the reliance on human observation, Adobe Premiere's fill tool was used to fill the backgrounds of the images with a pure white color. This made it possible to isolate artifacts precisely at the pixel level; the first non pure white pixel after background filling was taken to represent the edge of the artifact. Only artifacts that were visible on the LCD screen when it was initially viewed were considered after filling.

3.2 Dirt Configuration

The dust on the camera sensor was another constant; no dirt was added and no dirt was removed during the experiments. In fact, the camera's dust removal system was switched on for a significant period before the experiments were conducted and it was left on for the duration of the experiments. This meant that the observed dirt was probably stuck to the sensor; any new loose dirt that may have been introduced would, in all likelihood, have been shaken off.

One important issue was how to represent the dirt. A number of options were considered; dividing the sensor into a grid and identifying particles based on their grid positions seemed the most promising. One aspect that was not fully known before the work was started was the accuracy with which particle positions may be determined (this deserves attention in future work). The use of a grid makes it possible to determine the space (in pixels) between grid lines to a degree that is coarse enough to deal with possible imprecision in measurements but fine enough to yield reliable forensic conclusions.

The forensic use of particle positions requires a finely spaced grid; this issue is discussed in more detail in Section 4. However, the focus of this work was to evaluate the utility of the technique, not to make exact measurements. Consequently, a coarse grid of 15 × 10 pixels was employed in the experiments.

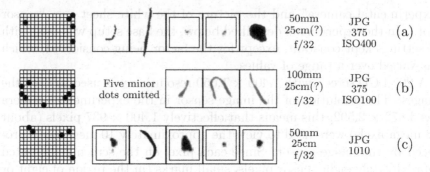

Figure 1. Comparison of three sensors.

Figure 1(c) uses such a grid to show the positions of dust particles in the experimental camera. A dot in a cell position indicates that some dust was observed on the corresponding portion of the sensor. To the right of the grid, individual dust particles are depicted in row-major order. We refer to such a diagram as a "sensor map."

Two scales are used to deal with different sized particles: smaller particles are doubled in size both horizontally and vertically. A double square frame around a particle indicates that doubling has been used. The second particle in Figure 1(c) starts at Row 301 from the top of the sensor and stretches over 54 pixel rows down to Row 355. (The middle row of this range corresponds to Row 2 of the grid.) 54 rows on the sensor correspond to a physical height for the dust particle of about 327μm. In contrast, the fourth particle in Figure 1(c) is much smaller; it occupies only six rows (about 36μm high), and is magnified in the figure to be visible at all.

Figure 1 shows the dirt on the experimental camera as well as dirt on two other sensors for comparison. Figure 1(a) is based on a sensor shot of the experimental camera that was taken some time before the experiments were conducted. The camera sensor was cleaned after this shot was taken and dirt was allowed to build up until the experiments were performed. Figure 1(b) is based on a sensor shot of a Pentax *ist DS also taken some time before the experiments. The sensor of the Pentax *ist DS only contained 6 megapixels; the figure has been adjusted so that similar sized particles are represented using similar sized images even though they cover fewer (but physically larger) pixels.

Figure 1 clearly illustrates that sensor dirt forms characteristic patterns. Even though a very low resolution grid is used, the patterns formed are very different. Moreover, the size and shape of the individual particles demonstrate unique characteristics.

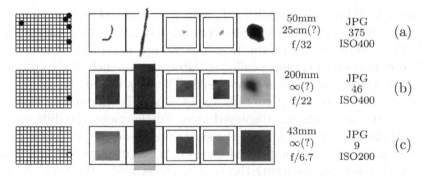

Figure 2. Spot occurrence in pictures.

On the negative side, the fact that two diagrams in the figure originated from the same camera clearly demonstrates that sensor patterns
are temporary. Sensors may be cleaned and may accumulate additional
dirt over time. Hence, such an analysis will only be useful if the camera
was seized soon after the picture of interest was taken. This limitation
may not be quite as serious as it seems. Cleaning a sensor requires some
dexterity and somewhat specialized tools. Hence, many people will allow
sensor dirt to accumulate until the effect becomes unbearable. Moreover,
some cameras are shipped with dirt on their sensors [3].

In fact, it is probable that the experimental camera was shipped with
dirt on its sensor. One spot, in particular, was visible from almost the
first picture taken. The sensor shot in Figure 1(a) was taken when the
camera was a few weeks old. Figure 2 repeats the sensor shot of Figure
1(a) and adds the corresponding regions from two early pictures taken
with the camera. A region consists of the pixels corresponding to the
observed particle and some additional bits around it. In the case of the
larger particles, ten additional bits were added on each side and, if space
permitted, ten more bits were added at the top and bottom. For smaller
particles, five bits were included at the sides, top and bottom. They were
then enlarged with the smaller picture, as was the case for the smaller
particles discussed earlier. The question is whether the sensor pattern in
Figure 2(a) and the corresponding areas from the pictures (contained in
Figures 2(b) and 2(c)) prove that they were taken with the same camera.

Figure 2 demonstrates the difficulty of using sensor dirt for camera
identification. The first four areas of the picture in Figure 2(b) are
simply too dark to observe any spots. The fifth spot is clearly present
and has a similar shape. However, it seems to be shifted to the left and is,
perhaps, a little higher and a little smaller. Is this enough to declare that
the picture matches the sensor? The remainder of this paper attempts
to address this question.

Figure 2(c) illustrates additional challenges involved in camera identification. Some of the areas are lighter and may have shown some spots
if particles were present at the time the picture was taken. Note that
since dirt particles may have collected later, the absence of a spot does
not prove that the camera was not used. The area in the extreme right
of Figure 2(c) does indeed contain a spot, but it is enlarged to the extent that it almost fills the displayed area. Furthermore, the differences
between the tone of the spot and the surrounding area are so subtle that
the spot disappears in the printed version. When displayed on a screen
(and with some imagination) the spot is discernible. However, it becomes clearer when a larger area is considered and when it is displayed
more densely. This suggests that our choice to use a border of five or ten
pixels may be too conservative. Nevertheless, it is not clear that a larger
area would be sufficient to link the picture positively to the sensor.

Some details about the camera settings appear to the right of the
sensor maps in Figure 2. Clearly, there are several differences between
the various cases, e.g., different focal lengths (50mm, an 18–200mm zoom
lens at 200mm and a 28–70mm zoom lens at 43mm), different sensor
speeds (ISO 200 and ISO 400) and different apertures (f/32, f/22 and
f/6.7). The impact of these factors on sensor shots is discussed below.

3.3   Encoding

The first issue to consider is the encoding format used to record an
image. Most high-end digital cameras offer a lossy compression encoding
(typically JPEG abbreviated as JPG), and a format in which all the
pixels (and some other information) are recorded without loss. While
TIFF was used in the past, most current cameras use a proprietary
RAW format. The experimental camera offers a RAW format known as
PEF. It also supports Adobe's DNG format, which may be used without
paying royalties and could lead the drive towards standardization [1].

The recording format must be considered because a lossy compression
technique (e.g., that used by JPG) may lose information about sensor
dirt, which may not be desirable. We say "may" because it is not clear if
it is best to use the same compression technique that was used to create
the suspect picture.

In fact, the situation is even more complex – cameras offer different compression levels, with higher compression levels typically yielding
lower quality images and vice versa. Our experiments did not test the
effect of different compression levels, but simply used the highest quality
level offered by the camera. Any differences seen between the JPG and
RAW images should be significantly more pronounced when lower qual-

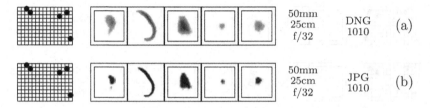

Figure 3. Comparison of JPG and DNG images.

ity levels are used. Since it did not seem to matter which RAW format was used (all RAW formats record all pixels), we decided to use DNG in our experiments.

Figure 3 shows the results of an experiment performed in this regard. As expected, JPG compression smoothed the transition between the blank sensor and the dark dirt, resulting in smaller – albeit apparently darker – marks on the image (Figure 3(b)). JPG compression removed between two and six pixels from the height or width of the mark. This is rather significant given the fact that the marks (in JPG) ranged in length dimension from four pixels to 51 pixels. Given the fact that the JPG encoding modifies the observed particles, we decided to use DNG in the remainder of our work.

3.4   Focus Distance

The second experiment with encoding in the previous section suggests another issue that needs to be considered: Does focus distance have an impact on how marks are rendered? In fact, focus distance had a minor effect on the rendering of the artifacts. However, space limitations do not permit a full discussion in this paper.

A more important observation was that the positions of the marks were affected by focus distance. This observation is predicted by the model of Zamfir, *et al.* [13]. The observation suggests that the sensor shot should ideally be taken with focus distance set to the same range as that for the suspect picture. Further study is required to determine whether marks recorded at different focus distances can be matched reliably. This could determine the finest grid resolution that may be used to match mark positions.

3.5   Lighting

Lighting was considered as a possible reason for mark size variations in the previous section. Artificial lighting can be better controlled than natural light that was used in that particular case. Hence, that part

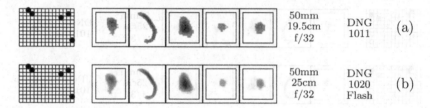

Figure 4. Comparison of flash and daylight photography.

of the experiment was repeated using an electronic flash. The results are presented in Figure 4. Note that the differences appear to be more pronounced than they were in reality. The sizes of most marks differed by zero, one or two pixels; one differed by three pixels. These variations did not seem to be significant enough to warrant further investigation. We assumed natural light suffices, which is useful when longer lenses are tested (as discussed below).

3.6   Aperture

As suggested earlier in the paper, focal length may affect the rendering of marks. Many of the lenses available for the experiments could not be set to an aperture of f/32 – as was used in the testing procedure up to this point. Hence, the smallest common aperture setting of f/22 was used. Before discussing the impact of focal length, we examine the effect of aperture on the experimental observations.

It is well known that sensor dirt causes the most problems at small apertures, primarily because dirt is most visible at small apertures. Consequently, small apertures were chosen in the experimental study (f/32, in general, and f/22 for the tests involving focal lengths). Experience has shown that sensor marks quickly become less defined at larger apertures, but they remain observable and their positions are clearly marked. Filling the background with white helped us to conduct the experiments in a repeatable manner and enabled precise measurements of the position, size and shape of dirt marks down to the pixel level.

Since it was known that larger apertures would not provide such precision, aperture testing was scheduled as the last test in the current series. However, we were surprised at the rate at which precision was lost.

The 50mm lens focused at infinity was still used in the aperture tests; it was set to apertures of f/32, f/22, f/16, f/11, f/5.6, f/4 and f/2.8. As expected, the dirt marks became "softer."

At the f/22 setting, all five sensor marks were visible in the original image; however, filling the background with white erased the two smaller marks and drastically reduced the size of the three remaining marks. At aperture settings larger than f/22, filling the background erased all the marks, which rendered exact comparative testing impossible.

The three larger marks remained visible up to f/5.6, and some at f/4. Even at f/5.6, the color variation between mark and background was so subtle that observability depended on specific screen settings. At f/4, it was only possible to observe the marks after "tweaking," which, of course, touches on the fundamental premises of experimentation. Obviously, a specialized tool that could identify marks more objectively would be very useful in future experiments.

The shape of the most distinctive mark was still recognizable at f/16 and, perhaps, even f/11; the other marks lost their distinctive shapes at f/22. The sizes of the marks were (according to a subjective assessment) significantly affected by aperture. Consequently, it appears that mark position is the most useful attribute. Size may have to be adjusted depending on various factors in order for it to be useful. Shape offers, perhaps, the most convincing proof, when it is observable, especially when smaller apertures are used.

In summary, larger apertures cause a loss of shape and an increase in the size of marks, and may cause some marks to disappear. Many marks remain discernible up to fairly large apertures (even f/4). Moreover, the marks that remain visible do not change their position. These observations are interesting, but their quantification requires a tool that can objectively isolate marks.

3.7   Focal Lengths

The following focal lengths were tested: 500mm, 170mm, 100mm, 50mm, 40mm, 17mm and 10mm. The first two and last two used zoom lenses at their extreme settings; the others used fixed focal length lenses. The fisheye zoom lens was used for the 17mm and 10mm settings.

Observations were harder to make than expected. One difficulty stemmed from the fact that an aperture of f/22 was used. In all cases this eliminated the smaller two marks once the background was filled with white. (Subjectively, all marks were initially present.) Another problem arose because the white plane used in the experiments proved to be too small at the shorter focal lengths. This was easily remedied in the case of the 40mm lens However, for the 10mm lens, the field of view across the diagonal was 180° and it was not possible to obtain an evenly lit white background. The same problem occurred for the 17mm setting. While the marks were clearly visible, the edges introduced by the borders of the light tent and the fact that all the sides of the light tent were not evenly lit caused the background filling to fail.

For some reason, only one mark remained for the 500mm lens after filling. Its position moved 16 pixels horizontally and 13 pixels vertically between the 500mm and 50mm settings, with most of the movement (12 and 12 pixels, respectively) occurring from 500mm to 170mm. The other marks that were present from 170mm down, showed very little movement (up to four pixels horizontally and six pixels vertically) until the point where measurement became an issue given the background edge marks. Size remained virtually unchanged (with a four pixel change in one case). However, as mentioned above, comparing these results with others in the paper is questionable given the impact of the f/22 aperture used.

4.   Camera Identification

It was argued earlier in the paper that matching an image to a sensor may be based on the position, shape and size of dirt marks. We have pointed out that particle shape requires a suitable aperture and further investigation of the effects of particle size is required. Consequently, the primary attribute for matching at this point is particle position.

As discussed above, a grid is very useful for comparing the positions of dirt particles. We propose that the grid be placed so that a mark does not move from one grid cell to another due to the focal length or focus distance or other factors. Having assumed that an $m \times n$ grid has been overlaid in such a manner, the question is: Given some marks on the image and given some marks on the sensor, what is the probability that the image has been produced by the sensor? To quantify the probability, we assume that a dirt particle will stick to any part of the sensor with equal probability.

In the following calculations, for $k, j \in I\!N$, the term $k^{!j}$ denotes $k \times (k-1) \times (k-2) \times (k-j+1)$, i.e., the product of the j successive integers ranging from k to $k-j+1$. Note that $k^{!j} = \frac{k!}{(k-j)!}$.

Assume that the picture displays p marks and that there are s (visible) particles on the sensor. Further, assume that c of these marks are in corresponding cells of the overlaid grid.

The probability of a Type I (false positive) error is given by:

$$P(c) = \binom{s}{c} \frac{(mn - p)^{!(s-c)} \cdot p^{!c}}{(mn)^{!s}}.$$

The derivation of this probability expression is not provided due to a shortage of space. Interested readers may contact the author for the derivation.

Type II errors (false negatives) are expected to occur frequently. A dust particle may be deposited on the sensor, appear in a single picture and then fall from the sensor. Alternatively, the sensor may be cleaned between pictures. Also, camera settings, such as aperture, may cause some particles not to appear in the picture.

Given these considerations, what do the formulas in this section mean in practice? The marks observed in this study suggest that a 300×200 (or finer) grid may be practical. A match of exactly one cell on such a grid implies false positives for 0.0017% of such cases based on position alone. A false positive match of exactly two cells ($s = p = c$) occurs with a frequency of 2.7×10^{-8}%. Partial matches may not be as convincing, but may be perfectly adequate. In fact, our experiments indicate that a sensor with two marks that matches the position of one mark correctly links a picture to a camera in more than 99.996% of test cases.

5. Conclusions

Dirt particles on a camera sensor can be used as toolmarks to link a picture to the camera. Several factors, including focus distance and aperture, affect the rendering of dirt marks on camera images. A matching technique involving grid overlay was proposed and the probability of false positive matches was quantified. The results indicate that toolmark analysis based on sensor dirt is a promising technique for camera identification.

More work needs to be done to fully understand the effects of individual factors and combinations of factors on image rendering. Experiments should also be conducted on multiple cameras and dirt configurations. Additionally, some of the assumptions used in this preliminary work, e.g., the random distribution of dirt particles, should be verified empirically.

Camera dust removal systems are being continuously improved. However, because a few isolated marks appear to be more useful than myriad marks, sensor cleaning may, in fact, have a positive impact on the potential of the technique, as long as dust removal systems are not 100% effective.

References

[1] Adobe Systems, Digital Negative (DNG) Specification (version 1.1.0.0), San Jose, California (www.adobe.com/products/dng/pdfs /dng_spec.pdf), 2005.

[2] P. Alvarez, Using extended file information (EXIF) file headers in digital evidence analysis, *International Journal of Digital Evidence*, vol. 2(3), pp. 1–5, 2004.

[3] Anonymous, Pentax K10D, *Practical Photography*, pp. 110–113, February 2007.

[4] Delkin, *SensorScope and Digital Duster System Cleaning Guide*, Inglewood, California, 2006.

[5] A. Dirik, H. Sencar and N. Memon, Source camera identification based on sensor dust characteristics, *Proceedings of the IEEE Workshop on Signal Processing Applications for Public Security and Forensics*, pp. 1–6, 2007.

[6] J. Freeman, *Collins Digital SLR Handbook*, Collins, London, United Kingdom, 2007.

[7] N. Genge, *The Forensic Casebook: The Science of Crime Scene Investigation*, Ballantine Books, New York, 2002.

[8] J. Hedgecoe, *The New Manual of Photography*, DK Publishing, New York, 2003.

[9] S. James and J. Nordby (Eds.), *Forensic Science: An Introduction to Scientific and Investigative Techniques*, CRC Press, Boca Raton, Florida, 2005.

[10] J. Lukas, J. Fridrich and M. Goljan, Digital camera identification from sensor pattern noise, *IEEE Transactions on Information Forensics and Security*, vol. 1(2), pp. 205–214, 2006.

[11] Pentax Corporation, *K10D Operating Manual*, Tokyo, Japan (www .pentaxslr.com/files/scms_docs/K10D_Manual.pdf), 2006.

[12] R. Saferstein, *Criminalistics – An Introduction to Forensic Science*, Prentice-Hall, Englewood Cliffs, New Jersey, 2007.

[13] A. Zamfir, A. Drimbarean, M. Zamfir, V. Buzuloiu, E. Steinberg and D. Ursu, An optical model of the appearance of blemishes in digital photographs, in *Proceedings of SPIE (Volume 6502) – Digital Photography III*, R. Martin, J. DiCarlo and N. Sampat (Eds.), SPIE, Bellingham, Washington, 2007.

[14] C. Zhou and S. Lin, Removal of image artifacts due to sensor dust, *Proceedings of the IEEE Conference on Computer Vision and Pattern Recognition*, pp. 1–8, 2007.

Chapter 17

A NEW FEATURE-BASED METHOD FOR SOURCE CAMERA IDENTIFICATION

Fanjie Meng, Xiangwei Kong and Xingang You

Abstract   The identification of image acquisition sources is an important problem in digital image forensics. This paper introduces a new feature-based method for digital camera identification. The method, which is based on an analysis of the imaging pipeline and digital camera processing operations, employs bi-coherence and wavelet coefficient features extracted from digital images. The sequential forward feature selection algorithm is used to select features, and a support vector machine is used as the classifier for source camera identification. Experiments indicate that the source camera identification method based on bi-coherence and wavelet coefficient features is both efficient and reliable.

Keywords: Source camera identification, bi-coherence, wavelet coefficients

1.   Introduction

The improving performance and the falling cost of digital cameras have led to their widespread use. Compared with their analog counterparts, digital cameras provide photographers with immediate visual feedback and the pictures can be shared conveniently by electronic means. Because of these advantages, the general public as well as law enforcement agencies are rapidly replacing analog cameras with digital versions [14]. On the other hand, it is easy even for amateurs to manipulate the content of digital images without leaving any obvious traces. Thus, a digital image may not be an accurate record of reality and its authenticity can be questioned, especially in legal proceedings [15]. Reliable techniques for identifying digital cameras are, therefore, important to establishing the origin of images presented as evidence.

The simplest method for source camera identification is to inspect the header file of an image. The EXIF header of an image, for example,

Please use the following format when citing this chapter:

Meng, F., Kong, X. and You, X., 2008, in IFIP International Federation for Information Processing, Volume 285;
Advances in Digital Forensics IV; Indrajit Ray, Sujeet Shenoi; (Boston: Springer), pp. 207–218.

provides information about the camera make and model, and details about image capture (e.g., exposure and time). However, this method has limited credibility because header data is easily modified and may not be available after the image is recompressed or saved in a new format.

Source cameras can also be identified based on digital watermarks. Some cameras (e.g., Kodak DC290) embed visible watermarks while others (e.g., Epson PhotoPC 700/750Z) embed invisible watermarks. However, the use of watermarks for camera identification is limited to special situations (e.g., "secure digital cameras" [3]). In any case, few digital cameras embed watermarks in their images, so watermark-based identification is not a general solution to the source camera problem.

Several researchers have investigated passive methods such as identification based on camera pixel defects. Geradts, *et al.* [12] note that manufacturing defects in CCD sensor arrays can be used to construct unique patterns for digital cameras. However, this approach fails when strong light is incident on a CCD array, when there are not enough dark frames, or when there is camera movement.

CCD noise is another camera characteristic that can be used in passive identification. Operating under the assumption that CCD noise is unique to cameras, Lukas and co-workers [17–19] have developed an identification method that uses photo-response non-uniformity (PRNU) noise caused by pixel non-uniformities. In their approach, the noise component of images is extracted using a wavelet-based denoising filter and the denoising residual from several sample images is averaged to produce a PRNU pattern that represents the camera signature. This signature acts as a high frequency spread spectrum watermark whose presence in the image is established using a correlation detector. While the method is robust to JPEG compression, the authors note that geometrical operations and noise attacks may prevent correct camera classification [19].

Kharrazi, *et al.* [15] have proposed a feature-based technique in which a classifier is used to identify the source camera based on pattern recognition principles. The feature vector used for classification contains image color characteristics, image quality metrics and the mean of wavelet coefficients. Although the method has been shown to achieve nearly 92% average classification accuracy for six different cameras, it fails to identify cameras of the same make but different models (these experimental results are presented later in this paper).

Choi and co-workers [5, 6] have augmented the feature-based approach by incorporating the lens radial distortion coefficients of digital cameras. The classification accuracy is improved. However, it is necessary to extract distorted line segments in Devernay's straight line method [7] in

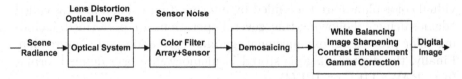

Figure 1. Imaging pipeline.

order to estimate the distortion coefficients. Thus, the image samples are limited to those containing distorted line segments.

This paper proposes a new passive feature-based method for source camera identification. It considers the influence of non-linear distortions caused by the imaging pipeline on higher-order image statistics and the impact of image processing operations on the wavelet domain. The method uses bi-coherence and wavelet coefficient statistics as distinguishing features and a support vector machine (SVM) as the classifier for source camera identification. Experimental results demonstrate that the method is both efficient and reliable. Also, it has better accuracy than the methods of Kharrazi, *et al.* [15] and Choi, *et al.* [5, 6] without placing constraints on the sample images.

2. Imaging Pipeline

The imaging pipeline of a digital camera is presented in Figure 1 [22].

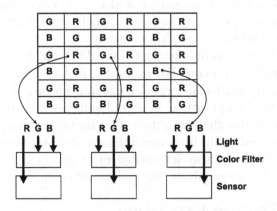

Figure 2. Color filter array.

Light entering the camera through the lens is captured by a sensor (usually a CCD detector). Most cameras employ one CCD detector at each pixel; however, each pixel has a different RGB color filter based on the color filter array (CFA) used by the camera (Figure 2). The individual color planes are then filled by interpolation using a process called "demosaicing." Following this, several operations are performed, including color processing, enhancement, gamma correction and compression. Finally, the digital image is stored in memory in a user-defined format (e.g., RAW, TIFF or JPEG).

Differences in the image capture and processing operations of camera models produce distinguishing features in digital images. We attempt to quantify these image features using statistical techniques and use the results for source camera identification.

3.   Identification Based on Image Features

In order to identify the source camera of a particular digital image, it is necessary to extract statistical features that can be used to discriminate between cameras. Kharrazi, *et al.* [15] use image color statistics to quantify the impact of interpolation and color processing. They also use image quality metrics to quantify differences arising from image processing operations.

Most cameras also introduce certain geometric and luminance non-linearities (e.g., due to lens distortion and gamma correction). These non-linearities introduce higher-order correlations in the frequency domain, which can be detected using polyspectral analysis tools [10]. Farid and colleagues [9–11] have used bi-coherence statistics to estimate geometric and luminance non-linearities and to calibrate digital images. We employ polyspectral analysis and higher-order statistics as discriminating features primarily because of their sensitivity to the non-linear distortions produced by digital cameras.

Digital images can be represented in additional detail using features in a transformation domain. For example, photographic images have been modeled using multiscale wavelet decomposition. Image capture and image processing operations in digital cameras have different influences on the regularities that are inherent to natural scenes; these differences can be captured using first- and higher-order statistics of wavelet coefficients. Our use of wavelet coefficient statistics is motivated by their effectiveness in steganalysis [20] and image origin identification [21].

3.1   Feature Extraction

Our identification method uses the magnitude and phase statistics of bi-coherence along with wavelet coefficient statistics to capture the unique non-linear distortions in images produced by different cameras. This section discusses the methods used to extract these statistical features.

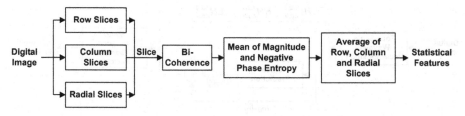

Figure 3. Extraction of bi-coherence features.

3.1.1 Bi-Coherence Features.

Non-linear distortions produced by digital cameras are characterized using statistical features of image bi-coherence. Consider, for example, a one-dimensional signal $f(x)$. The bi-spectrum of the signal is estimated by dividing the signal into N (possibly overlapping) segments, computing the Fourier transform of each segment, and averaging the individual estimates. This is given by:

$$\widehat{B}(\omega_1, \omega_2) = \frac{1}{N} \sum_{k=1}^{N} F_k(\omega_1) F_k(\omega_2) F_k^*(\omega_1 + \omega_2) \tag{1}$$

where $F_k(\cdot)$ is the Fourier transform of the kth segment. In order to make the variance at each bi-frequency (ω_1, ω_2) independent of $P(\omega_1)$, $P(\omega_2)$ and $P(\omega_1 + \omega_2)$, we employ the bi-coherence (i.e., normalized bi-spectrum) [16]:

$$\widehat{b}(\omega_1 + \omega_2) = \frac{\frac{1}{N} \sum_k F_k(\omega_1) F_k(\omega_2) F_k^*(\omega_1 + \omega_2)}{\sqrt{\frac{1}{N} \sum_k |F_k(\omega_1) F_k(\omega_2)|^2 \frac{1}{N} \sum_k |F_k(\omega_1 + \omega_2|^2)}}$$

$$= |\widehat{b}(\omega_1 + \omega_2)| e^{j\phi(\widehat{b}(\omega_1 + \omega_2))}. \tag{2}$$

Next, we compute the mean of the magnitude and the negative phase entropy [23] of the bi-coherence as statistic features.

The extraction of bi-coherence features is illustrated in Figure 3. To reduce memory and the computational overhead involved in calculating the full four-dimensional bi-coherence of images, we restrict our analysis to one-dimensional row, column and radial slices through the center of images. For each slice, we use segments of 64 pixels in length with an overlap of 32 pixels with adjacent segments. To reduce the frequency leakage and obtain better frequency resolution, each segment is multiplied with a Hamming window and padded with zeros from the end before computing the 128-point discrete Fourier transform. Then, the

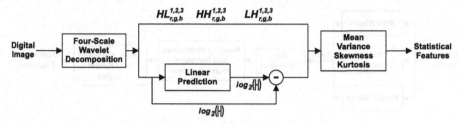

Figure 4. Extraction of wavelet coefficient features.

estimates of bi-coherence statistics (mean of the magnitude and negative phase entropy) for a slice are calculated. The statistics for the entire image are computed by averaging the estimates for a subset of row, column and radial slices for each RGB color component.

Note that it is not necessary to extract the information associated with image content (e.g., line segments) when applying bi-coherence statistics to quantify the non-linear distortions produced by cameras. Therefore, no rigorous constraint is placed on image sample selection.

3.1.2 Wavelet Coefficient Features.

Wavelet coefficients are used to characterize the impact of image processing on digital camera images. Four-scale wavelet decomposition is employed (Figure 4). This splits the frequency space into four scales and the orientations (HH, HL, LH). Next, four statistics (mean, variance, skewness and kurtosis) of the sub-band coefficients and the linear prediction errors at each orientation, scale and color channel are computed. These statistics form the second group of statistical feature vectors used for source camera identification.

Note that the method of Kharrazi, *et al.* [15] uses only the first-order statistic (mean) of the sub-band coefficients; also, it does consider linear prediction errors. Therefore, the prediction of wavelet coefficients can be regarded as a filtering operation in the wavelet domain and the prediction errors are basically independent of image content. As a result, the dependence between the prediction error features and image content is lower, producing more stable performance for arbitrary image samples.

3.2 Source Camera Identification Framework

The sequential forward feature selection algorithm [24] is used to reduce the correlation among features and improve the accuracy of source camera identification. The algorithm provides reliable results with reasonable computational cost.

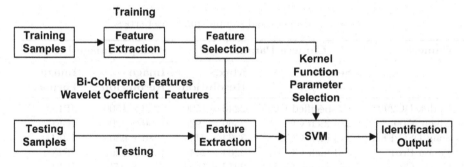

Figure 5. Source camera identification framework.

The algorithm analyzes all the features and constructs the most significant feature set by adding or removing features until no further improvement is obtained. The steps in the algorithm are as follows:

1. Initialize the current feature vector with the pair of features that produce the best classification results.

2. Add the most significant feature from the remaining features to the current feature set.

3. Remove the least significant feature from the current feature set. (The least significant feature is the feature whose removal improves the classification result the most.)

4. Check if the removal of the feature improves the classification result. If the classification result is improved, remove the feature and return to Step 3. Otherwise, do not remove the feature and return to Step 2.

A support vector machine (SVM) is used as the classifier. In our experiments, we used the SVM implementation provided by the LIBSVM toolbox [4].

The source camera identification framework is shown in Figure 5. First, the bi-coherence and wavelet coefficient features are extracted from the training samples for use in feature selection and classifier design. When using SVM classification, a certain amount of pre-processing of the feature data can increase the accuracy of classification; in our scheme, this is accomplished by linearly scaling feature values to the range [0,1].

Our experiments used C-support vector classification with the nonlinear RBF kernel and the tunable parameters, C and γ. The two parameters are obtained by performing a grid search using v-fold cross validation [13]. In the cross validation procedure, all the training samples are randomly divided into v subsets of equal size. Each subset is

Table 1. Camera and sample image properties.

Camera	Camera Parameters		Sample Image Parms.	
	Sensor	Max. Resolution	Image Resolution	Image Format
Kodak DC290	Unspecified CCD	2240 × 1500	2240 × 1500	JPEG
Nikon 5700	2/3-inch CCD	2560 × 1920	1600 × 1200	JPEG
Sony DSC-F828	2/3-inch CCD	3264 × 2448	1280 × 960	JPEG
Canon Pro1	2/3-inch CCD	3264 × 2448	1600 × 1200	JPEG
Canon G2	1/1.8-inch CCD	2272 × 1704	2272 × 1704	JPEG
			1600 × 1200	
			1024 × 768	
Canon G3	1/1.8-inch CCD	2272 × 1704	2272 × 1704	JPEG

tested using the classifier trained with the remaining $v-1$ subsets. Thus, every sample in the entire training set is predicted once so that the cross validation accuracy is the percentage of data that is correctly classified. In our experiments, a 5-fold cross validation was performed for each (C, γ) pair with values in the set $\{2^{-5}, 2^{-4}, \ldots, 2^5\}$. The parameter value pair with the highest cross validation accuracy was selected.

4. Experimental Setup and Results

This section describes the experimental setup for testing the source camera identification method and the results that were obtained.

4.1 Experimental Setup

Six different cameras were used in the experiments (Table 1). Three resolutions were used for the Canon G2 images in order to eliminate the influence of the properties of the sample images on the experimental results. The JPEG format was used for all the images because of its popularity and concerns about degradation in image quality caused by image compression in other formats. Furthermore, upon estimating the JPEG tables of all the image samples, no regularities were found within every class; this implies that JPEG compression has no impact on the experimental results.

A total of 2,100 image samples were used (350 images for each camera). The images were captured using the auto-focus mode and stored in the JPEG format. The images were typical shots varying from nature scenes to close-ups of people. The training set contained 1,200 images and the classifier was tested using the remaining 900 images. Images were randomly assigned to the training and testing sets. Camera identi-

Table 2. Experimental results.

Camera	Kodak	Nikon	Sony	Canon Pro1	Canon G2	Canon G3	Accy.
Kodak	**150**	0	0	0	0	0	100%
Nikon	0	**148**	0	2	0	0	98.7%
Sony	0	2	**148**	0	0	0	98.7%
Canon Pro1	0	1	1	**148**	0	1	98.7%
Canon G2	0	0	0	5	**139**	6	92.7%
Canon G3	0	0	0	0	2	**148**	98.7%

fication features were extracted for all the images and fed to a support vector machine for training and testing.

4.2   Experimental Results

Table 2 presents the results obtained after computing the image features and applying the feature selection method discussed in Section 3.2. The confusion matrix shows that the average identification accuracy for all the cameras exceeds 97% and that for the three Canon cameras is at least 96%. Note that the Canon G2 camera has the lowest identification accuracy, most likely because its images had three resolutions; using multiple resolutions negatively affects classifier training and, consequently, the accuracy of identification.

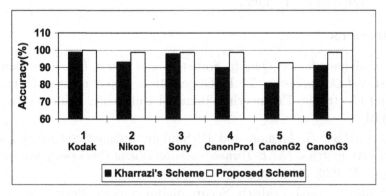

Figure 6. Comparison of results.

Figure 6 compares the results obtained using our method with those obtained using the method of Kharrazi, *et al.* [15] for the same image samples. Note that the average accuracy obtained with Kharrazi's method is 92%, but the accuracy for the Canon G2 camera is only about

80%. We can, therefore, conclude that bi-coherence and wavelet domain statistical features improve the identification accuracy, especially for cameras of the same brand but different models.

5.   Conclusions

The source camera identification method, which engages statistical characteristics of bi-coherence and wavelet coefficients as distinguishing features, the sequential forward feature selection algorithm for feature selection and a support vector machine for classification, is both efficient and reliable. The accuracy of identification is also much better than that obtained using the method of Kharrazi, *et al.* [15], especially for cameras of the same brand but different models. Furthermore, no constraints are imposed on image samples as in the case of the method proposed by Choi, *et al.* [5, 6].

Our future research will attempt to enhance the identification method by incorporating features from other techniques (e.g., PRNU [19], which is more effective at distinguishing between cameras of the same model but less robust for geometrical transformations). We will also attempt to expand the feature vector to accommodate camera images of varying content and texture.

Acknowledgements

This research was supported by Grant No. 60572111 from the National Science Foundation of China.

References

[1] I. Avcibas, *Image Quality Statistics and Their Use in Steganalysis and Compression*, Ph.D. Dissertation, Department of Electrical and Electronics Engineering, Bogazici University, Istanbul, Turkey, 2001.

[2] I. Avcibas, N. Memon and B. Sankur, Steganalysis using image quality metrics, *IEEE Transactions on Image Processing*, vol. 12(2), pp. 221–229, 2003.

[3] P. Blythe and J. Fridrich, Secure digital camera, *Proceedings of the Fourth Digital Forensic Research Workshop*, 2004.

[4] C. Chang and C. Lin, LIBSVM: A Library for Support Vector Machines (www.csie.ntu.edu.tw/~cjlin/libsvm).

[5] K. Choi, E. Lam and K. Wong, Automatic source camera identification using the intrinsic lens radial distortion, *Optics Express*, vol. 14(24), pp. 11551–11565, 2006.

[6] K. Choi, E. Lam and K. Wong, Source camera identification using footprints from lens aberration, *Proceedings of the SPIE*, vol. 6069, pp. 172–179, 2006.

[7] F. Devernay and O. Faugeras, Automatic calibration and removal of distortion from scenes of structured environments, *Proceedings of the SPIE*, vol. 2567, pp. 62–72, 1995.

[8] J. Fackrell and S. McLaughlin, Detecting nonlinearities in speech sounds using bi-coherence, *Proceedings of the Institute of Acoustics*, vol. 18(9), pp. 123–130, 1996.

[9] H. Farid, Blind inverse gamma correction, *IEEE Transactions on Image Processing*, vol. 10(10), pp. 1428–1433, 2001.

[10] H. Farid and A. Popescu, Blind removal of image non-linearities, *Proceedings of the Eighth International Conference on Computer Vision*, vol. 1, pp. 76–81, 2001.

[11] H. Farid and A. Popescu, Blind removal of lens distortion, *Journal of the Optical Society of America – A*, vol. 18(9), pp. 2072–2078, 2001.

[12] Z. Geradts, J. Bijhold, M. Kieft, K. Kurosawa, K. Kuroki and N. Saitoh, Methods for identification of images acquired with digital cameras, *Proceedings of the SPIE*, vol. 4232, pp. 505–512, 2001.

[13] C. Hsu, C. Chang and C. Lin, A Practical Guide to Support Vector Classification, Department of Computer Science and Information Engineering, National Taiwan University, Taipei, Taiwan (www .csie.ntu.edu.tw/~cjlin/papers/guide/guide.pdf), 2008.

[14] N. Khanna, A. Mikkilineni, A. Martone, G. Ali, G. Chiu, J. Allebach and E. Delp, A survey of forensics characterization methods for physical devices, *Digital Investigation*, vol. 3(S1), pp. 17–18, 2006.

[15] M. Kharrazi, H. Sencar and N. Memon, Blind source camera identification, *Proceedings of the International Conference on Image Processing*, vol. 1, pp. 709–712, 2004.

[16] Y. Kim and E. Powers, Digital bispectral analysis and its applications to nonlinear wave interactions, *IEEE Transactions on Plasma Science*, vol. 7(2), pp. 120–131, 1979.

[17] J. Lukas, J. Fridrich and M. Goljan, Determining digital image origin using sensor imperfections, *Proceedings of the SPIE*, vol. 5685, pp. 249–260, 2005.

[18] J. Lukas, J. Fridrich and M. Goljan, Digital "bullet scratches" for images, *Proceedings of the International Conference on Image Processing*, vol. 3, pp. 65-68, 2005.

[19] J. Lukas, J. Fridrich and M. Goljan, Digital camera identification from sensor pattern noise, *IEEE Transactions on Information Forensics and Security*, vol. 1(2), pp. 205–214, 2005.

[20] S. Lyu and H. Farid, Detecting hidden messages using higher-order statistics and support vector machines, *Proceedings of the Fifth International Workshop on Information Hiding*, pp. 340–354, 2002.

[21] S. Lyu and H. Farid, How realistic is photorealistic? *IEEE Transactions on Signal Processing*, vol. 53(2-2), pp. 845–850, 2005.

[22] T. Ng and S. Chang, Passive-blind image forensics, in W. Zeng, H. Yu and C. Lin (Eds.), *Multimedia Security Technologies for Digital Rights*, Academic Press, New York, pp. 383–412, 2006.

[23] T. Ng, S. Chang and Q. Sun, Blind detection of photomontage using higher order statistics, *Proceedings of the International Symposium on Circuits and Systems*, vol. 5, pp. 688–691, 2004.

[24] P. Pudil, F. Ferri, J. Novovicova and J. Kittler, Floating search methods for feature selection with nonmonotonic criterion functions, *Proceedings of Twelfth IEEE International Conference on Pattern Recognition*, vol. 2, pp. 279–283, 1994.

Chapter 18

DATA RECOVERY FROM WINDOWS CE BASED HANDHELD DEVICES

Antonio Savoldi and Paolo Gubian

Abstract   Data hiding creates serious problems for digital forensic practitioners attempting to recover evidence. It is possible to conceal large amounts of sensitive data in handheld devices in a manner that prevents their recovery using standard forensic tools. This paper describes a technique for recovering data stored in the slack memory of Windows CE based devices. A case study involving data hiding in a Toshiba E740 PDA is discussed.

Keywords: Data recovery, handheld devices, Windows CE, Toshiba E740 PDA

1.   Introduction

Personal digital assistants (PDAs) and cell phones are the most pervasive pieces of electronic equipment in modern society. These devices contain a wealth of information of evidentiary value – subscriber data, call data, contact lists, SMS and email messages, images, audio and video files, as well as sensitive data concealed by exploiting weaknesses in the operating system and/or hardware. Data can be hidden in a variety of ways, usually for illicit purposes. Two common techniques involve hiding data in images, audio or video files using steganography and allocating sensitive data in the slack memory of electronic devices [11, 12].

Covert channels [14] are frequently used for the surreptitious transfer of sensitive data in a manner that violates the security policy of a computer system. In the case of a storage channel, data is transferred from one party to another by writing to shared storage; a timing channel signals sensitive data by modulating temporal system resources. Due to their popularity and functionality, PDAs and cell phones are attractive devices for implementing storage channels. It is common to find such communications devices with 256 MB RAM and 128 MB flash ROM, var-

Please use the following format when citing this chapter:

Savoldi, A. and Gubian, P., 2008, in IFIP International Federation for Information Processing, Volume 285; *Advances in Digital Forensics IV*; Indrajit Ray, Sujeet Shenoi; (Boston: Springer), pp. 219–230.

ious built-in wireless capabilities (Wi-Fi, Bluetooth, IrDa, GSM, UMTS, HSDPA) along with a high resolution camera and a GPS receiver. Large amounts of data can be hidden in these handheld devices in a manner that prevents their recovery using standard forensic tools.

This paper describes techniques for data concealment and recovery from devices running Windows CE (WinCE) [9], one of the most popular operating systems for handheld devices. A case study involving data hidden in the slack memory of a Toshiba E740 PDA is presented. Also, guidelines are provided to assist digital forensic practitioners in identifying and recovering hidden data in WinCE devices.

2.   Background

This section describes Windows CE and the Toshiba E740 PDA used in our case study.

2.1   Windows CE Operating System

Windows CE [9], often referred to as WinCE, is a modular operating system, which serves as the foundation for several classes of embedded devices. It is supported by Intel Xscale processors and compatibles, and MIPS, ARM and Hitachi SH processors. WinCE is optimized for devices with minimal storage and small scale factors (small-scale digital devices); its kernel requires less than 1 MB of memory. WinCE devices are often configured without any disk storage and may be configured as closed systems, with the operating system burned on a flash ROM. WinCE is compliant with the definition of a real-time operating system with deterministic interrupt latency. It supports 256 priority levels and uses priority inheritance to deal with priority inversion. Furthermore, WinCE is a multitasking operating system, where the fundamental unit of execution is a "thread." Since the first edition of WinCE (called Pegasus) was released in 1996, the operating system has evolved to support platforms other than handheld devices. The basic WinCE core is used in AutoPC, PocketPC 2000/2002, Mobile 2003, Mobile 2003 SE, Mobile 5.0/6.0, Smartphone 2002/2003 and many other embedded systems and industrial devices.

The WinCE kernel uses a paged virtual memory system to manage and allocate program memory. The virtual memory system provides contiguous blocks of memory, between 1 KB and 4 KB within 64 KB regions, so that applications do not have to deal with memory allocation. In a WinCE device, the operating system and the applications bundled with the operating system are stored in ROM. The entire operating system is mapped to a binary ROM image divided logically into two types of modules. The first type corresponds to executable in place (XIP) modules; these modules save RAM space and reduce the time needed to start applications. The second type includes compressed modules, which are decompressed by the operating system and paged into RAM before execution.

In WinCE devices, the RAM is divided into two regions, "object store" and "program memory." The object store resembles a permanent, virtual RAM disk. Data in the object store is retained when the system is suspended or when a soft reset operation is performed. Normally, devices have a backup power supply for the RAM to preserve data when the main power supply is interrupted. When operations resume, the system searches for a previously-created object store in RAM and uses it (if one is found). Devices without battery-backed RAM may use a special flag in the registry to preserve data during multiple boot processes.

The remaining portion of the RAM on a WinCE device is designated for program memory. This space holds various stacks and heaps belonging to executing applications.

WinCE has a virtual memory address space of 4 GB. The operating system is able to manage at most 32 processes by assigning a "slot" corresponding to 32 MB of virtual address space to each process. This is partly due to the fact that Windows CE keeps the address spaces of all processes available at all times, even when the processes are not running. Thus, the lower portion of the address space is split into 32 MB slots. The address space is divided as follows (note that 32 MB corresponds to 0x02000000 in hexadecimal code):

- Slot 0 is assigned the memory locations in the range 0x00000000 to 0x01FFFFFF.

- Slot 1 is assigned the memory locations in the range 0x02000000 to 0x03FFFFFF.

- Slot 31 (last slot) ends at memory location 0x41FFFFFF.

- Memory locations in the range 0x42000000 to 0x7FFFFFFF mostly correspond to the "shared area" used for VirtualAlloc functions and memory-mapped files.

- Memory locations above 0x80000000 are reserved for the kernel. The kernel and the DLLs that load into the kernel (e.g., installable interrupt service routine (ISR) DLLs) execute from this memory space.

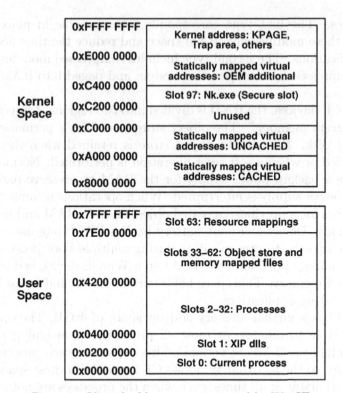

Figure 1. Virtual address space managed by WinCE.

Figure 1 shows the layout of the virtual memory managed by WinCE. Note that the kernel and user space each have 2 GB of addressable memory.

The Remote Application Program Interface (RAPI) protocol [8] is often used by tools to extract the ROM and RAM contents of WinCE devices. The RAPI library enables applications running on a desktop computer to perform actions on a remote WinCE device; these include manipulating the file system on the remote device (e.g., creating and deleting files and directories). RAPI interfaces can be used to create and modify databases, either in the object store or in mounted database volumes. RAPI applications can also query and modify registry keys as well as launch applications and invoke methods on the remote device.

2.2   WinCE Test Device

A Toshiba E740 PDA equipped with the PocketPC 2002 OS (a WinCE derivative) was used in our investigation of data hiding and recovery at the firmware level. It has an Intel PXA240 (400 Hz) processor, 64 MB of SDRAM (main memory) and 32 MB of CMOS flash memory (ROM), which holds the operating system. The device also has built-in Wi-Fi and IrDa transceivers. Two slots for secure digital and compact flash cards are available for memory expansion. Later in this paper we will demonstrate the ease with which data can be hidden in the ROM and RAM in a manner that precludes its recovery using commercial digital forensic tools.

2.3   Data Extraction Techniques

The two main classes of data extraction techniques are logical extraction and physical extraction. A logical extraction technique focuses only on the visible content at the file system level, i.e., data pertaining to files, databases and registry along with other file system data. Device Seizure [10] is a popular logical data extraction tool for PDAs and cell phones (although it can access some physical data from certain devices).

A physical extraction technique, on the other hand, is attractive because it can recover all the data stored in an electronic device. In most cases, however, only the flash ROM and the RAM content are recovered using a special operating mode of the device (e.g., Palm OS debugger mode) or by communicating with the operating system (e.g. using the RAPI protocol [8]).

According to Breeuwsma and co-workers [2], three techniques may be used to obtain a complete copy of flash memory: (i) using "flasher" tools, (ii) using JTAG test access ports, and (iii) using forensic de-soldering.

Flasher tools are designed to copy the memory of certain families of electronic devices. They employ APIs that interact with the addressable memory. Generally, these tools originate from manufacturers, who use them for debugging purposes, or they come from the hacker community, which creates the tools to modify the functionality of handheld devices. An important advantage of this technique is that flash memory can be imaged without de-soldering the chip. However, many flasher tools do not make complete forensic copies of flash memory, mostly because of the limited functionality of the API provided by the embedded device. Furthermore, it is important to acknowledge Locard's Exchange Principle [3] in that a data extraction process executing in device memory can potentially affect the integrity of the memory. Gershteyn and co-workers [4] have used flasher tools to recover hidden data from BIOS chips. Savoldi and Gubian [11] have used similar tools to extract data from SIM/USIM cards.

The second physical extraction method involves the use of JTAG test access ports of embedded devices. JTAG ports in most devices are designed for debugging purposes, but they can also be used to access the flash memory [1]. The JTAG extraction technique is complex and time consuming; however, it is possible to guarantee that no data is written to memory during the data recovery phase.

The third physical extraction technique is to de-solder the memory chip and use a chip programmer or reader to extract the data. This method is expensive, time consuming and the most invasive; however, it can be used to recover data from damaged devices.

3.   Data Extraction Methodology

This section discusses the use of open source tools based on the RAPI protocol [8] for acquiring the binary ROM image and major portions of the RAM of a WinCE device. The software-based approach falls in the category of using flasher tools. It can be used to extract data in a non-invasive manner from a variety of WinCE devices.

Our experiments employed a set of open source tools [6] based on the RAPI and ActiveSync protocols. Two tools, pmemdump and pmemmap, are particularly useful.

The pmemdump tool is very effective at extracting ROM and RAM data. To use the tool, it is necessary to copy a DLL library to the device file system. The following options are provided by pmemdump:

```
Usage: pmemdump [ -m | -p procname | -h prochandle] start length
                [ filename ]
    numbers can be specified as 0x1234abcd
    -1 -2 -4 : dump as bytes/words/dwords
    -w NUM   : specify number of words per line
    -s SIZE  : step with SIZE through memory
    -a       : ascdump iso hexdump
    -f       : full -- do not summarize identical lines
    -c       : print raw memory to stdout
    -x       : print only hex
    -xx      : print only fixed length ascii dumps
    -v       : verbose
    -n NAME  : view memory in the context of process NAME
    -h NUM   : view memory in the context of process with handle NUM
    -m       : directly access memory -- not using ReadProcessMemory
    -p       : access physical memory instead of virtual memory
    if -p, -h and -m are not specified, memory is read from the
    context of rapisrv.exe
```

By specifying the virtual starting address (in hexadecimal notation) with the length of the memory block, it is possible to obtain, for example, the entire ROM image (32 MB). This is saved in the file rom_pda.bin as follows:

```
pmemdump.exe 0x80000000 0x02000000 rom_pda.bin
```

Table 1. Complete dump of the system pagetable.

Virtual Address	Physical Address	Size	KB
v160f9000-160fa000	pa3f77000-a3f78000	1000_{16}	4
v1649f000-164a0000	pa3f60000-a3f61000	1000_{16}	4
v1686f000-16870000	pa3d1f000-a3d20000	1000_{16}	4
v17f66000-17f67000	pa3d54000-a3d55000	1000_{16}	4
v80000000-80400000	**pa0100000-a0500000**	**400000_{16}**	**4096**
v80400000-82000000	**p00400000-02000000**	**$1c00000_{16}$**	**28672**
v88200000-88300000	p48000000-48100000	100000_{16}	1024
v88300000-88400000	p44000000-44100000	100000_{16}	1024
v88400000-89800000	p40000000-41400000	1400000_{16}	20480
v8b400000-8b500000	p28000000-28100000	100000_{16}	1024
v8b500000-8b600000	p20000000-20100000	100000_{16}	1024
v8b600000-8b700000	p38000000-38100000	100000_{16}	1024
v8b700000-8b800000	p30000000-30100000	100000_{16}	1024
v8c000000-8d000000	p0c000000-0d000000	1000000_{16}	16384
v90000000-90100000	pa0000000-a0100000	100000_{16}	1024
v90100000-90500000	p00000000-00400000	400000_{16}	4096
v90500000-94000000	**pa0500000-a4000000**	**$3b00000_{16}$**	**61440**
v98000000-9c000000	p2c000000-30000000	4000000_{16}	65536
v9c000000-a0000000	p3c000000-40000000	4000000_{16}	65536
va0000000-a0400000	pa0100000-a0500000	400000_{16}	4096
va0400000-a2000000	p00400000-02000000	$1c00000_{16}$	29696
va8200000-a8300000	p48000000-48100000	100000_{16}	1024
va8300000-a8400000	p44000000-44100000	100000_{16}	1024
va8400000-a9800000	p40000000-41400000	1400000_{16}	20480
vab400000-ab500000	p28000000-28100000	100000_{16}	1024
vab500000-ab600000	p20000000-20100000	100000_{16}	1024
vab600000-ab700000	p38000000-38100000	100000_{16}	1024
vab700000-ab800000	p30000000-30100000	100000_{16}	1024
vac000000-ad000000	p0c000000-0d000000	1000000_{16}	16384
vb0000000-b0100000	pa0000000-a0100000	100000_{16}	1024
vb0100000-b0500000	p00000000-00400000	400000_{16}	4096
vb0500000-b4000000	pa0500000-a4000000	$3b00000_{16}$	61440
vb8000000-bc000000	p2c000000-30000000	4000000_{16}	65536
vbc000000-c0000000	p3c000000-40000000	4000000_{16}	65536
vfffd0000-fffd1000	pa05a0000-a05a1000	1000_{16}	4
vfffd1000-fffd2000	pa05a0000-a05a1000	1000_{16}	4
vfffd2000-fffd3000	pa05a0000-a05a1000	1000_{16}	4
vfffd3000-fffd4000	pa05a0000-a05a1000	1000_{16}	4
vfffd4000-fffd5000	pa05a0000-a05a1000	1000_{16}	4
vfffd5000-fffd6000	pa05a0000-a05a1000	1000_{16}	4
vfffd6000-fffd7000	pa05a0000-a05a1000	1000_{16}	4
vfffd7000-fffd8000	pa05a0000-a05a1000	1000_{16}	4
vffff0000-ffff1000	pa05a8000-a05a9000	1000_{16}	4
vffff2000-ffff3000	pa05a8000-a05a9000	1000_{16}	4
vffff4000-ffff5000	pa05a8000-a05a9000	1000_{16}	4
vffff6000-ffff7000	pa05a8000-a05a9000	1000_{16}	4
vffffc000-ffffd000	pa05a9000-a05aa000	1000_{16}	4

The `pmemmap` tool can be used to sample the entire 4 GB of virtual memory as follows (each step of 16 MB takes 16 bytes):

```
pmemmap.exe -s 0x01000000 0 0xfff00000
```

An important task is to locate the starting and ending addresses of the ROM and RAM memory blocks. These addresses can be identified by analyzing the content of the system pagetable (Table 1), which was obtained using the `pmemmap` tool.

The entire binary ROM image is obtained by starting with the virtual address 0x80000000 and specifying a length of 32 MB (0x02000000). This can be verified by summing up the two physical block sizes identified with the virtual and physical addresses as shown below. Note that only one virtual memory block is present, which is mapped to two physical ROM blocks; the two physical blocks together constitute the 32 MB ROM block.

```
v80000000-80400000 -- pa0100000-a0500000  4096 KB
v80400000-82000000 -- p00400000-02000000 28672 KB
```

Extracting the RAM contents is important, especially as the RAM contains all the installed programs along with sensitive user data. Unfortunately, as will be explained below, it is not possible to obtain a complete forensically-sound copy of the RAM. Also, according to Locard's Exchange Principle, the integrity of the RAM memory image cannot be guaranteed because the acquisition process executes in the same memory from where data is being extracted. The pagetable shows a 60 MB block, which contains the object file store (32 MB) along with a substantial portion of the program memory (except for the kernel area). The portion of the pagetable presented below shows six virtual blocks that refer to three physical blocks.

```
v90500000-94000000 -- pa0500000-a4000000    60 MB

v98000000-9c000000 -- p2c000000-30000000    64 MB
v9c000000-a0000000 -- p3c000000-40000000    64 MB

vb0500000-b4000000 -- pa0500000-a4000000    60 MB
vb8000000-bc000000 -- p2c000000-30000000    64 MB
vbc000000-c0000000 -- p3c000000-40000000    64 MB
```

Our experiments indicate that only the 60 MB block is related to the main RAM. Therefore, it is possible to carve the signatures of all the known programs that are present in memory to verify the correctness of the extracted RAM block.

The main drawback of this data recovery technique is the possible lack of integrity of the extracted program memory. This is because the stack and heap portions of the memory are modified as the data extraction process executes. However, the memory portion related to the object store should not change because it is not influenced by the extraction process. Thus, the most important portions of the RAM can be successfully extracted if some integrity loss is acceptable. In any case, the integrity of the extracted data can be verified by analyzing the RAM contents and carving all the signatures related to user objects (programs, sensitive data, etc.).

An important point worth noting is that it is not necessary to scan the entire 4 GB virtual address space, which can take more than two hours. It is much more efficient to analyze the pagetable and focus on the memory blocks that have forensic value; this requires no more than 20 minutes to obtain the entire ROM and RAM contents. We believe that this methodology is applicable to the full range of WinCE devices.

4. Experimental Results

This section presents the results of the case study involving data hiding in WinCE devices. It shows how data can be hidden in the slack portion of the binary ROM of a Toshiba E740 PDA in a manner that prevents its recovery using standard digital forensic tools.

4.1 Binary ROM Image

The Toshiba E740 PDA has a regular binary ROM image of 32 MB. The ROM has a section allocated to the boot loader; the remaining portion of the memory holds the operating system kernel. Inspection of the ROM image released by Toshiba reveals that about 40% of the binary image is empty – this corresponds to about 12 MB of slack space.

Two principal techniques may be used to hide data in the slack portion of the binary ROM image. One approach is to use a flasher tool that has been modified using reverse engineering techniques. The second, simpler approach is use a compact flash card.

Generally, tools for upgrading the operating system are released by the manufacturer. They incorporate a checksum mechanism to verify the integrity of the official binary ROM image and, consequently, to permit its upload. In order to upload a modified version of the binary ROM image, it is necessary to remove this control in the original executable file using reverse engineering techniques. Other checksum tests may be implemented at the boot loader level to verify that a trusted ROM image is loaded into the PDA. It is also necessary to defeat these protection schemes in order to upload arbitrary ROM images.

In the case of the Toshiba E740 PDA, we have developed a technique for re-flashing the device without modifying the executable file or the boot loader. Specifically, it is possible to initiate the re-flashing process by uploading a ROM image on a compact flash card and performing a soft reset with the card inserted in the PDA. This bypasses all the integrity controls, enabling a modified ROM image to be installed in the device.

The binary ROM image is a sequence of contiguous blocks, some of which may be empty; these empty blocks can be used to hide sensitive data. To simplify memory allocation, we used only the empty blocks with size greater than 1 KB to hide data. Since about 40% of the ROM image is empty, approximately 12 MB is available to hide data. Of course, it is necessary to first identify all the empty and usable blocks and locate their starting and ending addresses.

4.2   Hiding Data

Standard strategies used for allocating pages in main memory (e.g., first fit, best fit and worst fit techniques [5, 13]) may be used to hide data within the slack portion of the ROM. We recommend the following data hiding strategy to accommodate the fact that empty blocks in the ROM are of varying size.

- A script (e.g., written in Perl) is used to identify all the empty blocks with size above a certain threshold (e.g., 1 KB). Each block has a starting and an ending address. In addition, a unique number is assigned to each block in order to apply a steganographic scheme. The total slack space, S_{tot}, is represented as:

$$S_{tot} = \{(n_1, s_1, e_1), (n_2, s_2, e_2), ..., (n_K, s_K, e_K)\} \tag{1}$$

  where n_k is the number assigned to the kth empty block for steganographic purposes, and s_k and e_k are its starting and ending addresses, respectively.

- A file, F, is created with size less than or equal to $Dim(S_{tot})$ $(F \mid Dim(F) \leq Dim(S_{tot}))$, where $Dim()$ is the space occupied by a specific block of data. Next, an allocation policy is chosen based on a block sequence specified according to Equation 1. Thus, the file F is mapped as follows:

$$F^1 = \{(n_1, s_1, e_1), ..., (n_p, s_p, e_p)\} \tag{2}$$

  where $\binom{K}{p} = \frac{K!}{p!(K-p)!}$ possibilities exist for selecting the p blocks from the K possible blocks. The F^1 file is the result of allocation using an arbitrary sequence of blocks in the set $\{1, ..., K\}$:

$$Dim(F^1) = \sum_{i=1}^{p} b(i) \mid Dim(F^1) \geq Dim(F). \tag{3}$$

Note that F^1 differs from F in the last block used, which can be greater than the last chunk of the file. The sequence of used blocks forms the steganographic key for recovering the original file.

4.3   Recovering Hidden Data

Every certified binary ROM image has a unique MD5/SHA1 signature that may be used to verify its integrity. An image with a different signature potentially contains hidden data.

The first step in recovering hidden data is to analyze the differences between the two images. Next, data carving techniques and a steganalysis approach are used to recover the hidden data. The procedure for recovering hidden data can be summarized as follows:

- Having verified that the extracted binary image is not original, analyze the differences between the certified ROM image and the extracted image.

- Apply data carving techniques [7] to obtain headers and fragments that might indicate the type of the data and the techniques used to hide it.

- If it is evident that scrambling techniques have been applied, attempt to identify the correct sequence of blocks used for data hiding.

Standard commercial tools such as Device Seizure [10] can be be used for logical data extraction. However, logical data extraction does not recover hidden data allocated within the slack portion of the ROM; only standard objects present at the file system level (e.g., user files, registry and installed programs) are visible and, consequently, recoverable. Unfortunately, Device Seizure was not very effective at physcial data extraction – it was unable to reveal any hidden data.

5.   Conclusions

Large amounts of illicit data may be concealed in handheld devices in a manner that prevents their recovery using standard forensic tools. Due to the ubiquity of WinCE devices, digital forensic practitioners must be aware of techniques used for hiding data and for recovering this data. As verified in the case study involving a Toshiba E740 PDA, the methodology proposed for discovering and extracting hidden data from the slack portion of flash ROM and RAM is both sound and efficient. Moreover, the guidelines proposed for identifying and recovering hidden data hold for WinCE devices in general. Our future work will investigate data hiding and recovery techniques for embedded devices using other operating systems (e.g., Symbian OS and iPhone OS X).

References

[1] M. Breeuwsma, Forensic imaging of embedded systems using JTAG (boundary-scan), *Digital Investigation*, vol. 3(1), pp. 32–42, 2006.

[2] M. Breeuwsma, M. De Jongh, C. Klaver, R. van der Knijff and M. Roeloffs, Forensics data recovery from flash memory, *Small Scale Device Forensics Journal*, vol. 1(1), pp. 1–17, 2007.

[3] W. Chisum and B. Turvey, Evidence dynamics: Locard's exchange principle and crime reconstruction, *Journal of Behavioral Profiling*, vol. 1(1), 2000.

[4] P. Gershteyn, M. Davis and S. Shenoi, Forensic analysis of BIOS chips, in *Advances in Digital Forensics II*, M. Olivier and S. Shenoi (Eds.), Springer, New York, pp. 301–314, 2006.

[5] M. Gorman, *Understanding the Linux Virtual Memory Manager*, Prentice-Hall, Upper Saddle River, New Jersey, 2004.

[6] W. Hengeveld, RAPI tools (www.xs4all.nl/~itsme/projects/xda/tools.html), 2003.

[7] K. Kendall and J. Kornblum, Foremost (version 1.5.3) (foremost.sourceforge.net).

[8] Microsoft Corporation, Remote API 2 (RAPI2), Redmond, Washington (msdn2.microsoft.com/en-us/library/aa920150.aspx).

[9] Microsoft Corporation, Windows CE overview, Redmond, Washington (msdn2.microsoft.com/en-us/library/ms899235.aspx).

[10] Paraben Corporation, Device Seizure v1.2, Orem, Utah (www.paraben-forensics.com/catalog).

[11] A. Savoldi and P. Gubian, Data hiding in SIM/USIM cards: A steganographic approach, *Proceedings of the Second International Workshop on Systematic Approaches to Digital Forensic Engineering*, pp. 86–100, 2007.

[12] A. Savoldi and P. Gubian, SIM and USIM file system: A forensics perspective, *Proceedings of the ACM Symposium on Applied Computing*, pp. 181–187, 2007.

[13] A. Silberschatz, P. Galvin and G. Gagne, *Operating System Concepts*, John Wiley and Sons, Hoboken, New Jersey, 2005.

[14] U.S. Department of Defense, Department of Defense Trusted Computer System Evaluation Criteria, Technical Report DOD 5200.28-STD, Washington, DC, 1985.

Chapter 19

LEGAL ISSUES PERTAINING TO THE USE OF CELL PHONE DATA

Charles Adams, Anthony Whitledge and Sujeet Shenoi

Abstract   This paper examines the principal legal issues related to the use of cell phone data as evidence at trial and to establish a basis for obtaining wiretap orders or call detail records from service providers. Four scenarios are considered. The first three scenarios explore evidentiary issues related to data extracted from damaged SIM cards, partial data recovered from memory chips and deleted data obtained from handsets. The fourth scenario, which focuses on the so-called "Trojan defense," clarifies the important distinction between evidence admissibility and evidence sufficiency.

Keywords: Cell phone forensics, evidence, admissibility, sufficiency

1.   Introduction

Cell phones contain large amounts of information – subscriber data, call logs, address books, text and email messages, images, and audio and video recordings [1, 3]. Due to the ubiquity of cell phones and the nature of their use, information recovered from cell phones can be vital in criminal investigations [2, 4]. Law enforcement agencies may use this information to establish a basis for obtaining wiretap orders or call detail records from service providers, and, of course, as evidence at trial.

Obtaining a search warrant or wiretap order requires a factual showing of "probable cause." Such a showing only requires the presentation of enough information to support a conclusion by a judge that there is a fair probability of finding evidence of criminal activity. On the other hand, the admissibility of cell phone data as evidence in a trial requires some verification that the data extracted from the cell phone was obtained by reliable scientific methods and is relevant to the material issues in the case.

Please use the following format when citing this chapter:

Adams, C., Whitledge, A. and Shenoi, S., 2008, in IFIP International Federation for Information Processing, Volume 285; *Advances in Digital Forensics IV*; Indrajit Ray, Sujeet Shenoi; (Boston: Springer), pp. 231–243.

This paper uses four scenarios to explore the principal legal issues related to the use of cell phone data to obtain wiretap orders and call records, and as evidence at trial. The first three scenarios examine evidentiary issues related to data extracted from damaged SIM cards, partial data recovered from memory chips, and deleted data obtained from handsets. The fourth scenario, which involves a "Trojan defense," clarifies the difference between admissibility and sufficiency of evidence.

2.   Data from a Damaged SIM Card

Consider the following scenario involving the use of data extracted from a damaged Subscriber Identity Module (SIM) card in a cell phone.

> *Before FBI agents arrest him, a suspect in a kidnapping case throws his cell phone into a fireplace. The agents recover some melted plastic, burned electronic components and a damaged SIM card, which cannot be read by conventional means. Using a classified technique, the FBI is able to recover the International Mobile Subscriber Identifier (IMSI) and the name of the service provider from the SIM card. These facts form the basis of an application for a Section 2703(d) order to obtain from the provider the name and address of the subscriber and information about all calls made during the last thirty days. Phone company records show that a call was made to the kidnap victim's parents from a cell phone with that SIM card at the very same time they received a ransom call. Does the defendant have any basis to move to suppress the phone company records at his trial because they were the fruit of an unconventional and possibly improper forensic examination?*

The defendant would not have any basis for a motion to suppress the phone company records if they were offered against him at trial.

This scenario demonstrates the use of SIM card data for investigative leads, but not as direct evidence at a trial. Forensic data must meet evidentiary standards for authenticity and reliability before it may be introduced at trial. However, information used to develop leads or further an investigation does not have to meet these standards. Thus, the phone company records would have to satisfy the standards for admissibility in court, but the SIM card data used to obtain a search warrant or court order does not.

Section 2703(d) of Title 18 of the United States Code authorizes a court to issue an order to a phone company to disclose call records if law enforcement "offers specific and articulable facts showing that there are reasonable grounds to believe that ... the records ... are relevant and material to an ongoing criminal investigation" [16]. The House report that accompanied the legislation described the standard for Section 2703(d) as higher than that required for a subpoena in order to guard against "fishing expeditions" by law enforcement, but less than that required for a search warrant based on probable cause [17].

The IMSI and service provider information recovered from the damaged SIM card are certainly "specific and articulable facts." Moreover, the circumstances under which the cell phone was retrieved would provide reasonable grounds for a judicial officer to believe that the phone company records would be relevant to the kidnapping investigation.

Even if the Section 2703(d) order was improperly issued, the defendant's only remedy would be a civil suit for damages, not the suppression of evidence in his criminal case. Under traditional Fourth Amendment principles, an individual does not have a sufficient expectation of privacy in a third party's records to challenge the use of the records against him at a trial, no matter how they were obtained [22–24].

In addition, there is an impediment to the defendant raising a Fourth Amendment challenge to the use of information obtained from the SIM card. Since the defendant abandoned his cell phone when he threw it into the fireplace, he does not retain an expectation of privacy regarding the abandoned property [9, 27]. Thus, the defendant can look only to the statute for any remedy for its violation. However, Section 2708 of Title 18 states that the only remedies are a civil action for damages and disciplinary actions against federal agencies or departments for willful or intentional violations [11]. Consequently, there would be no basis for the suspect to move to suppress the phone company records on the grounds that the forensic examination of the damaged SIM card was improper.

In addition, the defendant could not force the government to disclose the classified technique used to recover SIM card data. The U.S. Supreme Court has recognized a state secrecy privilege. Also, it has noted that, in certain circumstances, the government may have to drop a criminal case in order to protect the privilege. In United States v. Reynolds, the court explained that "since the Government which prosecutes an accused also has the duty to see that justice is done, it is unconscionable to allow it to undertake prosecution and then invoke its governmental privileges to deprive the accused of anything which might be material to his defense" [18].

The data from the damaged SIM card would not be material to the suspect's defense, if the data was used only to obtain the Section 2703(d) order, rather than being admitted at trial as evidence against the suspect. The disclosure of a classified technique is analogous to the disclosure of the identity of an informant where there is a public interest in law enforcement maintaining the secrecy of the identity. The U.S. Supreme Court has ruled that the government is not required to disclose the identity of an informant if it relied on information from the informant to provide a basis for the issuance of a search or arrest warrant [21]. In contrast, disclosure would be required if the informant is to provide testimony relevant to the guilt or innocence of the accused [19].

Thus, the government could prosecute the suspect without having to reveal the means it used to extract the SIM card data, if these means were a valid state secret. If the government sought to introduce the SIM card data at trial, the judicial officer might require some information about the classified technique to verify its relevance and reliability. However, any disclosure could be made under seal in order to protect the classified recovery technique [12, 15].

3.   Partial Data from Cell Phone Memory

Consider the following scenario involving the extrapolation of partial data recovered from cell phone memory.

> After an explosion at a Metro station, law enforcement personnel re-
> cover a memory chip from a cell phone that they reasonably believe was
> used to detonate the bomb. A forensic examiner uses a chip programmer
> to recover data from the memory chip, including fragments of the call
> log. Many of the calls in the log were made to or received from known
> members of radical groups. More importantly, the last call was made to
> the phone from the number 789-012-XXXX immediately before the bomb
> exploded. Unfortunately, the last four digits of the phone number, indi-
> cated by XXXX, were unrecoverable. Further investigation reveals that
> Jane Roe, an individual with links to radical groups, has a cell phone
> number of 789-012-3456. Law enforcement agents use this information
> to obtain a wiretap order for Jane Roe's phone. The indictment charg-
> ing her with participating in the bombing is based on the partial phone
> number in the call log as well as on the conversations recorded during
> the wiretap. Jane Roe moves to suppress all the evidence because the
> numbers recovered from the memory chip were obtained using uncon-
> ventional and unreliable means and did not provide probable cause for
> the wiretap. How should the court rule on the motion to suppress?

Unlike the previous scenario, law enforcement agents used the data recovered from the cell phone as a basis for a wiretap order and also as evidence at trial.

Only evidence that can be shown to have been derived from reliable scientific processes is admissible under the rules of evidence. Thus, if the court decided that the unconventional forensic technique used by the examiner was not scientifically sound and could not be shown to produce reliable results, the court would not allow the partial data recovered from the memory chip to be admitted into evidence. In contrast, the conversations were the product of a valid wiretap order and would not be suppressed, even though the information that identified the defendant came from the examination of the chip.

A court may issue a wiretap order under Section 2518 of Title 18 if the judge concludes that there is probable cause to believe that an individual has committed one of the crimes specified in the wiretap statute and that particular communications concerning the crime will be obtained from the wiretap. The U.S. Supreme Court has held that "probable cause does not demand the certainty we associate with formal trials" and that the probable cause requirement is satisfied if there is a "fair probability" based on the totality of the circumstances presented to the judge that evidence of a crime will be found [26]. The information that the judge may consider in issuing a wiretap order does not have to comply with the Federal Rules of Evidence because these rules are not applicable to the issuance of search warrants, and the requirements for wiretap orders are similar to those for search warrants [14]. Hearsay, for example, may furnish a basis for a wiretap order, even though, as a general rule, hearsay is not admissible at trial [7, 20]. The reliability of the information presented to the judge factors into the decision whether probable cause exists. The assessment of reliability is made on the basis of all the information presented, rather than on the basis of each item of information, so that the various items of information can corroborate each other to enhance their reliability [26].

Once a wiretap order has been issued, the determination of probable cause should be given great deference at a hearing on a motion to suppress the evidence obtained from the wiretap [26]. As long as there was a substantial basis for the conclusion that probable cause existed, a motion to suppress the evidence would be denied.

It is clear that there was a plausible basis for a determination of probable cause for the issuance of a wiretap order. The technique the forensic examiner used to recover data from the chip was outside the norm and, therefore, its reliability may be challenged. Nevertheless, the forensic examiner was able to recover the partial number of the phone that "called" the cell phone detonator along with phone numbers of members of radical groups. This information, coupled with the fact that the interpolated phone number belonged to a person affiliated with radical groups, furnish a plausible basis to believe that a wiretap on that phone number would capture communications concerning the bombing. Consequently, the court would reject the challenge to suppress the conversations recorded during the wiretap.

The court must apply a different standard to determine whether to admit the data from the memory chip into evidence. In the scenario, the defendant is challenging the scientific basis of the extraction technique upon which the examiner's testimony about the partial phone number and the other calls will be based. As a general rule, the results of a forensic examination done using standard tools are considered to be reliable and are admissible because the tools have been tested, show consistent results, and are generally accepted by the forensic community.

As we discuss in the next scenario, in order to be admissible, expert testimony based on scientific evidence must meet the standards of Federal Rule of Evidence 702 and the Supreme Court's Daubert [25] and Kumho Tire [28] cases. These authorities permit the admission of testimony based on scientific evidence that can be demonstrated to be reliable, while denying litigants the use as evidence of the results of non-scientific tests or procedures of dubious reliability. That is, the results of scientific tests or forensic procedures are admissible only when the proponent can show such evidence comes from the application of sound science, and tools and techniques that can be demonstrated to produce accurate and reliable information.

The technique used in this case lies somewhere between an accepted digital forensic technique and a wholly untested approach that was developed for another purpose. Engineers and software developers routinely use chip programmers to read and write data to memory chips. Their use in cell phone forensics to extract data from memory chips is becoming more common [1, 3, 4], and the prosecution will rely on this fact. Nevertheless, the resolution of the issue will probably require a "Daubert hearing" in which experts testify regarding the soundness and reliability of the data extraction technique.

4.   Deleted Data from Cell Phone Memory

Consider the following scenario where a programming interface that directly interacts with cell phone memory is used to recover deleted data.

> *Law enforcement agents have identified several members of a drug gang, but not the kingpin. During the execution of a search warrant on a night-club frequented by crime bosses, law enforcement agents seize several cell phones. A forensic examiner uses a programming interface to recover deleted data from the seized phones. Deleted data from one of the phones indicates that it belongs to the kingpin. At his trial, the kingpin objects to the introduction of the data taken from his phone as evidence because the process that was used to recover deleted data is not reliable.*

Forensic examiners use many tools to extract data from electronic devices. In the early days of digital forensics, hex editors and utilities designed for administrators and software analysts were routinely used to recover data. Over the years, numerous tools and scripts written for other purposes have proved useful to forensic examiners. The main concern about unconventional tools and methods is their reliability. Does the tool or method do what the examiner expects and intends for it to do? More importantly, does it do anything unintended – such as change data on the target system? The rules of evidence condition admissibility of evidence on a showing that it is reliable. Data recovered using unreliable tools or methods cannot be admitted into evidence.

Rule 702 of the Federal Rules of Evidence, which govern trials in U.S. federal courts, requires scientific evidence to be based on reliable principles and methods for it to be admissible at trial. The main factors used to determine reliability are: (i) whether the technique has been tested and was subjected to peer review and evaluation, (ii) the known or potential rate of error for the technique, (iii) whether standards and controls exist and have been maintained for the technique, and (iv) whether the technique is generally accepted by the scientific community. These factors were refined and articulated by the U.S. Supreme Court in Daubert v. Merrell Dow Pharmaceuticals, Inc. [25]. The Daubert notion of reliability was incorporated into Federal Rule of Evidence 702 in 2000. It requires the trial judge to serve as a gatekeeper in order to keep the jury from considering unreliable expert testimony and scientific evidence that is misleading or not helpful.

The programming interface technique would not satisfy the Daubert factors unless it has been extensively tested. The technique must be subjected to peer review and evaluation, and the rate of error should be known. Also, standards and controls must be enforced on its proper use, and it should be generally accepted by the scientific community.

Nevertheless, the Supreme Court emphasized in a later case, Kumho Tire Co. v. Carmichael [28], that the Daubert factors were never intended to be a definitive checklist. Instead, the trial court's inquiry into the reliability of scientific evidence should be flexible, and recognize that the Daubert factors are not the only tests of reliability. Thus, it may be possible for the government to make a case for the reliability of the programming interface technique even though it has not been subjected to peer review and evaluation and may not be generally accepted by the scientific community.

Repeated tests with consistent results may be necessary to convince a trial judge that the programming interface technique is reliable. Also, it would be desirable to provide as much information about the technique as possible, e.g., whether it had been used in other cases and whether other forensic examiners had used or tested it. If the source code of the software were available, testimony about what it does and how it was used would be important to asserting that it produces reliable and consistent results.

Even if the trial court was inclined to admit the data taken from the cell phone over the kingpin's objections, the kingpin could argue that the data should not be believed – or given "weight" – by the jury.

5.   Trojan Defense

The following scenario clarifies the important distinction between admissibility and sufficiency of evidence:

> *An executive of a high-tech company has been indicted for securities fraud. The centerpiece of the prosecution's case is a document discussing improper changes to accounting records to improve the company's quarterly reports. The document was recovered from the executive's smart phone, which was seized during a search warrant executed on his corporate office. The executive objects to the introduction of the document on the ground that it was placed on his phone by a rival. To support his argument, the executive points out that many company employees have the technical skills and equipment to hack his phone. Would the document recovered from the smart phone be admissible as evidence against the executive? May the executive raise the "hacker did it" defense if the document is introduced in evidence?*

The document recovered from the executive's smart phone would be admissible as evidence and the executive could claim that someone else put it on his phone. However, the jury would be free to believe or reject his defense as it chooses. As noted above, the threshold for admissibility is relatively low and the admissibility of an item of evidence depends on its relevance to the material issues in the case. Under Federal Rule of Evidence 401, an item of evidence is relevant if it has "any tendency to make the existence of any fact that is of consequence to the determination of the action more probable or less probable than it would be without the evidence" [13].

The facts that the document was found on the executive's cell phone and the phone was in the executive's possession are probably sufficient to connect the document to the executive and meet the admissibility standard. Proof that the document was recovered from the executive's smart phone would be relevant to establishing that the executive was the author or recipient of the document, because it would have some tendency to make it more probable that the executive had knowledge of the document. Even though there is no direct evidence to connect the executive to the document, the fact that the document was recovered from his smart phone is circumstantial evidence that he was aware of its contents. It is up to the jury to decide whether the executive was connected to the document because of its presence on his smart phone.

An inference may be used to connect an item of evidence to a material issue in a case only if the inference is reasonable and consistent with experience, science and logic. If a case is tried by a jury, both the judge and jury have a role in deciding whether an item of evidence is admissible and relevant. First, the judge must decide whether the inferences on which the relevance of the item of evidence is based are reasonable and consistent with experience, science and logic so that it would be possible for a reasonable juror to conclude that there is a tendency to make a material issue in the case more probable or less probable. If the judge decides that this requirement is satisfied, the item may be admitted as evidence. It is then up to the jury to determine whether to believe the evidence, what weight to give to it and what inferences to draw from it. Thus, the jury has the ultimate responsibility for deciding factual issues, such as whether the executive was the author or intended recipient of the document, but the judge has authority to keep the jury from seeing a particular item of evidence if there is no reasonable connection between the evidence and the material issues in the case.

Two cases involving a "Trojan defense" illustrate these evidentiary principles. In the first case, Aaron Caffrey, a hacker from the United Kingdom, was charged with launching a distributed denial of service attack that brought down the navigation system at the Port of Houston, Texas on September 20, 2001. Law enforcement agents traced the attack to a computer in Caffrey's home. A forensic examination of the computer uncovered a denial of service script and a file containing the IP addresses of more than 11,000 servers that were vulnerable to the attack. When the denial of service software was executed in a controlled environment, it displayed the message: "IIS Unicode exploiter coded by Aaron." Law enforcement agents also recovered chatroom logs from Caffrey's computer stating that a chatroom user named "Aaron" had launched the attack at another user in South Africa in retaliation for insults against his girlfriend.

At his trial, Caffrey denied responsibility for the attacks, and claimed that two other hackers had installed a Trojan program on his computer so that they could remotely control his computer, and that they used it to launch the attack without his knowledge. The prosecution countered with expert testimony that there was no indication of a Trojan on the computer and no known software that could install such a Trojan without leaving a trace. The jury returned a not guilty verdict.

Although there was sufficient evidence to allow the jury to conclude that Caffrey initiated the attack and find him guilty beyond a reasonable doubt, the jury was not required to do so. It is wholly within the province of the jury to decide what weight to give to evidence, to decide what the facts really are, and to decide guilt or innocence based on these facts. The members of the Caffrey jury may have believed Caffrey's claim rather than the prosecution's expert testimony. On the other hand, the jurors may have voted to acquit Caffrey for other reasons without resolving the Trojan defense issue [5, 6].

A jury reached a different conclusion in United States v. Ray [8]. Thomas Ray was accused of attempting to extort $2.5 million from Best Buy by sending email messages that threatened to exploit a computer vulnerability. After tracing the emails to three AOL accounts, one of which belonged to Ray, the FBI obtained search warrants and conducted forensic examinations of the computers associated with the AOL accounts. The forensic examiner found portions of three of the sixteen extortion emails sent to Best Buy on Ray's computer. Ray raised the Trojan defense at his trial. An expert witness for the defense testified that Ray's computer had no firewall and an outdated anti-virus program, that the Internet Explorer 5.5 browser on Ray's computer had various security problems, and that traces of a Trojan were found on the hard drive. Despite this evidence, the jury convicted Ray on two counts of extortion, and the conviction was affirmed on appeal.

The appellate court ruled that the following evidence supported the jury's decision: (i) Ray admitted he used the computer to connect to the Internet several times a day, (ii) three of the emails sent to Best Buy were traced to the IP address he was using when the emails were sent, (iii) portions of three of the extortion letters were found on Ray's hard drive, (iv) the emails were created by someone typing on Ray's computer who connected to the Internet using Ray's screen name and password to send the emails, (v) no evidence of remote access or hacking was found on Ray's computer, and (vi) Ray had the knowledge and ability to process the monetary transactions that the extortion emails demanded. On the other hand, the decision whether to convict Ray was a matter for the jury, and the jury would not have been compelled to return a conviction.

These two cases and a recent "somebody else used my computer to do it" case (United States v. Shea [10]) demonstrate that, even in cases involving sophisticated technical issues, the jury is free to choose which evidence to believe and which evidence to reject. Where the prosecution can prove the defendant had access to the computer or device at the proper time, the technical ability to do what was done and the motive, the jury is free to infer guilt and reject defense claims that a hacker did it. Conversely, the jury is also free to believe the defense claims and acquit if the prosecution has not proved the negative.

In the case of the high-tech executive, the document would be relevant and admissible into evidence because its recovery from his smart phone would make it more probable that he knew about the document. The executive would likewise be able to present evidence about the hacking skills of his associates and anything else relevant to his defense.

To overcome this defense, the prosecution might attempt to show that there was no evidence the phone had been hacked. It might also analyze the call log to show that the phone was always in the executive's possession and that it was unlikely that someone else had access to the phone to place the incriminating document.

6.   Conclusions

The widespread use of cell phones provides new sources of evidence for criminal investigations. Law enforcement agencies may use this evidence at trial as well as to establish a basis for obtaining wiretap orders or call detail records from service providers. The legal standards for the admissibility of evidence at trial differ substantially from those for obtaining wiretaps or call detail records. The showing required for a wiretap order is essentially probable cause, which means that there is a fair probability based on the totality of the circumstances that the wiretap will produce evidence of a crime. The showing required for a Section 2703(d) order to obtain call detail records consists of specific and articulable facts that there are reasonable grounds to believe that the records are relevant and material to an ongoing criminal investigation. In contrast, admissibility at trial requires proof that the evidence offered has been obtained by reliable scientific methods and is relevant to the issues in the case. It is, therefore, extremely important that law enforcement agencies employ scientifically sound and reliable forensic tools and techniques to ensure that cell phone data recovered using new and evolving technologies will be admissible and useful in judicial proceedings.

References

[1] R. Ayers, W. Jansen, N. Cilleros and R. Daniellou, Cell Phone Forensic Tools: An Overview and Analysis, NIST Publication NISTIR 7250, National Institute of Standards and Technology, Gaithersburg, Maryland, 2005.

[2] Computer Crime and Intellectual Property Section, Searching and Seizing Computers and Obtaining Electronic Evidence in Criminal Investigations, U.S. Department of Justice, Washington, DC (www.usdoj.gov/criminal/cybercrime/s&smanual2002.htm), 2002.

[3] D. Harrill and R. Mislan, A small scale digital device forensics ontology, *Small Scale Digital Device Forensics Journal*, vol. 1(1), 2007.

[4] W. Jansen and R. Ayers, Guidelines on Cell Phone Forensics: Recommendations of the National Institute of Standards and Technology, NIST Special Publication 800-101, National Institute of Standards and Technology, Gaithersburg, Maryland, 2007.

[5] J. Leyden, Caffrey acquittal a setback for cybercrime prosecutions, *The Register* (www.theregister.co.uk/2003/10/17/caffrey _acquittal_a_setback), October 17, 2003.

[6] A. McCue, Revenge hack downed US port systems, ZDNet.co.uk (news.zdnet.co.uk/security/0,1000000189,39116978,00.htm), October 7, 2003.

[7] U.S. Court of Appeals (Eighth Circuit), United States v. Garcia, *Federal Reporter Second Series*, vol. 785, pp. 214–218, 1986.

[8] U.S. Court of Appeals (Eighth Circuit), United States v. Ray, *Federal Reporter Third Series*, vol. 428, pp. 1172–1175, 2005.

[9] U.S. Court of Appeals (First Circuit), United States v. Scott, *Federal Reporter Second Series*, vol. 975, pp. 927–931, 1992.

[10] U.S. Court of Appeals (Ninth Circuit), United States v. Shea, *Federal Reporter Third Series*, vol. 493, pp. 1110–1119, 2007.

[11] U.S. District Court (District of Kansas), United States v. Kennedy, *Federal Supplement Second Series*, vol. 81, 1103–1115, 2000.

[12] U.S. District Court (District of New Jersey), United States v. Scarfo, *Federal Supplement Second Series*, vol. 180, pp. 572–583, 2001.

[13] U.S. Government, Rule 401, Definition of Relevant Evidence, Title 28, Appendix – Rules of Evidence, Judiciary and Judicial Procedures, *United States Code (Volume 16)*, Washington, DC, pp. 863–864, 2001.

[14] U.S. Government, Rule 1101, Applicability of Rules, Title 28, Appendix – Rules of Evidence, Judiciary and Judicial Procedures, *United States Code (Volume 16)*, Washington, DC, pp. 930–931, 2001.

[15] U.S. Government, Classified Information Procedures Act, Title 18, Appendix, Crimes and Criminal Procedure, *United States Code (2000 Edition) Supplement V*, Washington, DC, pp. 1524–1529, 2007.

[16] U.S. Government, Section 2703, Required Disclosure of Customer Communications Records, Title 18, Crimes and Criminal Procedure, *United States Code (2000 Edition) Supplement V*, Washington, DC, pp. 1073–1075, 2007.

[17] U.S. House Judiciary Committee, Communications Assistance for Law Enforcement Act, Public Law No. 103-414, *United States Code Congressional and Administrative News, 103rd Congress, Second Session 1994 (Volume 5)*, West Publishing Company, St. Paul, Minnesota, pp. 3489–3515, 1995.

[18] U.S. Supreme Court, United States v. Reynolds, *United States Reports*, vol. 345, pp. 1–12, 1953.

[19] U.S. Supreme Court, Roviaro v. United States, *United States Reports*, vol. 353, pp. 53–71, 1957.

[20] U.S. Supreme Court, Jones v. United States, *United States Reports*, vol. 362, pp. 257–273, 1960.

[21] U.S. Supreme Court, McCray v. Illinois, *United States Reports*, vol. 386, pp. 300–316, 1967.

[22] U.S. Supreme Court, Smith v. Maryland, *United States Reports*, vol. 442, pp. 735–752, 1979.

[23] U.S. Supreme Court, Rawlings v. Kentucky, *United States Reports*, vol. 448, pp. 98–121, 1980.

[24] U.S. Supreme Court, United States v. Payner, *United States Reports*, vol. 447, pp. 727–751, 1980.

[25] U.S. Supreme Court, Daubert v. Merrell Dow Pharmaceuticals, Inc., *United States Reports*, vol. 509, pp. 579–601, 1983.

[26] U.S. Supreme Court, Illinois v. Gates, *United States Reports*, vol. 462, pp. 213–295, 1983.

[27] U.S. Supreme Court, California v. Greenwood, *United States Reports*, vol. 486, pp. 35–56, 1988.

[28] U.S. Supreme Court, Kumho Tire Co. v. Carmichael, *United States Reports*, vol. 526, pp. 137–159, 1999.

VIII

EVENT DATA RECORDER FORENSICS

Chapter 20

PROTECTION AND RECOVERY OF RAILROAD EVENT RECORDER DATA

Mark Hartong, Rajni Goel and Duminda Wijesekera

Abstract   Passenger and freight locomotives in the United States are required to carry event recorders for collecting data that can be used in post-accident investigations. There are, however, shared management, labor and government concerns about maintaining the integrity, confidentiality and non-repudiation properties of the collected data. This paper proposes a cryptographic technique based on secret sharing that protects event recorder data while supporting data recovery by authorized parties.

Keywords: Event data recorders, railroad accident investigations, secret shares

1.   Introduction

Railroad accidents are relatively rare events in the United States. In 2006, the total incident rate was 16.25 per million train miles [13]. This rate is very low, but it still equates to more than 13,100 separate incidents. Train accidents (collisions or derailments) and highway grade crossing incidents accounted for 22.2% of the incidents; the remaining 55.6% involved trespassers on railroad property or railroad personnel performing their job-related activities.

Locomotive event data recorders are used by railroad companies, the Federal Railroad Administration (FRA) and the National Transportation Safety Board (NTSB) to determine the root cause of incidents. In fact, the lead locomotive of any train operating faster than 30 mph is required to be equipped with an event recorder [34]. But the regulations only require event data recorders to capture information about a limited number of parameters; they do not mandate the recording of onboard communications or the crash hardening of all recorders until 2009.

Please use the following format when citing this chapter:

Hartong, M., Goel, R. and Wijesekera, D., 2008, in IFIP International Federation for Information Processing, Volume 285; Advances in Digital Forensics IV; Indrajit Ray, Sujeet Shenoi; (Boston: Springer), pp. 247–260.

The lack of evidence pertaining to crew actions was highlighted in the aftermath of the February 1996 collision of MARC and AMTRAK trains in Silver Spring, Maryland. In particular, the NTSB/FRA investigation was hampered by the lack of voice records of the train crew in the moments leading up to the accident. Indeed, the NTSB subsequently recommended that voice communications of crew members be recorded for exclusive use in accident investigations [27].

Railroad management, labor organizations and the government have strong interests in using event data recorders to collect forensic data about railroad incidents and to maintain the integrity and confidentiality of the data. This paper discusses the current requirements for locomotive event recorders and proposes cryptographic mechanisms for protecting the recorded data from unauthorized release, tampering and misuse.

2.   Railroad Event Recorder Requirements

The use of event data recorders to assist in accident investigations goes back almost 50 years. Aircraft flight data recorders capture critical flight parameters while cockpit voice recorders record all flight deck communications. Without information from these devices, the sequences of events that resulted in several major aviation incidents (e.g., the ValueJet Flight 592 crash in Miami, Florida on May 11, 1996) would have remained unknown.

The use of event data recorders in railroads is a more recent development. The Rail Safety Improvement Act of 1988 [35] provides statutory authority for the use of event recorders in the United States. Based on this statutory authority, Section 229.135 of Title 49 of the Code of Federal Regulations [34] defines the minimum requirements for locomotive event recorders. It differs from the original regulations by adding the requirement for a certified survivable version and phasing out magnetic tape recordings by 2010. The federal technical performance standards generally mirror the IEEE standard for event recorders [15]. The recovery of data from locomotive event recorders is governed by Association of American Railroads (AAR) standards [5]. These mandatory industry standards define manufacturer-independent physical and logical download interfaces, download methods and the serial protocol used to recover data from event recorders.

There are six original equipment manufacturers (OEMs) for locomotive event recorders in the United States (Table 1). While the data storage formats used by the manufacturers may differ, the primary method of data download is a serial DB-9 RS232 (19,200 bps) interface to a personal computer using the Xmodem 1K CRC file transfer protocol [9].

Table 1. Event recorder manufacturers.

Manufacturer	URL
Bach Simpson	www.bach-simpson.com
Electromotive Diesel	www.emdiesels.com
GE Transportation Systems	www.getransportation.com
Q-tron – A WABTEC Company	www.wabtec.com
Quantum Engineering	www.qei.biz
WABTEC Railway Electronics	www.wabtec.com

This simple file transfer protocol, which does not distinguish between text and binary files, uses a 16-bit cyclic redundancy check for error detection. Other approved downloading mechanisms include a PCMCIA interface using the ANSI AT Attachment (ATA) protocol and a serial download data port connected to a radio for wireless download using the Xmodem protocol.

3. Cryptographic Protection of Data

This paper proposes the use of cryptographic techniques to achieve data integrity, authentication and non-repudiation. Currently, all event recorder manufacturers utilize checksums to provide integrity protection against accidental and non-malicious errors, but not against malicious attacks. Also, checksums (on their own) do not provide for data non-repudiation and confidentiality. Event recorder data is not random and is interpreted within a particular context; consequently, the surreptitious modification of checksums is extremely difficult. Nevertheless, certain bit manipulations are possible [21].

Table 2 presents the minimum requirements for data collection by event recorders for the purposes of accident reconstruction, disciplinary actions or locomotive health monitoring. In all cases, it is critical that data integrity and confidentiality be maintained and that the data be attributed to particular entities without non-repudiation. Unfortunately, tampering with event recorder data has been observed. In a 1982 collision, the crew reported that the event recorder was working properly prior to the accident. However, several hours after the accident, a railroad official discovered that the case had been broken open and the tape was missing (the locomotive cab itself was not damaged) [26]. In another collision [25], certain attributes of the recorded data were found to have been modified. The union that represents railroad engineers has agreed, in principle, to the use of event recorders, but it is concerned about the

Table 2. Minimum data required to be collected by event recorders.

Train Speed
Direction of Motion
Time
Distance
Throttle Position
Application and Operation of Automatic Air Brakes by Engineer
Application and Operation of Automatic Air Brakes by On-Board Computer
Application and Operation of Independent Brakes
Application and Operation of Dynamic Brakes (if equipped)
Cab Signal Aspects (if equipped)
Loss of End of Train (EOT) Communications
Electronic Controlled Pneumatic (ECP) Braking Messages (if equipped)
EOT Armed Emergency Brake Command and Emergency Brake Application
Indication of EOT Valve Failure
EOT Brake Pipe Pressure
EOT Marker Light Status
EOT "Low Battery" Status
Status of Lead Locomotive Headlights
Status of Lead Locomotive Auxiliary Lights (Ditch Lights)
Horn Control Activation
Locomotive Number
Locomotive Position in the Consist
Tractive Effort (Pulling Capability)
Cruise Control Status
Safety Critical Train Control Information Routed to Engineer's Display

misuse, improper interpretation, public disclosure, tampering and use of the data beyond the purposes of accident investigation [8].

Most of these concerns can be addressed by having at least two entities actively participate in the recovery of event recorder data. Railroad management and labor, for example, could jointly obtain data to evaluate locomotive performance and determine maintenance requirements, an activity in which the government has no regulatory interest. Labor and government could retrieve locomotive operating parameters (e.g., speed and horn settings) to support or refute labor claims during a federal locomotive engineer review board hearing. Likewise, railroad management and government could obtain locomotive operating parameters to support or refute the validity of railroad violations identified by the government.

The secret sharing technique [7, 30] – also known as secret splitting or split knowledge – enables cryptographic keys to be distributed between the various stakeholders. In secret sharing, N secrets (e.g., pieces of the

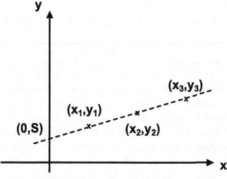

Figure 1. Secret shares.

key used to encrypt data) are shared among M entities where $M < N$ such that all M entities can collaborate to recover the original data, but no group with $M - 1$ or fewer entities can do so.

Multiple mathematical results are available to support the creation and reconstruction of secret shares [32]. In the case of event recorder data, any two of the three stakeholders (management, labor and government) should be able to recover the data by combining their secret shares. This situation is modeled using three distributed secrets (S_1, S_2, S_3). Each stakeholder is given two of the three secrets, (S_1, S_2), (S_1, S_3) or (S_2, S_3), and agreement by any two of the three stakeholders is sufficient to recover all three distributed secrets, enabling the key to be reconstituted and the data to be recovered.

4.   Secret Sharing and the Primary Use Case

The critical use case in the forensic analysis of a railroad incident is the recovery of encrypted event recorder data. We use an implementation of Shamir's N of M secret sharing scheme to ensure that no single party can unilaterally recover the cryptographic key and modify or release the data. Three parties are involved, railroad management, railroad labor and government ($M = 3$). Any pair of the secret shares held by management, labor and government is sufficient to reconstruct the cryptographic key (i.e., $N = 2$).

The secret sharing technique is illustrated in Figure 1. First, the point $(0, S)$ on the y-axis corresponding to the cryptographic key S is located. A line containing the point $(0, S)$ is then drawn, and three points, (x_1, y_1), (x_2, y_2) and (x_3, y_3), on the line are selected. These three points represent the shares that are distributed to railroad management, labor and government.

Table 3.   Recovery of event recorder data use case.

Number	Description
1	**Summary**: Railroad management, labor or government recovers cryptographically-protected data from a locomotive event recorder for forensic analysis of a locomotive accident (collision/derailment), locomotive health monitoring or crew disciplinary actions.
2	**Basic Path**: The event recorder captures forensic data. After a locomotive collision or derailment, government accident investigators combine their secret share with the secret share held by railroad management or labor to generate the cryptographic key. Cryptographically-protected data is downloaded from the event recorder. Using the cryptographic key, the government decrypts the downloaded data and verifies its authenticity and integrity; the data is then forensically analyzed.
3	**Alternate Paths**: (1) Health Analysis – The event recorder captures forensic data. Railroad management combines its secret share with the secret share held by railroad labor to generate the cryptographic key. Cryptographically-protected data is downloaded from the event recorder. Using the cryptographic key, railroad management decrypts the downloaded data and verifies its authenticity and integrity. Railroad management conducts locomotive health analysis using the decrypted data. (2) Engineer Discipline – The event recorder captures forensic data. Railroad management combines its secret share with the secret share held by the government to generate the cryptographic key. Cryptographically-protected data is downloaded from the event recorder. Using the cryptographic key, railroad management and government decrypt the downloaded data and verify its authenticity and integrity. Railroad management and government review the data to determine if engineer decertification is warranted.
4	**Capture Points**: The event recorder captures recorder attributes. Management, labor and government analyze the downloaded and decrypted forensic data.

At least two of the three shares must be known in order to recover the key S. Knowing two shares means that two points on the line are available, enabling the specification of the equation of the line. The cryptographic key S is then obtained by determining the intersection of the line with the y-axis. One share (or point) is insufficient to determine S. An infinite number of lines go through this point, corresponding to an infinite number of intersections with the y-axis (possible key values). The key is secure because, regardless of the computing power available, the key cannot be reconstructed without at least two shares (points).

The secret sharing technique enables the use case described in Tables 3 and 4. However, it does not protect against data corruption due to

Table 4. Recovery of event recorder data use case (continued).

Number	Description
5	**Triggers:** (1) Management and labor determine the need for forensic analysis of the event recorder data. (2) Management and government determine the need for forensic analysis of the event recorder data. (3) Labor and government determine the need for forensic analysis of the event recorder data.
6	**Attacker Profile:** Not applicable.
7	**Preconditions:** (1) Railroad management, labor and government each have a secret share. (2) Event recorder attributes have been successfully captured in the event recorder.
8	**Post Conditions (Worst Case):** (1) Event recorder is damaged and data cannot be recovered. (2) Data confidentiality, integrity and non-repudiation are lost. (3) Event recorder is not damaged, but data has been manipulated to preclude data recovery.
9	**Post Conditions (Best Case):** (1) Data is recovered from the event recorder. (2) Data confidentiality, integrity and non-repudiation are maintained.
10	**Business Rules:** (1) Management, labor and government place their secret shares in escrow. (2) Secret shares held in escrow must be released if ordered by a court. (3) In the case of an accident, data that is recovered may not be used in civil suits by the affected parties (management, labor, government or the public).

event recorder damage or the deliberate manipulation of data. Storing event recorder data in a crash-hardened memory module reduces the probability of data loss, but does not completely address data corruption and malicious data modification. Data loss can be mitigated using a fault tolerant storage mechanism such as Rabin's Information Dispersal Algorithm (IDA) [28]. This algorithm is conceptually similar to the secret sharing technique in that it breaks a file or block of data into M pieces and permits complete data recovery using any N pieces. This requires that event recorder designs implement multiple independent storage mechanisms, each of which holds one of the M pieces. Note, however, that IDA does not protect against malicious data modification.

Protection against unauthorized data alteration can be achieved by storing a hash value of each of the M pieces. The hash value of each piece is validated prior to using the piece to recover the complete file or block. If a hash value is determined to be invalid, it is assumed that the corresponding piece has been altered and that piece is not used to reconstruct the original file or block. Only subsets of the M pieces that have not been corrupted are used in reconstruction. The original

---

Algorithm 1 Data collection.

---

  while *event_recorder_is_enabled* **do**
    for *required_event_attributes* **do**
      Read(*required_event_attribute*)
      Store(*required_event_attribute*)
    end for
  end while

---

data can be reconstructed as long as the cardinality of the subset of uncorrupted pieces is no less than N.

5.   Implementation Issues

This section discusses the principal implementation issues related to data collection and recovery. These include modifications to the event recorder as well as trust management and key escrow.

5.1   Data Collection

Event recorders capture continuous streams of data. Algorithm 1 specifies the steps involved in data collection.

Algorithm 2 Secure data collection.

  Process_command_line_options
  while *event_recorder_is_enabled* **do**
    for all *required_event_attributes* **do**
      Read(*required_event_attribute*)
      encrypted_required_event_attribute ←
        Encrypt(*required_event_attribute*, *common_key*)
      Store(*encrypted_required_event_attribute*)
    end for
  end while

Algorithm 2 incorporates an additional encryption step to protect event recorder data. Encryption would be implemented using a cryptographic module that is resistant to reverse engineering. The device would have to be programmed after mass production so that the key and key escrow information are entered once and maintained without external electrical power. Data written to the EEPROM must be prevented from being erased, altered or cleared by service personnel or crash investigators. Detailed technical standards for cryptographic modules have been specified [23] along with compliant implementations [22]. Using such a cryptographic module with an appropriate trust management system can ensure that event recorder data is adequately protected.

A major technical issue arises because IDA operates on blocks of data. This precludes its use with analog data and also limits its application to digital data. Digital event recorders capture their information as continuous streams of closely-spaced "snapshots" in time. Therefore, the cryptographic module must encrypt each snapshot and write the encrypted information to the EEPROM before the next snapshot arrives. Consequently, the sampling rate of event recorder inputs is limited by the cycle time for encryption and storage. But reducing the sampling rate decreases the fidelity of the collected data. Specifying the required fidelity of event recorder data is, therefore, an important issue.

The worst-case scenario occurs when an event recorder captures crew conversations. The sampling rate must be high enough for the recorded conversations to be intelligible on replay. According to the Shannon-Nyquist theory [31], the sampling rate should be twice the frequency of the highest frequency that is sampled. A frequency range of 0-4 kHz is required for most phonemes, which corresponds to a sampling rate of 8 kHz or a cycle time of 125 microseconds. Assuming that 8-bit pulse coded modulation (PCM) is used, the required system throughput is 64 kbps. FPGA-based encryption engines can support throughputs that are two magnitudes higher [11]. Therefore, an FPGA coupled with EEPROM technology with fast write times [36] would satisfy the 125 microsecond cycle time requirement.

5.2   Data Recovery

Several standards have been established for trust management in operational environments [2–4, 16–20]. While a detailed discussion of trust management is beyond the scope of this paper, an examination of the use cases for normal and abnormal data recovery provides valuable insights into the requirements of a trust management system.

Algorithm 3 presents the steps involved in normal event recorder data recovery for the purposes of monitoring locomotive health and engineer discipline. The data recovery process uses a non-secure network connection or a direct connection to the event recorder. A non-secure connection can be used because the AAR data transfer protocol, which is data-format neutral, allows data to be transferred in encrypted form. Likewise, when a direct connection is employed, data can be recovered in an encrypted format and is decrypted only in a secure environment during an investigation.

In the case of data recovery for the purpose of evaluating locomotive health, the *recovered_common_key* in Algorithm 3 is reconstructed from the key shares held by railroad management and labor. The recovered

---

Algorithm 3 Normal data recovery.

---
  if *locomotive_healh_recovery* **then**
    recovered_common_key ←
      Recover_key(*railroad_management_share*, *railroad_labor_share*)
    for all *encrypted_required_event_attributes* **do**
      Read(*encrypted_required_event_attribute*)
      required_event_attribute ←
        Decrypt(*encrypted_required_event_attribute*, *shared_key*)
    end for
  else if *engineer_discipline* **then**
    recovered_common_key ←
      Recover_key(*railroad_management_share*, *government_share*)
    for all *encrypted_required_event_attributes* **do**
      Read(*encrypted_required_event_attribute*)
      required_event_attribute ←
        Decrypt(*encrypted_required_event_attribute*, *recovered_key*)
    end for
  end if

---

data enables management to proactively determine degradations in locomotive behavior that may have an adverse impact on the capability of a crew to operate a train safely, which would, of course, be of great interest to labor. However, in the unlikely event that labor refuses to participate and provide its key shares (e.g., during a strike), data recovery could still proceed by management obtaining key shares from the government.

In scenarios involving engineer discipline, the *recovered_common_key* is reconstructed using the key shares held by labor and government or by management and government. The government serves as the neutral party in these scenarios, which involve the certification, recertification or decertification of locomotive engineers [33]. Both management and labor have a vested interest in these proceedings and would, therefore, provide their key shares to government upon request.

The steps involved in accident data recovery (Algorithm 4) are similar to those performed during normal data recovery. However, there are two primary differences. First, data recovery is conducted in a controlled environment (i.e., the event recorder is moved from the accident site to a laboratory). Second, because the determination of the cause of an accident is in the interest of all three stakeholders, there would be few objections to providing key shares. Damage to the event recorder may complicate the task of data recovery. Possible solutions are to implement data distribution schemes or to perform off-board recording of data [14].

Management and labor could collude to prevent the recovery of accident data, but this is unlikely because of the mutual distrust that exists

---

Algorithm 4 Accident data recovery.

---

if key shares held by government and labor **then**
  recovered_common_key ← Recover_key(*railroad_labor_share*,
    government_share)
else if key shares held by government and management **then**
  recovered_common_key ← Recover_key(*railroad_management_share*,
    government_share)
  for all *encrypted_required_event_attributes* **do**
    Read(*encrypted_required_event_attribute*)
    required_event_attribute ← Decrypt(*encrypted_required_event_attribute*,
      recovered_common_key)
  end for
end if

---

between labor and management. Collusion could be mitigated by having a trusted third party hold all the key shares and release them to an authorized entity only upon receiving a court order. However, this escrow approach has several problems that would have to be resolved [1].

6.   Conclusions

Evidence recovered from locomotive event data recorders is extremely important in accident investigations. Secret sharing provides an elegant cryptographic mechanism for preserving the integrity, confidentiality and non-repudiability of accident data. Indeed, it is expected that cryptography will be broadly adopted in devices that store potentially valuable data [10, 24, 29]. However, secret sharing introduces additional costs. These include adapting event data recorders to support encryption, securing the secret shares and operating the required infrastructure. Nevertheless, secret sharing is an attractive solution to the problem of securing critical shared data [6, 12].

Note that the views and opinions expressed in this paper are those of the authors. They do not reflect any official policy or position of the Federal Railroad Administration, U.S. Department of Transportation or the U.S. Government, and shall not be used for advertising or product endorsement purposes.

References

[1] H. Abelson, R. Anderson, S. Bellovin, J. Benaloh, M. Blaze, W. Diffie, J. Gilmore, P. Neumann, R. Rivest, J. Schiller and B. Schneier, The risks of key recovery, key escrow and trusted third-party encryption, *World Wide Web Journal*, vol. 2(3), pp. 241–257, 1997.

[2] American National Standards Institute, Financial Institution Multiple Center Key Management, ANSI Standard X9.28:1991, Washington, DC, 1991.

[3] American National Standards Institute, Financial Institution Key Management (Wholesale), ANSI Standard X9.17:1995, Washington, DC, 1995.

[4] American National Standards Institute, Public Key Cryptography for the Financial Services Industry, Key Agreement and Key Transport Using Elliptic Curve Cryptography, ANSI Standard X9.63:2001, Washington, DC, 2001.

[5] Association of American Railroads, Locomotive Event Recorder Download Standard, AAR Standard S-5512, Section M, *AAR Manual of Standards and Practices*, Washington, DC, 2004.

[6] M. Azer, S. El-Kassas and M. El-Soudani, Threshold cryptography and authentication in ad hoc networks: Survey and challenges, *Proceedings of the Second International Conference on Systems and Network Communications*, p. 5, 2007.

[7] G. Blakely, Safeguarding cryptographic keys, *Proceedings of the National Computer Conference*, vol. 48, pp. 313–317, 1979.

[8] Brotherhood of Locomotive Engineers, Locomotive event recorders seeking a balance of safety and privacy in the real world of railroad operations, presented at the *NTSB/SAE Vehicle Recorder Topical Technical Symposium*, 2003.

[9] J Campbell, *C Programmer's Guide to Serial Communications*, Sams, Indianapolis, Indiana, 1993.

[10] E Casey, Practical approaches to recovering encrypted digital evidence, *International Journal of Digital Evidence*, vol. 1(3), 2002.

[11] A. Dandalis, V. Prasanna and J. Rolim, A comparative study of performance of AES final candidiates using FPGAs, *Proceedings of the Second International Workshop on Cryptographic Hardware and Embedded Systems*, pp. 125–140, 2000.

[12] Y. Desmedt, Some recent research aspects of threshold cryptography, *Proceedings of the First International Workshop on Information Security*, pp. 158–173, 1997.

[13] Federal Railroad Agency, Accident/Incident Overview, 2006, Office of Safety Analysis, U.S. Department of Transportation, Washington, DC (safetydata.fra.dot.gov/OfficeofSafety), 2007.

[14] M. Hartong, R. Goel and D. Wijesekera, A framework for investigating railroad accidents, in *Advances in Digital Forensics III*, P. Craiger and S. Shenoi (Eds.), Boston, Massachusetts, pp. 255–265, 2007.

[15] Institute of Electrical and Electronics Engineers, IEEE Standard for Rail Transit Vehicle Event Recorders, IEEE Standard 1482.1-1999, Piscataway, New Jersey, 1999.

[16] International Organization for Standardization, Banking – Key Management (Retail) – Parts 1, 2 and 5, ISO Standards 11568-1:2005, 11568-2:2005, 11568-1:2007, Geneva, Switzerland, 2005–2007.

[17] International Organization for Standardization, Information Technology – Open Systems Interconnection – The Directory: Public Key and Attribute Certificate Frameworks, ISO Standard ISO/IEC 9594-8:2005, Geneva, Switzerland, 2005.

[18] International Organization for Standardization, Health Informatics – Public Key Infrastructure – Parts 1, 2 and 3, ISO Standards ISO/TS 17090-1:2008, 17090-2:2008, 17090-3:2008, Geneva, Switzerland, 2008.

[19] Internet Engineering Task Force, RFC 1422: Privacy Enhancement for Internet Electronic Mail Part II: Certificate-Based Key Management, 1993.

[20] Internet Engineering Task Force, RFC 1424: Privacy Enhancement for Internet Electronic Mail Part IV: Key Certificate and Related Services (Standard), 1993.

[21] A. Menezes, P. van Oorschot and S. Vanstone *Handbook of Applied Cryptography*, CRC Press, Boca Raton, Florida, 2001.

[22] National Institute of Standards and Technology, Module Validation Lists, Gaithersburg, Maryland (csrc.nist.gov/groups/STM/cmvp/validation.html).

[23] National Institute of Standards and Technology, Security Requirements for Cryptographic Modules, FIPS PUB 140-1, Gaithersburg, Maryland, 2001.

[24] National Research Council, *Cryptography's Role in Securing the Information Society*, National Academy Press, Washington, DC, 1996.

[25] National Transportation Safety Board, Railroad Accident Report – Side Collision of Two Missouri Pacific Railroad Company Freight Trains at Glasie Junction near Possum Grape, Arkansas, October 3, 1982, NTSB-RAR-83-06, U.S. Department of Transportation, Washington, DC, 1983.

[26] National Transportation Safety Board, Railroad Accident Report – Head-on Collision of National Railroad Passenger Corporation (Amtrak) Passenger Trains Nos. 151 and 168, Astoria, Queens, New York, July 23, 1984, NTSB-RAR-85-09, U.S. Department of Transportation, Washington, DC, 1985.

[27] National Transportation Safety Board, Railroad Accident Report – Collision and Derailment of Maryland Rail Commuter MARC Train 286 and National Railroad Passenger Corporation Amtrak Train 29 Near Silver Spring, Maryland on February 16, 1996, NTSB-RAR-97-02, U.S. Department of Transportation, Washington, DC, 1997.

[28] M. Rabin, Efficient dispersal of information for security, load balancing and fault tolerance, Journal of the ACM, vol. 36(2), pp. 335–348, 1989.

[29] Scientific Working Group on Digital Evidence, Proposed standards for the exchange of digital evidence, Forensic Science Communications, vol. 2(2), 2000.

[30] A. Shamir, How to share a secret, Communications of the ACM, vol. 22(11), pp. 612–613, 1979.

[31] C. Shannon, A mathematical theory of communication, Bell System Technical Journal, vol. 27, pp. 379–423 and pp. 623–656, 1948.

[32] D. Stinson and R. Wei, Bibliography on Secret Sharing Schemes, Research Report CORR 98-50, Department of Combinatorics and Optimization, University of Waterloo, Waterloo, Canada, 1998.

[33] U.S. Government, Qualification and Certification of Locomotive Engineers, Title 49, Code of Federal Regulations, Part 240, Washington, DC, pp. 743–791, 2006.

[34] U.S. Government, Railroad Locomotive Safety Standards, Title 49, Code of Federal Regulations, Part 229, Washington, DC, pp. 229–385, 2006.

[35] U.S. Government, Rail Safety Improvement Act of 1988, Title 49, Code of Federal Regulations, Part 1.49(m), Washington, DC, pp. 25–26, 2007.

[36] J. Wilson, Solid-state memory takes over niche military and aerospace applications, Military and Aerospace Electronics, vol. 12(12), 2001.

Chapter 21

AUTOMOBILE EVENT DATA RECORDER FORENSICS

Nathan Singleton, Jeremy Daily and Gavin Manes

Abstract   Automobile event data recorders (EDRs) provide vital information for reconstructing traffic crashes. This paper examines the primary issues related to evidence recovery from EDRs and its use in crash reconstruction. Recommendations related to the use of EDR data in court proceedings are also presented.

Keywords: Automobile event data recorders, evidence extraction

1.   Introduction

Vehicle collisions cause significant personal injuries and financial losses on a daily basis. Several techniques and tools have been developed for traffic crash reconstruction, which involves the scientific interpretation of physical evidence to determine the events that precipitated a crash [3]. Event data recorders (EDRs) in passenger vehicles provide detailed data about vehicular operation and state. EDR data, which varies according to the make, model and year of vehicles, can augment the physical evidence used in crash investigations.

Methods for retrieving data stored in EDRs are generally proprietary in nature. The Bosch crash data retrieval (CDR) system is used for automobiles from General Motors, Ford, Chrysler and partner companies. Data contained in EDRs of other vehicles is usually recovered using manufacturer-specific hexadecimal translation tools (HTTs).

This paper focuses on the recovery of digital evidence from EDRs. A case study involving a 2001 Chevrolet 1500 pickup is used to clarify recovery techniques and digital forensic practices.

Please use the following format when citing this chapter:

Singleton, N., Daily, J. and Manes, G., 2008, in IFIP International Federation for Information Processing, Volume 285; *Advances in Digital Forensics IV*; Indrajit Ray, Sujeet Shenoi; (Boston: Springer), pp. 261–272.

2.   Automobile Event Data Recorders

Modern automobile event data recorders (EDRs) record pre-crash vehicle performance data and system status, accelerations during a crash, safety restraint system data, driver control inputs and post-crash information such as automatic crash notification. The development of EDRs can be traced back to 1990, when General Motors introduced the diagnostic energy reserve module (DERM) to record data about airbag systems. Evidence from DERMs has been used in litigation related to the design and operation of airbag systems [8].

The next generation of EDRs, called sensing and diagnostic modules (SDMs), were introduced in 1994. These modules were designed to perform three main functions in the following prioritized order: (i) deploy airbags in the event of a crash, (ii) perform airbag system diagnostics, and (iii) monitor and record system and event data during an "event." An "event," in this context, is a sudden change in vehicle acceleration that initiates an algorithm in the airbag module. Depending on the decision logic, the event may or may not cause the airbags to deploy.

Early SDMs also recorded system status data related to seat belt use and accelerations during a crash. In 1999, SDMs began to record pre-crash data such as vehicle speed, engine rpm, brake light switch status, throttle position, warning indications and seat belt use. The data is measured external to the SDM and is transferred to the module via a vehicle system bus.

In 2006, the U.S. National Highway Traffic Safety Administration (NHTSA) estimated that about 64% of new passenger vehicles were equipped with EDRs [9]. EDR use is rising due its voluntary inclusion in vehicles by manufacturers. Indeed, it is rare for automobiles manufactured in 2008 not to have some form of EDR. There is no standard location for positioning an EDR; however, it is usually located inside the vehicle cabin, near the centerline of the vehicle or under/in one of the front seats. Physical removal of an EDR typically requires the disassembly of a vehicle's interior.

In a typical EDR, vehicle system data and crash information are continuously stored in a volatile data buffer during normal operation. Depending on the module and the type of event, the volatile data may be flashed to an EEPROM. In the event of an airbag deployment in a General Motors vehicle, this data is permanently written to the EEPROM (and the module has to be replaced). However, if the airbag is not deployed, EEPROM data is cleared after the SDM is turned on 250 times. These characteristics vary for modules from different manufacturers; interested readers are referred to [1] for additional information about SDMs used in General Motors automobiles.

Driven by the need to ensure the accuracy, reliability and privacy of automobile event data, the Society of Automotive Engineers (SAE) and the Institute for Electrical and Electronics Engineers (IEEE) joined with NHSTA to form working groups to address policy issues and standardization [6]. Interested readers are referred to the NHTSA website [7] for information about these working groups and their activities.

Historically, the primary concern has been the reliability of automobile event data as it pertains to supporting physical evidence in crash investigations [10]. Consequently, the majority of studies related to EDRs have focused on using data after it has been recovered and decoded [2, 4, 11]. However, it is just as important to ensure that event data used in legal proceedings accurately reflects the data captured by the EDR. This paper is motivated by the need to develop sound forensic techniques for evidence recovery from EDRs.

3.   Crash Data Retrieval System

General Motors initiated the development of the crash data retrieval (CDR) system; this system is now also licensed to Ford and Chrysler. At this time, a CDR can only download data from EDRs in select General Motors automobiles manufactured after 1994, Ford vehicles built in 2001 or later, and Chrysler automobiles from 2004 onwards.

3.1   System Connections

The system connections for data recovery are presented in Figure 1. A standard nine-pin RS-232 cable is used to connect a CDR interface module to a computer. However, a special 15-wire cable is required to connect the interface module to the EDR. The interface module end has a modified 15-pin serial connector with only the pins required to make the EDR connection, typically two for power and one for the signal. The other end of the cable has a specialized connector that mates to the EDR or directly connects to the OBD-II or DLC diagnostic ports of an automobile.

EDR connections may be established in two ways. In the field, the primary method is to connect through the OBD-II or DLC diagnostic ports located under the driver side dashboard. However, this requires the EDR to have electrical power. The second method requires direct access to the EDR; this is used performed when the electrical system is non-functional.

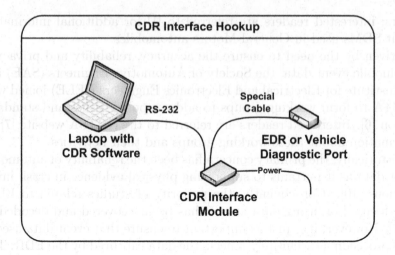

Figure 1.   Data recovery system connections.

Having established the CDR-EDR connections, the CDR interface module is connected to a computer with CDR software via an RS-232 cable. Power is applied to the EDR through a lead attached to the CDR interface module (Figure 1).

3.2   Data Recovery

After the CDR software (version 2.8) is initialized, it communicates with the serial communications port using the standard 41 54 0D (AT) command. The software then checks for the presence of the CDR interface module by sending the data: D3 56 00 D7. Upon receiving a satisfactory response, the software opens an existing file or starts a new case depending on the investigator's selection.

When a new case is started, the investigator is required to enter case-specific information such as the vehicle identification number (VIN), investigator name, case number, investigation date, crash date and comments (e.g., accident location and details). The investigator may save the report as a file; the default file name is the VIN.

After the case-related information has been entered, the CDR software sends an initial polling signal, 53 56 47 10, which retrieves EDR variant identifier code from the EDR register. For example, a 2001 GMC Sierra 1500 EDR returns the code 88 59 91 17 00 00 77; the 91 17 sequence corresponds to the specific SDMG2000 EDR, which is a GM product (G2000 refers to the version). On the other hand, a 2001 Oldsmobile Alero EDR returns the sequence 88 59 08 23 00 00 F4, where the 08 23 corresponds to an SDMG2001 EDR. The EDR variant identifier code specifies the type of EDR installed, which dictates the cabling and CDR setup requirements and the specific commands that can be used.

Next, the CDR sends a dump command corresponding to the EDR model. For example, the SDMG2000 dump command is 47 56 01 62 while the SDMG2001 dump command is 47 56 06 5D. The dump command downloads the non-volatile memory from the EDR to the CDR interface module; the sequence D0 56 47 93 is sent to the CDR when the process is completed. At this point, the recovered data is stored in volatile memory on the CDR interface module. The CDR then sends a command to transfer approximately half of the downloaded data for processing. In the case of the SDMG2000 EDR, this command is EF 5A 01 1F 00 80 00 17. The EF 5A 01 1F portion is the download command; 00 marks the starting location and 80 is the ending location. This command returns the following hexadecimal data:

```
EF D6 01 91 17 00 00 A7 18 41 53 30 33 34 30 4B 46 33 42 39 32
00 15 76 31 80 A3 A5 A4 F8 AC 00 03 A4 34 80 83 81 85 70 FF 00
FA FA FA FA FA FA FA FA FA FA FA FA FA FA FF 02 00 00 00 FF FF
FF FF FF FF FF FF FF FF FF FF FF FF FF FF FF FF FF FF FF FF FF
FF FF FF FF FF FF FF FF FF FF FF FF FF FF FF FF FF FF FF FF FF
FF FF FF FF FF FF FF FF FF FF FF FF FF FF FF FF FF FF FF FF FF
FF FF FF FF FF 81
```

Data at the beginning of the file (EF D6 01) and at the end of file (81) is not downloaded by the CDR; however, it is appended to the data in the CDR interface module. The code 91 17 following the beginning of the file marker corresponds to the EDR type. The rest of the data is downloaded with sequence EF 5A 01 1F 80 5E 00 B9. Note that 80 and 5E mark the starting and ending locations, respectively.

The CDR interface module then transmits the following data:

```
EF B4 01 FF FF FF FF FF FF 80 00 00 FF 80 FE FF BF FF FF FF FF
FF FF FF FF FF FF 7C 04 03 01 01 02 00 00 00 00 00 00 00 00 FF
FF FF FF FF 0A 10 00 61 70 70 6E 6C 6A 00 80 00 00 73 73 73 73
00 20 20 20 20 20 00 F8 25 FE 00 00 00 04 00 FF FF FF FF FF FF
FF FF FF FF FF FF FF FF FF FF FF FF FF 98
```

The sequences EF B4 01 and 98 are the beginning of file and end of file markers, respectively; the two markers are appended to the data by the CDR interface module. The entire retrieval process, which begins with the CDR sending the EDR a dump command, is repeated two more times for a total of three passes.

3.3   Retrieved Data

After the CDR software completes the retrieval process, it analyzes the EDR data and generates a report. The report is placed in a temporary file, which is deleted unless it is explicitly saved prior to exiting the program. A saved report is stored in a proprietary format (*.CDR) or as a *.pdf file. In addition to the data in the report, the *.CDR file contains formatting data and error checking data (hash value and field size counts).

Analysis of the CDR file reveals that the data is stored in a simple file format. A common element in the hex data is the sequence 0D 0A, which is used as a delimiter to separate fields and as the carriage return/line feed. Additionally, hex 20 is used as the space character and to fill fixed-size fields.

Three sources of data are contained in the dump: user-entered data, CDR-supplied data and hash values. The user-entered data includes the VIN, investigator's name, case number, comments, etc. The user-entered fields, "Investigator," "Case Number," "Investigation Date" and "Crash Date" have a maximum of 64 characters. The "Comments" field can have a variable amount of data; preceding the actual data is a data-size marker of two bytes that indicates its length.

The CDR-supplied data is also variable in size and incorporates a data-size marker at the beginning of each field. This is most likely due to the fact that the "Interface Used to Collect Data" field has carriage returns inserted in the data, which have the same hex code as delimiters. When the size of the field is calculated, all carriage returns/line feeds in the entered data are counted as two bytes and ignored as field delimiters.

Two hash values are included in the hex dump. The hash value that appears toward the middle of the hex is used to ensure the data has not been altered. The last hex code value corresponds to the Reporting Program Verification Number and the Collecting Program Verification Number, both of which are displayed in the CDR report.

The first 17 bytes of data recovered from a 2001 GMC Sierra 1500 contain the VIN. Once the program is running, this is the first information requested as user input by the CDR software:

```
32 47 54 45 43 31 39 54 35 31 31 32 34 34 39 38 39

 2  G  T  E  C  1  9  T  5  1  1  2  4  4  9  8  9
```

Following the VIN is the delimiter 0D 0A, which is used to separate fields. The next field is inserted by the CDR software and contains information about the EDR type and model. Note that hex code 20 is used to fill the field:

```
53 44 4D 47 32 30 30 30 20 20 20 20 20 20 20 20
```

```
S  D  M  G  2  0  0  0

39 31 31 37 20 20 20 20 20 20 20 20 20 20 20 20

9  1  1  7
```

This data is followed by the investigators's name and other user-entered data such as the investigation date. The actual EDR data appears later and is preceded by a size field in big endian. Note that **A7** below computes to 167 bytes, which is the number of bytes stored on the EDR including the initial padding of six sets of zeros. The reason for the padding is unknown.

```
00 00 00 00 00 00 91 17 00 00 A7 18 41 53 30 33 34 30 4B 46 33
42 39 32 00 15 76 31 80 A4 A6 A5 F8 AD 00 03 A4 34 80 84 81 85
70 FF 00 FA FA FA FA FA FA FA FA FA FA FA FA FA FF 02 00 00
00 FF FF FF FF FF FF FF FF FF FF FF FF FF FF FF FF FF FF FF
FF FF FF FF FF FF FF FF FF FF FF FF FF FF FF FF FF FF FF FF
FF FF FF FF FF FF FF FF FF FF FF FF FF FF FF FF FF FF FF FF
FF FF FF FF FF FF FF FF FF FF FF FF FF 80 00 00 FF 80 FE FF
BF FF FF FF FF FF FF FF FF FF FF 7C 04 03 01 01 02 00 00 00 00
00 00 00 00 FF FF FF FF FF 0A 10 00 61 70 70 6E 6C 6A 00 80 00
00 73 73 73 73 00 20 20 20 20 20 00 F8 25 FE 00 00 00 04 00 FF
FF FF FF FF FF FF FF FF FF FF FF FF FF FF FF FF FF
```

The file have two hash values that are used to verify the integrity of the data. The exact hash functions are unknown. Based on experimentation, including trial-and-error attempts at determining the hash functions used by manipulating the data, it appears that the data is rehashed every time the CDR software is asked to open the document. The new hash value is then compared with the old value; if the hash comparison fails, an error is reported and the program exits.

Although this file format appears to be simple, no public description of the format exists and there is no method to review many of these fields using the CDR software. Furthermore, the human-readable reports do not contain hash values or any file verification data that a digital forensic examiner would come to expect.

4. Digital Forensic Issues

EDR evidence must be introduced in court by an expert witness. The expert must provide testimony that relates to knowledge or experience beyond that possessed by lay persons. Furthermore, the individual must have specialized knowledge, skill, training or education regarding the subject matter of the testimony, which must be based on reliable scientific, technical or other specialized information.

EDR data introduced in court must pass the well-known Daubert and Frye tests of scientific evidence. The first criminal case to introduce

EDR data as evidence was Colorado v. Cain in 2002; since then, numerous criminal and civil cases have employed EDR evidence [5]. Due to the increased use of EDR data, many jurisdictions have create statutes regarding EDRs. This section examines some of the major issues pertaining to EDR data and data collection that may impact the quality of the recovered evidence.

4.1   Missing and Uninterpreted Data

The CDR report includes downloaded hex data with the presumed register numbers from where the data was pulled. The registers for the 2001 GMC Sierra 1500 system contain six bytes of data, but those for other automobile EDRs have fewer bytes. Also, certain segments of these registers are missing. The system documentation does not explain this anomaly.

The CDR report also displays uninterpreted data, possibly proprietary information such as deployment thresholds. However, when the data transfer is monitored with a sniffer, discrepancies appear between different passes. The method used by the system to select and insert data is unknown, making it difficult to verify the repeatability of extraction process and the results.

Despite these somewhat disturbing findings, the information provided in a CDR report appears to be complete. Without additional techniques and translation tools, it must be assumed that all data that is available is being translated. However, it would be very useful to have an alternative HTT to compare the results.

4.2   Data Collection Discrepancies

Discrepancies were observed in the bytes obtained during the three data dump passes. The number of discrepancies increased when multiple downloads were performed in short order (each download takes three to five minutes). The changed bytes were found in the first portion of the download from the CDR interface module.

Analysis revealed that the values were random and not due to a clock or counter. For example, the CDR interface module sent the same data during the first two of six runs. However, there were discrepancies when comparing the three passes in each run. The remaining four runs also contained discrepancies. These discrepancies were discovered by comparing the hex values in the final CDR report to those collected by a sniffer.

Additionally, the *.CDR file does not contain the original data collected during the three passes. This implies that the data read from the EDR is transformed by the CDR software (possibly by performing certain calculations on the data) before being displayed in the CDR report.

4.3 Unexplained Methods

The final data in a CDR report is processed by an algorithm before it is displayed. In fact, the following statement is provided at the beginning of a CDR report:

> Once the crash data is downloaded, the CDR tool mathematically adjusts the recorded algorithm forward velocity data to generate an adjusted algorithm forward velocity change that may more closely approximate the forward velocity change the sensing system experienced during the recorded portion of the event. The adjustment takes place within the downloading tool and does not affect the crash data, which remains stored in the SDM. The SDM Adjusted Algorithm Forward Velocity Change may not closely approximate what the sensing system experienced in all types of events.

It is important to note that the description of the algorithm is not provided by the manufacturer. Also, terms such as "more closely approximate" are undefined. Furthermore, the original data stored in the SDM is not displayed in a human-readable format and it may not be possible to verify the data.

4.4 Evidence Identifiers

Initially, it was believed that the CDR software employed VIN data ("World Manufacturer Identifier," "Vehicle Attributes," "Model Year") to determine the type and version of the EDR being read. However, we discovered that any data may be entered as long as the "World Manufacturer Identifier" corresponds to a manufacturer supported by the CDR and follows the VIN formatting requirements. Thus, it is possible to spoof a CDR system in an attempt to download data from a different module than intended.

4.5 Unwiped Media

There are indications that the CDR interface module memory is not wiped between downloads. We attempted to verify this fact by experimentation. Power was applied to the CDR interface module and the data in CDR memory was requested prior to performing a download of the EDR.

When the following data was sent by the CDR interface module to the SDMG2000 EDR (see Section 3.2):

    EF 5A 01 1F 00 80 00 17

the following block of data was returned:

```
EF D6 01 00 01 02 03 04 05 06 07 08 09 0A 0B 0C 0D 0E 0F 10 11
12 13 14 15 16 17 18 19 1A 1B 1C 1D 1E 1F 20 21 22 23 24 25 26
27 28 29 2A 2B 2C 2D 2E 2F 30 31 32 33 34 35 36 37 38 39 3A 3B
3C 3D 3E 3F 40 41 42 43 44 45 46 47 48 49 4A 4B 4C 4D 4E 4F 50
51 52 53 54 55 56 57 58 59 5A 5B 5C 5D 5E 5F 60 61 62 63 64 65
66 67 68 69 6A 6B 6C 6D 6E 6F 70 71 72 73 74 75 76 77 78 79 7A
7B 7C 7D 7E 7F 7A
```

When the following data was sent by the CDR interface module:

```
EF 5A 01 1F 80 5E 00 B9
```

the following block of data was returned:

```
EF B4 01 80 81 82 83 84 85 86 87 88 89 8A 8B 8C 8D 8E 8F 90 91
92 93 94 95 96 97 98 99 9A 9B 9C 9D 9E 9F A0 A1 A2 A3 A4 A5 A6
A7 A8 A9 AA AB AC AD AE AF B0 B1 B2 B3 B4 B5 B6 B7 B8 B9 BA BB
BC BD BE BF C0 C1 C2 C3 C4 C5 C6 C7 C8 C9 CA CB CC CD CE CF D0
D1 D2 D3 D4 D5 D6 D7 D8 D9 DA DB DC DD 49
```

This suggests that the memory in the CDR interface module is not reset and unknown data is available for download as authentic data.

5.   Recommendations

EDRs provide vital data for reconstructing traffic crashes. However, during a crash reconstruction, it is important to also consider the physical evidence that is always present instead of relying solely on digital evidence.

Digital forensic professionals should be cognizant of the following recommendations related to EDRs and EDR data:

- Maintain a detailed record of the chain of custody of an EDR. This specifically includes documenting all physical extractions from the module because there are no unique identification marks on the EDR that tie it to the vehicle.

- Preserve and maintain the original human-readable report as this document becomes the evidence used in the legal context. Note that the original data in the EDR device could be erased, overwritten or corrupted. For example, an SDM does not write its memory to a permanent record for a non-deployment event and the memory is erased after the unit is turned on a certain number of times.

- Understand when and how the data is erased, overwritten or corrupted. For example, some powertrain control modules on Ford vehicles retain 25 seconds of data (including vehicular speed) in a circular buffer. However, the data is not "locked" in the event of a crash and the reapplication of power to the module causes the data to be overwritten. Note that modules from different manufacturers vary considerably in terms of their operational characteristics.

■ Learn how current vehicular technology is used to generate data for the EDR. Many EDRs rely on external sensors and advanced vehicular systems for data. For example, the speed sensor actually measures the rotation of the driveshaft, not the true speed. This means that the speed of a vehicle that is sliding sideways on ice is not reported correctly in the EDR.

6.   Conclusions

EDR data is extremely valuable in reconstructing the physical events leading to automoble crashes. However, the case study involving the extraction of data from a 2001 Chevrolet 1500 pickup EDR using the Bosch CDR system has revealed several problems that may impact evidentiary quality. The problems include missing data and uninterpreted data, data collection discrepancies, unexplained methods, and issues with evidence identifiers and unwiped media. Investigators should be aware of these problems and should use sound forensic procedures and tools to ensure that EDR evidence is not excluded in legal proceedings.

References

[1] A. Chidester, J. Hinch, T. Mercer and K. Schultz, Recording automotive crash event data, *Proceedings of the International Symposium on Transportation Recorders*, 1999.

[2] J. Correia, K. Iliadis, E. McCarron and M. Smolej, Utilizing data from automotive event data recorders, *Proceedings of the Twelfth Canadian Multidisciplinary Road Safety Conference*, 2001.

[3] J. Daily, N. Shigemura and J. Daily, *Fundamentals of Traffic Crash Reconstruction*, Institute of Police Technology and Management, University of North Florida, Jacksonville, Florida, 2006.

[4] R. Fay, R. Robinette, J. Scott and D. Deering, Using event data recorders in collision reconstruction, *Proceedings of the Society of Automotive Engineers World Congress and Exhibition*, SAE Technical Paper Series 2002-01-0535, Society of Automotive Engineers, Warrendale, Pennsylvania, 2002.

[5] Harris Technical Services, EDR Case Law, Port St. Lucie, Florida (harristechnical.com/cdr5.htm).

[6] IEEE Vehicular Technology Society, IEEE Project 1616: Draft Standard Motor Vehicle Event Data Recorders, Piscataway, New Jersey (grouper.ieee.org/groups/1616/home.htm).

[7] National Highway Traffic Safety Administration, Event Data Recorder (EDR) Applications of Highway and Traffic Safety, U.S. Department of Transportation, Washington, DC (www-nrd.nhtsa .dot.gov/edr-site).

[8] U.S. Court of Appeals (Sixth Circuit), Harris v. General Motors Corporation, *Federal Reporter Third Series*, vol. 201, pp. 800–805, 2000.

[9] U.S. Government, Event Data Recorders, Department of Transportation, National Highway Traffic Safety Administration, *Federal Register*, vol. 71(166), pp. 50998–51048, 2006.

[10] S. van Nooten and J. Hrycay, The application and reliability of commercial vehicle event data recorders for accident investigation and analysis, *Proceedings of the Society of Automotive Engineers World Congress and Exhibition*, SAE Technical Paper Series 2005-01-1177, Society of Automotive Engineers, Warrendale, Pennsylvania, 2005.

[11] C. Wilkinson, J. Lawrence, B. Heinrichs and D. King, The accuracy and sensitivity of 2003 and 2004 General Motors event data recorders in low-speed barrier and vehicle collisions, *Proceedings of the Society of Automotive Engineers World Congress and Exhibition*, SAE Technical Paper Series 2005-01-1190, Society of Automotive Engineers, Warrendale, Pennsylvania, 2005.

IX

NOVEL INVESTIGATIVE TECHNIQUES

Chapter 22

REASONING ABOUT EVIDENCE USING BAYESIAN NETWORKS

Michael Kwan, Kam-Pui Chow, Frank Law and Pierre Lai

Abstract   There is an escalating perception in some quarters that the conclusions drawn from digital evidence are the subjective views of individuals and have limited scientific justification. This paper attempts to address this problem by presenting a formal model for reasoning about digital evidence. A Bayesian network is used to quantify the evidential strengths of hypotheses and, thus, enhance the reliability and traceability of the results produced by digital forensic investigations. The validity of the model is tested using a real court case. The test uses objective probability assignments obtained by aggregating the responses of experienced law enforcement agents and analysts. The results confirmed the guilty verdict in the court case with a probability value of 92.7%.

Keywords: Digital evidence, hypotheses, probability, Bayesian networks

1.   Introduction

Like other forensic disciplines, digital forensics involves the formulation of hypotheses based on the available evidence and facts, and the assessment of the likelihood that they support or refute the hypotheses. Although substantial research has focused on principles and tools for retrieving digital evidence [7, 8, 10], little, if any, work has examined the accuracy of hypotheses based on the evidence.

Without reliable and scientific models, the conclusions made by digital forensic analysts can be challenged on the grounds that they are mere speculation. The problem is acerbated by the fact that forensic conclusions derived from the same digital evidence can vary from analyst to analyst. This can severely impact the reliability of digital forensic findings as well as the credibility of analysts. Speculation and subjective

Please use the following format when citing this chapter:

Kwan, M., Chow, K.-P., Law, F. and Lai, P., 2008, in IFIP International Federation for Information Processing, Volume 285; *Advances in Digital Forensics IV*; Indrajit Ray, Sujeet Shenoi; (Boston: Springer), pp. 275–289.

views offered by forensic analysts under the guise of expert opinion have little (if any) value in legal proceedings [6].

This paper presents a formal model for reasoning about digital evidence. The model, which is based on probability distributions of hypotheses in a Bayesian network, quantifies the evidential strengths of the hypotheses and, thereby, enhances the reliability and traceability of the analytical results produced by digital forensic investigations. The validity of the model is investigated using a real court case involving the illegal dissemination of a movie using the BitTorrent peer-to-peer network.

2. Background

Forensics is the process of analyzing and interpreting evidence to determine the likelihood that a crime occurred. Many researchers (see, e.g., [4, 12, 15, 19, 20]) argue that that this process should cover the formulation of hypotheses from evidence and the evaluation of the likelihood of the hypotheses for the purpose of legal proceedings.

Aitken and Taroni [1] state that likelihood is an exercise in hypothetical reasoning. It denotes the degree of belief in the truth of a hypothesis. In the scientific community, belief is often expressed in terms of probability. Probability theories provide mechanisms for deducing the likelihood of hypotheses from assumptions. Although probabilistic methods may be useful for proving or refuting the hypotheses involved in a criminal investigation, Jones and co-workers [9] argue that obtaining all the probability distributions for the entailing evidence is impractical. Given the large volume of evidence involved, it is not feasible to obtain the joint probability distributions for all possible evidential variables. Moreover, simple probabilistic methods do not capture the complex dependencies that exist between items of evidence; therefore, the methods have limited value from an analytical point of view [5]. Indeed, many researchers [5, 11, 16] emphasize that comprehensive probabilistic models should accurately model the conditional dependencies existing between items of evidence.

A criminal investigation is an abductive diagnosis problem [16]. However, it is difficult to design a model that can deterministically describe all the assumptions involved in an investigation. Poole [18] has attempted to address this issue by proposing a model that describes crime scenarios non-deterministically using symbolic logic and probabilistic Bayesian methods. Unfortunately, Poole's model is too abstract to be applied in real scenarios.

It is important to observe that digital events are discrete computer events that are deterministic in nature and have a temporal causal sequence. Therefore, it is common practice for digital forensic analysts to establish their abductive reasoning based on the existence or validity of the causal events that entail their hypotheses. However, it is difficult to have consistent models that determine the supporting events for hypotheses. Different analysts may attach different events to the same hypothesis. Even if they agree on the same set of events, they usually assign different (subjective) probabilities to the events.

Analysts also must reason about hypotheses in the face of missing and/or uncertain information about events. The events for which evidence is available may not prove the complete truth of the hypotheses; however, they can be used very effectively to compute degrees of likelihood for the hypotheses. Consequently, probabilistic approaches are well suited to developing formal models for reasoning about digital evidence in criminal investigations.

3. Bayesian Networks

Before we discuss Bayesian networks, it is important to emphasize that digital evidence deals with "past" events that were caused by some other hypothetical events that have to be verified. For example, if a suspect had child pornography on his computer, he may have downloaded it from a pornographic web site, which could be verified by the presence of the URL in the history file of his browser.

A Bayesian network uses probability theory and graph theory to construct probabilistic inference and reasoning models. It is defined as a directed acyclic graph with nodes and arcs. Nodes represent variables, events or evidence. An arc between two nodes represents a conditional dependency between the nodes. Arcs are unidirectional and feedback loops are not permitted. Because of this feature, it is easy to identify the parent-child relationship or the probability dependency between two nodes.

A Bayesian network operates on conditional probability. For example, if the occurrence of some evidence E is dependent on a hypothesis H, the probability that both H and E occurred, $P(H, E)$, is given by:

$$P(H, E) = P(H)P(E|H). \tag{1}$$

According to the multiplication law of probability, which expresses commutativity, if H is relevant for E, then E must also be relevant for

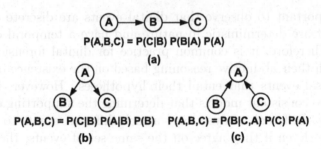

$$P(A,B,C) = P(C|B)\, P(B|A)\, P(A)$$

(a)

$$P(A,B,C) = P(C|B)\, P(A|B)\, P(B)$$

(b)

$$P(A,B,C) = P(B|C,A)\, P(C)\, P(A)$$

(c)

Figure 1. Bayesian network connections: (a) Serial; (b) Diverging; (c) Converging.

H. The corresponding joint probability expression is:

$$P(H,E) = P(H)P(E|H) = P(E)P(H|E),\tag{2}$$

and, hence,

$$P(E|H) = \frac{P(E)P(H|E)}{P(H)}.\tag{3}$$

Equation (3) is the celebrated Bayes' Theorem. From a statistical point of view, it denotes the conditional probability of E caused by H. This is also referred as the likelihood ratio of H given E. It denotes the degree of belief that E will occur given a situation where H is true.

$P(H|E)$ is the posterior probability, i.e., the probability that when E is detected H has actually occurred. $P(H)$ denotes the prior probability of H at a stage where the evidence is not yet presented. $P(E)$ is the prior probability of E, which is sometimes referred to as a normalizing constant. Therefore, the above expression can be formalized as:

$$likelihood\ ratio = \frac{posterior\ probability \times normalizing\ constant}{hypothesis\ prior\ probability}.\tag{4}$$

Since the likelihood ratio is proportional to the posterior probability, a larger posterior probability denotes a higher likelihood ratio. In the evidentiary context, it also means that the greater the evidence supporting the hypothesis, the more likely that the hypothesis is true.

A Bayesian network has three elementary connections between its nodes that represent three different types of probability distributions (Figure 1). For a serial connection, if B's evidential state is unknown, then A and C are dependent on each other. In other words, there is an evidential influence between A and C if the evidential state of B is unknown. However, if B's state is known, then A and C are independent of each other; this means that A and C are conditionally independent of each other given B. In a diverging connection, the same conditional independence is observed for A and C, i.e., if B's state is known, then A and C are independent. In a converging connection, if B's state is unknown, then A and C are independent. In other words, unless the state of B is known, A and C can influence each other.

4. Proposed Model

A real case involving the distribution of a pirated movie via the BitTorrent peer-to-peer network is used to demonstrate the utility of the Bayesian network model. The digital evidence discussed in this paper was presented in court during the criminal trial.

4.1 The BitTorrent Case

The defendant in the case was alleged to have used his computer to distribute a pirated movie on the Internet using BitTorrent [13]. The defendant had the optical disk of the movie in his possession. He copied the movie from the optical disk to his computer and then used BitTorrent to create a "torrent file" from the movie file. The torrent file contained metadata of the source file (movie file) and the URL of the BitTorrent tracker server.

To distribute the movie, the defendant sent the torrent file to several newsgroups. He then activated the torrent file on his computer, which caused his computer to connect to the tracker server. The tracker server queried the defendant's computer about the metadata of the torrent file. The tracker server then returned a list with the IP addresses of peer machines on the network and the percentages of the target file that existed on the peer machines.

Since the defendant's computer had a complete copy of the movie, the tracker server labeled it as a "seeder computer." The defendant maintained the connection between the tracker server and his computer so that other peers could download the movie from his computer.

4.2 Building the Model

The construction of a Bayesian network model begins with the main hypothesis that the analyst intends to determine. In order to prove the illegal act in the BitTorrent case, we use the following hypothesis:

H: The seized computer was used as the initial seeder to share the pirated file on a BitTorrent network.

Next, we express the possible states of the hypothesis (Yes, No and Uncertain) and assign probability values to these states. The values are also called the prior probabilities of the hypothesis.

Hypothesis H is the root node in the Bayesian network. Since it has no parent nodes, its prior probabilities are unconditional. To begin with, the probabilities of H are evenly distributed among its three states, i.e., $P(H) = (0.333, 0.333, 0.333)$ (Table 1).

Table 1. Prior probability of the root node.

Node	State	$P(H)$
	Yes	0.333
H	No	0.333
	Uncertain	0.333

Having established the root node, we proceed to explore evidence or events that are causally dependent on H. These are usually observable variables. However, note that sub-hypotheses may also be added under the root node. Although these sub-hypotheses do not have observable states, they are useful because they refine the model by producing a graph with more structure and increased clarity. Five sub-hypotheses are created to support the root hypothesis:

- H_1: The pirated file was copied from the seized optical disk (found at the crime scene) to the seized computer.

- H_2: A torrent file was created from the copied file.

- H_3: The torrent file was sent to newsgroups for publishing.

- H_4: The torrent file was activated, which caused the seized computer to connect to the tracker server.

- H_5: The connection between the seized computer and the tracker server was maintained.

Table 2. Conditional probabilities of H_1.

State	Yes	No	Uncertain
H = Yes	0.6	0.35	0.05
H = No	0.35	0.6	0.05
H = Uncertain	0.05	0.05	0.9

Since the sub-hypotheses are dependent on H, they are assigned conditional probability values. Table 2 presents the conditional probability values of Hypothesis H_1 given the state of H. Initial or prior probability values are assigned to the possible states of H_1 for different states of H. For example, an initial value of 0.6 is assigned for the situation when H and H_1 are both Yes. This means that when the seized computer has been used as an initial seeder, the probability that the pirated file found on the computer had been copied from the optical disk seized at the crime scene is 0.6. However, it is also possible that, although the seized computer was the initial seeder, the pirated file was downloaded from the Internet or copied from another computer in a local network; a probability value of 0.35 is assigned to these scenarios.

Finally, there is the possibility that, even though the seized computer was the initial seeder, the evidence may not be able to confirm a Yes or No state for H_1. Therefore, there is a chance that the seized computer was the initial seeder, but the source from where the pirated movie was copied is Uncertain.

Table 3. Conditional probabilities of H_2, H_3, H_4 and H_5.

State	Yes	No	Uncertain
H = Yes	0.6	0.35	0.05
H = No	0.35	0.6	0.05
H = Uncertain	0.05	0.05	0.9

Table 3 presents the conditional probabilities of Hypotheses H_2, H_3, H_4 and H_5 given the state of H.

Following the assignment of conditional probabilities to the five sub-hypotheses, we proceed to develop the entailing casual events or evidence for the sub-hypotheses. This is because a Bayesian network propagates probabilities for linked hypotheses based on the states of events or evidence.

Hypothesis H and the five sub-hypotheses have a diverging connection. The nodes in a diverging connection influence each other when the state of their parent node is still unknown. Therefore, the five sub-hypotheses are related to each other in a probabilistic manner. Also, their probabilities are affected by all the child events or evidence under them.

To illustrate the Bayesian network methodology, we focus on Hypothesis H_1: The pirated file was copied from the seized optical disk (found at the crime scene) to the seized computer.

5. Assigning Prior Probabilities

Items of digital evidence correspond to past digital events (or posterior evidence) that can be used to support or refute the five sub-hypotheses,

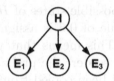

Figure 2.   Partial Bayesian network for H_1.

which, in turn, support or refute H. One of the main challenges in applying a Bayesian network to evaluate evidence is assigning probability values to posterior evidence. This is because the assignments are usually based on subjective personal beliefs. Although the personal beliefs (regarding a case) of a digital forensic analyst are assumed to arise from professional knowledge and experience, there is no means to determine whether they truly represent the accepted views of the digital forensic discipline, let alone whether or not the probability values assigned to posterior evidence are, in fact, accurate.

To enhance the reliability and accuracy of the probability assignments for posterior evidence, we attempted to use objective probability assignments obtained by aggregating the responses of experienced law enforcement agents and analysts. A questionnaire (available at www.cs.hku.hk/kylai/qr.pdf) was created to obtain the required information from personnel with the Technical Crime Bureau of the Hong Kong Police and the Computer Forensic Laboratory of Hong Kong Customs. The questionnaire solicited the following information from the respondents: (i) digital forensics training and experience, (ii) degree of belief in digital evidence resulting from general computer operations, and (iii) degree of belief in the digital evidence related to the operation of the BitTorrent protocol.

Responses were received from 31 law enforcement personnel. The weighted average approach was used to aggregate the probability values. For example, Item 7 of the questionnaire required respondents to gauge the probability range that the URLs and access times of web sites would be stored in the file named `index.dat` in the folder `History.IE5`. The answers received were: 20-40%: 1 respondent, 40-60%: 1 respondent, 60-80%: 6 respondents, 80-100%: 22 respondents, and Uncertain: 1 respondent. The weighted average of the probability of the Yes state was computed as: $(1 \times 0.3) + (1 \times 0.5) + (6 \times 0.7) + (22 \times 0.9) = 24.8$, which yielded a probability value $24.8/31 = 0.8$. The probability of the Uncertain state was computed as $1/31 = 0.03$. Therefore, the probability of the No state was $1 - 0.8 - 0.03 = 0.17$.

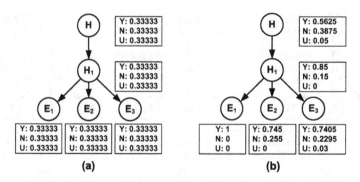

Figure 3. Probability values: (a) Initial; (b) Updated.

6.   Analyzing Hypothesis H_1

The partial Bayesian network for Hypothesis H_1 is presented in Figure 2. The arguments describing events or evidence that would be caused by copying a file from an optical disk to a local hard disk are : (i) E_1: Modification time of the destination file equals that of the source file (states: Yes, No, Uncertain), (ii) E_2: Creation time of the destination file is after its own modification time (states: Yes, No, Uncertain) and (iii) E_3: Hash value of the destination file matches that of the source file (states: Yes, No, Uncertain).

Table 4. Conditional probabilities of E_1, E_2 and E_3

	E_1			E_2			E_3		
State	**Y**	**N**	**U**	**Y**	**N**	**U**	**Y**	**N**	**U**
$H = Y$	0.85	0.15	0	0.85	0.15	0	0.85	0.12	1.03
$H = N$	0.15	0.85	0	0.85	0.15	0	0.12	0.85	0.03
$H = U$	0	0	1	0	0	1	0.03	0.03	0.94

The next task is to assign conditional probability values to the events or evidence. Table 4 lists the conditional probabilities of E_1, E_2 and E_3, given the state of H_1.

Next, the probability of H_1 based on the observed probabilities of E_1, E_2 and E_3 is calculated. The MSBNx Bayesian Network Editor and Tool Kit [14] was used to calculate this probability and to propagate probability values within the Bayesian network.

The probability values for the network nodes are presented in Figure 3. Figure 3(a) presents the initial probability values in the network without any observed evidence. Figure 3(b) shows the updated probabilities

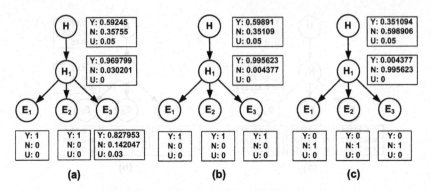

Figure 4. Propagated probability values.

assuming that evidence E_1 is observed to be Yes while E_2 and E_3 are still unobservable.

Hypothesis H_1 is in a diverging connection with E_1, E_2 and E_3. Therefore, if the state of H_1 is unobserved, any change in the probability of E_1 will change the probability of H_1. When H_1 changes, the likelihood ratios of E_2 and E_3 also change. Similarly, since H, H_1 and E_1 are in a serial connection, a change in the probability of E_1 will propagate to H if H_1 remains unobservable.

The Bayesian network has two more serial connections, $H \longrightarrow H_1 \longrightarrow E_2$ and $H \longrightarrow H_1 \longrightarrow E_3$. Therefore, any changes in the states of E_2 and E_3 will also affect the probabilities of H and H_1.

Suppose we examine the state of the posterior evidence E_2 and find it to be Yes. The corresponding propagated probabilities in the network are shown in Figure 4(a). If the final posterior evidence E_3 is also observed to be Yes, the probabilities that result are shown in Figure 4(b). Note that when all the evidence states are Yes, the propagated probability for H_1 = Yes is 99.6% and the corresponding probability for H = Yes is 59.9%. In other words, if the states of E_1, E_2 and E_3 are all Yes, then the digital forensic analyst can confirm that there is a 99.6% probability that H_1 (the pirated file was copied from the seized optical disk to the seized computer) is true. Furthermore, based on the 99.6% probability value for H_1, the forensic analyst can conclude that H (the seized computer was used as the initial seeder to share the pirated file on a BitTorrent network) is true with probability 59.9%.

Figure 4(c) shows the resulting probabilities for the case where all the evidence states are No. The probability that H_1 is true drops to 0.4% and the probability that H_1 is false rises to 99.6%. Unless a posterior event or evidence exists, the probability that H is true drops to 35.1% and the probability that H is false rises to 59.9%.

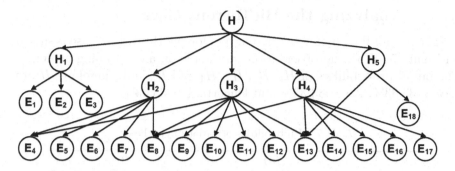

HYPOTHESES:

H   The seized computer was used as the initial seeder to share the pirated file on a BitTorrent network

H₁   The pirated file was copied from the seized optical disk to the seized computer

H₂   A torrent file was created from the copied file

H₃   The torrent file was sent to newsgroups for publishing

H₄   The torrent file was activated, which caused the seized computer to connect to the tracker server

H₅   The connection between the seized computer and the tracker was maintained

EVIDENCE:

E₁   Modification time of the destination file equals that of the source file

E₂   Creation time of the destination file is after its own modification time

E₃   Hash value of the destination file matches that of the source file

E₄   BitTorrent client software is installed on the seized computer

E₅   File link for the shared file is created

E₆   Shared file exists on the hard disk

E₇   Torrent file creation record is found

E₈   Torrent file exists on the hard disk

E₉   Peer connection information is found

E₁₀   Tracker server login record is found

E₁₁   Torrent file activation time is corroborated by its MAC time and link file

E₁₂   Internet history record about publishing website is found

E₁₃   Internet connection is available

E₁₄   Cookie of the publishing website is found

E₁₅   URL of the publishing website is stored in the web browser

E₁₆   Web browser software is available

E₁₇   Internet cache record about the publishing of the torrent file is found

E₁₈   Internet history record about the tracker server connection is found

Figure 5.   Bayesian network diagram.

7.   Analyzing the BitTorrent Case

The overall Bayesian network diagram for the BitTorrent case is shown in Figure 5. When no observations are made on any entailing evidence, the initial probabilities of H_1, H_2, H_3, H_4 and H_5 and, therefore, H are Yes = 33.33%, No = 33.33% and Uncertain = 33.33%.

Table 5.   Probabilities of various hypotheses.

Hypothesis	(a)			(b)		
	Y(%)	N(%)	U(%)	Y(%)	N(%)	U(%)
H	92.54	7.45	0.01	92.27	7.72	0.01
H_1	99.71	0.29	0.00	99.70	0.30	0.00
H_2	99.98	0.0015	0.0185	99.92	0.07	0.01
H_3	99.98	0.02	0.00	99.80	2.20	0.00
H_4	99.93	0.07	0.00	99.51	0.49	0.00
H_5	89.31	10.47	0.22	99.45	10.33	0.22

When all the entailing evidence is switched to the state Yes, the propagated probabilities for the various hypotheses are as presented in Table 5(a).

Media reports about the BitTorrent trial mentioned that there was no indication that the torrent file was present on the seized computer. Also, there was no mention of cookies that are required to publish the torrent file in newsgroups. Therefore, the corresponding observations about the existence of the created torrent file (node E_8 in Figure 5) and cookies of newsgroups (node E_{14}) should be amended from Yes to No in order to reveal their impact on the hypotheses.

It is worth mentioning that the "torrent file node" (E_8) is a common node for H_2, H_3 and H_4. In other words, there is a converging connection to E_8 from these three hypotheses. According to the rules of probability propagation for a converging connection, when the state of E_8 is known, the probabilities of H_2, H_3 and H_4 will influence each other. Therefore, a change in the state of E_8 changes the probabilities of these three hypotheses.

Furthermore, since H_1, H_2, H_3, H_4 and H_5 are in a diverging connection with the parent hypothesis H, changes to the probabilities of H_2, H_3 and H_4 influence the probabilities of H_1 and H_5. Table 5(b) shows the probability values obtained after the states of E_8 and E_{14} are changed from Yes to No. The propagated probability for H from the available evidence is 92.27%. In other words, based on the observed evidence, there is a probability of 92.27% that the seized computer was used as the initial seeder to distribute the pirated movie on a BitTorrent network. This is the most that a digital forensic analyst can provide. It is up to the court to decide whether or not this probability value is sufficient to support the Hypothesis *H*.

Note that other evidence exists in the BitTorrent case. This includes email exchanges, detailed comparisons of the torrent file metadata with computer trails, and timeline analysis. However, as the focus of this paper is to demonstrate the utility of Bayesian networks in digital forensic investigations, only the most important pieces of digital evidence were considered in the discussion.

8. Conclusions

A Bayesian network is a useful formalism for quantifying and propagating the strengths of investigative hypotheses and supporting evidence. The Internet piracy trial provides an excellent case study for validating the approach. The hypotheses in the case and their supporting events and evidence are clearly specified, along with their causal relationships and probability values. Thus, the Bayesian network model is not only an analytical tool for evaluating evidence, but also a tracking tool that enables digital forensic practitioners to review and analyze the original findings.

The subjectivity involved in assigning probabilities can be alleviated to some extent by using a survey instrument and aggregating the responses obtained from expert investigators. However, it is difficult to completely eliminate the subjective aspects, especially with regard to the assignment of prior probabilities to posterior evidence. Our future research will investigate this aspect in more detail with the goal of enhancing the accuracy, precision and reliability of the Bayesian network model for reasoning about digital evidence.

References

[1] C. Aitken and F. Taroni, *Statistics and the Evaluation of Evidence for Forensic Scientists*, John Wiley and Sons, New York, 2004.

[2] V. Baryamureeba and F. Tushabe, The enhanced digital investigation process model, *Proceedings of the Fourth Digital Forensic Research Workshop*, 2004.

[3] S. Ciardhuain, An extended model of cybercrime investigations, *International Journal of Digital Evidence*, vol. 3(1), 2004.

[4] R. Cook, I. Evett, G. Jackson, P. Jones and J. Lambert, A model for case assessment and interpretation, *Science and Justice*, vol. 38, pp. 151–156, 1998.

[5] R. Cowell, Introduction to inference for Bayesian networks, *Proceedings of the NATO Advanced Study Institute on Learning in Graphical Models*, pp. 9–26, 1998.

[6] P. Good, *Applying Statistics in the Courtroom: A New Approach for Attorneys and Expert Witnesses*, Chapman and Hall/CRC Press, Boca Raton, Florida, 2001.

[7] International Association of Computer Investigative Specialists, Forensic procedures, Fairmont, West Virginia (www.cops.org/for ensicprocedures), 2007.

[8] International Organization on Computer Evidence, International principles for computer evidence, *Forensic Science Communications*, vol. 2(2), 2000.

[9] J. Jones, Y. Xiang and S. Joseph, Bayesian probabilistic reasoning in design, *Proceedings of the IEEE Pacific Rim Conference on Communications, Computers and Signal Processing*, pp. 501–504, 1993.

[10] K. Kent, S. Chevalier, T. Grance and H. Dang, Guide to Integrating Forensic Techniques into Incident Response, Special Publication 800-86, National Institute of Standards and Technology, Gaithersburg, Maryland, 2006.

[11] J. Keppens and J. Zeleznikow, A model based reasoning approach for generating plausible crime scenarios from evidence, *Proceedings of the Ninth International Conference on Artificial Intelligence and Law*, pp. 51–59, 2003.

[12] R. Loui, J. Norman, J. Altepeter, D. Pinkard, D. Craven, J. Linsday and M. Foltz, Progress on Room 5: A testbed for public interactive semi-formal legal argumentation, *Proceedings of the Sixth International Conference on Artificial Intelligence and Law*, pp. 207–214, 1997.

[13] Magistrates' Court at Tuen Mun, Hong Kong Special Administrative Region v. Chan Nai Ming, TMCC 1268/2005, Hong Kong, China (www.hklii.hk/hk/jud/en/hksc/2005/TMCC001268A_2005 .html), 2005.

[14] Microsoft Research, MSBNx: Bayesian Network Editor and Tool Kit, Microsoft Corporation, Redmond, Washington (research.micro soft.com/adapt/MSBNx).

[15] J. Mortera, A. Dawid and S. Lauritzen, Probabilistic expert systems for DNA mixture profiling, *Theoretical Population Biology*, vol. 63(3), pp. 191–206, 2003.

[16] J. Pearl, *Probabilistic Reasoning in Intelligent Systems: Networks of Plausible Inference*, Morgan Kaufmann, San Mateo, California, 1988.

[17] S. Peisert, M. Bishop, S. Karin, M. Bishop and K. Marzullo, Principles-driven forensic analysis, *Proceedings of the New Security Paradigms Workshop*, pp. 85–93, 2005.

[18] D. Poole, Probabilistic Horn abduction and Bayesian networks, *Artificial Intelligence*, vol. 64(1), pp. 81–129, 1993.

[19] H. Prakken, C. Reed and D. Walton, Argumentation schemes and generalizations in reasoning about evidence, *Proceedings of the Ninth International Conference on Artificial Intelligence and Law*, pp. 32–41, 2003.

[20] D. Walton, Argumentation and theory of evidence, in *New Trends in Criminal Investigation and Evidence – Volume II*, C. Breur, M. Kommer, J. Nijboer and J. Reijntjes (Eds.), Intersentia, Antwerp, Belgium, pp. 711–732, 2000.

Chapter 23

INFERRING SOURCES OF LEAKS IN DOCUMENT MANAGEMENT SYSTEMS

Madhusudhanan Chandrasekaran, Vidyaraman Sankaranarayanan and Shambhu Upadhyaya

Abstract   A document management system (DMS) provides for secure operations on a distributed repository of digital documents. This paper presents a two-phase approach to address the problem of locating the sources of information leaks in a DMS. The initial monitoring phase treats user interactions in a DMS as a series of transactions, each involving content manipulation by a user; in addition to standard audit logging, relevant contextual information and user-related metrics for transactions are recorded. In the detection phase, leaked information is correlated with the existing document repository and context information to identify the sources of leaks. The monitoring and detecting phases are incorporated in a forensic extension module (FEM) to a DMS to combat the insider threat.

Keywords: Document management system, insider threat, information leaks

1.   Introduction

Digital documents have become the principal vehicle through which organizational information such as email, public memos and proprietary information are created and shared. Initially, digital documents were shared using portable media (floppy disks). Eventually, loosely-structured networked collaborations were created where documents were emailed in order to share information. However, as the value of the exchanged information grew, so did the security threats. Prompted by the increasing threat level and the importance of document content, sophisticated document management systems (DMSs) were developed to automate and secure document creation, check-in and check-out processes. Authentica [4] and Microsoft Information Rights Management [9]

Please use the following format when citing this chapter:

Chandrasekaran, M., Sankaranarayanan, V. and Upadhyaya, S., 2008, in IFIP International Federation for Information Processing, Volume 285; *Advances in Digital Forensics IV*; Indrajit Ray, Sujeet Shenoi; (Boston: Springer), pp. 291–306.

are examples of DMSs. These systems protect the documents from external threats, e.g., by automatically encrypting every document. Thus, even if the file server containing the documents is compromised, information in the documents is not compromised. While numerous security mechanisms have been designed to safeguard documents from external intruders, DMSs and the documents they contain remain vulnerable to insider attacks.

This paper describes a two-phase extension to an existing DMS, called the forensic extension module (FEM), that identifies the sources of information leaks – a common form of insider abuse. During the first phase, every user action is logged by a monitoring component. In the second phase, when an information leak is discovered, audit data along with data gathered during the monitoring phase are used to attribute the sources of the leak. As a proof of concept, the FEM is implemented as an add-on to Word 2003, where it is seamlessly integrated into the process flow and conducts evaluations in a virtual environment.

2.   Related Work

Incidents of information leaks involving Microsoft Word documents have led to the development of several add-ons for document editors to combat the threat. For example, Microsoft's Remove Hidden Data tool [8] removes all meta tags, field codes and revision information from Word documents. Microsoft's Word Redaction tool [7] is an add-on that redacts information from Word 2003 documents. Note that these add-ons were not created for forensic purposes; they are merely filters that prevent unintentional information leaks from documents that have been declared fit for public consumption. In the context of our work, these tools are important for two reasons: (i) they expose and cleanse information in documents that is not immediately visible to end users, and (ii) they may leak information and, therefore, should be considered when performing forensic analysis.

Recent efforts in document forensics have focused on several issues, including document reconstruction from deleted fragments [15], retrieval of hidden documents via file system analysis [3], detection of masquerades for the purpose of document access [13], and mitigation of illicit system and log file tampering [14]. Although these techniques can enhance the overall detection capabilities in a DMS, they do not specially address the problem of information leaks, which is the crux of our research. In fact, our focus is on "information leak forensics" in a DMS rather than traditional "document forensics."

3. Document Management Systems

A document management system (DMS) is a repository of digital documents that provides the functionality for shared editing, collaboration, check-in and check-out, and various security features. The predominant security features are document encryption and custom security policy settings. Note that the DMS security features are document-format-specific and viewer-specific as opposed to file-system-specific. In a typical DMS, users interact with a secure document editor like Microsoft Word 2003 or Adobe Acrobat. The editor is responsible for authenticating users, communicating with the file server, retrieving documents and enforcing custom security policies on the documents. The security policies are mostly static policies that dictate user rights to documents. Read, edit and print permissions may be assigned for documents. Additional fine-grained policies may be set for specialized document formats.

Each document in a DMS is assigned a type and classification. The document type usually indicates the nature of the information content (e.g., Financial, News, Technology). The classification, on the other hand, indicates the sensitivity of the document (e.g., Top Secret, Secret, Classified, Unclassified, Declassified, Public). In addition, user roles (e.g., Secretary, Software Developer, Project Manager, Board Member, Chief Executive Officer) are usually defined based on the organization's functions. Security policies are defined based on user roles and document classifications and types. In some DMS architectures, documents may also be watermarked or digitally signed to establish the authenticity of their content, proof of ownership and non-repudiable statements pertaining to access histories.

3.1 Characterizing Information Leaks

Modern document formats, most notably the format used by Microsoft Word, have provisions for storing data in various sections that may not be immediately visible to users:

- **Actual Document Content:** This section, which contains text, pictures, embedded objects and comments, is usually what the author and the readers view.

- **Document Metadata:** This information, e.g., document author, time of last edit and time of last printing, is not immediately visible to users. However, the metadata can unintentionally reveal confidential information such as author name and document classification.

- **Content Change/Revision Information:** Modern document editors have a provision for tracking changes to documents. This is usually the starting point for shared document editing, where a document is marked with "Track Changes." All changes are recorded, but the final document may not present the earlier versions. However, the original content and all the revisions are embedded in the document unless they are explicitly removed.

- **Content Versions:** This feature enables a single document to store multiple versions of the same document over time.

Information leaks involve the release of these different types of information contained in documents. Depending on the nature of the leak, the revealed information can cause considerable damage to the concerned organization.

3.2   Protection from Inadvertent Leaks

Document management systems are designed to enable collaborative document editing by ensuring workflow integration and incorporating security mechanisms where necessary. The dual goals of workflow integration and security control are at the root of any information leak.

Consider a scenario where a document D1 has type Financial and is classified as Secret. A user with the role of Accountant is authorized to work on the document with read and edit permissions. At the end of the financial year, the user transfers some summary information from D1 to a public document D2 for a press release. Since the user has read and edit permissions on D1, he can perform this information transfer, which involves the use of copy and paste commands using the document editor. This scenario illustrates two important characteristics of a DMS:

- The DMS must permit information transfer from document D1 to a public document. This is in accordance with the organization's workflow requirements (i.e., non-interference).

- The DMS must protect D1 by ensuring that only authorized users are allowed to access it. In accordance with the prevailing security policies, it must prevent the Accountant from executing a print operation on document D1.

Many commercial entities tout tight integration with workflow (and non-interference) as a feature of their DMS products. However, it is trivial to observe that the Accountant is in a position to transfer information from document D1. While security policies can be implemented to pre-

Table 1. Notation used for modeling leaks.

U	Set of DMS users: $u_i \in U$
D	Set of DMS documents: $d_i \in D$
C	Set of DMS document classifications: $c_i \in C$
S_D	Set of DMS document security identifiers (DSIDs): $s_d \in S_D$ such that $\forall d \in D, \exists s_d \in S_D$ specifying the corresponding security level
S_U	Set of DMS user security identifiers (SIDs): $s_u \in S_U$ such that $\forall u \in U, \exists s_u \in S_U$ specifying the corresponding security level
$u_i \rightarrow d_j$	User u_i accesses document d_j
d_{open}	Leaked document is found in the open

vent this information transfer [11], it is, nevertheless, possible for a malicious insider to leak information within the purview of normal workflow processes. On the other hand, a security policy that completely prevents such information flow would interfere with normal workflow processes.

An information leak occurs when information at a higher classification level becomes available at a lower level. Information leaks may be categorized as inadvertent or premeditated. Any undesirable information transfer occurring as part of a legitimate workflow process is termed as inadvertent. For example, if the Accountant wishes to create a new public document D2 with the same formatting as D1, he may initiate a file copy of D1 to D2, which replaces the original content of D2. Then, he proceeds to edit the content and create the public document D2. However, documents D1 and D2 have the same metadata (author information, original creation time, last printed time, etc.). Absent DMS detection and mitigation functionality, this metadata is leaked when document D2 is published on the corporate website.

4. Modeling Information Leaks

This section formally characterizes information leaks. Table 1 presents the notation used for modeling leaks.

DEFINITION 1 *Information Potential (IP): The information potential of a document $d_i \in D$ is defined by:*

$$IP(d_i) = (s_{d_i} \sum s_{u_j}) / \sum u_j \qquad \forall u_j \in U : u_j \rightarrow d_i.$$

The information potential of a document expresses the importance of the information it contains. Note that the information potential of a document can be trivially defined to be its DSID. The SID of a document is generally assigned a value in the range [0,1] depending on its criticality; Public documents are assigned a value of zero while Top Secret documents are assigned a value of one. The relative importance of a document is expressed by including a weighting for the levels of the users who access the document. Thus, a document is accorded importance based on its SID as well as on the levels of the users who access it [5].

DEFINITION 2 *Document Similarity Set* (D_{sim})*: The document similarity set* D_{sim}*, corresponding to a document* d_{open} *found in the open, is a set of documents that have contributed to* d_{open} *along with their respective similarity scores. Thus,* D_{sim} *is a set of tuples of the form* <document, score> *defined by:*

$$D_{sim}(d_{open}) \quad = \quad <d_1, sc_1>, <d_2, sc_2>, \ldots, <d_k, sc_k>$$
$$\text{where } d_k \in D \text{ and } sc_1 \geq sc_2 \geq \ldots \geq sc_k.$$

DEFINITION 3 *Information Leakage Value* (IL_{val})*: The value of the information leaked in* d_{open} *is defined by:*

$$IL_{val}(d_{open}) = \sum_{i=1}^{|D_{sim}|} IP(d_i) \times sc_i.$$

IL_{val} represents the information similarity measure for the document d_{open} with respect to the documents contained in D_{sim}. This definition depends only on the information potential of documents, not on the quantity of information transferred. Thus, a single word transferred from d_1 to d_2 is equivalent to the transfer of a sentence or paragraph or section. Since we do not have a mechanism to detect the importance of the content of a document, this definition is the best we can use to quantify information transfer in a DMS.

4.1   Problem Definition

Given a document d_{open}, constructed by the complete or partial composition of one or more documents in $D = d_1, d_2, \ldots, d_n$, that constitutes an information leak, return a list of suspects, i.e., users $U_{suspects}$ = $u_1, \ldots, u_k : u_i \in U$. Thus, the goal is to deduce the list of suspects, possibly a single user, whose actions resulted in the information leak.

The document d_{open} could be a confidential piece of information leaked intentionally and discovered by a network trace or by examining log files. The insider could create d_{open} as a composition of the documents to which he has access. Thus, d_{open} may contain some confidential information and mostly public information; the idea being to mix information so that the leak is not detected and traced to the insider.

It is also possible that an information leak could be inadvertent, i.e., the information transfer was intended for legitimate purposes but was later found to be in violation of the security policy. Generally, we assume that $d_{open} = d_1 \circ d_2 \circ \ldots \circ d_k$, where $d_1, d_2, \ldots, d_k \in D$, i.e., d_{open} is the composition of documents d_1 through d_k. For simplicity, we assume that d_{open} only contains information from $d_1, d_2, \ldots, d_k \in D$, although the insider might add other commonly available information to create document d_{open}. However, as discussed below, adding spurious information does not impact the detection of information leaks.

4.2   FEM Algorithm Preliminaries

To attribute the source of an information leak, it is essential to capture all the changes made to documents in a DMS, preferably in a succinct way. We use rooted, labeled trees to model the transmutations that documents undergo in their lifetime. We denote the tree as $T = (D, E, \epsilon)$ where D is a set of nodes representing different versions of the documents after edit sessions. Node $r \in D$ is a special node that forms the root of the tree.

All the documents contained in a DMS at any point in time correspond to nodes that are connected directly to the root r. $E \subseteq D \times D$ is the set of edges in the tree. An edge $(d_{i_j}, d_{i_k}) \in E$ denotes the transition that a document d_i undergoes as a result of edit operations. In other words, d_{i_k} is a version of the document that has evolved from its previous version d_{i_j}. The sequence $\epsilon = e_1, e_2, e_3, \ldots, e_k$ is the edit script that transforms the document from one version d_{i_j} to another d_{i_k}. In turn, each e_i represents an edit operation that is applied as a part of an edit script ϵ. L is a set of version labels. Each version of the document $d_i \in D$ after a successful edit operation is uniquely identified with a different name d_{i_l} corresponding to its label l (version).

Any sensitive information that could have leaked from a document with a higher classification to a document with a lower classification is encapsulated by the edit script. We define the set of edit operations [2] that can be applied in an edit script ϵ_1 to transform document version d_i to document version d_j (i.e., $d_i \rightarrow^{\epsilon_1} d_j$).

- **Insertion:** Each DMS document is considered to be a flat file represented as a $p \times q$ rectangular grid where p is the column width of the document and q is the number of lines in the document. Each $p \times q$ point in the grid is mapped to a single ASCII character. The insert operation $INS(p_1, q_1, content)$ inserts the ASCII characters dictated by the content beginning at (p_1, q_1) in the grid. The content previously located at (p_1, q_1) and beyond is shifted and concatenated with the inserted content.

- **Deletion:** Deletion is the inverse of insertion. $DEL(p_1, q_1, p_2, q_2)$ truncates the content located between (p_1, q_1) and (p_2, q_2).

- **Update:** The $UPD(p_1, q_1, p_2, q_2, content)$ operation replaces the content between (p_1, q_1) and (p_2, q_2) with the specified content. An update operation is equivalent to successively applying the $DEL(p_1, q_1, p_2, q_2)$ and $INS(p_1, q_1, content)$ operations.

- **Copy:** $CPY(p, q, d_s)$ is a special operation that does not change the content of document d_s. It is used to capture "content highlighting" and "copy to clipboard" events, which occur when information is transferred within a document or between documents.

- **Glue:** $GLU(p_1, q_1, p_2, q_2, content, d_s)$ is similar to the update operation. The only difference is that the content between (p_1, q_1) and (p_2, q_2) is replaced with the content copied from the clipboard taken from document d_s using the CPY operation. If (p_1, q_1) is equal to (p_2, q_2), the GLU operation becomes equivalent to $INS(p_1, q_1, content)$. It is possible that content is manually transferred from document d_u to d_v. Such an information transfer is recorded as an INS operation instead of the CPY and GLU operations.

4.3   FEM Trace-Back Algorithm

This section describes the algorithm for tracing the sources $(U_{suspects})$ of an information leak.

First, the leaked information is correlated with a set of documents D_{sim} in the DMS. Next, it is determined if the leak is caused by CPY and GLU operations in an edit script ϵ that transfer information from a document d_k with a higher classification to a document d_i with a lower classification to produce a new version d_j. In such an instance, the content pasted from the clipboard by the GLU operation is checked to see if it matches the leaked content.

An information leak can also take place across multiple edit sessions spanning multiple documents. This is similar to a "slow poisoning" attack where D_{sim} only matches the final version of the document, say d_j, even though the information leak could have occurred in part during previous editing sessions.

Algorithm 1 Malicious Insider Detection Algorithm

Require: IL_{tsh} and audit logs as specified in the monitoring phase
Ensure: Output of $U_{suspects}$

1: Evaluate $D_{sim}(d_{open}) = <d_1, sc_1>, <d_2, sc_2>, \ldots, <d_k, sc_k>$
2: Calculate $D_{high} = d_i \in D_{sim} : IL_{val} > IL_{tsh}$
   Calculate $D_{low} = d_i \in D_{sim} : IL_{val} \leq IL_{tsh}$
3: Calculate $U_{high} = u_i \in U : \forall d_j \in D_{high}, u_i \to d_j$
   Calculate $U_{low} = u_i \in U : \forall d_j \in D_{low}, u_i \to d_j$
4: **for all** d_i in D_{sim} **do**
5: $\quad <d_{i1}, d_{i2}, \ldots, d_{ik}> = $ Greedy-Collate(GLU/CPY)
6: $\quad U_{suspects} += u : u_l \to d_{ij}$ where $d_{ij} \to^{\epsilon} d_{ik}, \forall u_l \in U, \forall d_{ik} \in D_{sim}$
7: **end for**

The algorithm collates the contents of GLU operations from edit scripts from previous sessions in a greedy manner to check if the collated content matches the leaked content. All the users who initiated the edit script are deemed as suspects. However, not all information leaks occur due to CPY and GLU operations. For example, a user might try to reproduce a document by reading it and typing its content ("content jacking"). The algorithm only considers the content involved in the INS and UPD operations and generates an information graph [11] to determine the documents in D_{sim} that were opened concurrently with the public document d_j that contains the leaked information.

Algorithm 1 presents the steps involved when only GLU operations are considered. The sub-procedure Greedy-Collate is self explanatory.

The algorithm is easily extended to incorporate content collation implemented by the INS and UPD operations. The algorithm also (optionally) takes as input an information leak threshold value (IL_{tsh}) beyond which any information transfer is considered to be a leak. If IL_{tsh} is specified, then D_{sim} in Step 4 can be replaced by D_{high} and U in Step 6 can be replaced by U_{high}.

5. Forensic Extension Module

The forensic extension module (FEM) has two phases, monitoring and analysis. The monitoring phase is an online process, i.e., it takes place whenever there is user activity. The components used in this phase augment standard DMS auditing procedures. Each user action/interaction with the documents in the repository is recorded and relevant context information is collected. Along with each activity, information about the document classification, time of transfer, etc. is also logged. Various metrics are computed from the logs to understand the specific actions

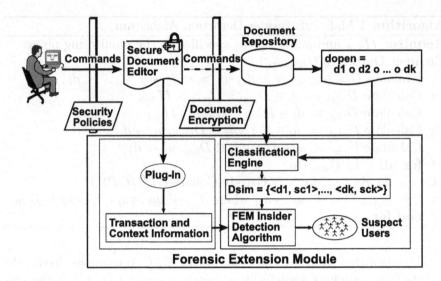

Figure 1. Incorporation of a FEM in a DMS.

taken by users and their intent. For example, a flurry of document accesses (reads and searches) may indicate exploratory activities that are not part of the workflow process. A simple query submitted to the logs can provide all the instances of these document accesses. Similarly, transaction time and transaction origin (within the organizational perimeter or external access via a VPN connection) are indicators of surreptitious activity.

The second FEM phase, which involves offline analysis, is initiated whenever a leaked document is found in the open. The leaked document is first correlated with the document repository. Based on the correlation, the set D_{sim} is constructed (as in Definition 3). Finally, the DMS audit logs and the metrics computed during the monitoring phase are used to obtain the list of suspects $U_{suspects}$.

5.1   Integration Issues

Microsoft Word 2003 was chosen as the DMS hosting platform. It (i.e., Office 2003) comes with a digital rights management feature (Information Rights Management), which enables document protection, including the specification and enforcement of custom policies. Most of the Word Object Model interfaces are exposed as standard SDKs, which facilitate the addition of custom plug-ins (called "add-ins" in Microsoft's documentation). Thus, the FEM was implemented as an add-in to Word 2003 and integrated with the DMS process flow as shown in Figure 1.

5.2   Implementation Issues

During the monitoring phase, the FEM is supposed to log information on all user transactions involving DMS documents. However, this is difficult to implement because document editors such as Microsoft Word and OpenOffice were designed primarily as document editing tools rather than inhibition tools. Over the years, they have evolved from using simple text documents with formatting tags to supporting complex documents with embedded software that provides advanced features. Thus, a Microsoft Word document is specified as an XML schema with tags and binary-encoded streams for various portions of the document. A side effect of these tags is that, from a document editing viewpoint, they do not form part of the content, but can conveniently be used to transfer critical information. The interface exposed by the Word Object Model enables notification for certain document operations (e.g., opening and printing) but does not provide a hook for logging information transfer. For example, if a user were to copy and paste information from one document to another, no API is available to hook the copy and paste events. To overcome this limitation, information required during the monitoring phase is obtained by enabling the "Track Changes" feature for every document edited by a user and creating a log of all the files modified in a session.

6.   Evaluation

The following components were used to emulate a DMS in order to evaluate the effectiveness of the FEM trace-back algorithm.

- **Document Corpus:** The corpus contained Microsoft Word 2003 documents created using the 20 newsgroup data set [12]. The documents were classified into five categories: Top Secret, Secret, Confidential, Classified and Public. The twenty newsgroups in the data set were uniformly distributed among the five document classifications. For example, the posts (in plain text format) in **talk.politics.guns** were converted to Microsoft Word documents and were uniformly distributed under the five classifications. Note that converting the posts to Word document format is slightly more involved than merely renaming the files with a .doc extension. A simple helper tool that instantiates a Word Application Object and seamlessly converts plain text files in a given directory to Microsoft Word 2003 documents was used for this purpose. This tool performs the equivalent of manually renaming the newsgroup post with a .doc extension, opening the renamed document

Table 2.   Access control matrix.

	Admin	Manager	Pgmmr	Intern	Contr	Secy
Top Secret	r, w, p	r, w, p	-	-	-	-
Secret	r, w, p	r, w, p	r	-	-	-
Confidential	r, w, p	r, w, p	r, w	r	-	-
Classified	r, w, p	r, w, p	r, w, p	r, w	r, w	-
Public	r, w, p	r, w, p	r, w, p	r, w, p	r, w	r, w, p

in Word, accepting the default encoding, and saving the file in the
latest Word format.

- **User Set:** Five classes of users were defined: Administrator ≻
  Manager ≻ Programmer ≻ Intern ≻ Contractor ≻ Secretary. Note
  that these roles do not naturally produce a linear hierarchy; this
  hierarchy was chosen only for the proof-of-concept implementation.
  A fixed access control matrix was used to specify the rights (r:
  read, w: write and p: print) possessed by the five classes of users
  to the five document categories (Table 2).

- **FEM:** The FEM add-in for Microsoft Word 2003 provides audit logging and forensic capabilities. It was implemented in C#
  using Visual Studio 2005 under .NET Framework 2.0 and Windows Vista. When installed, the add-in places a "FEM toolbar"
  in Word.

  The FEM toolbar has three controls:

  - A drop-down combo box titled "Role Choice," which enables
    the user to choose a role (e.g., Intern) for the particular ses-
    sion. Based on the role, access control policies are applied
    that allow a test subject to open documents with the classi-
    fications dictated by the access control matrix in Table 2.

  - A button titled "Start FEM Logging," which is used to initi-
    ate logging after a role is chosen. Note that the logging is not
    performed by a third-party process, but by Microsoft Word,
    whose functionality is extended by the FEM add-in. Thus,
    the FEM add-in is truly an extension to the DMS (where Mi-
    crosoft Word serves as the document viewer and editor). The
    FEM add-in can be extended to dump the logs to a remote
    database or a server (e.g., Windows 2003 Server).

– A "Send Logs" button is available to (optionally) send the log by email upon completion of a session. This feature can be eliminated if a trusted DMS platform is used.

The FEM evaluation experiment gathered data from thirteen virtual users, each with an assigned role. The users were asked to transfer information from the highest classification level to which they had access (based on the access control matrix in Table 2) to a Public document. They were allowed to browse the Internet and copy and paste information from the Internet to obfuscate detection attempts. Note that because the users only performed the operations defined by the access control matrix, a simplified version of the detection algorithm was applied where the content derived from the "Track Changes" feature was merged with the log file to infer the actions performed by users that led to information leaks.

Document similarity was tested using a simplified "diff" algorithm [10] (other algorithms such as the Term Frequency Inverse Document Frequency (TF-IDF) algorithm [6] can also be used). Detection would have been much easier if the documents had been structured (e.g., using XML [1]).

Two of the thirteen users chose to not initiate any information leaks. Nine users who leaked a significant amount of information were detected by the FEM. Using the check-in and check-out feature of the DMS and the difference between the two versions of the documents, it was relatively straightforward to identify the nine users as final suspects. Two users who leaked information were not detected at all. One user transferred a single number from a Top Secret document. As this change was minute, the transfer did not score a high enough similarity score for the algorithm to investigate the user. The other user changed the content of a Public document without actually copying information directly from a Secret document. Furthermore, the content of the destination Public document was scattered throughout the document making it difficult for the FEM (or any computer program) to analyze the content.

The performance of the FEM was very reasonable; however, it has inherent limitations that stem from the nature of the problem and the myriad possibilities that exist for information leaks. Users cannot have their workflow affected. In a DMS, this translates to unhindered information flow subject to static and context-specific security policies. If an information leak occurs, the FEM can narrow the list of suspects and, in favorable circumstances, can identify the single malicious insider. The FEM relies on the similarity between the leaked document and the document repository; this is correlated with the information transfer initiated by users. However, a major limitation arises from the fact that the similarity score is computed for raw text while information transfer may (also) be in terms of pictures, WordArt, AutoShapes, or even custom embedded objects. These types of information transfer can be regarded as steganographic in nature; they are simple for a human to perform but very difficult for a computing system to recognize or categorize. Although this problem has some resemblance to the (reverse) Turing test [16], its scope is much larger. Indeed, the lack of computing approaches (possibly based on artificial intelligence) for recognizing such "information" significantly impacts the efficacy of a FEM-like approach for detecting steganographic forms of information transfer.

7. Conclusions

Information leaks in DMSs are a major security threat, but little work has been done on detecting and mitigating them. Current approaches, which are effective at detecting infractions when information is transferred between documents of different classifications, are impractical for two reasons. First, defense mechanisms are intrusive and can significantly hinder workflow processes. Second, loosely-framed DMS policies may permit actions that result in information leaks. Our FEM solution addresses these two issues using an information leak metric and coupling it with audit data collected during the monitoring phase. Its proof-of-concept implementation as an add-in to Microsoft Word 2003 is likely the first time that forensic functionality is integrated in an environment where a threat vector (malicious insider) is not addressed. Our future research will investigate extensions to the FEM framework for detecting and mitigating information leaks propagated through other mechanisms such as printed materials, steganography and human channels.

References

[1] S. Chawathe and H. Garcia-Molina, Meaningful change detection in structured data, *ACM SIGMOD Record*, vol. 26(2), pp. 26–37, 1997.

[2] S. Chawathe, A. Rajaraman, H. Garcia-Molina and J. Widom, Change detection in hierarchically structured information, *Proceedings of the ACM SIGMOD International Conference on Management of Data*, pp. 493–504, 1996.

[3] K. Eckstein and M. Jahnke, Data hiding in journaling file systems, *Proceedings of the Fifth Annual Digital Forensics Research Workshop*, 2005.

[4] EMC Corporation, Authentica Software, Hopkinton, Massachusetts (software.emc.com/microsites/regional/authentica).

[5] A. Garg, S. Pramanik, V. Shankaranarayanan and S. Upadhyaya, Dynamic document reclassification for preventing insider abuse, *Proceedings of the Fifth Annual IEEE SMC Information Assurance Workshop*, pp. 218–225, 2004.

[6] D. Grossman and O. Frieder, *Information Retrieval: Algorithms and Heuristics*, Springer, Dordrecht, The Netherlands, 2004.

[7] Microsoft Corporation, Office 2003 Add-In: Word Redactionv1.2, Redmond, Washington (www.microsoft.com/downloads/details.a spx?FamilyID=028c0fd7-67c2-4b51-8e87-65cc9f30f2ed&displaylang =en).

[8] Microsoft Corporation, Office 2003/XP Add-In: Remove Hidden Data, Redmond, Washington (www.microsoft.com/downloads/deta ils.aspx?FamilyId=144E54ED-D43E-42CA-BC7B-5446D34E5360& displaylang=en).

[9] A. Mehta, Office Space: Information rights management in Office 2003, TechNet, Microsoft Corporation, Redmond, Washington (technet.microsoft.com/en-us/magazine/cc160822.aspx), 2003.

[10] E. Myers, An O(ND) difference algorithm and its variations, *Algorithmica*, vol. 1(2), pp. 251–266, 1986.

[11] S. Pramanik, V. Sankaranarayanan and S. Upadhyaya, Security policies to mitigate insider threats in the document control domain, *Proceedings of the Twentieth Annual Computer Security Applications Conference*, pp. 304–313, 2004.

[12] J. Rennie, 20 Newsgroups (people.csail.mit.edu/jrennie/20Newsgr oups).

[13] V. Sankaranarayanan, S. Pramanik and S. Upadhyaya, Detecting masquerading users in a document management system, *Proceedings of the IEEE International Conference on Communications*, pp. 2296–2301, 2006.

[14] B. Schneier and J. Kelsey, Secure audit logs to support computer forensics, *ACM Transactions on Information and System Security*, vol. 2(2), pp. 159–176, 1999.

[15] K. Shanmugasundaram and N. Memon, Automatic reassembly of document fragments via context based statistical models, *Proceedings of the Nineteenth Annual Computer Security Applications Conference*, pp. 152–159, 2003.

[16] L. von Ahn, M. Blum and J. Langford, Telling humans and computers apart automatically, *Communications of the ACM*, vol.47(2), pp. 56–60, 2004.

[17] W. Wang and T. Daniels, Building evidence graphs for network forensics analysis, *Proceedings of the Twenty-First Annual Computer Security Applications Conference*, pp. 254–266, 2005.

Chapter 24

IMAGE BACKGROUND MATCHING FOR IDENTIFYING SUSPECTS

Paul Fogg, Gilbert Peterson and Michael Veth

Abstract   Thousands of digital images may exist of a given location, some of which may show a crime in progress. One technique for identifying suspects and witnesses is to collect images of specific crime scenes from computers, cell phones, cameras and other electronic devices, and perform image matching based on image backgrounds. This paper describes an image matching technique that is used in conjunction with feature generation methodologies, such as the Scale Invariant Feature Transform (SIFT) and the Speeded Up Robust Features (SURF) algorithms. The technique identifies keypoints in images of a given location with minor differences in viewpoint and content. After calculating keypoints for the images, the technique stores only the "good" features for each image to minimize space and matching requirements. Test results indicate that matching accuracy exceeding 80% is obtained with the SIFT and SURF algorithms.

Keywords: Image background matching, SIFT, SURF, keypoint reduction

1.   Introduction

Electronic matching is commonly performed for fingerprints [5], shoe imprints [1] and facial features [13]. Image feature generation techniques, such as the scale invariant feature transform (SIFT) [7] and speeded up robust features (SURF) [2] algorithms can be used to automate the process of digital image matching. Persons of interest can be identified by grouping and matching multiple images of a crime scene, even when the images are taken from different viewpoints. For example, crime scene images can be used to identify and place suspects and victims at the scene. Alternatively, background details from child pornography images can be used to establish where the pictures were taken.

Please use the following format when citing this chapter:

Fogg, P., Peterson, G. and Veth, M., 2008, in IFIP International Federation for Information Processing, Volume 285; *Advances in Digital Forensics IV*; Indrajit Ray, Sujeet Shenoi; (Boston: Springer), pp. 307–321.

This paper describes a technique for image matching that is used in conjunction with the scale invariant feature transform (SIFT) and speeded up robust features (SURF) algorithms. The first step involves the generation of keypoints for each algorithm. The next step reduces the number of keypoints to minimize storage requirements and improve matching speeds. The third step performs match comparison, which removes poor quality keypoint matches. The final step analyzes images taken of the same location to identify features and/or persons of interest. Testing indicates that better than 80% matching accuracy is achieved using the SIFT and SURF algorithms.

2.   Image Matching Algorithms

This section provides an overview of several image matching algorithms, including the Scale Invariant Feature Transform (SIFT) [7, 8] and Speeded Up Robust Features (SURF) [2] algorithms.

2.1   SIFT Algorithm

The SIFT algorithm [7] performs image recognition by calculating a local image feature vector. The feature vector is used for matching scaled, translated and/or rotated images under low illumination and affine transformations. This technique is inspired by neuronal activities in the inferior temporal cortex of primates, which implement object recognition.

The SIFT algorithm uses four steps to extract image keypoints: scale-space extrema detection, keypoint localization, orientation assignment and keypoint descriptor generation [8].

1. Scale-Space Extrema Detection: In this step, Gaussian kernels of increasing variance are convolved with the image. A total of $s+3$ images are produced (s is the number of scales); each image has an increased amount of blur. Next, the difference of Gaussians is computed for each pair of blurred images by subtracting each image from the next most blurred image; this produces $s+2$ differences of Gaussians. Each difference of Gaussians is then bilinearly interpolated to generate the next reduced scale for the total of s scales.

2. Keypoint Localization: Each pixel in a difference of Gaussians is compared with its eight neighbors. A pixel is designated as a keypoint if it is a maximum or minimum at this level and the related pixels at all other scales are also maxima or minima. An improve-

ment to this technique proposed by Lowe [8] fits a 3D quadratic function to the pixels and their neighbors across scales.

3. Orientation Assignment: For each keypoint, the Gaussian blurred image with a value closest to the scale of the keypoint is selected. In this image, the gradient magnitude and orientation of the image are calculated over 36 bins around the keypoint pixel. These 36 vectors, which are weighted by the keypoint scale, identify the orientation of the keypoint.

4. Keypoint Descriptor Generation: The keypoint descriptor is determined by calculating the gradient magnitude and orientation of each pixel in a 16×16 pixel patch around the keypoint. These vectors are weighted by a Gaussian distribution centered at the keypoint and are combined in 4×4 pixel patches. The 16 combined gradients are reduced to eight vectors in each of the cardinal directions. The magnitudes of these vectors become the 128-element keypoint descriptor.

Lowe [8] identified a marked decrease in matching performance for 112 images as the number of keypoints approaches 100,000 per image. However, the effect of a reduction in the number of keypoints per image on matching performance has not been investigated. This is an important issue because a child pornography case, for example, may have tens of thousands of images; an average of 3,000 keypoints per image results in more than 30,000,000 keypoints. Our strategy is to reduce the number of keypoints per image (which saves time and memory) while achieving satisfactory image matching percentages.

2.2 SURF Algorithm

The SURF algorithm incorporates enhancements to the SIFT algorithm that increase the overall speed [2]. The enhancements are described below in the context of the four steps of the SIFT algorithm.

1. Scale-Space Extrema Detection: SURF uses a 2×2 Hessian matrix, whose components are the convolution of the second-order Gaussian derivative with an area of the image centered at each pixel. To speed this process, a box filter approximation of the second-order Gaussian derivatives is used. The reduction in the scale of the images (to generate multiple scales) is then performed by increasing the size of the box filter approximation [2].

2. Keypoint Localization: SURF uses SIFT's 3D quadratic function to extract localized keypoints [2].

3. Orientation Assignment: Haar wavelet responses in the x and y directions are calculated over a circular neighborhood of radius $6s$ around each keypoint (s is the scale of the image). The Haar responses are weighted with a Gaussian distribution centered at the keypoint and are summed to generate the orientation vector [2].

4. Keypoint Descriptor Generation: The keypoint descriptor is calculated over a $20s$ pixel area around the keypoint oriented according to the orientation assignment. The area is divided into 16 square patches that are evenly spaced over the keypoint descriptor area. In each patch, the Haar wavelet responses in the x and y directions are calculated over a 4×4 pixel square for each pixel in the patch. The response vectors from each pixel in a patch are then combined. The four component vectors from each of the 16 patches give rise to the 64-element keypoint descriptor [2].

The SURF descriptor has similar properties to the SIFT descriptor but is less complex and is, therefore, faster to compute. The times required for keypoint descriptor generation are 354 ms, 391 ms and 1,036 ms for SURF (with a 64-element descriptor), SURF-128 (128-element descriptor) and SIFT, respectively [2]. The average recognition rates or accuracy of detecting repeat locations for SURF, SURF-128 and SIFT are 82.6%, 85.7% and 78.1%, respectively [2].

2.3   Other Image Matching Algorithms

An alternative image matching algorithm is PCA-SIFT [12], which incorporates principal components analysis. PCA-SIFT applies a normalized gradient patch instead of smoothed weighted histograms to generate the keypoint feature vector. This provides users with the ability to specify the size of the feature vector. The default feature vector size in PCA-SIFT is 20 [12]. Experiments show that SIFT runs slightly faster during keypoint generation, 1.59 sec vs. 1.64 sec [12]. However, the experiments also show that PCA-SIFT has a large performance advantage during image matching, 0.58 sec vs. 2.20 sec [12]. This improvement is due to a significant reduction in keypoint feature size (20 vs. 128).

The Shi-Tomasi algorithm [10] selects features that are suitable for tracking between image frames. Keypoints are generated over 7×7 blocks of pixels. The second-order partial derivatives of the intensity of the pixels are calculated for each pixel block. The eigenvalues of the derivatives are identified as an interest point if their minimum exceeds a user-specified threshold. The algorithm is most suitable for small camera position changes, but is not robust enough to handle the large displacements found in our application domain.

3. Keypoint Reduction and Matching

This section presents the methods used to reduce the number of keypoints and to identify a location match given variations in the viewpoint and content.

3.1 Keypoint Reduction

The SIFT and SURF algorithms generate an average of 3,000 keypoints per image. Reducing the number of keypoints significantly reduces memory requirements and image matching times but negatively impacts the matching accuracy. This problem can be addressed by choosing "stronger" keypoints that are well distributed in the image. A distance function helps ensure a good keypoint spread, which prevents keypoint clustering and subsequent image occlusion.

Keypoints are selected using an iterative approach. The SIFT algorithm selects the first two points based on the scale of the detected keypoints. For the SURF algorithm, the first two points are selected based on the log of the cardinality of the non zero (Nz) elements of the second moment matrix $\log\left(\frac{1}{\sqrt{|Nz|^2}}\right)$. Consequent keypoints are selected based on a weighted sum of the scale (SIFT) or second moment (SURF) of the keypoint and of the Mahalanobis distance between the keypoint and all previously chosen keypoints [11]. Keypoints are obtained by evaluating each available point (x_i, y_i) using $W_1 D_M(x_i, y_i) + W_2 \sigma(x_i, y_i)$ to obtain the largest value. Note that $\sigma(x_i, y_i)$ is the scale/second moment, $D_M(x_i, y_i)$ is the Mahalanobis distance at point (x_i, y_i), W_1 is the weighting on the Mahalanobis distance function, and W_2 is the weighting on the scale/second moment of the keypoint. This process continues until the desired number of keypoints is selected.

The best settings for the distance weighting (W_1) and scale/second moment weighting (W_2) were determined by tests using distance weightings from 0.5 to 100 and a constant scale weighting of 1. The goal was to ensure that the selected keypoints are spread uniformly to prevent partial occlusion but still provide a strong probability of matching. Keypoints tend to cluster when the distance weighting is much greater than the scale/second moment weighting; equal weights generally result in a better distribution of keypoints.

This trend is seen in Figure 1, where the settings of the distance weighting and the scale/second moment weighting of 0:1 (Figure 1(a)) produce a larger spread of keypoints than settings of 5:1 (Figure 1(b)). The figures show feature distributions of 102 keypoints; the figure axes are the x and y coordinates of pixels. The best settings for the distance

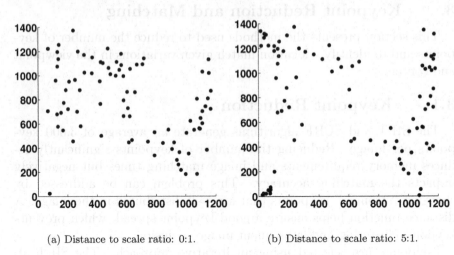

(a) Distance to scale ratio: 0:1.   (b) Distance to scale ratio: 5:1.

Figure 1.   Feature distributions of 102 keypoints.

weighting and the scale/second moment weighting were determined subjectively by overlaying the keypoint distributions and observing the levels of spread and clustering. The setting that results in the greatest spread of keypoints occurs when W_1 and W_2 are both equal to 1.

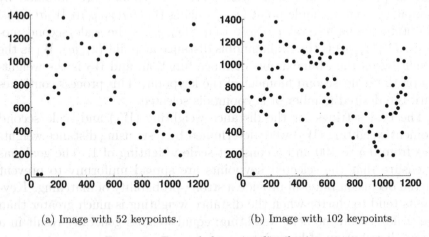

(a) Image with 52 keypoints.   (b) Image with 102 keypoints.

Figure 2.   Example keypoint distributions.

Limited testing was conducted to identify the best number of keypoints to select from an image. The tests compared the image keypoint distribution between selecting 52 keypoints (Figure 2(a)) versus 102 keypoints (Figure 2(b)). Both distributions were generated using distance

(W_1) and scale (W_2) weights of 1. The larger number of keypoints (102) provides a more uniform distribution along both axes.

The more uniform the distribution of points, the better the matching opportunities. Using a large number of keypoints was considered to address background occlusion. However, the computational cost of keypoint reduction is high, so a decision was made to limit the number of keypoints in subsequent tests to 102. More research is required to identify the optimal number of keypoints.

3.2   Background Matching Using SIFT

Image background matching with the SIFT algorithm involves an extension of Hess' SIFT implementation [6]. Each image is processed using the SIFT keypoint generation algorithm to produce 102 keypoints as described in Section 3.1. The image keypoints are stored in a database that is used for match comparisons. Next, the keypoints corresponding to each pair of images are compared. The best candidate match is found by calculating the nearest neighbor using a minimum Euclidean distance for the descriptor vector. The distance from the second-closest neighbor is used to define the distance ratio such that 90% of the bad matches are pruned with a distance ratio greater than 0.8 [8]. The Best Bin First algorithm is used to implement the nearest neighbor search; the Hough transform is used to identify clusters of features that help enhance the recognition of small or occluded objects [8].

Two quality checks are performed to eliminate poor matches; both checks use the same initial framework. First, each pair of match points are converted into lines calculated as if the two images are stacked on top of each other (see Figure 3 in Section 4.1). The intersection points for each line are then computed; these intersection points are used to identify poor matches. The first quality check removes a match if it produces intersection points within the frame of the match image. The second check calculates the mean and standard deviation of the intersection points; a line is a poor match when 90% or more of its intersection points lie outside one standard deviation from the mean.

3.3   Background Matching Using SURF

SURF image background matching is similar to that of SIFT with the exception that the MATLAB® keypoint generation software created by Alvaro and Guerrero [3] is employed. However, the quality checks developed for SIFT do not perform as well as those for SURF. The reason is that SIFT generates a significantly larger number of false matches; most matches are accepted because the standard deviation of the intersection points is quite large. An additional check is incorporated prior to match filtering to improve the quality of matching. This check tests the slopes of the match lines against a threshold of 0.4; a match line is eliminated when its slope exceeds the threshold.

4.   Experimental Results

A Fuji FinePix E550 was used to acquire the 125 images used to test the image background matching algorithms. The images were taken at six locations (home office, guest bedroom office, stairwell, living room, home exterior and computer laboratory). 119 images were taken at 1,600×1,200 resolution and six were taken at 640×480 resolution.

The images were taken from various vantage points with different points of view (POV). The camera distance for the indoor images varied between 2.75 feet and 11 feet; the rotation varied approximately ±15 degrees and the camera angle variation was more than ±50 degrees. The home office was the only location where images were taken at two resolutions (1,600×1,200 and 640×480). The outdoor images had much larger variations; the distance varied 50 feet and the rotation and camera angle varied ±10 degrees and more than ±180 degrees, respectively.

The images were divided into seven groups for testing. Images taken at each of the six locations were placed in a separate group, except for those taken at the home office, which were placed into two groups because the camera viewpoint for these images differed by 180 degrees.

The 125 images were converted to gray scale prior to matching. This is because the two matching algorithms use the intensity of each pixel $I(x, y)$ in keypoint calculations. It is possible to create keypoints in color images using each of the three color channels (red, green, blue) as separate intensity values, but the matching performance for both algorithms degrades.

The first step in the matching technique involved the extraction of the keypoints for each image using the SIFT and SURF algorithms. Next, keypoint reduction was performed using the method described in Section 3.1; the reduced keypoints were stored in a data file to facilitate matching. After matching, the keypoint comparison technique presented in Section 3.2 was performed on the matched keypoint lines in an effort to prune "bad" matches.

To verify the accuracy of the technique, each of 125 images was compared with every other image, resulting in a total of image 7,750 comparisons for each of the algorithms. However, before the algorithms were applied, a human who had not seen any of the image locations was asked to group the images based on location. The individual placed the images into 24 groups using prominent reference points to distinguish image locations. Six of the 24 groups contained just one image. The accuracy of identification was 55% mainly due to the creation of extra groups.

The performance of the human could not be compared with that of SIFT and SURF because he grouped images individually instead of performing 7,750 comparisons (like the algorithms). Nevertheless, the experiment demonstrates the difficulty involved in matching images.

Reducing the number of the keypoints saved for each image conserves storage space. We demonstrate that this technique reduces storage as well as the time required for matching image locations. Specifically, we compare the storage and time requirements for our image matching technique with those for the SIFT and SURF algorithms. The tests were conducted using a dual core Xeon 3 GHz workstation with 3 GB RAM.

Table 1. Storage required by the SIFT and SURF algorithms.

Algorithm	Size On Disk	Percent Reduction
SIFT Files	197 MB	
Reduced SIFT Files	4.88 MB	97.5%
SURF Files	290 MB	
Reduced SURF Files	16.1 MB	94.4%

Table 1 shows the storage required by the SIFT and SURF algorithms before and after keypoint reduction. The storage requirements are for the 125 SIFT/SURF keypoint files generated from the 125 images used in the experiment. Keypoint reduction yields a 97.5% reduction in the storage requirements for SIFT. Similar results are obtained for the SURF algorithm (94.4% reduction).

Table 2. Execution time for the SIFT algorithm.

SIFT Algorithm	Approximate Execution Time	Percent Reduction
Match	24 hours 39 minutes	N/A
Reduced Match	6 hours 23 minutes	74.1%
Keypoint Reduction	3 hours 27 minutes	86.0%
Reduced Match and Keypoint Reduction	9 hours 50 minutes	60.1%

Using 102 well-selected keypoints per image instead of several thousand keypoints (which would otherwise be used) significantly reduces the time required to perform image matching. Table 2 presents the time required to run a complete matching experiment for the SIFT algorithm.

SIFT matching of the 125 images takes more than 24 hours whereas the time required for keypoint reduction and subsequent matching requires just 9 hours and 50 minutes, a 60.1% reduction.

Table 3.   Execution time for the SURF algorithm.

SURF Algorithm	Approximate Execution Time	Percent Reduction
Match	12 hours 19 minutes	N/A
Reduced Match	2 hours 16 minutes	81.6%
Keypoint Reduction	1 hours 39 minutes	86.6%
Reduced Match and Keypoint Reduction	3 hours 55 minutes	68.2%

Table 3 shows that similar reductions in computational time are obtained for the SURF algorithm. SURF requires 12 hours and 19 minutes to perform a full match on the 125 test images. On the other hand, keypoint reduction and match requires only 3 hours and 55 minutes, a 68.2% reduction. Below we show that the storage and time savings come without significant loss of image matching accuracy.

4.1   SIFT Algorithm Results

Figure 3 shows that the SIFT match algorithm deals well with occlusion. A total of six matches were found in the two images in Figure 3. One of them – the one on the individual's arm – is an incorrect match. This incorrect match is pruned by both SIFT quality check methods.

Figures 4 and 5 indicate that relatively few images are incorrectly matched – this occurs when images of different locations are identified as being of the same location. Figure 4 shows that the Type I error (false positives) drops dramatically until a threshold of 4. As shown in Figure 5, 81.0% accuracy is obtained using a threshold (η) of 5. However, lower resolution images matched poorly with an accuracy of 72.5%.

The highest accuracy (81.1%) for the SIFT algorithm is obtained using a threshold of 6. In fact, correct matches were obtained even for a large threshold of 98 (not shown in Figure 5). However, using a threshold of 102 incorrectly drops some image matches; this is because the matching algorithm uses a nearest neighbor algorithm to identify keypoint matches and some of the neighbors are pruned during keypoint reduction [8].

There was no difference in the maximum accuracy obtained for the two quality checks. Note that the data in Figures 4 and 5 were computed using only the intersection standard deviation quality check.

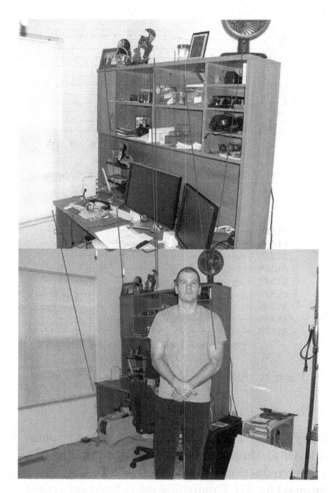

Figure 3.   SIFT image showing reduced keypoint matches with occlusion.

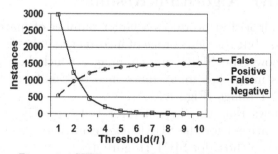

Figure 4.   SIFT error with reduced keypoints.

The matching performance obtained with the keypoint reduction technique compares well against that obtained when using the full unreduced

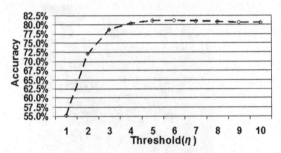

Figure 5.   SIFT accuracy with reduced keypoints.

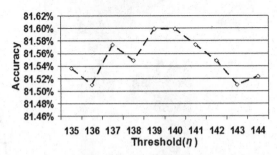

Figure 6.   SIFT accuracy with unreduced features.

set of SIFT keypoints. Figure 6 shows that the maximum accuracy of 81.6% is achieved at thresholds of 139 and 140 for the SIFT algorithm without keypoint reduction. This accuracy (81.6%) is marginally better than that obtained for SIFT matching using keypoint reduction (81.1%).

4.2   SURF Algorithm Results

The SURF algorithm produces a larger number of matches than the SIFT algorithm, but the percentage of incorrect matches is much higher.

Figure 7 shows the SURF match image, which has a total of 44 matches. This image has many more incorrect matches than the corresponding SIFT image (Figure 3).

Figure 8 shows that the Type I error (false positives) and Type II error (false negatives) for the SURF algorithm with reduced keypoints are comparable to those for SIFT (Figure 4).

Figure 9 shows that the maximum accuracy of 79.6% for the SURF algorithm occurs at a threshold of 57, where the unreduced SURF accuracy is 78.3%. However, by adding the slope threshold of 0.4, the accuracy is improved to 80.7%.

Figure 7. SURF image showing reduced keypoint matches with occlusion.

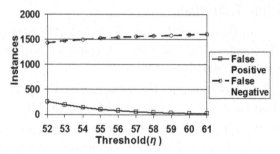

Figure 8. SURF error with reduced keypoints.

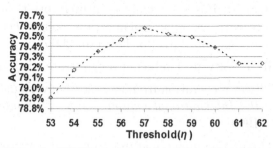

Figure 9. SURF accuracy with reduced keypoints.

5. Conclusions

Automating image background matching for the task of grouping images based on location is, indeed, feasible. Good results are obtained using the SIFT algorithm augmented with keypoint reduction. Specifically, the SIFT algorithm provides a maximum accuracy of 81.1% whereas the SURF algorithm has a maximum accuracy is 79.6%. Significant space and time savings are obtained using keypoint reduction. The storage reduction for the SIFT and SURF algorithms are 97.5% and 94.4%, respectively. The corresponding savings in computational time for SIFT and SURF are 60.1% and 68.2%, respectively.

Additional work is needed to enhance image background matching with reduced keypoints. This includes analyzing match points to improve matching accuracy and identifying optimal threshold values for the SIFT and SURF quality check methods. Furthermore, tests need to be run on large databases of images with varying content, size and quality.

References

[1] W. Ashley, What shoe was that? The use of a computerized image database to assist in identification, *Forensic Science International,* vol. 82(1), pp. 7–20, 1996.

[2] H. Bay, L. Van Gool and T. Tuytelaars, SURF: Speeded up robust features, *Proceedings of the Ninth European Conference on Computer Vision,* pp. 404–417, 2006.

[3] H. Bay, L. Van Gool and T. Tuytelaars, SURF: Speeded Up Robust Features Software (www.vision.ee.ethz.ch/~surf/index.html).

[4] S. Birchfield, KLT: An Implementation of the Kanade-Lucas-Tomasi Feature Tracker (www.ces.clemson.edu/~stb/klt).

[5] J. Gonzalez-Rodriguez, J. Fierrez-Aguilar, D. Ramos-Castro and J. Ortega-Garcia, Bayesian analysis of fingerprint, face and signature evidence with automatic biometric systems, *Forensic Science International,* vol. 155(2-3), pp. 126–140, 2005.

[6] R. Hess, SIFT Software (web.engr.oregonstate.edu/~hess).

[7] D. Lowe, Object recognition from local scale-invariant features, *Proceedings of the International Conference on Computer Vision,* pp. 1150–1157, 1999.

[8] D. Lowe, Distinctive image features from scale-invariant keypoints, *International Journal of Computer Vision,* vol. 60(2), pp. 91–110, 2004.

[9] F. Murtagh, Z. Geradts, J. Bijhold and R. Hermsen. Image matching algorithms for breech face marks and firing pins in a database of spent cartridge cases of firearms, *Forensic Science International,* vol. 119(1), pp. 97–106, 2001.

[10] J. Shi and C. Tomasi, Good features to track, *Proceedings of the IEEE Conference on Computer Vision and Pattern Recognition,* pp. 593–600, 1994.

[11] M. Veth and J. Raquet, Fusion of low-cost imaging and inertial sensors for navigation, *Proceedings of the Institute of Navigation Global Navigation Satellite System Conference,* 2006.

[12] S. Zickler and A. Efros, Detection of multiple deformable objects using PCA-SIFT, *Proceedings of the Twenty-Second National Conference on Artificial Intelligence,* pp. 1127–1132, 2007.

[13] W. Zhao, R. Chellappa, P. Phillips and A. Rosenfeld, Face recognition: A literature survey, *ACM Computing Surveys,* vol. 35(4), pp. 399–458, 2003.

X

FORENSIC TOOLS

Chapter 25

AN EVIDENCE ACQUISITION TOOL FOR LIVE SYSTEMS

Renico Koen and Martin Olivier

Abstract   Evidence acquisition is concerned with the collection of evidence from digital devices for subsequent analysis and presentation. It is extremely important that the digital evidence is collected in a forensically-sound manner using acquisition tools that do not affect the integrity of the evidence. This paper describes a forensic acquisition tool that may be used to access files on a live system without compromising the state of the files in question. This is done in the context of the Reco Platform, an open source forensic framework that was used to develop the prototype evidence acquisition tool both quickly and efficiently. The paper also discusses the implementation of the prototype and the results obtained.

Keywords: Live systems, evidence acquisition, Reco Platform

1.   Introduction

Traditional or "dead" forensics involves the recovery of evidence from computer systems that have been powered down [1, 3]. Unfortunately, shutting down a system results in the loss of important volatile data. Also, it may not be possible to shut down vital enterprise systems to conduct forensic investigations.

Live forensics [1, 3] is an attractive alternative to dead analysis, enabling an investigator to recover and analyze data while a computer system is running. However, this technique does have limitations due to the possible presence of an intermediary, such as a rootkit, which may modify data before it is presented to the investigator. Even if a rootkit is not present, the mere fact that an untrusted piece of code, in the form of a normal operating system service, was used to retrieve the forensic data may cast doubt on the validity of the data.

Please use the following format when citing this chapter:

Koen, R. and Olivier, M., 2008, in IFIP International Federation for Information Processing, Volume 285; *Advances in Digital Forensics IV*; Indrajit Ray, Sujeet Shenoi; (Boston: Springer), pp. 325–334.

Operating system services execute in various layers. Depending on its location and functionality, a rootkit may hijack services in any of these layers. In particular, a rootkit hides its presence by modifying system services. For example it may exclude itself from the list of processes displayed to users or it may remove the names of its own files from file lists. In order to do this effectively, a rootkit ideally operates at the lowest possible layer (kernel layer); if it knows what information has been requested, it is easier to remove traces of itself.

Given this fact, the reliability of digital evidence retrieved from a lower layer is potentially higher than that retrieved from a higher layer. Obtaining information from a lower layer not only bypasses rootkits in the higher layers, but also shortens the chain of services used to answer a query. If fewer services are involved, the probability that one of them has been modified is lower than in the case of a longer chain of services. However, if data is to be retrieved from a lower layer, it is necessary to reconstruct the higher-level information structures – ideally using code that is known to be reliable.

This paper describes a prototype forensic acquisition tool that accesses low level information from a disk during live analysis. The tool uses its own code to reconstruct the logical files that exist above the low level information on disk. The implementation is based on the Reco Platform [7], which was designed to allow rapid prototyping of forensic tools, including tools that emerge from academic research and one-of-a-kind tools needed for special investigations. The platform ensures that as much code as possible is reused; this increases the reliability of evidence and its potential admissibility in legal proceedings. The Reco Platform also enables investigators to utilize other tools built using the platform, thereby increasing the range of collection and analysis possibilities.

2.   Live Evidence Acquisition

It is important to ensure that digital evidence is not modified during a live acquisition process. Walker [17] observes that even a single file timestamp found to be later than the date of acquisition may cause digital evidence to be declared inadmissible in court. Any file accessed from a logical partition, which is mounted in standard read/write mode, may have some of its attributes (e.g., access time) modified by the operating system when it is accessed. The ability of the operating system to update the file access time is useful for system administrators, but it is highly undesirable for digital forensic investigators. The use of standard file access routines supplied by the operating system should, therefore, be avoided during live evidence acquisition.

Casey [5] notes that standard operating system copy routines should also be avoided due to presence of rootkits. Live acquisition software should, therefore, have the capability to perform low-level file access without the help of the operating system. Moreover, all files should be accessed in read-only mode to preserve the integrity of file data and metadata [5]. This is because the state of a file system mounted in read/write mode is implicitly modified whenever a file is accessed.

Another, more technical, requirement for a live acquisition tool is static compilation and storage of binaries used to perform acquisitions. According to Adelstein [1], an investigator should never trust binaries stored on the system in question; rather, the investigator should employ statically-compiled binaries that do not use external libraries. The binaries should, therefore, be stored on CD-ROM to ensure that they cannot be altered.

3. Reco Platform

The Reco Platform was designed to provide the low-level functionality required by digital forensic tools, thereby decreasing the time and expertise required to develop prototypes. The platform is written in C++ and compiles under Linux and Windows. It is published under the popular GNU license [6], which enables the code to be used freely in open source projects. Like other open source software [12], the Reco source code can be inspected by programmers, helping create a stable, forensically-sound platform that will compare favorably with expensive commercial toolkits in terms of quality.

The Reco Platform provides multiple layers of software abstraction to support forensic applications development and rapid prototyping. The lower layers offer core functionality, giving developers limited abstraction but more control; the upper layers supply a higher degree of abstraction, but little control. Developers may choose the software layer that strikes the right balance between abstraction and control. This section provides an abbreviated discussion of the Reco architecture; interested readers are referred to [8] for additional details.

The Reco Platform currently consists of five layers: (i) physical, (ii) interpretation, (iii) abstraction, (iv) access, and (v) logging (Figure 1). The physical layer, which offers the lowest degree of abstraction, emulates the hardware devices from where digital evidence is collected. Digital evidence in a popular forensic format (e.g., disk image or TCP-Dump trace) is supplied to the physical layer. The physical layer uses this digital evidence to emulate the functionality expected by the device

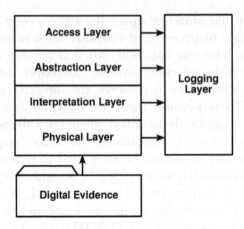

Figure 1. Reco Platform layers.

drivers that provide access to the evidence. This simplifies the task of modifying third-party software drivers for use with the Reco Platform.

The interpretation layer is the second layer in the Reco hierarchy. This layer typically models device drivers. The purpose of the interpretation layer is to read low-level data supplied by the physical layer in block or stream formats and convert it to a higher level of abstraction such as file-based information (for block devices) and temporal information (for stream-based devices).

The third layer is the abstraction layer. Its purpose is to supply functionality that is not specific to any operating system or computing platform. This is done in order to hide unnecessary details that may obscure an investigator's perception of the information conveyed by digital evidence. Another purpose is to enable investigators to identify relationships that may exist among different pieces of digital evidence. Tallard and Levitt [16] note that this functionality is crucial to filtering data that is not relevant and to creating abstract objects that can be interpreted in a relational manner with other objects.

The fourth Reco layer, the access layer, provides access to information generated by the lower layers. Searching, indexing and access control functionality are implemented at this layer. Visual abstraction may also be implemented at this layer to display digital information in a human-oriented format. Wang [18] has observed that digital evidence is not well perceived by the human senses. The access layer enables investigators to view digital evidence in an organized and understandable manner, helping increase their efficiency.

The uppermost logging layer provides the logging facilities needed in digital forensic environments. Logging is an important part of any

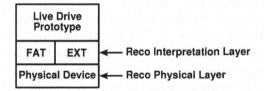

Figure 2. Dependence of the prototype on the Reco Platform.

digital forensics tool. According to NIST [11], tools used for backing-up disk data should log all errors and resolve the errors. The logging layer is used at every level of abstraction in the Reco hierarchy to document the actions applied to digital evidence.

4. Prototype Development

This section describes the prototype used for live analysis based on the Reco Platform. The prototype relies on the Reco physical layer to provide access to file system images and on the interpretation layer to supply file access routines for accessing files in read-only mode (Figure 2).

The Reco Platform is designed to work with Linux and Windows. In keeping with the Reco philosophy, the prototype was developed to permit source code to compile and run under both operating systems. The Reco Platform supports the FAT12, FAT16, FAT 32, EXT2 and EXT3 file systems, which were more than adequate for developing the prototype.

The next two subsections discuss issues related to the Linux and Windows prototypes. Note that the low-level implementation details are different for the two prototypes, but the higher-level algorithms are the same.

4.1 Linux-Based Prototype

A device that contains a Linux file system is referred to as a block device [15]. Block devices may be opened like any other file in the Linux environment except that administrative privileges are required. Since a block device can be opened as a file, it is possible to read data from the device; this process is similar to reading data from an acquired hard drive image.

The partition in which a file of interest exists is first located and opened in read-only mode. The Reco Platform is then instructed to use the opened file as the target for analysis. The easiest way to determine which block device represents the logical partition in question is to inspect the contents of the file /etc/mtab [2]. This file contains information about mounted partition types, their mount points and the locations of the block devices containing the partitions. Unfortunately, this technique has certain disadvantages. In particular, administrator (root) privileges are required when a device is opened as a file and access to the /etc/mtab file changes the state of the file system. One way to access the /etc/mtab file without altering its access time is to open the device on which the file is located via the Reco Platform, access the file in read-only mode and then close the device. This method allows file access without compromising the integrity of the file system, but prior knowledge of the block device that maps to the mounted root partition is required.

4.2   Windows-Based Prototype

In the case of a Windows environment, a logical device is opened as a file and the Reco Platform is instructed to mount the open file as the forensic target. Specifically, the logical device is opened as a file using the CreateFile() API call with the filename "\\.\N" where N is the drive letter representing the logical partition [13]. Note that administrator privileges are required to perform this operation.

Next, the GetLogicalDrives() API call is used to determine which logical drives are mounted [14]. The call returns a bitmap representing the drive letters of the mounted logical partitions. Using this information in combination with the CreateFile() method, it is possible to obtain access to a logical partition as in the case of the Linux prototype. Having determined the partition containing the file of interest, the file is located and opened. The Reco Platform is then instructed to use the opened file as the source of analysis, after which the files stored on the partition become accessible to applications using the Reco framework.

4.3   Implementation

The prototype was written in the C++ programming language; its graphical user interface was implemented using the wxWidgets framework [19]. The prototype involves very little code (not including the Reco code) and was developed in a very short time.

Source files were designed to compile in both Linux and Windows without requiring a special makefile or changing the project source code. Platform-specific sections of code were marked for compilation using preprocessor flags specific to the operating system in question. The combination of the two approaches allowed for the development of code

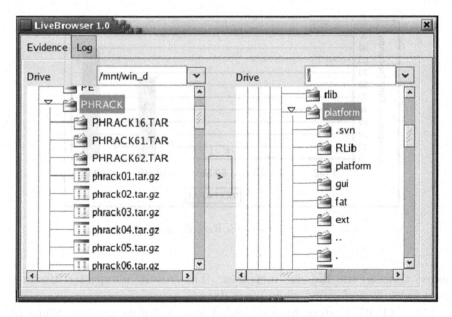

Figure 3. Screenshot of the prototype.

that runs under Linux and Windows without any major compatibility issues.

5. Results

The tool was tested on Linux Fedora Core 4 and Windows XP. Executables were generated that statically linked to the Reco library; this was done to minimize dependence on external libraries.

The results obtained with the two operating systems were similar: regular files could be accessed without modifying them or their metadata. A mounted logical partition could be opened by the prototype, the directories in the partition in question could be browsed and files could be copied to another partition to allow forensic examiners to inspect their contents. Figure 3 shows a screenshot of the prototype.

A comparison was conducted of the access times required by the file system drivers used by the prototype. An application was developed that created images of different sizes on the logical partitions targeted by the file system drivers. The created files were then read, and the time taken to read each consecutive file was recorded for each distinct logical partition.

The graph in Figure 4 shows the efficiency of the drivers used by the Reco Platform. The EXT file system driver shows a linear increase in

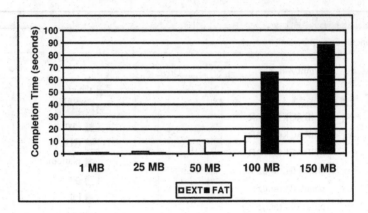

Figure 4.   Access times for Reco file system drivers.

access time as the file size increases. This result is expected because more work is performed when more data is accessed.

The FAT file system driver yielded less desirable results. Signs of an exponential increase are seen when the amount of data accessed increases. This is unfortunate because it shows that the Reco Platform is unable to provide fast access to large files stored in a FAT partition.

Because the higher-level operating system layers were bypassed when the acquisitions were performed, it can be assumed that the results obtained would be immune to most rootkits. Note that although rootkits are bypassed using this method, it is by no means a comprehensive way to neutralize rootkits in general. This is largely due to the limited involvement that an operating system has in controlling logical devices.

When access is required to a logical device, the prototype sends a request to the underlying operating system for permission to open a logical drive as a file. When data needs to be read from the logical drive, a read request is sent to the operating system to perform the task. A sophisticated kernel rootkit that has the same file processing capabilities as the Reco Platform could, in theory, return blocks of code that were maliciously engineered to hide traces of data, or it could inject falsified information. Although such a rootkit would be rare due to its complexity, it might be possible for a malicious programmer to develop one using enabling tools like the Reco Platform.

6.   Conclusions

The live evidence acquisition tool described in this paper can be used to access files on a live target without compromising the state of the files. The evidence acquisition tool leverages the Reco Platform, an open source framework designed for the rapid prototyping of forensic tools. With only a few lines of code, it was possible to quickly and efficiently develop Linux and Windows prototypes that provide true read-only access to FAT12/16/36 and EXT2/3 partitions without modifying files and their metadata.

However, two principal limitations exist, both of which should be considered in the context of live analysis. First, access to files stored in a logical partition requires administrator privileges. Second, access to file system data is by no means absolute – the low-level data access mechanisms can be bypassed by sophisticated kernel rootkits.

References

[1] F. Adelstein, Live forensics: Diagnosing your system without killing it first, *Communications of the ACM*, vol. 49(2), pp. 63–66, 2006.

[2] BrunoLinux.com, FSTAB and MTAB (www.brunolinux.com/02-The_Terminal/Fstab_and_Mtab.html).

[3] B. Carrier, Risks of live digital forensic analysis, *Communications of the ACM*, vol. 49(2), pp. 56–61, 2006.

[4] E. Casey, Error, uncertainty and loss in digital evidence, *International Journal of Digital Evidence*, vol. 1(2), 2002.

[5] E. Casey and A. Stanley, Tool review – Remote forensic preservation and examination tools, *Digital Investigation*, vol. 1(4), pp. 284–297, 2006.

[6] Free Software Foundation, GNU general public license, Boston, Massachusetts (www.gnu.org/copyleft/gpl.html).

[7] R. Koen, Reco Platform (sourceforge.net/projects/reco).

[8] R. Koen and M. Olivier, An open-source forensics platform, *Proceedings of the Southern African Telecommunication Network and Applications Conference*, 2007.

[9] W. Kuhnhauser, Root kits: An operating systems viewpoint, *ACM SIGOPS Operating Systems Review*, vol. 38(1), pp. 12–23, 2004.

[10] Linux Journal Staff, Take command: What is dd? *Linux Journal*, vol. 1996(32es), no. 11, 1996.

[11] J. Lyle, NIST CFTT: Testing disk imaging tools, *International Journal of Digital Evidence*, vol. 1(4), 2003.

[12] D. Manson, A. Carlin, S. Ramos, A. Gyger, M. Kaufman and J. Treichelt, Is the open way a better way? Digital forensics using open source tools, *Proceedings of the Fortieth Annual Hawaii International Conference on System Sciences*, p. 266b, 2007.

[13] Microsoft Corporation, CreateFile Function, Redmond, Washington (msdn2.microsoft.com/en-us/library/aa363858.aspx).

[14] Microsoft Corporation, GetLogicalDrives Function, Redmond, Washington (msdn2.microsoft.com/en-us/library/aa364972.aspx).

[15] D. Rusling, The File System (www.science.unitn.it/~fiorella/guide linux/tlk/node94.html).

[16] T. Stallard and K. Levitt, Automated analysis for digital forensic science: Semantic integrity checking, *Proceedings of the Nineteenth Annual Computer Security Applications Conference*, pp. 160–167, 2003.

[17] C. Walker, Computer forensics: Bringing the evidence to court (www.infosecwriters.com/text_resources/pdf/Computer_Forensics_to_Court.pdf), 2007.

[18] S. Wang, Measures of retaining digital evidence to prosecute computer-based cyber-crimes, *Computer Standards and Interfaces*, vol. 29(2), pp. 216–223, 2007.

[19] wxWidgets, What is wxWidgets? (www.wxwidgets.org).

Chapter 26

TIME ANALYSIS OF HARD DRIVE IMAGING TOOLS

Jack Riley, David Dampier and Rayford Vaughn

Abstract   Computer hard drives often contain evidence that is vital to digital forensic investigations. However, an authenticated working copy or "forensic image" of a suspect hard drive must be created before any data can be analyzed. As the capacities of modern hard drives increase, the time taken to create a forensic image, let alone analyze the data, increases significantly. This paper investigates two popular hard drive imaging tools, ICS ImageMASSter SOLO III and Logicube Talon. The results of the imaging experiments and timing analysis provide valuable guidance on selecting the appropriate imaging tool for digital forensic investigations.

Keywords: Imaging tools, hard drives, time analysis

1.   Introduction

Digital forensic activities, at the highest level of abstraction, can be grouped into three basic tasks: acquisition, authentication and analysis. Acquisition involves seizing media and equipment that might contain digital evidence and processing the items to recover the evidence. During this process, at least two copies of all source media are made for purposes of analysis; the original evidentiary items are then catalogued and stored securely. Authentication is necessary to prove that the working copy of the digital evidence used for analysis is identical to the original. This is generally done by computing cryptographic hash values of the original and copy; the integrity of the copy is verified when its hash value matches that of the original. The final process, analysis, explores the copies of the original media to identify potential evidence and provide corroborating support for non-digital evidence. This pa-

---

Please use the following format when citing this chapter:

Riley, J., Dampier, D. and Vaughn, R., 2008, in IFIP International Federation for Information Processing, Volume 285; *Advances in Digital Forensics IV*; Indrajit Ray, Sujeet Shenoi; (Boston: Springer), pp. 335–344.

per focuses primarily on acquisition and secondarily on the process of authentication.

Hard disk imaging devices create exact (bit-for-bit) duplicates of an original hard drive and, at the same time, calculate a cryptographic hash value of the original and copy. The time requirements for imaging hard drives is a serious issue, especially as cases frequently involve massive volumes of digital evidence and hard drive capacities are increasing significantly. Meanwhile, new demands on evidence acquisition are imposed by legislation such as the Sarbanes-Oxley Act, which requires mandatory document retention [3]. Since the analysis of digital forensic data is time intensive, time saved during the evidence acquisition phase can be leveraged during the analysis phase.

Several hardware and software tools have been designed for imaging hard drives, but they have greatly varying capabilities. Few, if any, researchers have analyzed the time requirements for these tools using rigorous experimental methods. This paper investigates two of the most commonly used hardware-based imaging tools, ICS ImageMASSter SOLO III and Logicube Talon. In particular, it describes the results of imaging experiments and timing analysis. The comparative study provides valuable insights into the performance of hard drive imaging tools and offers guidance for tool selection in digital forensic investigations.

2.   Background

Hard disk storage capacities have increased significantly over the past ten years. Currently, two terabytes of storage can be purchased for under $1,000 [4], and the cost per terabyte of storage continues to drop rapidly. The availability of massive volumes of inexpensive storage is a boon to all types of computer users, but it also serves to increase the amount of electronic evidence that the digital forensic investigator has to sort through in civil and criminal cases.

Digital forensic investigators need efficient methods for acquiring and analyzing data. Roussev and Richard [4] report that one of the most widely accepted forensic examination systems took more than four days to organize case data on an 80 GB hard drive. Their results indicate that this was mainly due to I/O limitations of large capacity drives. Only after a case is opened and the data is indexed can investigation and analysis proceed. These steps also take a considerable amount of time, especially for cases involving data in the order of terabytes.

Several researchers have focused on making forensic analysis more efficient. Dandass [2] has used field programmable gate arrays (FPGAs) to implement pipelined pattern matching algorithms for speeding up the search for image files on hard drives at line speed. In laboratory tests, the FPGA implementation required a little over 600 seconds to locate 24 image files placed in random clusters on a 40 GB hard drive; in contrast, state-of-the-art software-based methods running on a Pentium 4 2.8 GHz computer under Windows XP took more than 4,700 seconds [2]. The FPGA implementation also supports sector-by-sector copying of hard drives at speeds approaching 6 GB per minute.

Roussev and Richard [4] have sought to reduce the time needed for forensic analysis, especially in the face of the slow linear growth of I/O systems compared with the exponential growth of CPU performance and data storage capacity. Their research has shown that it is more efficient to access a hard drive once and perform analysis from a cached copy in memory. Unfortunately, the standard practice of using a single forensic workstation does not allow for a cached copy of any significant size to be analyzed due to constraints on the memory capacity of a single system. Roussev and Richard obtained good results using a specialized, distributed approach to forensic analysis. In particular, their approach produced significant reductions in data preprocessing and search times.

Unfortunately, these research results, while promising, have not yet transitioned to forensic practice. A need still exists for a practical technique to efficiently copy vast amounts of data in the least amount of time. Our work evaluates the time requirements of two leading hardware drive imagers, with the goal of assisting practitioners in choosing the right tool for an imaging task.

3. Experimental Design

Our experiments on hard drive imaging tools were designed to evaluate the base times required to create exact authenticated copies of hard drives. Two imaging tools, the ICS ImageMASSter Solo Forensics III and the Logicube Talon, were used in this study. Non-imaging functions provided by the tools, including hash value checks, were disabled or disregarded when the timing data was collected. Since timing display capabilities were an unknown variable in the study, a software stopwatch [1] was used for timing purposes. Using a stopwatch introduces human reaction time error, however, the error was assumed to be consistent and was minimized to the extent possible. In any case, the time measurements made in the experiments were much larger than the fractions of a second introduced by human error.

The timing analysis was conducted using ImageMASSter and Talon for one-to-one drive transfers. The experiments were carried out in two stages: (i) one-to-one IDE trials, and (ii) one-to-one SATA trials. The

IDE and SATA trials were both conducted using 80, 120 and 250 GB drives. These sizes were chosen because they are representative of the drives used in digital forensic investigations. Each trial involved ten iterations per drive, and both the tools were tested on the same drives.

3.1   IDE Hard Drive Trials

This section presents the results obtained using the Talon and Image-MASSter tools on 80, 120 and 250 GB IDE hard drives.

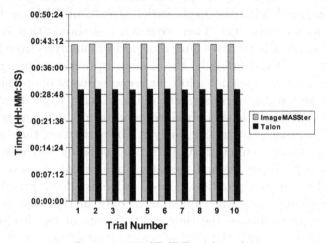

Figure 1. 80 GB IDE trial results.

Figure 1 presents the results obtained for the 80 GB IDE hard drives. Note that the experiment used two Western Digital WD800BB hard drives as the source and destination drives. The data shows that Talon outperforms ImageMASSter by about 30%, with an average time over ten iterations of 30 minutes, 7 seconds as opposed to 42 minutes, 22 seconds.

Figure 2 shows the results for the 120 GB IDE drives; 120 GB Seagate Barracuda 7200.9 drives were used as the source and destination drives. Once again, Talon was faster than ImageMASSter, with an average time over ten iterations of 45 minutes, 24 seconds compared with 54 minutes, 32 seconds. These results show a difference of 9 minutes, 8 seconds, which is less than the difference achieved for the 80 GB IDE trials; this indicates a possible scaling factor.

Figure 3 presents the results for the 250 GB IDE pair of hard drives (the source drive was a Seagate Barracuda 7200.9 and the destination drive was a Western Digital WD2500). As before, Talon is faster than ImageMASSter; however, the difference in performance is significantly less than that observed in the 120 GB IDE trials. The average times

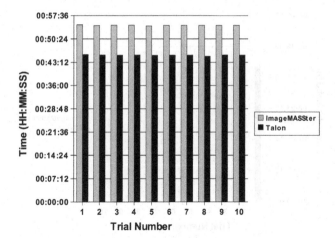

Figure 2.   120 GB IDE trial results.

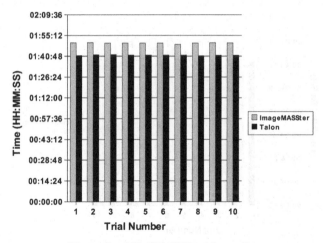

Figure 3.   250 GB IDE trial results.

over ten interations for Talon and ImageMASSter were 101 minutes, 32 seconds and 110 minutes, 8 seconds, respectively.

3.2   SATA Hard Drive Trials

This section presents the results obtained using the Talon and Image-MASSter tools on 80, 120 and 250 GB Serial ATA hard drives.

Figure 4 shows the results obtained for a pair of 80 GB Western Digital WD800JD SATA drives. Talon proved to be faster than ImageMASSter, with an average time over ten iterations of 31 minutes 18 seconds as opposed to 34 minutes, 39 seconds.

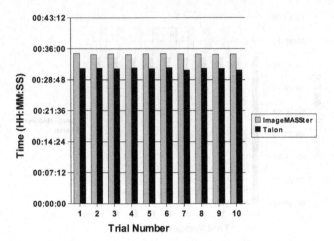

Figure 4.   80 GB SATA trial results.

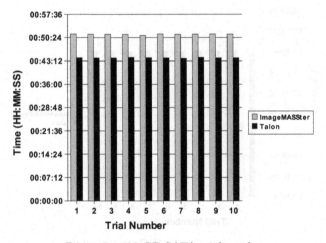

Figure 5.   120 GB SATA trial results.

Figure 5 presents the results for a pair of 120 GB Western Digital WD1200JS SATA drives. The difference between the average times over ten iterations in this experiment was 7 minutes, 13 seconds, once again in Talon's favor. The actual recorded average times were 44 minutes, 11 seconds for Talon and 51 minutes, 24 seconds for ImageMASSter.

Figure 6 shows the results obtained for a pair of 250 GB Western Digital WD2500KS SATA drives. The difference in average times over ten iterations between the two imaging tools was nearly 13 minutes, with Talon averaging 93 minutes, 45 seconds and ImageMASSter averaging 106 minutes, 39 seconds.

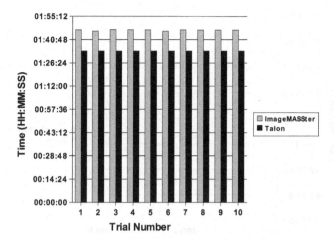

Figure 6. 250 GB SATA trial results.

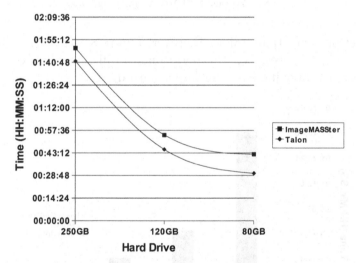

Figure 7. Average IDE drive imaging times.

4. Analysis of Results

The analysis of experimental data reveals three important observations. First, Talon performs better than ImageMASSter on IDE and SATA drives. Figures 7 and 8 show the average times for Talon and ImageMASSter; it is clear that Talon performed better on the drives used in the experiments.

Second, as seen in Figure 7, as IDE drive capacity increases, the difference in the imaging times for Talon and ImageMASSter decreases. The potential exists that, for very large drives, ImageMASSter may exhibit

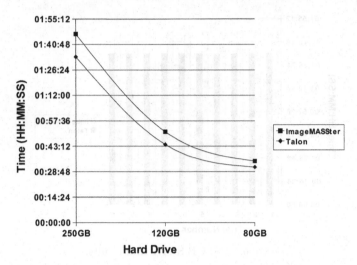

Figure 8. Average SATA drive imaging times.

better performance than Talon. However, Figure 8 reveals the opposite trend for SATA drives, i.e., the performance difference between Talon and ImageMASSter increases for larger hard drives.

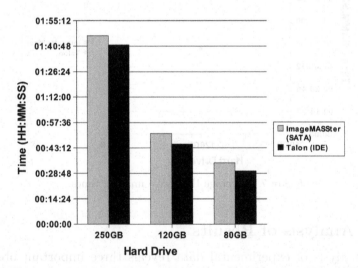

Figure 9. Average times for ImageMASSter (SATA) versus Talon (IDE).

The third observation is that not only does Talon exhibit better performance than ImageMASSter for IDE and SATA drives, but Talon actually performs better on IDE drives than ImageMASSter performs on SATA drives. This result, shown in Figure 9, is unexpected because SATA drives are supposed to be much faster than IDE drives.

Table 1.   Computed *t*-values for test groups.

Test Group	Computed *t*-value
250 GB IDE	64.28
120 GB IDE	124.30
80 GB IDE	410.29
250 GB SATA	124.84
120 GB SATA	153.49
80 GB SATA	113.69

5.   Statistical Analysis

A *t*-test was conducted to determine whether or not the difference in the results observed is statistically significant. The null hypothesis was that there is no significant difference between the data from the Image-MASSter and Talon trials. The respective means, standard deviations and variances were calculated for each data group. The variance for both groups of data was less than 6%.

Ten iterations were performed for each group (n1 = n2 = 10), yielding a degrees of freedom value of 18 (= n1 + n2 − 2) with p = 0.001. The proposed *t*-value for each group of data, referenced from the aforementioned degrees of freedom and p-value, was 3.92. The *t*-value was computed for each paired group of data using Microsoft Excel 2003; the results are reported in Table 1. If the computed *t*-value is larger than the proposed *t*-value, it can be concluded that there is a 99.9% probability of that the two groups of data are statistically different. Table 1 shows that the computed *t*-value for each test group exceeds the proposed *t*-value for the given p-value (0.001) and degrees of freedom. From these results, the null hypothesis can be rejected and the observed values are, in fact, statistically different.

6.   Conclusions

Imaging speed is important to digital forensic investigators because of the large volumes of electronic evidence that are involved in civil and criminal cases. With storage capacities certain to increase in the future, the ability of imaging tools to quickly make authentic copies of hard drives will become even more critical. The experiments demonstrate a marked difference in the speeds of two popular hardware-based imaging tools, with the Logicube Talon outperforming the ICS ImageMASSter. While the difference in speeds might appear small, it is important to note that the time savings achieved when using a faster imaging tool can be significant for large capacity hard drives.

References

[1] Arantius.com, Stopwatch (tools.arantius.com/stopwatch).

[2] Y. Dandass, Hardware-assisted scanning for signature patterns in image file fragments, *Proceedings of the Fortieth Hawaii International Conference on System Sciences*, p. 268, 2007.

[3] M. Lange, Sarbanes-Oxley has major impact on electronic evidence, *The National Law Journal* (www.law.com/jsp/article.jsp?id =1039054510969), January 2, 2003.

[4] V. Roussev and G. Richard III, Breaking the performance wall: The case for distributed digital forensics, *Proceedings of the Fourth Digital Forensics Research Workshop*, 2004.

Chapter 27

FUSION OF STEGANALYSIS SYSTEMS USING BAYESIAN MODEL AVERAGING

Benjamin Rodriguez, Gilbert Peterson and Kenneth Bauer

Abstract   The increasing use of steganography requires digital forensic examiners to consider the extraction of hidden information from digital images encountered during investigations. The first step in extraction is to identify the embedding method. Several steganalysis systems have been developed for this purpose, but each system only identifies a subset of the available embedding methods and with varying degrees of accuracy. This paper applies Bayesian model averaging to fuse multiple steganalysis systems and identify the embedding used to create a stego JPEG image. Experimental results indicate that the steganalysis fusion system has an accuracy of 90% compared with 80% accuracy for the individual steganalysis systems.

Keywords: Steganalysis, multi-class fusion, Bayesian model averaging

1.   Introduction

The problem of steganalysis has moved from simply determining if an image contains hidden information to extracting the hidden message. However, it is not possible to extract the hidden information without first identifying the method used to create the steganographic image. With more 250 steganography tools available on the Internet it is important to develop multi-class steganalysis systems that can label a suspect image as containing a specific type of steganography.

Several steganography detection systems are available, including research prototypes [4, 9, 11, 14, 18, 21] and commercially-available tools (e.g., ILook Investigator, Inforenz Forager, SecureStego, StegDetect [12] and WetStone Stego Suite). Each system has its own advantages and disadvantages. But with so many detection systems available to the steganalyst, a problem arises in deciding which system is best to use. A

Please use the following format when citing this chapter:

Rodriguez, B., Peterson, G. and Bauer, K., 2008, in IFIP International Federation for Information Processing, Volume 285; *Advances in Digital Forensics IV*; Indrajit Ray, Sujeet Shenoi; (Boston: Springer), pp. 345–355.

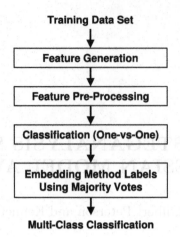

Training Data Set

Feature Generation

Feature Pre-Processing

Classification (One-vs-One)

Embedding Method Labels Using Majority Votes

Multi-Class Classification

Figure 1. Multi-class detection system.

solution to this problem is to fuse the results from the various detection systems to more accurately identify the embedding method.

This paper focuses on the detection of six steganography methods: F5 [22], JP Hide and Seek [8], JSteg [20], Model Based [16], OutGuess [13] and StegHide [5]. Bayesian model averaging [6] is used to combine four multi-class steganalysis detection systems. The first steganalysis system is StegDetect [12], which is capable of detecting F5, JP Hide and Seek, JSteg and OutGuess. The remaining three systems are one-vs-one multi-class classifiers [4, 9, 15] that use a two-class support vector machine (SVM) for classification. Test results show that the steganalysis fusion system has an accuracy of 90% compared with 80% accuracy for the individual multi-class steganalysis systems.

2.   Related Work

Commercially available steganography detection tools are designed to give the analyst an initial indication if a set of images contains hidden information. These tools include ILook Investigator, Inforenz Forager, SecureStego, StegDetect [12] and WetStone Stego Suite. However, no tool targets all the common embedding methods. For example, StegDetect detects four (F5, JP Hide and Seek, JSteg and OutGuess) of the six common embedding methods.

The steps involved in multi-class steganalysis detection are illustrated in Figure 1. A data set containing clean and stego images is used to train a multi-class detection system.

The first step involves the generation of features from the input images; feature generation significantly reduces the amount of information sent to the classifier. The feature generation techniques used in our work are the wavelet-based method of Lyu and Farid [9], a DCT-based feature generation method [11], and a method that generates features from DCT decomposed coefficients [15].

The next step, feature pre-processing, employs two procedures. The first procedure normalizes the set of input features; this reduces the likelihood that features with large values would have a greater influence on the cost function than features with small values. The second procedure eliminates the less important features while retaining satisfactory class discrimination capability.

Many multi-class classifiers for steganalysis [11, 14] use a two-class SVM classification method in conjunction with a one-vs-one approach to combine individual classifiers. Multiple SVM classifiers are trained to distinguish clean images and images created with specific embedding methods. The overall multi-class classification system counts the votes from each SVM classifier; the final classification (identification of the embedding method used) is determined as the classification with the most number of votes.

The next section describes our steganalysis fusion system. It incorporates four systems discussed in this section: StegDetect [12], wavelet feature generation [9], DCT-based feature generation [11], and DCT decomposition feature generation [15].

3.   Steganalysis Fusion System

The fused multi-class steganalysis detection system uses multi-class classifiers with Bayesian model averaging. The steganography techniques targeted by the detection system include F5 [22], JP Hide and Seek [8], JSteg [20], Model Based [16], OutGuess [13] and StegHide[5]. All these embedding methods hide data by manipulating the quantized discrete cosine transform (DCT) values generated during the JPEG image compression process. This section provides details of the feature generation, classification and labeling steps involved in multi-class detection (Figure 1).

3.1   Feature Generation

Three feature generation methods – wavelet feature generation [9], DCT based feature generation [11] and DCT decomposition feature generation [15] – are used to create a multi-class steganalysis classification system.

Wavelet feature generation first performs a multi-scale Haar wavelet decomposition of an image [9]. Next, higher-order statistics are calculated over each pixel in the wavelet and the pixel's relationship to its neighbors in the current and higher scales. 36 coefficient statistics and 36 error statistics are computed to yield a total of 72 statistics. These statistics form the feature vectors used to discriminate between clean and stego images.

DCT based feature generation calculates first- and second-order features over the DCT values and pixel values (spatial domain) of an image [11]. The features in the DCT and spatial domains are calculated using several functions applied to the stego JPEG image. These functions include the global DCT coefficient histogram, co-occurrence matrix, spatial blockiness and others [11]. The stego image is decompressed to the spatial domain, cropped by four pixels in each direction and recompressed with the same quantization table used in decompression. An approximation of the hidden information is generated by applying the same functions to the cropped image. This feature generation technique produces 274 features.

DCT decomposition feature generation divides a processed DCT block into directional and frequency bands [15]. The DCT coefficients are separated into low, medium and high frequencies as well as in the vertical, diagonal and horizontal directions. This is referred to as DCT decomposition. In addition, the coefficients are categorized into raw, shifted and predicted coefficients. The shifted coefficients are used to identify embedding blockiness between neighboring 8×8 blocks. The predicted coefficients estimate the coefficients altered by an embedding method. The features are generated by calculating several higher-order statistics (first, second, third and fourth moments; second, third and fourth central moments; and entropy) for the sets of selected coefficients. This produces 234 total features consisting of 72 shifted coefficients, 72 raw coefficients, 72 predictors and 18 histogramming features.

3.2   Support Vector Machine

The support vector machine (SVM) is a classification algorithm that provides state-of-the-art performance in a variety of application domains [1, 17]. In particular, the SVM produces a model that predicts the class of data instances in a testing set given only the attributes. SVM performs pattern recognition for two-class problems by determining the separating hyperplane that has maximum distance between the closest points of each class in the training set; the closest points to the hyperplane are called support vectors. This is accomplished by performing a nonlinear separation of the input space using a nonlinear transformation $\phi(\cdot)$ that maps data instances x (with features x_i) from the input space into a higher-dimensional space called kernel space. The mapping, $\phi(\cdot) \rightarrow \phi(x_i)$, is performed by the SVM classifier using a kernel function $K(\cdot, \cdot)$. The SVM decision function is linear in the kernel space, albeit not in the feature space. We use LibSVM [2] in our work. This implementation employs sequential minimal optimization for a binary SVM with an L1-soft margin [3].

3.3   One-vs-One Methodology

Two-class classifiers are combined using a one-vs-one methodology [19]. This technique trains several classifiers; each individual classifier compares one class against one of the other classes. For k classes, this produces $k(k-1)/2$ classifiers that each vote on the class assignment for a data instance. The algorithm then identifies the final classification as the class with the highest vote. The goal is to train the multi-class rule based on the majority vote strategy. The method is fairly reliable when the feature space is separable for the various classes.

Seven classes (6 stego + 1 clean, i.e., $k = 7$) are targeted by the steganalysis fusion system; this requires 21 classifiers to be trained. The output of each SVM is a vote that is tallied. The classification with the majority of votes for a class wins.

3.4   Multi-Class Detection System

Multi-class detection requires a training set for which the number of classes have been assigned. In our work, we attempt to detect stego images created using six embedding methods (F5, JP Hide and Seek, JSteg, Model Based, OutGuess and StegHide). Consequently, the training set consisted of seven classes of images (6 stego and 1 clean). Multi-class detection based on the training set involves the following steps:

1. Feature Generation: This step generates features from each JPEG test image. Three feature generation methods [9, 11, 15] are used to develop three distinct multi-class systems.

2. Feature Pre-Processing: This step normalizes the feature values and selects a subset of features based on the Fisher's discriminant ratio ranking. Other pre-processing methods could be applied for outlier removal, data normalization, feature selection and feature extraction [7].

3. Classification: This step uses an SVM to train each one-vs-one classifier based on the training data set.

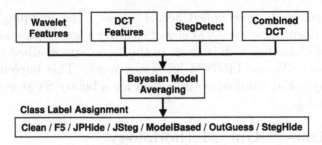

Figure 2. Bayesian model averaging structure.

4. Majority Vote Assignment: This step assigns a class label based on a majority vote from each classifier.

3.5   Bayesian Model Averaging

Bayesian model averaging merges several multi-class classifiers by combining the probability density estimation of each classifier's classification accuracy as a mixture of Gaussians [6, 10]. The Bayes Net Toolbox for Mathlab [10] was used to perform the model averaging computations. The probability density estimation specifies the local conditional probability distribution (CPD) for a classification model, M_k, where k is one of K classifiers and M is the set of all classifiers. The CPD of each model M_k is $p(M_k|T)$, which represents the probability that a classification model will classify a target instance T. For example, given a target image that contains data hidden using JP Hide and Seek, $p(M_k|T = \textit{JP Hide and Seek})$ represents the probability distribution over all of the possible classifications M_k could make, i.e., F5, JP Hide and Seek, etc. In our implementation, the confusion matrix, which represents the correct and incorrect classifications for a multi-class classifier, provides the probability density estimation for each classifier.

The fusion process uses the classifications from the classification models, M, to compute the joint probability distribution over each target classification $T = c$:

$$p(T = c|M) = \eta \prod_{k=1}^{K} p(M_k|T = c)p(T = c).$$

The final classification is designated as the target classification $T = c$ with the highest probability. The prior probabilities $p(T)$ are calculated based on the number of clean images and the number of images of each type of embedding used in the testing.

Figure 2 illustrates an example Bayesian model averaging system. The four nodes at the top represent the classifiers and CPDs for each M_k. The Bayesian model averaging node contains the $p(T)$ CPD that merges the results of the four models and makes the final classification.

The following seven steps are involved in using Bayesian model averaging for steganalysis:

1. Generate features.

2. Select relevant features.

3. Create the classification model based on one-vs-one training.

4. Use the majority vote strategy to populate the confusion matrix containing actual and predicted classified values for the clean, F5, JP Hide and Seek, JSteg, Model Based, OutGuess and StegHide training sets.

5. Repeat Steps 1 through 4 for each of the three feature generation methods [9, 11, 15].

6. Create a confusion matrix for StegDetect [12].

7. Use the four confusion matrices as classifier models for the Bayesian averaging technique.

This seven-step procedure produces a multi-class model that receives four inputs (three from each of the trained detection systems and one from StegDetect) in order to classify a suspect image. The resulting steganalysis fusion system is shown in Figure 2.

4. Results

The results presented in this section are based on a data set containing 1,000 512×512 RGB JPEG (stego and clean) images. The training set consisted of 200 clean images and 100 images for each of the six embedding methods (F5, JP Hide and Seek, JSteg, Model Based, OutGuess and StegHide). The test set contained 50 clean images and 25 images for each embedding method. The clean images in the test set did not overlap with the stego images, nor did any of the images from one stego type overlap with another; for example, none of the F5 images were the same as the JSteg images. Approximately one page of text (4,000 characters) was hidden in each stego image.

The following were the percentages of altered coefficients for the six embedding methods:

Table 1.   Test set classification accuracy for individual detection systems.

Image Type	Wavelet Features	DCT Features	StegDetect	Combined DCT Features
Clean	45.4 ± 1.1	42.6 ± 2.1	40.6 ± 1.1	42.8 ± 0.8
F5	21.4 ± 0.8	24.2 ± 1.8	25.0 ± 0.0	18.0 ± 0.7
JP Hide (JP)	22.2 ± 0.5	21.8 ± 0.8	17.4 ± 1.1	20.0 ± 1.0
JSteg (JS)	20.8 ± 0.8	22.0 ± 1.6	20.0 ± 2.1	22.8 ± 0.8
Model Based (MB)	13.2 ± 1.3	16.4 ± 0.5	0.0 ± 0.0	17.8 ± 0.5
Outguess (OG)	17.0 ± 0.7	13.8 ± 0.5	17.4 ± 2.1	18.4 ± 0.5
StegHide (SH)	17.6 ± 1.1	16.4 ± 0.5	0.0 ± 0.0	18.0 ± 0.7

- F5 had an average of 0.3% of the coefficients altered.

- JP Hide and Seek had an average of 2.8% of the coefficients altered.

- JSteg had an average of 6.7% of the coefficients altered.

- Model Based had an average of 7.8% of the coefficients altered.

- OutGuess and StegHide had an average of 1% of the coefficients altered.

The testing was performed using five-fold cross validation. Note that the results are not intended to benchmark one system against the others. Rather, they are used to show that the steganalysis fusion system takes advantage of the strengths of the individual systems and improves the overall accuracy.

Table 1 presents the results for the individual steganalysis systems. The results reveal that no multi-class classification algorithm outperforms the others. For example, StegDetect detects all the F5 images; wavelet feature generation (Wavelet) labels the fewest clean images as stego; DCT based feature generation (DCT) identifies the largest number of JP Hide and Seek images; and DCT decomposition feature generation (Combined DCT) identifies the most Model Based and OutGuess images.

Table 2 presents the results obtained for the steganalysis fusion system. It is clear that the fusion system consistently outperforms the individual systems. The only exception is for the F5 embedding, where the fusion system and StegDetect detect all the images.

5.   Conclusions

The steganalysis fusion system uses Bayesian model averaging to combine three multi-class SVM classifiers, each of which uses a different

Table 2. Confusion matrix obtained by Bayesian model averaging.

Actual		Predicted						
		Clean	F5	JP	JS	MB	OG	SH
Clean	Ave.	46.8±	0.8±	0.2±	0.2±	0.2±	1.6±	0.2±
	σ^2	0.8	0.5	0.5	0.5	0.5	0.9	0.5
F5	Ave.	0.0±	25.0±	0.0±	0.0±	0.0±	0.0±	0.0±
	σ^2	0.0	0.0	0.0	0.0	0.0	0.0	0.0
JP	Ave.	0.0±	0.0±	23.6±	1.4±	0.0±	0.0±	0.0±
	σ^2	0.0	0.0	0.6	0.6	0.0	0.0	0.0
JS	Ave.	0.0±	0.0±	1.4±	23.2±	0.0±	0.4±	0.0±
	σ^2	0.0	0.0	0.6	0.8	0.0	0.6	0.0
MB	Ave.	4.6±	1.6±	0.0±	0.0±	18.0±	0.2±	0.6±
	σ^2	0.6	0.6	0.0	0.0	0.7	0.5	0.6
OG	Ave.	1.8±	0.4±	0.0±	0.0±	0.0±	18.8±	4.0±
	σ^2	0.5	0.6	0.0	0.0	0.0	0.5	0.7
SH	Ave.	1.2±	0.0±	0.0±	0.0±	0.0±	2.6±	21.2±
	σ^2	0.5	0.0	0.0	0.0	0.0	0.6	0.8

feature extraction method. This strategy improves the overall accuracy with which steganography embedding algorithms are identified.

Future research will involve the addition of new steganalysis systems to the fused multi-class system, and the creation of richer JPEG data sets with images of various sizes and compression ratios. This work, which will utilize embedding signatures based on image size and compression changes, will further enhance the detection and identification of steganography embedding methods.

Acknowledgements

This research was partially supported by the Multi-Sensor Exploitation Branch, Information Directorate, U.S. Air Force Research Laboratory. The views expressed in this paper are those of the authors and do not reflect the official policy or position of the U.S. Air Force, U.S. Department of Defense or the U.S. Government.

References

[1] C. Burges, A tutorial on support vector machines for pattern recognition, *Data Mining and Knowledge Discovery*, vol. 2(2), pp. 121–167, 1998.

[2] C. Chang and C. Lin, LIBSVM: A Library for Support Vector Machines (www.csie.ntu.edu.tw/~cjlin/libsvm).

[3] N. Cristianini and J. Shawe-Taylor, *An Introduction to Support Vector Machines and Other Kernel-Based Learning Methods*, Cambridge University Press, Cambridge, United Kingdom, 2000.

[4] J. Fridrich, Feature-based steganalysis for JPEG images and its implications for future design of steganographic schemes, *Proceedings of the Sixth International Information Hiding Workshop*, pp. 67–81, 2004.

[5] S. Hetzl, StegHide (steghide.sourceforge.net).

[6] J. Hoeting, D. Madigan, A. Raftery and C. Volinsky, Bayesian model averaging: A tutorial (with discussion), *Statistical Science*, vol. 14(4), pp. 382–417, 1999.

[7] A. Jain, R. Duin and J. Mau, Statistical pattern recognition: A review, *IEEE Transactions on Pattern Analysis and Machine Intelligence*, vol. 22(1), pp. 4–37, 2000.

[8] A. Latham, Steganography – JP Hide and Seek (linux01.gwdg.de /~alatham/stego.html).

[9] S. Lyu and H. Farid, Steganalysis using color wavelet statistics and one-class support vector machines, *Proceedings of the SPIE Electronic Imaging Symposium*, 2004.

[10] K. Murphy, Bayes Net Toolbox for Matlab (www.cs.ubc.ca/~mur phyk/Software/BNT/bnt.html), 2007.

[11] T. Pevny and J. Fridrich, Merging Markov and DCT features for multi-class JPEG steganalysis, *Proceedings of the SPIE Electronic Imaging Symposium*, 2007.

[12] N. Provos, OutGuess (www.outguess.org).

[13] N. Provos and P. Honeyman, Hide and seek: An introduction to steganography, *IEEE Security & Privacy*, vol. 1(3), pp. 32–44, 2003.

[14] B. Rodriguez and G. Peterson, Steganography detection using multi-class classification, in *Advances in Digital Forensics III*, P. Craiger and S. Shenoi (Eds.), Springer, Boston, Massachusetts, pp. 193–204, 2007.

[15] B. Rodriguez, G. Peterson and R. Neher, DCT combined directional and frequency band distance measure features, submitted to *IEEE Transactions on Information Forensics and Security*.

[16] P. Sallee, Model-based steganography, *Proceedings of the Second International Workshop on Digital Watermarking*, pp. 154–167, 2003.

[17] B. Scholkopf and A. Smola, *Learning with Kernels: Support Vector Machines, Regularization, Optimization and Beyond*, MIT Press, Cambridge, Massachusetts, 2001.

[18] Y. Shi, G. Xuan, D. Zou, J. Gao, C. Yang, Z. Zhang, P. Chai, W. Chen and C. Chen, Image steganalysis based on moments of characteristic functions using wavelet decomposition, prediction-error images and neural networks, *Proceedings of the IEEE International Conference on Multimedia and Expo*, pp. 269–272, 2005.

[19] D. Tax and R. Duin, Using two-class classifiers for multi-class classification, *Proceedings of the Sixteenth International Conference on Pattern Recognition*, pp. 124–127, 2002.

[20] D. Upham, JPEG-JSteg (ftp.funet.fu/pub/crypt/steganography).

[21] Y. Wang and P. Moulin, Optimized feature extraction for learning-based image steganalysis, *IEEE Transactions on Information Forensics and Security*, vol. 2(1), pp. 31–45, 2007.

[22] A. Westfeld, F5 – A steganographic algorithm, *Proceedings of the Fourth International Workshop on Information Hiding*, pp. 289–302, 2001.

[23] G. Xuan, Y. Shi, J. Gao, D. Zou, C. Yang, Z. Zhang, P. Chai, C. Chen and W. Chen, Steganalysis based on multiple features formed by statistical moments of wavelet characteristic functions, *Proceedings of the Seventh International Workshop on Information Hiding*, pp. 262–277, 2005.

Chapter 28

A VIRTUAL DIGITAL FORENSICS LABORATORY

Philip Craiger, Paul Burke, Christopher Marberry and Mark Pollitt

Abstract   This paper discusses the concept of a virtual digital forensic laboratory, which incorporates networked examination and storage machines, secure communications, multi-factor authentication, role-based access control, and case management and digital asset management systems. Laboratory activities such as the examination, storage and presentation of digital evidence can be geographically distributed and accessed over a network by users with the appropriate credentials. The advantages of such a facility include reduced costs through shared resources and the availability of advanced expertise for specialized cases.

Keywords: Virtual laboratory, virtualization, storage area network

1.   Introduction

The collection, storage, examination and presentation of digital evidence typically occur in centralized laboratories. This is an inefficient model in that law enforcement agencies duplicate resources that are available elsewhere. A modest laboratory can cost tens of thousands of dollars, even more when the costs of computers, storage, forensic tools and training are considered.

The validation of forensic tools also poses problems. Proper forensic procedures require that the tools used in examinations be continually validated. Unfortunately, most examiners may not have the expertise to perform hardware and software validation. Additionally, there is a tremendous amount of duplication if every examiner has to validate the same tools.

Digital forensics laboratories of the future will be "virtual" in nature – they will not be limited by geographic boundaries. This paper proposes the concept of a virtual digital forensics laboratory (VDFL).

Please use the following format when citing this chapter:

Craiger, P., Burke, P., Marberry, C. and Pollitt, M., 2008, in IFIP International Federation for Information Processing, Volume 285; *Advances in Digital Forensics IV*; Indrajit Ray, Sujeet Shenoi; (Boston: Springer), pp. 357–365.

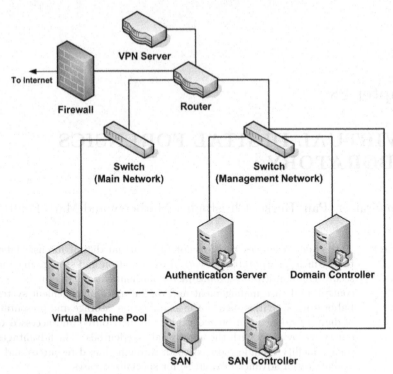

Figure 1.   Virtual digital forensics laboratory.

The proposal builds on previous work (e.g., [1]) by decentralizing forensic functionality while providing security and quality management processes. The virtual laboratory incorporates storage area network (SAN)
[7, 10] and virtualization [3, 4, 8, 9] technologies, forensic tools and security mechanisms to create a robust alternative to a physical laboratory.
Such a laboratory will reduce the duplication of resources and tasks,
provide law enforcement agents with cutting-edge tools, resources and
expertise, and lower the cost of forensic examinations.

2.   Virtual Laboratory Overview

The virtual digital forensics laboratory architecture attempts to leverage state-of-the-art networking and digital forensics technologies to support the acquisition, transportation, examination and storage of electronic evidence. This has resulted in somewhat unique problems that,
in turn, require unique solutions.

Figure 1 presents a schematic diagram of the virtual laboratory. The
laboratory provides facilities for examining, storing and presenting electronic evidence. The forensic examination component includes hardware, software and processes associated with the extraction, identifica-

tion and interpretation of evidence. The storage component incorporates large-scale, redundant magnetic storage that is logically separable by case. The presentation component includes extracted evidence, reports and other relevant information that may be accessed at various levels of detail by authorized parties (investigators, prosecutors, defense attorneys, judges and jury members).

The virtual laboratory employs a distributed model, which allows the complete functional separation of components. Each component is tied to the other components via a high-speed network. This approach is used very effectively in data centers, where physical and/or logical components are spread across multiple geographic locations.

The first step in defining system requirements is to identify the potential users. The user groups are law enforcement personnel, prosecution and defense attorneys, judges and jury members. Role-based access control allows each user to have the appropriate degree and type of access. For example, a law enforcement agent (examiner) might be granted full read/write access to each subsystem to perform imaging, upload images to long-term storage, conduct examinations of the evidence, and output intermediate results and final reports. Attorneys would not need access to the raw data or to examination tools, only to the intermediate results and final reports. Judges and jury members would only be able to view the final reports containing evidence prepared for trial.

Several other issues must be considered when specifying the system requirements. System performance is important in a distributed system because data has to travel over greater distances and on slower links than in a centralized facility. Security is equally important. Imaging, examination, storage and presentation involve machines in multiple locations, but the level of assurance provided must be just as high as that in a physical laboratory. Another issue is system management – every system component in every location must be maintained by an administrator who has the appropriate technical expertise and qualifications. The final issue is to create a system that is transparent to end users. Indeed, the system should look, feel and react as if it is a local examination computer.

System Performance A virtual system must provide the responsiveness and efficiency of a physical system. Even when high-speed networks are used, the transfer rates of forensic data to a remote location are much slower than the data transfer rates within an average computer, i.e., network speed is much slower than computer bus speed. Furthermore, in a multi-user environment, each data processing component must be capable of supporting multiple users reliably and with a satisfactory level of responsiveness.

Security   Security is paramount for a distributed forensic system. The legal requirements for evidence handling must be met, and there should be explicit guarantees about the confidentiality, integrity and availability of all data. The system must incorporate a strong user authentication mechanism, ideally one that relies on multi-factor authentication. The system must logically separate users to ensure that forensic data can only be accessed by authorized individuals. A logging system must be in place to provide accountability for user actions and to track system use because of the sensitive nature of the data and the applicable legal requirements (e.g., evidence handling and chain of custody).

System Management   System management is not a major concern for the typical forensics examiner. A distributed, multi-user system, however, requires a system administrator with demonstrable technical skills to create users, set access controls, maintain performance requirements, troubleshoot network problems and ensure system integrity.

Usability   Ease-of-use is also important. A distributed architecture leads to increased complexity for users; this must be addressed by making the system appear cohesive and familiar to all types of users, and by providing adequate documentation and support to ease the transition to a virtual laboratory. Additionally, the system should facilitate information sharing and collaboration.

3.   Virtual Laboratory Architecture

We have developed a prototype virtual laboratory that meets the requirements described above. However, it is only the laboratory users who are distributed; all the hardware and software components are currently situated in one geographic location. We chose to use a single location initially in order to evaluate the interactions between the hardware and software components, which would be more difficult to accomplish in a distributed environment. After the components are tested individually and as a complete system, the components will be distributed and the virtual laboratory will subsequently be tested.

Figure 2 presents the architecture of the virtual laboratory. The examination system uses a virtual machine pool with a variety of operating systems and complete user separation. SAN technology is used for local data storage because it can reliably store case data and is designed to support multiple users simultaneously. Authentication and security

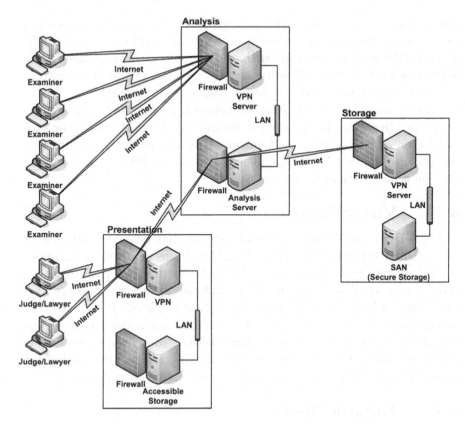

Figure 2. Virtual digital forensics laboratory architecture.

are implemented via a virtual private network (VPN) bound to a multi-factor authentication system. The next few sections discuss the design themes pertaining to the prototype laboratory.

3.1   Internal Network

A hardware-based firewall is used to control and filter inbound and outbound traffic. A gigabit Ethernet switch is used for internal network traffic. Multiple virtual LANs (VLANs) are employed on the switch to logically and securely segment management and user traffic. The switch also provides access control. Specifically, every port is configured to only accept connections from predefined hardware; this prevents a rogue user with physical access from connecting to the internal network.

3.2   Authentication and Access Control

The virtual laboratory uses multi-factor authentication and multiple access control techniques. Remote access to the network is controlled via two methods. One is a hardware-based VPN appliance that uses two-factor authentication (username/password and hardware token). The other is IP-based authentication that allows access to users from a pre-determined list of static IP addresses. Using these two methods in combination reduces the potential for system compromise [5].

Users connected to the internal network access their personalized workspace (e.g., user preferences, software and casework) using the same two-factor authentication mechanism. User authentication and access control are handled by a central management (LDAP) directory running on a non-virtualized system.

3.3   Virtualization

The VDFL has a pool of physical servers that host a number of virtual machines (Figure 2). These virtual machines are used by examiners to operate on the data stored in the SAN. Virtualization software was chosen instead of separate physical machines for several reasons. Virtualization allows for the logical separation of users. It reduces costs by consolidating hardware; also, deployment time is decreased because the virtual machine hardware is standardized. Moreover, virtualization allows administrators to move active virtual machines in the pool of host servers in real time to improve system performance and reliability.

3.4   Forensic Tools

Examiners using the virtual laboratory would have access to a variety of commercial and open source forensic tools running under virtual machines. Access would be available to multiple operating systems and related tools based on examination needs. Note that access control is role-based and determined by user credentials, not by the particular operating system or tool used. Costs would be reduced because forensic tools would be shared.

3.5   Storage

One of the principal issues is to provide an adequate storage pool for users. Another is to maintain satisfactory throughput for multiple simultaneous users. SAN technology was selected for its speed and reliability. Throughput is provided by a fibre channel connection running at 2 Gbps, which offers dedicated bandwidth for multiple users working with large data sets.

The SAN is partitioned into various logical storage roles to include virtual machine storage and case data (raw data, intermediate results and presentation data). Logical separation of storage allows access controls to be applied through the management directory. Law enforcement agencies are often required to retain case evidence for decades. Providing long-term storage is a goal for the virtual laboratory. However, using the SAN for this purpose should be considered carefully along with the possibility of using other archiving technologies.

3.6   Internal Network Security

Security is an integral part of the virtual laboratory architecture because of the sensitivity of the data and the requirements imposed by federal and state laws. Every component must be secured using applicable procedures and best practices [6]. Also, extensive logs must be maintained of user access and resource utilization. The current design uses segmented logging channels (separate from those used by the main network traffic) to send data to a central logging server.

4.   Challenges

Several challenges were encountered while designing and implementing the virtual laboratory. A major challenge was the inability of the current configuration to support the uploading of large data sets. This was largely due to the limited bandwidth available for consumer-level Internet connections. A promising solution is to use a high-speed network (e.g., Internet 2 Abilene/Florida LambdaRail [2]).

Another challenge is posed by popular forensic examination suites that rely on physical hardware locks (typically a USB key or "dongle"). Mapping and managing these dongles to individual virtual machines are problematic due to various physical and logical constraints (e.g., mapping identically-named devices to their virtual machines and coping with physical limitations of the available ports to connect these devices). A promising solution is to use special connectivity software that would allow a dongle to be remotely connected to a local virtual machine. This software would also enable users to use their own dongles and the virtual laboratory to host dongles.

Ultimately, however, the principal challenge is to address cultural and political barriers to the use of hardware and software resources located outside the local law enforcement agency jurisdiction. Furthermore, even if state-of-the-art technologies and best practices are employed to maintain the confidentiality, integrity and availability of digital evidence in the virtual laboratory environment, questions will persist. All the stakeholders – law enforcement agents, attorneys, judges and juries – will have to be educated about the benefits of the laboratory and the proper use of its facilities.

5. Conclusions

A virtual digital forensics laboratory is not limited by geographic boundaries – it decentralizes forensic functionality while providing security and quality management processes. As such, it would reduce the duplication of resources and tasks, provide law enforcement agents with cutting-edge tools, resources and expertise, and lower the cost of forensic examinations. Practically every crime now involves some aspect of digital evidence and the volume of digital evidence is growing faster than the ability of law enforcement to process it. Several challenges remain to be addressed before virtual digital forensics laboratories can become operational, let alone thrive. Nevertheless, these facilities may be the single best hope for law enforcement agencies to cope with the deluge of digital evidence.

Acknowledgements

This research was supported by the Electronic Crime Program of the National Institute of Justice under Contract No. 2005-MU-MU-K044.

References

[1] M. Davis, G. Manes and S. Shenoi, A network-based architecture for storing digital evidence, in *Advances in Digital Forensics*, M. Pollitt and S. Shenoi (Eds.), Springer, Boston, Massachusetts, pp. 33–42, 2005.

[2] Florida LambdaRail, Florida's Research and Education Network (www.flrnet.org).

[3] International Business Machines, IBM Systems Virtualization (Version 2, Release 1), Armonk, New York, 2005.

[4] N. McAllister, Server virtualization, *InfoWorld*, February 12, 2007.

[5] V. Mukhin, Multi-factor authentication as a protection mechanism in computer networks, *Cybernetics and Systems Analysis*, vol. 35(5), pp. 832–835, 1999.

[6] National Security Agency, NSA Security Configuration Guides, Fort Meade, Maryland (www.nsa.gov/snac), 2005.

[7] B. Phillips, Have storage area networks come of age? *IEEE Computer*, vol. 31(7), pp. 10–12, 1998.

[8] A. Singh, An Introduction to Virtualization (www.kernelthread.com/publications/virtualization), 2004.

[9] M. Stockman, J. Nyland and W. Weed, Centrally-stored and delivered virtual machines in the networking/system administration lab, *ACM SIGITE Newsletter*, vol. 2(2), pp. 4–6, 2005.

[10] J. Tate, F. Lucchese and R. Moore, *Introduction to Storage Area Networks*, IBM Redbooks/Vervante, Rolling Hills Estates, California, 2006.